An Illustrated Survey of Orchid Genera

North American orchids. Clockwise, from bottom, lower left: *Galearis spectabilis, Calypso bulbosa* var. *americana, Cypripedium guttatum* var. *guttatum, Spiranthes odorata, Calopogon tuberosus, Platanthera cristata, Arethusa bulbosa, Cleistes divaricata, Encyclia tampensis,* and *Polyrrhiza lindenii*. Center: *Cypripedium calceolus* var. *pubescens*.

AN ILLUSTRATED SURVEY OF
Orchid Genera

Tom and Marion Sheehan

TIMBER PRESS
Portland, Oregon

All illustrations by Marion Sheehan.

ISBN 0-88192-288-9

Printed in Hong Kong

TIMBER PRESS, INC.
The Haseltine Building
133 S.W. Second Ave., Suite 450
Portland, Oregon 97204-3527, U.S.A.

Library of Congress Cataloging-in-Publication Data
Sheehan, Thomas J. (Thomas John), 1924–
        An illustrated survey of orchid genera / Tom and Marion Sheehan.
            p.   cm.
        Rev. ed. of: Orchid genera illustrated. 1979.
        Includes bibliographical references (p.   ) and index.
        ISBN 0-88192-288-9
        1. Orchids. 2. Orchids—Pictorial works. 3. Orchid culture. 4. Botanical
illustration. I. Sheehan, Marion, II. Sheehan, Thomas J. (Thomas John),
1924– Orchid genera illustrated. III. Title.
QK 495.064S49   1994
584'.15—dc20   93-45569
                                                                  CIP

Contents

Color Plates

---

*These paintings, reprinted by courtesy of Mary Noble McQuerry, were originally published in *You Can Grow Cattleya Orchids* (1991) and *You Can Grow Phalaenopsis Orchids* (1971) by Mary Noble (McQuerry-Orchid Books).

Acknowledgments

This volume represents our endeavors for more than 26 years and could not have been accomplished without the support of many people. We are especially grateful to the late Gordon W. Dillon, who motivated us to undertake the project, and to the American Orchid Society, which published the original articles. We cannot overlook the generosity of our many orchid friends, hobbyists and commercial growers alike, who gave or loaned us flowering plants. They did this unselfishly knowing full well that their choice sprays of orchids would soon be cut up into small pieces for the sake of an illustration, as all the drawings were done from fresh flowers. The aforementioned list of individuals and firms is very extensive and to be certain that no one is overlooked, instead of listing each name, we say a collective "thanks again" to everyone who helped. We owe much to Bart Schutzman, whose extensive knowledge of computers saved us untold hours of time. He was always ready and willing to solve any computer problem as well as to offer help with this aspect of our work.

Introduction

While dissecting a flower of *Brassavola cucullata* a number of years ago, we found that all the flowers on the plant contained 12 pollinia. Because the available literature stated that the genera of Orchidaceae contained from two to eight pollinia per flower, we wondered whether the number of pollinia in our flowers was abnormal. Upon examining a number of flowers of the same species from fellow orchidists, however, we found that all plants of this species have 12 pollinia.

Convinced that the 12 pollinia of our flower were truly normal, we delved into the literature to see if we could find a description of the genus *Brassavola* and an explanation for this unusual condition. Our search was both interesting and frustrating, but it was not successful. We had hoped to find a complete description of the genus and sufficient illustrations to depict the important taxonomic characteristics. Instead, we found several descriptions that contained only two or three lines. Only one description stated that the genus *Brassavola* had "eight or more" pollinia, but it did not indicate how many "more" signified.

In general, most of the descriptions we found in the literature were brief and did not cover all the basic characteristics needed to separate the genus from close or similar genera. In many cases, illustrations were sketchy or lacking, and some contained only a leaf and flower in face view. Also, as we perused the literature, the same illustrations appeared again and again. The drawings we found were descriptive and accurate but generally not complete enough, and the illustrations did not depict the same flower parts for comparison.

The present volume was born from this experience. What we have endeavored to do is to depict in both words and illustrations the more commonly grown orchid genera. Each genus is described in terms the average person can understand without having a degree in botany or taxonomy. Occasionally, when a taxonomic word must be used, it is described and, where possible, illustrated in the Glossary.

Each generic illustration has habit and floral drawings, and several views of the column and pollinia, the major characteristics by which the various genera are separated. Since each genus illustration contains the same material in the same views, the reader can easily compare two genera to see how they vary. In addition to the descriptive material, a list of the more popular species and a map depicting the approximate native habitat of the genus is included. In cases where the genus is very large or shows great vegetative diversification, such as in *Oncidium* and *Dendrobium*, additional illustrations show vegetative and/or further flowering characteristics.

More than 150 orchid genera are illustrated in this volume. Since there are more than 800 genera in the Orchidaceae, this book is only a beginning. Hopefully it will enable orchidologists to become better acquainted with the plants of which they are so fond.

Orchid growers are often reluctant to cut up their blooms, but dissecting flowers is one of the best ways to study orchids. It should be easy for the reader to dissect an orchid flower and compare it with the illustrated material in this book and thus understand the flower better.

What is an Orchid?

When asked "What is an orchid?" the average person in the Western Hemisphere might develop a mental picture of a purple *Cattleya* flower, whereas the average person in Southeast Asia might think of a *Vanda* flower. In the United States it is natural to think of *Cattleya* flowers because they have been widely used by the florist trade and in advertising for many years. Yet the genus *Cattleya*, with less than 65 species, makes up only a minute portion of the family Orchidaceae. Thus, it appears many people are unable to answer the question, "What is an orchid?"

Orchidologists are aware of the multitude of orchids and their amazing array of flowers. The amateur orchid grower can choose from many sizes and forms of plants, a rainbow of flower colors, and a wide range of blooming seasons. Fragrance is another factor to consider in selecting plants to grow, as orchids offer a wide range of odors: delicate, strong, sweet, and pungent. Most taxonomists agree that there are probably more than 25,000 species of orchids in the world and over 100,000 hybrids.

The orchid family is widely distributed, being found in all parts of the world except the major deserts and arctic circles. Plants within the family may be epiphytes, terrestrials, lithophytes, or saprophytes. They may be with or without pseudobulbs and with linear, lanceolate, ovate, and many other forms of leaves. Some plants are leafless (e.g., *Vanilla dilloniana*) or have short-lived leaves. Mature plants range in height from less than 1 inch (2.5 cm) to over 15 feet (450 cm). Flowers range in size from 0.3 inch (3–4 mm) to over 12 inches (30 cm) in diameter. The more than 800 genera of orchids (some taxonomists say the figure is closer to 900) are grouped approximately into 74 subtribes, 20 tribes, and 5 subfamilies. How then, with this great diversity of vegetative forms and flower differentials, can the 25,000 known species be tied into one family, the Orchidaceae? What do these plants have in common?

Members of the Orchidaceae are related by floral characteristics. Becoming familiar with these characteristics makes identifying orchids easier. An orchidist should be able to look at an unknown plant in bloom and say, "That is an orchid." With knowledge and practice, the orchidist should be able to pinpoint the genus and possibly even the species of an unknown orchid by examining the flower.

There are tremendous differences between orchid flowers (Figs. 1, 2), which are more variable than vegetative characteristics, yet all can be grouped together in one family. It would be extremely difficult to describe the typical orchid plant. A *Phalaenopsis* grower might choose to describe *Phalaenopsis*; a *Cymbidium* grower, *Cymbidium*; and so on. Since most people are familiar with the genus *Cattleya*, and since its flowers are large and easy to dissect, it serves as a good example.

Five basic characteristics are associated with orchid flowers, and it is the combination of these five characteristics that separates orchids from other plant families: zygomorphic flowers; a white, stiff, waxy column containing the plant's reproductive structure; the rostellum, a gland that separates the pollinia from the stigmatic surface and thus prevents self-pollination while ensuring that visiting insects leave with pollinia; nonpowdery, agglutinated pollen; and the minute seeds, which, because they have no endosperm, require the aid of a fungus to germinate. Any plant with four of these charac-

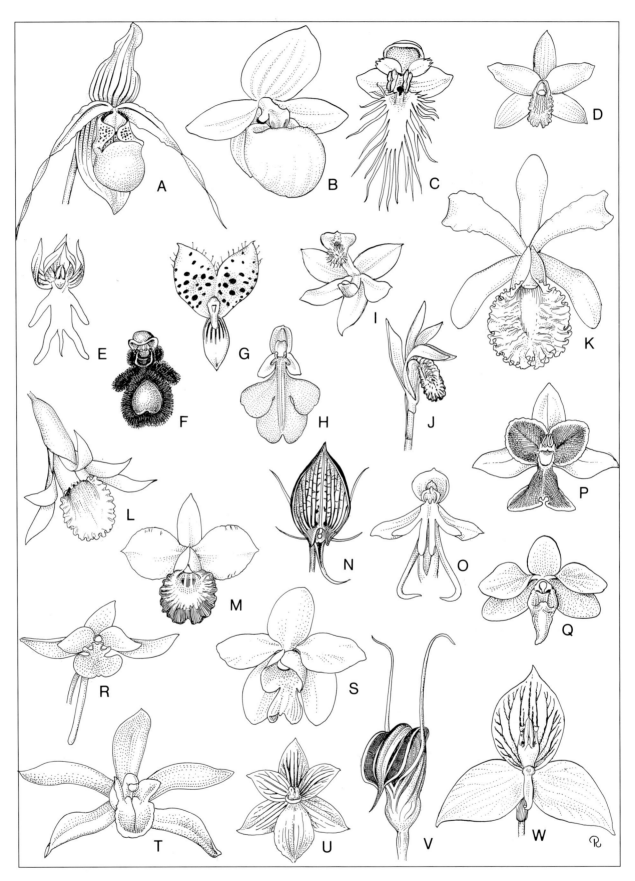

Figure 1. Flower variation in terrestrial orchids drawn at varying scales to show details. A: *Phragmipedium*.
B: *Cypripedium*. C: *Platanthera*. D: *Bletia*. E: *Orchis*. F: *Ophrys*. G: *Ponthieva*. H: *Habenaria*. I: *Calopogon*. J: *Arethusa*.
K: *Sobralia*. L: *Thunia*. M: *Arundina*. N: *Liparis*. O: *Bonatea*. P: *Brachycorythis*. Q: *Eulophia*. R: *Calanthe*. S: *Vanda*.
T: *Cymbidium*. U: *Thelymitra*. V: *Pterostylis*. W: *Disa*.

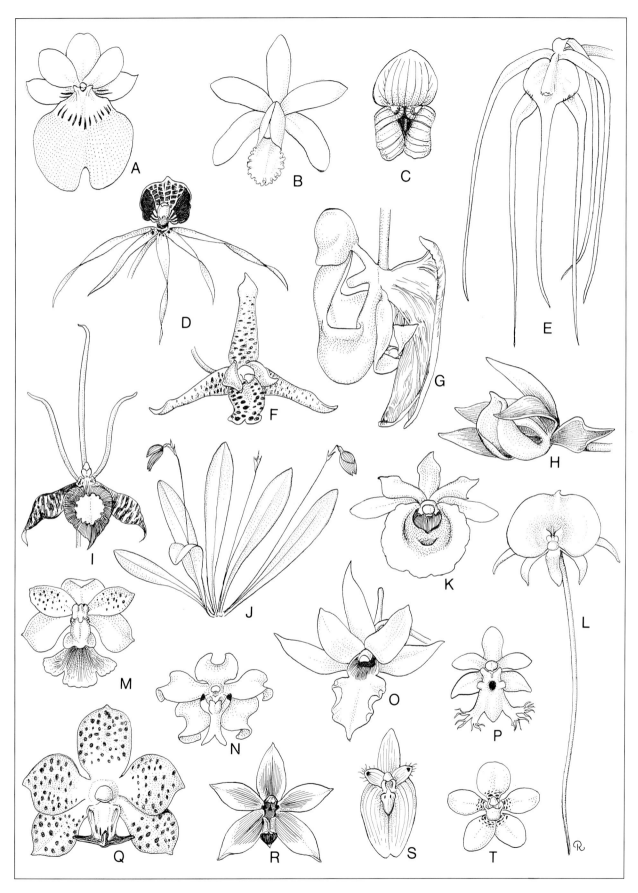

Figure 2. Flower variation in epiphytic orchids drawn at varying scales to show details. A: *Miltonia*. B: *Cattleya*.
C: *Trigonidium*. D: *Encyclia*. E: *Brassavola*. F: *Maxillaria*. G: *Coryanthes*. H: *Mormodes*. I: *Oncidium*. J: *Pleurothallis*.
K: *Eurychone*. L: *Angraecum*. M: *Aerides*. N: *Paraphalaenopsis*. O: *Dendrobium*. P: *Tridactyle*. Q: *Vandopsis*. R: *Phalaenopsis*.
S: *Bulbophyllum*. T: *Sarchochilus*.

teristics is an orchid, and since seeds are not always present, orchidists must rely heavily on the first four characteristics when checking an unknown plant to determine if it is an orchid.

Zygomorphic Flowers. Botanically, all flowers are divided into two major groups, regular and irregular. A regular flower, such as the tulip or Easter lily, is symmetrical and can be cut in any plane to divide it into two equal halves. An irregular flower, such as the canna or maranta, has segments that are different and thus dividing it in any plane will not produce equal halves. The orchid flower is a special type of irregular flower in that it can be cut in one plane, and one plane only, to produce two equal halves. This type of irregular flower is called *zygomorphic*, as it has bilateral symmetry.

Looking at an orchid in face view, it is easy to see the two equal halves (Fig. 3). By cutting the flower down through the center of the dorsal sepal, dividing the column and lip, the flower is split into two equal halves. Cutting an orchid flower in any other plane results in unequal halves.

Column. A waxy structure called the *column* (or gynandrium) is found in the center of the orchid flower, either exposed or enclosed by the labellum. The column contains the flower's reproductive structure. In the evolution of orchids the male (sta-

men) and female (pistil) segments of the flower fused to form the column. Most orchid columns have an anther cap at the apex and a concave stigmatic area just behind the anther cap on the underside of the column (Fig. 4). Although the column varies between and among genera, it is basically white, stiff, and waxy. In some species, the column is the same color as the sepals and petals. It should be noted that in some sections of the family, such as the Cypripedioideae (Fig. 14), there are two anthers and these are attached to the sides of the column rather than at the apex (see *Paphiopedilum*, *Phragmipedium*, and *Cypripedium*).

Rostellum. Often called "little beak," the *rostellum* is a sterile extension of the apex of the stigma. It lies between the stigmatic surface and the pollinia on the underside of the column (Fig. 4). This unique glandular structure serves two important purposes. First, it serves as a tissue dam to separate the pollen grains from the stigmatic surface. In this role it assures that self-pollination does not occur and that the flowers are cross-pollinated. (A few species of orchids, such as *Cattleya aurantiaca*, self-digest the rostellum so that self-pollination occurs.)

The rostellum's second role is to insure that insects or other pollinators visiting the flower take pollinia with them when they leave. As a gland, the rostellum is capable of dispensing a very viscid substance. When an insect (called a pollinator) enters a flower and forces its way beneath the column, the upper portion of its body comes in contact with the rostellum. A small amount of the sticky substance secreted by the rostellum is spread on the back of the pollinator as it withdraws from the flower. The caudicles or stipes of the pollinia come in contact with the glue on the insect's body, stick fast, and thus are removed. The insect carries the pollinia to other flowers, where they are deposited on the stigmatic surface as the insect enters the flower. An insect picks up more pollinia as its leaves the second flower, thus continuing the pollination process from flower to flower. Insects are a tool; they are not interested in carrying pollinia but in drinking nectar in the flower.

Pollinia. The pollen of the majority of orchid flowers is not powdery, as it is in most flowers, but rather agglutinated in masses called *pollinia* (singular, pollinium). Each orchid flower has from two to eight pollinia under the anther cap, depending on the genus. In one case, *Brassavola cucullata*, there are 12 pollinia. Each pollinium or pair of pollinia is attached to a stalk (caudicle or stipe), which comes in

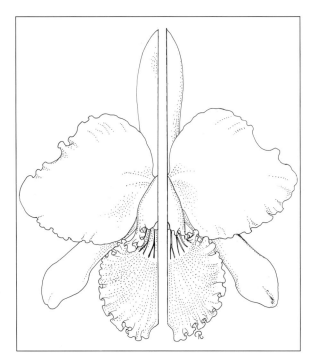

Figure 3. Zygomorphic flower (*Cattleya*) split into two halves.

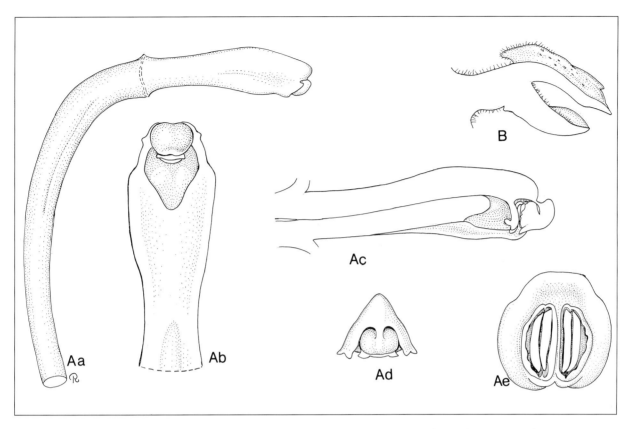

Figure 4. Reproductive structures. A: *Cattleya*. Aa: Column and ovary, side view. Ab: Column, ventral view. Ac: Column, vertical section. Ad: Column, end view. Ae: Anther cap with pollinia in place. B: *Paphiopedilum* column, vertical section.

contact with pollinators as they leave the flower. Pollinia and their stalks vary from genus to genus (Fig. 5). Most pollinia are yellowish in color and ovoid in shape. The caudicle or stipe may be a simple stalk or have an elaborate foot covered with a very viscid substance. In some cases, closely allied genera may be separated by their pollinia. *Cattleya*, for example, has four pollinia whereas *Laelia* has eight (Fig. 6). Therefore, to distinguish between the genera *Laelia* and *Cattleya*, count the pollinia. When these two genera are hybridized, the offspring have eight pollinia, but they, too, can be distinguished from their parents as the hybrid *Laeliocattleya* has four normal pollinia and four rudimentary pollinia.

Seed. The seeds of orchids (Fig. 7) are very minute and do not contain the normal endosperm (stored carbohydrates needed for growth) found in seeds of corn, beans, and peas. Because an orchid seed has no endosperm, it lacks the capability of germinating in the wild without the aid of a fungus.

Any plant that has four of the above characteristics qualifies as a member of the Orchidaceae. Unfortu-nately, seeds are not always present, so the first four characteristics must be relied upon heavily when checking an unknown plant to determine if it is is an orchid. Once these basic characteristics are memorized, however, there should be little difficulty recognizing whether or not a flower is an orchid. In addition to these basic characteristics, one should become familiar with the other floral segments and their arrangement, as these too will be helpful in identifying orchids.

Learning the components of the orchid flowers can be fascinating. The best way to learn to identify them is by dissecting flowers of different species and studying their various segments.

The flower of *Cattleya* is a familiar example of a typical orchid blossom (Fig. 8). Orchids are monocotyledonous plants and thus their floral segments are in threes, or threemerous (trimerous).

The unopened *Cattleya* bud as it emerges from the sheath (Fig. 9) is protected by an outer whorl of floral segments called *sepals*. The three sepals completely enclose the bud, but once the flower opens, the sepals also become an integral part of the floral display.

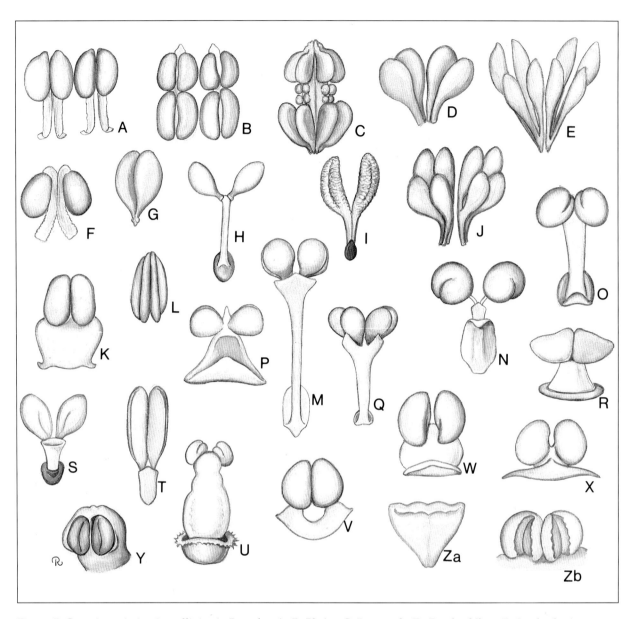

Figure 5. Generic variation in pollinia. A: *Broughtonia*. B: *Phaius*. C: *Brassavola*. D: *Dendrochilum*. E: *Spathoglottis*. F: *Hexisea*. G: *Masdevallia*. H: *Miltoniopsis*. I: *Ludisia*. J: *Calanthe*. K: *Bulbophyllum*. L: *Dendrobium*. M: *Doritis*. N: *Rhynchostylis*. O: *Rodriguezia*. P: *Arachnis*. Q: *Trichopilia*. R: *Eulophia*. S: *Brassia*. T: *Gongora*. U: *Cycnoches*. V: *Grammatophyllum*. W: *Maxillaria*. X: *Ansellia*. Y: *Phragmipedium*. Za: *Vanilla* pollen mass. Zb: *Vanilla* anthers.

The best way to understand an orchid blossom is to take a flower in hand and dissect it segment by segment. Looking at a *Cattleya* face view (Fig. 8), the labellum (lip) is the most prominent feature. This is true in many orchid species, but in other species the lip is small (e.g., *Masdevallia*, see color plate) or insignificant or hidden. The lip, in general, is a highly modified petal and is one of three petals that make up the inner whorl of the corolla (Fig. 8). Depending on the genus, the lip may or may not be distinctly three-lobed and it may or may not have other modifying structures or appendages. It may have a spur at its base, which may be very small (e.g., *Vanda*, see color plate), almost 12 inches (30 cm) long (e.g., *Angraecum sesquipedale*, see color plate), or shaped like a boot (e.g., *Cypripedium*, see color plate). Some lips have distinct discs, calli, and even antennae. Even though the lips of some genera may be small, they are highly modified structures. In other genera the lip is not greatly modified and is almost the same size, shape, and color as the other two petals (e.g., *Hexisea*, see color plate).

18

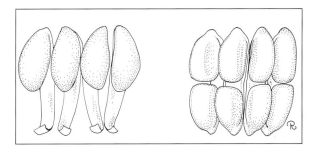

Figure 6. Pollinia of *Cattleya* (left) and *Laelia* (right).

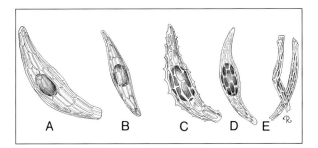

Figure 7. Seeds. A: *Phaius*. B: *Epidendrum*. C: *Ansellia*. D: *Dendrobium*. E: Undeveloped seeds or chaff.

The lip often acts as a landing platform for insects that come to visit the flower for nectar and, hopefully, to pollinate the flower. The callus tissue, antennae, and other modifications of the lip help to attract and guide insects into the proper area of the flower and to position them in such a manner that pollen removal and transfer are assured. In some cases, the lip is a very effective mimic. The lip of *Drakaea elastica*, native to Australia, is a good example; it resembles the posterior portion of a female wasp and is so cleverly arranged that it fools the male, who, in attempting to copulate, pollinates the flower.

Since the lip is so different from other floral segments, the question is, "How did it evolve?" Unfortunately, very few fossil records are available to show how the orchid flower evolved to its present state. From the meager information available, it could be assumed that at one time many, many years ago, the orchid flower looked more like an Easter lily. If so, then early in its evolution, the orchid flower had three sepals and three petals very similar in size, shape, and possibly color. It may have had three or six anthers. If this hypothesis is true, then the evolution of the orchid flower is relatively easy to imagine. Since most orchids including *Cattleya* contain only one anther, it could be assumed that two to five anthers disappeared in the evolutionary process. These anthers probably became petaloid and possibly two or more fused with one of the petals to form the lip. Since the petals of many flowers are larger than the sepals, there is also the possibility that one anther may have fused with

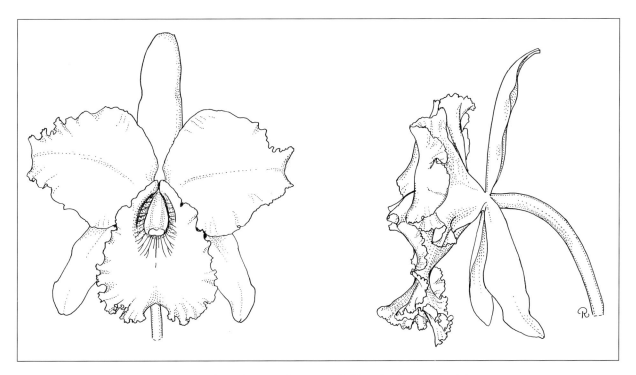

Figure 8. A typical orchid flower *(Cattleya)* showing face view (left) and side view (right).

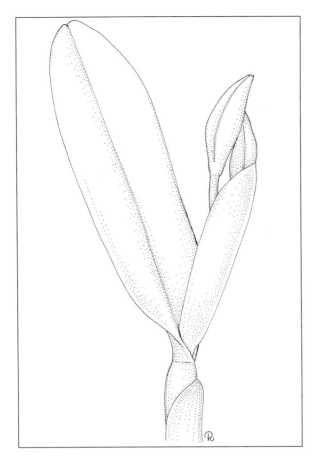

Figure 9. *Cattleya* buds emerging from the sheath. The visible floral parts are the sepals.

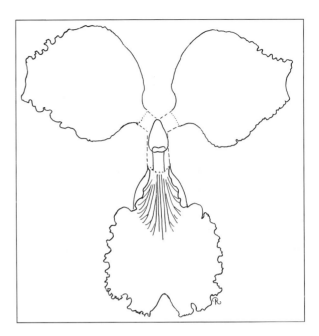

Figure 10. *Cattleya* flower showing inner whorl of floral segments.

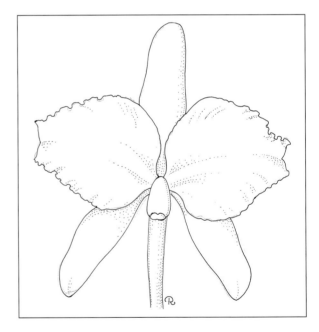

Figure 11. *Cattleya* flower with lip removed.

each of the lateral petals as well. This then would account for the missing anthers. Occasionally, a hard yellow structure that looks like anther tissue appears on the margins or other parts of the petals and the lips. This occurrence lends support to this theory.

The remainder of the inner whorl of floral segments in the orchid flower is composed of two petals (Fig. 10). When the lip is removed from the *Cattleya* flower, the petals are the dominant segments (Figs. 11, 12). The petals in general are smaller than the lip and are either equal to or larger than the sepals. In some orchid genera the petals are larger than the lip. In *Cattleya* the petals are usually arranged pinwheel fashion around the column and are spaced equidistant from each other; hence, their centerpoints of attachment are 120 degrees apart. In some species the petals are erect and stand between the dorsal and lateral sepals (e.g., *Cattleya*, see color plate). In others the petals may lie almost parallel to the column and sometimes enclose it (e.g., *Lycaste*, see color plate).

The outermost whorl of floral segments consists of three sepals, which generally are alike in size, shape, and color (Figs. 12, 13). In *Paphiopedilum* (see color plate) and its allied genera the two lateral sepals are fused in such a manner the flowers appear to have only two sepals. Together, the fused segments are called the *synsepal*. Genera such as *Masdevallia* (see color plate) and *Paphiopedilum* have

20

sepals that are the dominant portion of the flower. In *Cattleya* (see color plate), the sepals are spaced equidistant and lie between the petals, again in pinwheel fashion. In other genera, the arrangement of the sepals may be entirely different. The lateral sepals of *Maxillaria* (see color plate) are attached perpendicular to the dorsal sepal and almost form a cross. Thus, positioning of the sepals can sometimes be helpful in identifying an orchid.

When the two outer whorls of floral segments (sepals and petals) have been removed, all that remains is the inferior ovary with the column attached at its apex (Figs. 4, 13). In botanical terms, inferior means that the sepals and petals are attached at the top of the ovary rather than at the base. The column, as mentioned earlier, bears the reproductive organs of the flower. Thus, the column becomes an extremely important segment of the flower to the orchid breeder and should be examined in some detail. Columns, like orchid blossoms, vary widely in size and shape, but basically they are hard, waxy-looking structures. Often they are white or off-white, but they may be the same color as the flower.

At the apex of the column in *Cattleya*, as in most genera, is a movable structure called the anther cap (Fig. 4). This is the segment of the column that bears the pollinia. The anther cap of a *Cattleya* flower covers four pollinia. In other flowers there are anywhere from two to twelve pollinia under the anther cap depending on the genus and species. The anther cap of a *Cattleya* flower, as in most orchid flow-

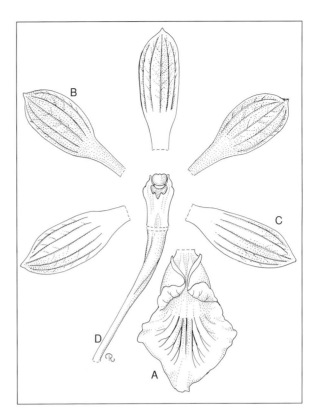

Figure 13. *Encyclia* flower dissected to show components. A: Lip. B: Petals. C: Sepals. D: Column and ovary.

ers, is hinged in such a manner that when a pollinating insect leaves the flower, the cap is lifted up and the pollinia with their caudicles or stipes are exposed and easily removed by the insect. When the insect enters the flower, the anther cap is not disturbed; therefore, the insect does not pick up pollinia as it enters the flower, but rather only as it leaves, thus assuring cross-pollination. In several genera, such as *Catasetum*, the pollinator hits a triggering mechanism; the pollinia are fired at the insect and become fastened to its body so that it flies off with them. The pollinia of the *Cypripedium* complex are borne on the sides of the column rather than on the apex (Fig. 14). In these flowers with bootlike lips (slippers), the insect enters from either side of the boot (slipper) and, when leaving, takes the pollinia along.

Just behind the anther cap on the under surface of the column is the rostellum (Fig. 4), which separates the pollinia from the stigmatic surface and prevents self-fertilization. The stigmatic surface lies just below the rostellum. Basically, the rostellum is a two-lobed structure of varying shape, covered with a very sticky substance, and connected to the ovary by a stylar canal (Fig. 4).

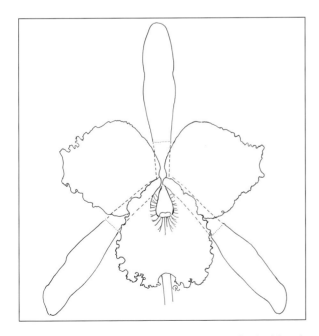

Figure 12. *Cattleya* flower showing outer whorl of floral segments removed.

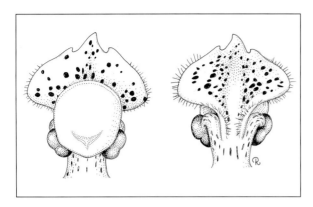

Figure 14. Column of *Paphiopedilum niveum* Ang Thong showing ventral view (left) and dorsal view (right) of pollinia.

One or more pollinia, when applied to the stigmatic surface by either humans or insects, bring about the eventual fertilization of the orchid flower. Soon after the pollinia have been placed on the stigmatic surface, the pollen grains germinate and the pollen tubes grow down the stylar canal and eventually enter the micropyle of the ovule. Depending on the species, it may take anywhere from a few days to as long as three months from the time the pollinia are applied to the stigmatic surface until actual fertilization of the ovules takes place. In the genus *Cattleya*, it may take as many as 90 days for the pollen tubes to penetrate the mature ovules.

If pollination and fertilization are effected, the seed pod matures after three to twelve months. At maturity, the *Cattleya* seed pod may contain well over 500,000 seeds.

The orchidist, whether a beginning hobbyist or a seasoned grower, can always profit by dismantling and studying orchid flowers to locate the features described here. The infinite variations among genera are fascinating to observe. Understanding the structures allows for greater appreciation of the complexities of orchids as well as greater success in cross-breeding. Thorough understanding of the orchid flower permits instant recognition of any unknown orchid as Orchidaceae. As genera in the family are studied, the recognition of numerous genera becomes easy.

Orchid Classification

Orchid classification has been developing for many years. The famous taxonomist John Lindley started the first major classification of the orchid family around 1825 and worked on it for approximately 40 years. He was followed by many other renowned taxonomists such as Heinrich G. L. Reichenbach, Ernst H. H. Pfitzer, Robert Rolfe, Oakes Ames, and Robert Dressler. Around the beginning of the 20th century, Rudolf Schlechter began his reclassification of the family based mainly on the work of Pfitzer. One might consider Schlechter a splitter because he maintained Pfitzer's basic classification but increased the number of subtribes. Since 1930, there has been almost continual modification of Schlechter's classification.

A large family such as the Orchidaceae is very complex and thus a challenge to taxonomists. Unfortunately, not all taxonomists agree on the total classification of this family. Hence, the only recourse for the orchidist faced with the dilemma of choosing among varying forms of classification that appear in the literature is to follow one taxonomist or taxonomic group and hopefully avoid some confusion. The classification followed in the present volume is based on the latest published work of Dressler (1993), who started reclassifying the orchid family around 1960 and is still modifying his system.

Fortunately, many of the changes found in various forms of classification of Orchidaceae are usually of a minor nature and do not greatly alter the major classification characteristics. Frequently, changes concern elevation of a subtribe to the higher status of a tribe. Other changes involve splitting a subtribe into two or more subtribes. Occasionally, a genus will be divided into two or more genera. There are also some taxonomists who would like to change the very basic family structure and split the family into two or more families. For the present, however, there is only one family Orchidaceae.

The Plant Kingdom
Division: Spermatophyta
Subdivision: Angiospermae
Class: Monocotyledonae
Order: Orchidales
Family: Orchidaceae
Subfamily: Orchidioideae
Tribe: Epidendreae
Subtribe: Laeliinae
Genus: *Cattleya*
Species: *dowiana*
Variety: *aurea*

Figure 15. The taxonomic relationship of *Cattleya dowiana* var. *aurea* to the plant kingdom and the family Orchidaceae.

Taxonomists use an orderly method of dividing a family in descending order from the family category to the species or even variety (Fig. 15). The divisions and the naming of these divisions are governed by the International Code of Botanical Nomenclature (ICBN). Using *Cattleya dowiana* var. *aurea* as an example, the orchid family is broken down as follows:

Family: Orchidaceae
The family category is a natural unit combining a number of characteristics that occur in the members

of this group. The plant kingdom is divided into many families, with over 300 families of flowering plants. According to the ICBN, family names end in *-aceae*.

Subfamily: Orchidioideae

Large families, such as Orchidaceae, are often divided into a number of subfamilies that combine those genera believed to have a common origin. The Orchidaceae is composed of at least five subfamilies. All subfamily designations end in *-oideae*.

Tribe: Epidendreae

Large subfamilies are often divided into more composite groups known as tribes. A tribe is a group of genera that are more alike than dissimilar. There are 20 tribes in the family Orchidaceae. Tribe designations end in *-eae*.

Subtribe: Laeliinae

Often tribes are subdivided into one or more subtribes with each subtribe containing one or more genera. There are 74 subtribes in the Orchidaceae. The designated ending for subtribe nomenclature is *-inae*.

Genus: *Cattleya*

A genus is a group of plants that have more characteristics in common with one another than they do with other members of the family. There are over 800 genera in Orchidaceae. Generic names have a variety of endings such as *-a*, *-um*, *-us*, and so forth.

Species: *dowiana*

A species is a group of plants that are nearly alike and differ only in very minor characteristics. The species designation ending should agree with the generic ending (e.g., *Cattleya dowiana*). There are over 65 species in the genus *Cattleya*.

Subspecies: *aurea*

Within some species there are groups of individuals that vary slightly but not significantly enough to be designated as another species. Subspecies names have endings that follow those of the genus and species (e.g., *Cattleya dowiana* subsp. *aurea*).

Variety (Latin Varietas): *aurea*

Plants with characteristics similar to those of subspecies are often designated as varieties. The term is widely used by horticulturists, sometimes erroneously, to designate any variant of the species. Again, the ending of the designated term, such as *aurea*, must agree with that of the genus and species.

Forma: *aurea*

Usually forma is used to designate a color variation, such as alba. Due to the variations in taxonomy, however, one taxonomist could list *aurea* as a subspecies, while another could designate it as a variety and still another as a forma. Forma is usually the smallest sector in any taxonomic grouping.

Although Dressler is continuing to update and revise his classification of the Orchidaceae, we feel his classification as outlined depicts the overall arrangement of the members of this family very well. Undoubtedly, this classification will continue to be altered. Publications by Carlyle A. Luer, for example, have divided the tribe Vandeae into four tribes. Since Vandeae is a very large tribe, additional alterations can be expected here and elsewhere in future classifications of the Orchidaceae.

Orchid Family Outline

The following outline of orchid classification with lists of genera is based on the work of Robert Dressler (1993). It should be pointed out, however, that several generic names in this book are no longer considered valid by Dressler. These genera appear in several books on cultivated orchids or have been moved between genera frequently in recent times so that the names still seem in a state of flux. Two examples are *Acacallis*, also called *Aganisia* (Alec Pridgeon 1992), and *Baptistonia*, also called *Oncidium* (Bechtel et al. 1992).

Apostasioideae: *Apostasia, Neuwiedia.*

Cypripedioideae: *Cypripedium, Paphiopedilum, Phragmipedium, Selenipedium.*

Spiranthoideae.

Diceratosteleae: *Diceratostele.*

Tropidieae: *Corymborkis, Tropidia.*

Cranichideae

Goodyerinae: *Anoectochilus, Aspidogyne, Chamaegastrodia, Cheirostylis, Cystorchis, Dicerostylis, Dossinia, Erythrodes, Eucosia, Eurycentrum, Evrardia, Gonatostylis, Goodyera, Gymnochilus, Herpysma, Hetaeria, Hylophila, Kreodanthus, Kuhlhasseltia, Lepidogyne, Ligeophila, Ludisia, Macodes, Moerenhoutia, Myrmechis, Orchipedum, Papuaea, Platylepis, Platythelys, Pristiglottis, Rhamphorhynchus, Stephanothelys, Tubilabium, Vrydagzynea, Zeuxine.*

Prescottiinae: *Aa, Altensteinia, Gomphichis, Myrosmodes, Porphyrostachys, Prescottia, Stenoptera.*

Spiranthinae: *Aracamunia, Aulosepalum, Beloglottis, Brachystele, Buchtienia, Coccineorchis, Cotylolabium, Cybebus, Cyclopogon, Degranvillea, Deiregyne, Dichromanthus, Discyphus, Dithyridanthus, Eltroplectris, Eurystyles, Funkiella, Galeottiella, Greenwoodia, Hapalorchis, Helonema, Kionophyton, Lankesterella, Lyroglossa, Mesadenella, Mesadenus, Odontorrhynchos, Oestlundorchis, Pelexia, Pseudogoodyera, Pteroglossa, Sacoila, Sarcoglottis, Sauroglossum, Schiedeella, Skeptrostachys, Spiranthes, Stalkya, Stenorrhynchus, Stigmatosema, Thelyschista.*

Manniellinae: *Manniella.*

Pachyplectroninae: *Pachyplectron.*

Cranichidinae: *Baskervilla, Cranichis, Fuertesiella, Nothostele, Ponthieva, Pseudocentrum, Pseudocranichis, Pterichis, Solenocentrum.*

Orchidoideae

Diurideae

Chloraeinae: *Bipinnula, Chloraea, Codonorchis, Gavilea, Geoblasta, Megastylis.*

Caladeniinae: *Adenochilus, Aporostylis, Burnettia, Caladenia, Elythranthera, Eriochilus, Glossodia, Leporella, Lyperanthus, Rimacola.*

Drakaeinae: *Arthrochilus, Caleana, Chiloglottis, Drakaea, Spiculaea.*

Pterostylidinae: *Pterostylis.*

Acianthinae: *Acianthus, Corybas, Cyrtostylis, Stigmatodactylus, Townsonia.*

Cryptostylidinae: *Coilochilus. Cryptostylis.*

Diuridinae: *Diuris, Epiblema, Orthoceras.*

Thelymitrinae: *Calochilus, Thelymitra.*

Rhizanthellinae: *Rhizanthella.*

Prasophyllinae: *Genoplesium, Microtis, Prasophyllum.*

Orchideae

Orchidinae: *Aceras, Aceratorchis, Amerorchis, Amitostigma, Anacamptis, Aorchis, Barlia, Bartholina, Brachycorythis, Chamorchis, Chondradenia, Chusua, Coeloglossum, Comperia, Dactylorhiza, Galearis, Gymnadenia, Hemipilia, Himantoglossum, Holothrix, Neobolusia, Neotinea, Neottianthe, Nigritella, Ophrys, Orchis, Piperia, Platanthera, Pseudodiphryllum, Pseudorchis, Schizochilus, Serapias, Steveniella, Symphyosepalum, Traunsteinera.*

Habenariinae: *Androcorys, Arnottia, Benthamia, Bonatea, Centrostigma, Cynorkis, Diphylax, Diplomeris, Gennaria, Habenaria, Herminium, Megalorchis, Oligophyton, Pecteilis, Peristylus, Physoceras, Platycoryne, Porolabium, Roeperocharis, Smithorchis, Stenoglottis, Thulinia, Tsaiorchis, Tylostigma.*

Diseae

Huttonaeinae: *Huttonaea.*

Satyriinae: *Pachites, Satyridium, Satyrium.*

Coryciinae: *Ceratandra, Corycium, Disperis, Evotella, Pterygodium.*

Disinae: *Brownleea, Disa, Herschelia, Monadenia, Schizodium.*

Epidendroideae

Neottieae

Limodorinae: *Aphyllorchis, Cephalanthera, Epipactis, Limodorum.*

Listerinae: *Listera, Neottia.*

Palmorchideae: *Palmorchis.*

Triphoreae: *Monophyllorchis, Psilochilus, Triphora.*

Vanilleae

Galeolinae: *Cyrtosia, Erythrorchis, Galeola, Pseudovanilla.*

Vanillinae: *Clematepistephium, Dictyophyllaria, Epistephium, Eriaxis, Vanilla.*

Lecanorchidinae: *Lecanorchis.*

Gastrodieae

Gastrodiinae: *Auxopus, Didymoplexiella, Didymoplexis, Gastrodia, Neoclemensia, Uleiorchis.*

Epipogiinae: *Epipogium, Silvorchis, Stereosandra.*

Wullschlaegeliinae: *Wullschlaegelia.*

Nervilieae: *Nervilia.*

Cymbidioid Phylad

Malaxideae: *Hippeophyllum, Liparis, Malaxis, Oberonia, Orestias, Risleya.*

Calypsoeae: *Aplectrum, Calypso, Corallorhiza, Cremastra, Dactylostalix, Ephippianthus, Oreorchis, Tipularia, Yoania.*

Cymbidieae

Goveniinae: *Govenia.*

Bromheadiinae: *Bromheadia.*

Eulophiinae: *Cyanaeorchis, Dipodium, Eulophia, Geodorum, Oeceoclades, Pteroglossaspis.*

Thecostelinae: *Thecopus, Thecostele.*

Cyrtopodiinae: *Acrolophia, Ansellia, Cymbidiella, Cymbidium, Cyrtopodium, Eulophiella, Galeandra, Grammangis, Grammatophyllum, Graphorkis, Grobya, Porphyroglottis.*

Acriopsidinae: *Acriopsis.*

Catasetinae: *Catasetum, Clowesia, Cycnoches, Dressleria, Mormodes.*

Maxillarieae

Cryptarrheninae: *Cryptarrhena.*

Zygopetalinae: *Aganisia (Acacallis), Batemannia, Benzingia, Bollea, Chaubardia, Chaubardiella, Cheiradenia, Chondrorhyncha, Cochleanthes, Dichaea, Dodsonia, Galeottia, Hoehneella, Huntleya, Kefersteinia, Koellensteinia, Neogardneria, Otostylis, Pabstia, Paradisianthus, Pescatorea, Promenaea, Scuticaria, Stenia, Vargasiella, Warrea, Warreella, Warreopsis, Zygopetalum, Zygosepalum.*

Lycastinae: *Anguloa, Bifrenaria, Horvatia, Lycaste, Neomoorea, Rudolfiella, Teuscheria, Xylobium.*

Maxillariinae: *Anthosiphon, Chrysocycnis, Cryptocentrum, Cyrtidiorchis, Maxillaria, Mormolyca, Pityphyllum, Trigonidium.*

Stanhopeinae: *Acineta, Braemia, Cirrhaea, Coeliopsis, Coryanthes, Embreea, Gongora, Horichia, Houlletia, Kegeliella, Lacaena, Lueddemannia, Lycomormium, Paphinia, Peristeria, Polycycnis, Schlimia, Sievekingia, Soterosanthus, Stanhopea, Trevoria, Vasqueziella.*

Telipogoninae: *Hofmeisterella, Stellilabium, Telipogon, Trichoceros.*

Ornithocephalinae: *Caluera, Centroglossa, Chytroglossa, Dipteranthus, Dunstervillea, Eloyella, Hintonella, Ornithocephalus, Phymatidium,*

Platyrhiza, Rauhiella, Sphyrastylis, Thysanoglossa, Zygostates.

Oncidiinae: *Ada, Amparoa, Antillanorchis, Aspasia, (Baptistonia), Binotia, Brachtia, Brassia, Buesiella, Capanemia, Caucaea, Cischweinfia, Cochlioda, Comparettia, Cuitlauzinia, Cypholoron, Diadenium, Dignathe, Erycina, Fernandezia, Gomesa, Helcia, Hybochilus, Ionopsis, Konantzia, Lemboglossum, Leochilus, Leucohyle, Lockhartia, Macradenia, Macroclinium, Mesoglossum, Mesospinidium, Mexicoa, Miltonia, Miltoniopsis, Neodryas, Neokoehleria, Notylia, Odontoglossum, Oliveriana, Oncidium, Osmoglossum, Otoglossum, Pachyphyllum, Palumbina, Papperitzia, Plectrophora, Polyotidium, Psychopsiella, Psychopsis, Psygmorchis, Pterostemma, Quekettia, Raycadenco, Rodriguezia, Rodrigueziella, Rodrigueziopsis, Rossioglossum, Rusbyella, Sanderella, Saundersia, Scelochiloides, Scelochilus, Sigmatostalix, Solenidiopsis, Solenidium, Stictophyllum, Suarezia, Sutrina, Symphyglossum, Systeloglossum, Ticoglossum, Tolumnia, Trichocentrum, Trichopilia, Trizeuxis, Warmingia.*

Epidendroid Phylad

Arethuseae

Arethusinae: *Arethusa, Eleorchis.*

Bletiinae: *Acanthephippium, Ancistrochilus, Anthogonium, Aulostylis, Bletia, Bletilla, Calanthe, Calopogon, Cephalantheropsis, Eriodes, Gastrorchis, Hancockia, Hexalectris, Ipsea, Mischobulbon, Nephelaphyllum, Pachystoma, Phaius, Plocoglottis, Spathoglottis, Tainia.*

Chysinae: *Chysis.*

Coelogyneae

Thuniinae: *Thunia.*

Coelogyninae: *Basigyne, Bracisepalum, Bulleyia, Chelonistele, Coelogyne, Dendrochilum, Dickasonia, Entomophobia, Forbesina, Geesinkorchis, Gynoglottis, Ischnogyne, Nabaluia, Neogyne, Otochilus, Panisea, Pholidota, Pleione, Pseudacoridium, Sigmatogyne.*

Epidendreae I (New World)

Sobraliinae: *Elleanthus, Epilyna, Sertifera, Sobralia.*

Arpophyllinae: *Arpophyllum.*

Meiracylliinae: *Meiracyllium.*

Coeliinae: *Coelia.*

Laeliinae: *Acrorchis, Alamania, Artorima, Barkeria, Basiphyllaea, Brassavola, Broughtonia, Cattleya, (Cattleyopsis), Caularthron, Constantia,* *Dilomilis, Dimerandra, Domingoa, Encyclia, Epidendrum, Hagsatera, Helleriella, Hexisea, Homalopetalum, Isabelia, Isochilus, Jacquiniella, Laelia, Leptotes, Loefgrenianthus, Myrmecophila, Nageliella, Neocogniauxia, Nidema, Oerstedella, Orleanesia, Pinelia, Platyglottis, Ponera, Pseudolaelia, Psychilis, Pygmaeorchis, Quisqueya, Reichenbachanthus, Rhyncholaelia, Scaphyglottis, Schomburgkia, Sophronitis, Tetramicra.*

Pleurothallidinae: *Acostaea, Barbosella, Barbrodria, Brachionidium, Chamelophyton, Condylago, Dracula, Dresslerella, Dryadella, Frondaria, Lepanthes, Lepanthopsis, Masdevallia, Myoxanthus, Octomeria, Ophidion, Platystele, Pleurothallis, Porroglossum, Restrepia, Restrepiella, Restrepiopsis, Salpistele, Scaphosepalum, Stelis, Teagueia, Trichosalpinx, Trisetella.*

Epidendreae II (Old World)

Glomerinae: *Aglossorhyncha, Agrostophyllum, Earina, Glomera, Glossorhyncha, Ischnocentrum, Sepalosiphon.*

Adrorhizinae: *Adrorhizon, Sirhookera.*

Polystachyinae: *Hederorkis, Imerinaea, Neobenthamia, Polystachya.*

Dendrobioid Subclade

Podochileae

Eriinae: *Ascidieria, Ceratostylis, Cryptochilus, Epiblastus, Eria, Mediocalcar, Porpax, Sarcostoma, Stolzia, Trichotosia.*

Podochilinae: *Appendicula, Chilopogon, Chitonochilus, Cyphochilus, Poaephyllum, Podochilus.*

Thelasiinae: *Chitonanthera, Octarrhena, Oxyanthera, Phreatia, Rhynchophreatia, Thelasis.*

Ridleyellinae: *Ridleyella.*

Dendrobieae

Dendrobiinae: *Cadetia, Dendrobium, Diplocaulobium, Epigeneium, Flickingeria, Pseuderia.*

Bulbophyllinae: *Bulbophyllum, Chaseella, Codonosiphon, Dactylorhynchus, Drymoda, Genyorchis, Hapalochilus, Jejosephia, Monomeria, Monosepalum, Pedilochilus, Saccoglossum, Sunipia, Tapeinoglossum, Trias.*

Vandeae

Aeridinae: *Abdominea, Acampe, Adenoncos, Aerides, Amesiella, Arachnis, Armodorum, Ascocentrum, Ascochilopsis, Ascochilus, Ascoglossum, Ascolabium, Biermannia, Bogoria, Brachypeza, Calymmanthera, Ceratocentron, Ceratochilus, Chamaeanthus, Chiloschista, Chroniochilus, Cleisocentron, Cleisomeria, Cleisostoma, Cordiglottis,*

Cottonia, Cryptopylos, Dimorphorchis, Diplocentrum, Diploprora, Doritis, Dryadorchis, Drymoanthus, Dyakia, Eparmatostigma, Esmeralda, (Euanthe), Gastrochilus, Grosourdya, Gunnarella, Haraella, Holcoglossum, Hygrochilus, Hymenorchis, (Kingidium), Lesliea, Loxoma, Luisia, Macropodanthus, Malleola, Megalotis, Micropera, Microsaccus, Microtatorchis, Mobilabium, Neofinetia, Nothodoritis, Omoea, Ornithochilus, Papilionanthe, Papillilabium, Paraphalaenopsis, Parapteroceras, Pelatantheria, Pennilabium, Peristeranthus, Phalaenopsis, Phragmorchis, Plectorhiza, Pomatocalpa, Porphyrodesme, Porrorachis, Proteroceras, Pteroceras, Renanthera, Renantherella, Rhinerrhiza, Rhynchogyna, Rhynchostylis, Robiquetia, Saccolabiopsis, Saccolabium, Sarcanthopsis, Sarcochilus, Sarcoglyphis, Sarcophyton, Schistotylus, Schoenorchis, Sedirea, Seidenfadenia, Smithsonia, Smitinandia, Staurochilus, Stereochilus, Taeniophyllum, Thrixspermum, Trichoglottis, Trudelia, Tuberolabium, Uncifera, Vanda, Vandopsis, Ventricularia, Xenicophyton.

Angraecinae: *Aeranthes, Ambrella, Angraecum, Bonniera, Calyptrochilum, Campylocentrum, Cryptopus, Dendrophylax, Harrisella, Jumellea, Lemurella, Lemurorchis, Neobathiea, Oeonia,* *Oeoniella, Ossiculum, Perrierella, Polyradicion (Polyrrhiza), Sobennikoffia.*

Aerangidinae: *Aerangis, Ancistrorhynchus, Angraecopsis, Azadehdelia, Beclardia, Bolusiella, Cardiochilus, Chamaeangis. Chauliodon, Cyrtorchis, Diaphananthe, Dinklageella, Distylodon, Eggelingia, Encheiridion, Eurychone, Holmesia, Listrostachys, Margelliantha, Microcoelia, Microterangis, Mystacidium, Nephrangis, Plectrelminthus, Podangis, Rangaeris, Rhaesteria, Rhipidoglossum, Sarcorhynchus, Solenangis, Sphyrarhynchus, Summerhayesia, Taeniorhiza, Triceratorhynchus, Tridactyle, Ypsilopus.*

Misfits and Problems

Arundinae: *Arundina, Dilochia.*

Collabiinae: *Chrysoglossum, Collabium, Diglyphosa.*

Claderia.

Eriopsis.

Pogoniinae: *Cleistes, Duckeella, Isotoria, Pogonia, Pogoniopsis.*

Thaia.

Xerorchis.

Orchid Genera Illustrated

For each genus that follows there is a diagrammatic color plate showing all the major floral details and the vegetative habit of a representative species. These illustrations were drawn from live material to assure accuracy of detail. In a few cases, a select clonal form of the chosen species was illustrated (e.g., a very colorful form of *Epigeneium lyonii* was used for illustrating the genus *Epigeneium*). In those cases where a genus is large and has great variability in vegetative or floral characteristics (e.g., *Dendrobium*), additional illustrations show some of the variations. When comparing specimens to the illustrations, the reader should keep in mind that the great variations within a species as well as between and among species in any given genus cannot be depicted using a single specimen.

The generic descriptions highlight the characteristics by which a given genus can be identified and also briefly summarize culture requirements for the genus. A list of the more popular species in the genus gives the flowering season (F = fall, W = winter, S = spring, SS = summer) and the general locale where the species is native. (The current official name has been used for places, although many readers are more familiar with Burma, for example, than they are with Myanmar.) The native locale is also depicted on a map. An × before a species name indicates that taxonomists consider it a natural hybrid.

Acacallis _____

GENUS: *Acacallis* Lindley (ak-ah-KAL-iss)
TRIBE: Maxillarieae   SUBTRIBE: Zygopetalinae
IDENTIFICATION CHARACTERISTICS: The genus *Acacallis* has only one species and is distinctly different from other orchid genera in several ways. From its unusual column to its beautiful blue flower, this one-of-a-kind genus is a worthy addition to any collection. The genus was first described in 1853 by John Lindley, who named it after Akakallis, a Greek nymph and Apollo's lover. Undoubtedly, Lindley adopted the name because of the beauty of the colorful flowers. Although *Acacallis* is closely allied to *Huntleya*, it differs in its lip, column, and pollinia characteristics.

Acacallis is a sympodial, epiphytic genus. The plants have a creeping rhizome and grow equally well in pots or on plaques. The small, ovoid pseudobulbs are spaced 1 to 2 inches (2.5–5 cm) apart on the rhizome and are topped by one or two almost-lanceolate leaves that have short petioles and may be up to 10 inches (25 cm) long. The inflorescence arises from the base of the pseudobulb and bears up to seven blue flowers with magenta-purple lips.

The large, up to 2.5 inches (6 cm) wide, attractive flowers tend to cup forward slightly. The sepals and petals are similar in size, shape, and color. The broad, three-lobed lip is not only showy but also exhibits several unusual features. Its fleshy callus has a number of fingerlike projections. The midlobe is distinctly ribbed and has a wavy, almost-serrate margin.

The column, which has a slender column foot, is also very distinct: it is triquetrous, that is, the tip of the column is three-parted or three-winged. Four yellow pollinia are superposed and appear almost as one pair atop a thin stipe.

CULTURE: Temperature, 60°F (15°C); light, 2400–3600 footcandles; humidity, 40–60%; media, tree fern, plaque; fertilization, monthly, with a 1–1–1 ratio.

COLOR PLATE: *Acacallis cyanea*

SPECIES	FLOWERING SEASON	GENERAL LOCALE
cyanea	S–SS	Brazil, Venezuela, Columbia

Acacallis cyanea
A: Plant in flower, × ½.
B: Flower, face view, × 1.
C: Flower, side view, × 1.
D: Lip, side view, × 2.
E: Lip, face view, × 2.
F: Flower, vertical section, × 2.
G: Column, ventral view, × 4.
H: Column, end view, × 4.
I: Column, side view, × 4.
J: Column, vertical section, × 4.
K, L, M: Pollinia, × 8.

Acampe

GENUS: *Acampe* Lindley (ah-KAM-pee)
TRIBE: Vandeae   SUBTRIBE: Aeridinae
IDENTIFICATION CHARACTERISTICS: The tight clusters of flowers in this genus make up for their diminutive nature with a delightful fragrance and long life. Well-grown plants often have several clusters of flowers open at one time. The genus, as described by John Lindley in 1853, includes about 12 monopodial, epiphytic species. The generic name, which comes from the Greek word *akampes* (rigid), describes the very stiff nature of the floral segments.

Vegetatively, *Acampe* species look like small *Arachnis* species. The stems are robust and erect but sometimes curve down gently, giving some plants an almost-pendent look. The stiff, leathery leaves, up to 12 inches (30 cm) long, are bilobed at the apex and generally curve downward. The short inflorescences, often bearing a dozen or more flowers, arise from the stem opposite from where the leaf is attached. Usually each leaf has one inflorescence.

The base color of most flowers, which are up to 1 inch (2.5 cm) wide, is yellow or cream with brown or reddish spots. The sepals and petals are alike in size and color, but the margins of the two petals recurve slightly, making the petals appear narrower than the sepals. The flared lip is attached to the base of the column and has a short spur. All floral segments are thick textured, making the flower very rigid.

The very short, broad column has a slight upward curve and is terminated by a distinct anther cap. Two yellow, almost-round pollinia are borne on a long, narrow stipe with a small foot.

CULTURE: Temperature, 60–65°F (15–18°C); light, 2400–3600 footcandles; humidity, 40–60%; media, tree fern, bark; fertilization, monthly, ratio depends on medium.

COLOR PLATE: *Acampe rigida*

SPECIES	FLOWERING SEASON	GENERAL LOCALE
dentata	SS	India
papillosa	F–W	India, Myanmar
rigida	F–W	Tropical Asia to East Africa

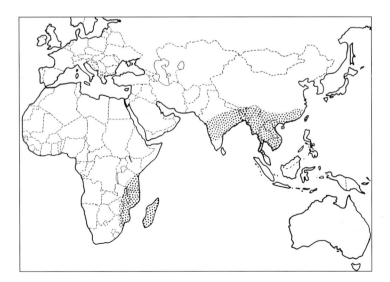

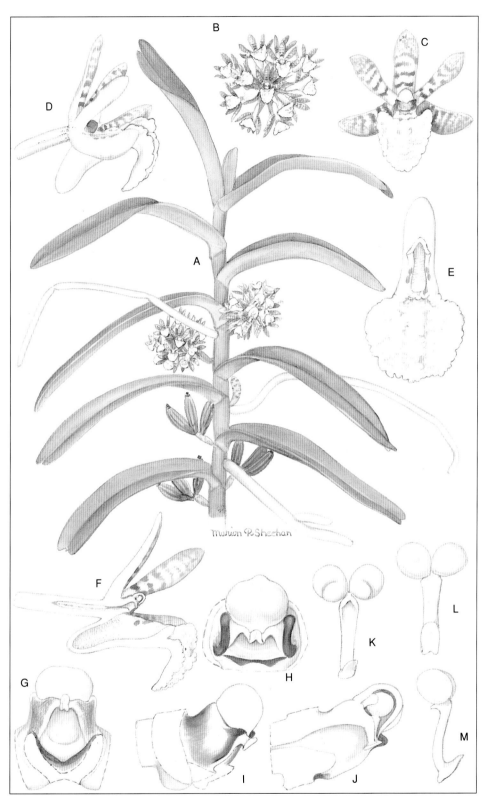

Acampe rigida
A: Plant in flower, × ½.
B: Inflorescence, × 1.
C: Flower, face view, × 3.
D: Flower, side view, × 3.
E: Lip, × 5.
F: Flower, vertical section, × 4.
G: Column, ventral view, × 12.
H: Column, end view, × 12.
I: Column, side view, × 12.
J: Column, vertical section, × 12.
K, L, M: Pollinia, × 20.

Acanthephippium

GENUS: *Acanthephippium* Blume (a-can-the-FIP-ee-um)

TRIBE: Arethuseae   SUBTRIBE: Bletiinae

IDENTIFICATION CHARACTERISTICS: The fleshy flowers of *Acanthephippium* almost belie that they are orchids. The fused sepals are inflated to form a somewhat-lopsided flower. Another unique quality is the odoriferous nature of some flowers. Close examination of the blooms reveals that they are truly orchids and their attempt at deception is over.

The genus was first described by Carl Blume in 1825, who derived the generic name from the Greek words *akantha* (thorn) and *ephippion* (saddle), a reference to the somewhat saddle-shaped lip. Blume originally misspelled the generic name as *Acanthophippium* and then corrected his error in 1828, yet occasionally the generic name is still found in the literature spelled with an *o* instead of an *e*. The genus is closely allied to *Calanthe* and *Phaius* and has about 15 species.

Vegetatively, these terrestrial species resemble *Calanthe* species at first glance. Closer examination, however, reveals that the pseudobulbs of *Acanthephippium* are larger, up to 12 inches (30 cm) tall, and consist of four or more nodes. The green, slightly fluted pseudobulbs are topped by two or more pleated, wrinkled leaves attached at the upper nodes. Each soft, medium green leaf may be up to 20 inches (60 cm) long and 6 inches (15 cm) wide. The leaves develop as the new pseudobulbs are elongating and maturing. The inflorescences (there may be more than one per pseudobulb) bear up to 5 flowers, 1.5 inches (3.75 cm) long, and arise from the base of the newly developing growth. The base flower color is light yellow to pink with reddish bars or spots.

The flowers are the unique part of this genus. The three sepals form a tube with a slight hint of a spur at the base, which is probably due to the curved column foot. The tube of sepals is slightly flared at the apex. The two petals are similar in shape to the sepals but slightly smaller and are barely exerted from the top of the cup. The petal tips are slightly reflexed. The three-lobed lip is attached to the column foot. The two distinct lateral lobes are erect and lie just beside and below the column apex.

The short column is broadest near the stigmatic area and then tapers to a blunt point near the anther cap. There are eight pollinia borne in two groups of four. Each group consists of two large and two small pollinia attached to an almost-granular caudicle with ragged margins. When removing the anther cap there appear to be only four small pollinia as the larger pollinia are folded back into a cavity above the stigmatic surface.

CULTURE: Temperature, 60–65°F (15–18°C) daytime, 55°F (12°C) at night; light, 3000–3600 footcandles; humidity, 40–60%; medium, any well-drained terrestrial medium containing 40% or more organic matter (keep salt concentration low, keep moist during growing season); fertilization, monthly, with any balanced fertilizer.

COLOR PLATE: *Acanthephippium mantinianum*

SPECIES	FLOWERING SEASON	GENERAL LOCALE
bicolor	S–SS	Sri Lanka
javanica	S–SS	Malaya, Java, Sumatra, Borneo
mantinianum	S–SS	Philippines
striatum	SS	Himalayas
sylhetehse	S–SS	Himalayas
unguiculatum	S	Taiwan
yamamotoi	S	Taiwan

Acanthephippium mantinianum

A: Plant in flower, × ⅖.
B: Flower, face view, × 1.
C: Flower, side view, × 1.
D: Lip, top view, × 2.
E: Lip, side view, × 2.
F: Petal, × 1½.
G: Flower, vertical section, × 1½.
H: Column, ventral view, × 3.
I: Column, end view, upper end only, × 3.
J: Column, side view, × 3.
K: Column, vertical section, × 3.
L, M, N: Pollinia × 6.

Acineta

GENUS: *Acineta* Lindley (ah-sin-EE-tuh)

TRIBE: Maxillarieae   SUBTRIBE: Stanhopeinae

IDENTIFICATION CHARACTERISTICS: A well-grown plant of *Acineta chrysantha* in a large hanging basket is a sight to behold. An array of pendent inflorescences, each bearing up to 20 large flowers, look like chains of golden globes. This species also can be very attractive when grown on plaques.

Approximately 15 species of robust plants comprise this New World genus, which John Lindley first described in 1843. Lindley derived the generic name from the Greek word *akinetos* (immovable), a reference to the rigid but jointless lip. *Acineta* is similar to *Stanhopea* vegetatively, but closer to *Pescatorea* in floral characteristics. Since its flower spikes grow down, like those of *Stanhopea*, *Acineta* is best grown in wire baskets.

Vegetatively, *Acineta* produces tight clusters of stout, furrowed pseudobulbs, which are for the most part sheathless and may be 4 inches (10 cm) tall and almost 3.5 inches (8 cm) wide. Each pseudobulb of these sympodial, epiphytic species is topped by one to four large, medium green leaves. The almost-lanceolate, plicate leaf blades can be up to 18 inches (45 cm) long and 3 inches (7.5 cm) wide. Each pendulous inflorescence arises from the base of the pseudobulb and bears numerous 2-inch (5-cm) wide flowers that seldom open fully.

The base flower color is yellow with various amounts of reddish spots. Some species, such as *Acineta erythroxantha*, have a spicy fragrance. The showy flowers of this genus have thick and fleshy sepals and petals that are alike in shape and color. The sepals, however, are more concave, and the petals are slightly smaller and often more densely spotted. The three-lobed, fleshy, rigid lip is more complex than the lip of many orchids, but not as complex as the lip of *Stanhopea*. The erect side lobes are much larger than the small midlobe, which is keeled and has a fleshy disc.

The short column often has the same but slightly paler color pattern as the other floral segments. It is slightly pubescent, is broadest near the stigmatic surface, and may be narrowly winged near the apex. Two yellow, waxy, elongate pollinia are borne on a single stipe with a small foot.

CULTURE: Temperature, 55°F (12°C) at night; light, 2400–3600 footcandles; humidity, 40–60%; medium, any good mix for epiphytes; fertilization, monthly, ratio depends on medium.

COLOR PLATE: *Acineta chrysantha*

SPECIES	FLOWERING SEASON	GENERAL LOCALE
alticola	S	Venezuela
barkeri	S	Mexico
chrysantha	S	Costa Rica, Panama
erythroxantha	S	Venezuela, Colombia
superba	S	Colombia, Venezuela, Ecuador

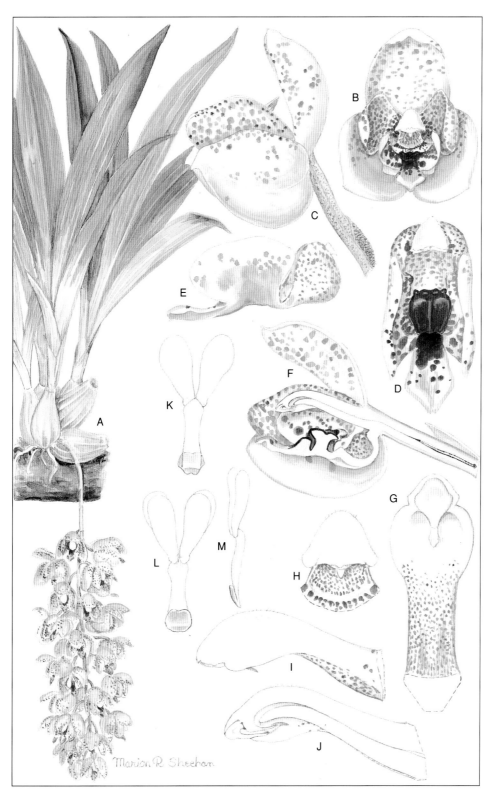

Acineta chrysantha
A: Plant in flower, × ¼.
B: Flower, face view, × 1.
C: Flower, side view, × 1.
D: Lip, face view, × 1½.
E: Lip, side view, × 1½.
F: Flower, vertical section, × 1.
G: Column, ventral view, × 2.
H: Column, end view, × 2.
I: Column, side view, × 2.
J: Column, vertical section, × 2.
K, L, M: Pollinia, × 5.

Ada

GENUS: *Ada* Lindley (A-duh)

TRIBE: Maxillarieae SUBTRIBE: Oncidiinae

IDENTIFICATION CHARACTERISTICS: In 1853 John Lindley founded the genus with one species, *Ada aurantiaca*. A few years later another species was added. Then in 1972, Norris Williams transferred a number of *Brassia* species to *Ada*. Today some taxonomists recognize up to eight species, although *A. aurantiaca* is the most widely recognized due to its very distinctive flowering habit. Lindley named the genus for Ada, sister of Artemisia in Caria, a character in ancient history.

Vegetatively, these sympodial, epiphytic (sometimes lithophytic) species resemble *Brassia* species. The flattened pseudobulbs are hidden by clasping leaf bases, so that plants appear to be pseudobulb-less. Approximately five to seven leaves are borne on each growth, with one leaf atop the pseudobulb and the rest attached at the base. Up to 12 inches (30 cm long), the soft, leathery leaves have variable, asymmetrical apices. The axillary inflorescence develops and flowers as the new growth matures.

Flower color is variable and includes orange, red, yellow-brown, and brown. The 1- to 3-inch (2.5- to 7.5-cm) wide flowers, although similar in component parts, vary considerably in the degree of opening. The sepals and petals of *Ada aurantiaca* barely separate near the apex, with only the tips slightly reflexed, giving the flower a tubular look. At the other extreme is the flower of *A. glumacea*, which opens fully and is almost flat. The sepals and petals of *Ada* species are alike in color and shape, with the petals often a little shorter and broader at the base. The sharp, pointed lip is almost lance-shaped, with a very distinct callus. In some species, lobes near the tip of the lip are rolled inward to form a short tube-like structure.

The column is very short and somewhat hour-glass-shaped when viewed from below. It has a large stigmatic area and a very distinct anther cap. The two yellow pollinia are attached to a single, almost-triangular stipe with a small viscidium. The viscidium of *Ada aurantiaca* is reddish maroon.

CULTURE: Temperature, 50°F (10°C); light, 2400–3600 footcandles; humidity, 40–60%; media, tree fern, bark, osmunda, peat and perlite; fertilization, monthly, ratio depends on medium.

COLOR PLATE: *Ada aurantiaca*

SPECIES	FLOWERING SEASON	GENERAL LOCALE
aurantiaca	W–S	Ecuador, Colombia, Venezuela
glumacea	W	Colombia, Venezuela
ishmanii	SS	Colombia
keiliana	SS	Colombia, Venezuela

Ada aurantiaca

A: Plant in flower, × ½.
B: Flower, face view, × 2.
C: Flower, side view, × 2.
D: Lip, face view, × 4.
E: Lip, side view, × 4.
F: Flower, vertical section, × 2.
G: Column, ventral view, × 6.
H: Column, end view, × 6.
I: Column, side view, × 6.
J: Column, vertical section, × 6.
K, L, M: Pollinia, × 12.

Aerangis

GENUS: *Aerangis* Reichenbach f. (air-ANG-giss)
TRIBE: Vandeae SUBTRIBE: Aerangidinae
IDENTIFICATION CHARACTERISTICS: More than 120 species of delightful plants comprise the African genus *Aerangis*, which was first described by H. G. Reichenbach in 1865. The generic name, formed by combining the Greek words *aer* (air) and *angos* (vessel), undoubtedly refers to the very pronounced spurs that are typical of so many species of this genus. *Aerangis* is closely related to *Angraecum*, but does not have the latter's deeply concave lip.

Vegetatively, two distinct types of monopodial habits are found in this epiphytic genus. The growth habit of many species (e.g., *Aerangis friesiorum*) is similar to that of *Phalaenopsis* species, while the growth habit of others (e.g., *A. thomsonii*) resembles that of *Vanda* species. *Vanda*-like species have stems covered with leaf bases; *Aerangis* species do not. The strap-shaped leaves of *Aerangis*, which vary in size and texture, may be bilobed at the apex and may be up to 10 inches (25 cm) long and 2 to 3 inches (5–7.5 cm) wide. The inflorescence arises from the axil of the leaf, is usually somewhat pendent, and has 10 or more whitish flowers, sometimes tinged pink or brown.

Each spurred flower may be up to 2 inches (5 cm) wide. The three sepals and two petals are usually alike in size, shape, and color. In a few species (e.g., *Aerangis luteoalba* var. *rhodosticta*), the two petals are slightly larger than the sepals. The lip is flat with a very distinct tubular spur. The midlobe of the lip is also flattened and may terminate in a sharp point or be rounded or blunt.

The short, erect column is often exposed by the reflexed floral segments. Usually this stubby structure, which is widest near the stigmatic surface, is white but sometimes it is orange-red (e.g., *Aerangis luteoalba* var. *rhodosticta*). Two yellowish, almost-elliptical pollinia are borne on a curved stipe with a small shieldlike base.

CULTURE: Temperature, 60°F (15°C); light, 2400–3600 footcandles; humidity, 40–60%; media, tree fern, bark; fertilization, monthly, ratio depends on medium.

COLOR PLATE: *Aerangis brachycarpa*

SPECIES	FLOWERING SEASON	GENERAL LOCALE
brachycarpa	S–SS	Tropical Africa
citrata	F–W–S	Madagascar
friesiorum	S–F	Kenya
luteoalba var.		
rhodosticta	S–SS–F	Uganda, Kenya, Congo, Ethiopia, Cameroon
mystacidii	S	South Africa
thomsonii	S–SS	Kenya, Uganda, Tanzania
ugandensis	S–SS	Uganda, Kenya

Aerangis brachycarpa

A: Plant in flower, × ½.
B: Flower, face view, × ½.
C: Flower, face view, × 1.
D: Flower, side view, × 1.
E: Lip, × 1½.
F: Flower, vertical section, × 2.
G: Column, ventral view, × 5.
H: Column, end view, × 5.
I: Column, side view, × 5.
J: Column, vertical section, × 5.
K, L, M: Pollinia, × 10.

Aeranthes

GENUS: *Aeranthes* Lindley (air-ANN-theez)
TRIBE: Vandeae SUBTRIBE: Angraecinae
IDENTIFICATION CHARACTERISTICS: The islands off the east coast of Africa are unusual in many ways, and one of the more interesting orchid genera endemic to this area is *Aeranthes*. Of the 30 species known today, 27 are found on Madagascar, 3 in the Mascarene Islands, and 1 on Comoro. When John Lindley first described the genus in 1824, he coined the generic name from the Greek words *aer* (air) and *anthos* (flower). Undoubtedly, he was referring to the flowers, like those of *A. grandiflora*, which may be at the tip of a 3-foot (90-cm) tall, slender, wiry stem such that they appear to be floating in the air.

Monopodial and epiphytic, *Aeranthes* species are always found growing on the trunks or limbs of trees. The linear-to-lanceolate, leathery leaves, up to 12 inches (30 cm) long, are unequally bilobed at the apex, clasp the stem, and usually are jointed a short distance above the point where they clasp. A thin, often wiry peduncle arises from the leaf axil bearing a racemose inflorescence. Although flowers generally open one at a time, flowering continues for a very long time. An inflorescence may be up to 3 feet (90 cm) long, either pendent or upright, and is covered with brown or tan papery bracts.

White, cream, and green are dominant colors for flowers, which vary considerably in size, up to 4 inches (10 cm) wide and 5 inches (12.5 cm) tall. Often slightly fragrant, the flowers usually are characterized by an insectlike or spiderlike appearance that is not unattractive. The three sepals and two petals are alike basically in shape and color. They flair at the base and are drawn out into long, attenuated points at the apices. The two lateral sepals are fused to the foot of the column. The lip has a broad, flaring or pointed midlobe with an often club-shaped spur at the base.

The very short column is almost as broad as it is long, with a major portion of the underside made up of the stigmatic surface. The two yellow pollinia, each with its own twisted stipe, are almost round. The stipes are twisted around the beak of the rostellum, but are easily removed by insects.

CULTURE: Temperature, 60–65°F (15–18°C); light, 2400–3600 footcandles; humidity, 40–60%; media, tree fern, osmunda, bark; fertilization, monthly, ratio depends on medium.

COLOR PLATE: *Aeranthes arachnites*

SPECIES	FLOWERING SEASON	GENERAL LOCALE
arachnites	SS–F	Madagascar
denticulata	F	Madagascar
filipes	S	Madagascar
grandiflora	SS–F	Madagascar
henrici	W	Madagascar
imerinensis	SS–F	Madagascar
longipes	SS	Madagascar
peyrotii	SS–F	Madagascar
ramosa	F	Madagascar

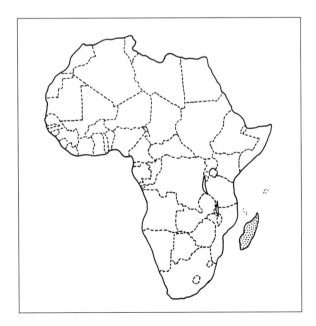

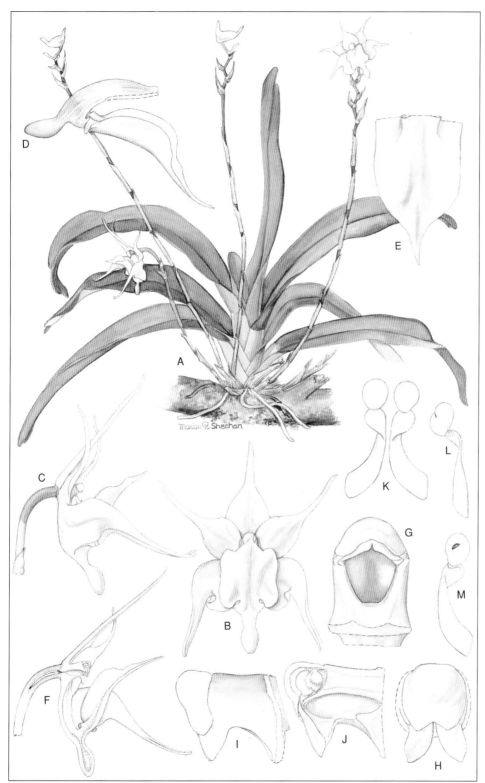

Aeranthes arachnites
A: Plant in flower, × ½.
B: Flower, face view, × 1½.
C: Flower, side view, × 1½.
D: Lip with spur, side view, × 2.
E: Lip, face view, × 2.
F: Flower, vertical section, × 1½.
G: Column, ventral view, × 6.
H: Column, end view, × 6.
I: Column, side view, × 6.
J: Column, vertical section, × 6.
K, L, M: Pollinia, × 8.

Aerides

GENUS: *Aerides* Loureiro (AIR-ih-deez)
TRIBE: Vandeae   SUBTRIBE: Aeridinae
IDENTIFICATION CHARACTERISTICS: *Aerides*, a genus of over 60 easy-to-grow species, has long been popular among orchidists due, probably, more to its flowering habit than to its ease of culture. Like *Rhynchostylis* species, *Aerides* species are called foxtail orchids in some areas. The genus was founded by Portuguese botanist João Loureiro before 1790, when he discovered *A. odorata* in Cochin, China. The literal translation of the generic name is "children of the air."

These monopodial, epiphytic orchids are found growing on trunks and branches of trees. The stems are round and seldom thicker than an ordinary lead pencil. The strap-shaped leaves are keeled and bilobed at the apex. They are thick, leathery, up to 14 inches (35.5 cm) long and 2 inches (5 cm) wide, and closely arranged on the stems with the leaf bases clasping the stem. The plants produce a large number of aerial roots that are robust and often branched. Viscid inflorescences arise from the axils of the leaves, are drooping, and usually are longer than the leaves. Although flowers are borne upside down, the pendulous inflorescences, up to 2 feet (60 cm) long in some species, display the flowers in the proper perspective for the viewer. Many 0.75-inch (2-cm) wide flowers are borne on an inflorescence, often very close together. Most of the flowers are white with rose or purple patterns. The dorsal sepal and the petals are similar and usually narrower than the two lateral sepals. The three-lobed lip is spurred and attached to the column foot. The two lateral lobes are almost perpendicular to the sepals and often toothed at the apex. The apex lobe curves upward toward the column and has a wavy and toothed margin.

The column is short, has a foot at the base and a beak at the apex, and is broadest near the foot and narrowest near the stigmatic surface. The stigmatic area is broadest near the foot and narrows down rapidly near the beak. Two roundish, usually yellow pollinia are borne on a narrow stipe with an almost-transparent, shield-shaped foot.

CULTURE: Temperature, 60–70°F (15–21°C); light, 2400–3600 footcandles; humidity, 40–70%; media, tree fern, bark, tree fern and charcoal; fertilization, monthly, ratio depends on medium.

COLOR PLATE: *Aerides odorata*

SPECIES	FLOWERING SEASON	GENERAL LOCALE
crassifolia	SS	Myanmar
crispa	SS	India, Himalayas
emerici	SS	Andaman Islands
falcata	SS	India, Myanmar, Thailand, Laos
flabellata	SS	Thailand
huttoni	F	Celebes
lawrenciae	F–W	Philippines
longicornu	F	Bhutan
maculosa	SS	India
odorata	SS–F	Philippines, Indonesia, Southeast Asia
quinquevulnera	S–F	Philippines
radicosa	SS	India
rosea	SS	Himalayas

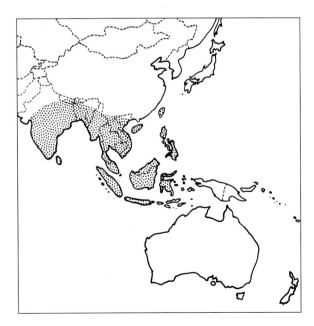

Aerides odorata
A: Plant in flower, × ½.
B: Flower, face view, × 1½.
C: Flower, side view, × 1½.
D: Lip, face view, × 2.
E: Lip, side view, × 2.
F: Flower, vertical section, × 1½.
G: Column, ventral view, × 8.
H: Column, end view, × 8.
I: Column, side view, × 8.
J: Column, vertical section, × 8.
K, L, M: Pollinia, × 10.

Amesiella

GENUS: *Amesiella* Garay (aim-zee-ELL-uh)

TRIBE: Vandeae   SUBTRIBE: Aeridinae

IDENTIFICATION CHARACTERISTICS: At first glance this orchid plant looks like a small *Phalaenopsis* seedling, but when the large spurred flowers appear there is no longer any confusion. *Amesiella* is in a class by itself. Oakes Ames of Harvard University originally described this unique Philippine plant as an *Angraecum*, but in 1972 Leslie Garay found sufficient characteristics to establish a new genus. The genus was named to honor Ames, who worked with Philippine orchids. Under the present taxonomic divisions, *Amesiella* has one species and is confined to the Philippines. It is closely related to *Angraecum* and *Neofinetia*.

This monopodial epiphyte appears stemless and often has up to six fleshy leaves. Each elliptic-to-obtuse leaf may be up to 2.5 inches (6 cm) long and about half as wide. The very short stem is hidden by the clasping leaf bases. One to a few nonfragrant, large, strikingly white flowers are borne on very short, somewhat pendulous inflorescences. In cultivation, the flowers often rest on the rim of the pot. A well-grown mature plant in a 2-inch (5-cm) pot may have one, two, or occasionally more inflorescences.

The flowers, up to 2 inches (5 cm) wide, have sepals and petals that are very much alike in size and color. The sepals often have a distinct notch at their apices. The three-lobed lip has a very long (up to 1.5 inches [4 cm]) slightly curved spur. The lateral lobes of the lip are smaller than the long, flat midlobe and curve upwards slightly.

The column is interesting because a major portion of the underside is covered by stigmatic surface. The two yellow pollinia are borne on a single stipe ending in an almost-flat, circular viscidium.

CULTURE: Temperature, 70°F (21°C); light, 1500–2000 footcandles; humidity, 40–60%; media, tree fern, bark, peat and perlite; fertilization, monthly, ratio depends on medium.

COLOR PLATE: *Amesiella philippinensis*

SPECIES	FLOWERING SEASON	GENERAL LOCALE
philippinensis	F–W	Philippines

Amesiella philippinensis
A: Plant in flower, × 1.
B: Flower, face view, × 1.
C: Flower, side view, × 1.
D: Lip, × 1¼.
E: Flower, vertical section, × 1½.
F: Column, ventral view, × 5.
G: Column, end view, × 5.
H: Column, side view, × 5.
I: Column, vertical section, × 5.
J, K, L: Pollinia, × 10.

Angraecum

GENUS: *Angraecum* Bory (an-GRAY-kum)
TRIBE: Vandeae SUBTRIBE: Angraecinae
IDENTIFICATION CHARACTERISTICS: Around 200 species of white or greenish, generally star-shaped flowers with pronounced spurs form the genus *Angraecum*. The generic name is a latinized form of the Malayan word *angrek*, used to describe orchids of vandaceous habit. Early specimens were introduced by French botanist Aubert Du Petit-Thouars, who is credited by some as founder of the genus. The name, however, was given by Colonel Jean Baptiste Bory in 1804. *Angraecum* was the first genus in this group to be described.

Despite some variations in vegetative growth (Fig. 16), *Angraecum* species are typical monopodial growers. Plants vary from a few inches in height (e.g., *A. distichum*) to 6 or more feet (180 cm) (e.g., *A. superbum*). The broad, often leathery, strap-shaped leaves clasp the stem and often have bilobed apices. One or more pronounced, spurred flowers from 0.25 to 7 inches (0.5–17.5 cm) in diameter are borne on axillary inflorescences.

The flowers vary slightly in overall shape. The sepals form a triangle, tapering from a broad base to a sharp point at the apex. The two petals are similar to the sepals in color and shape. The three-lobed lip has two small lateral lobes and a large apical lobe. The lip, with a large basal spur, is attached to the base of the column. *Angraecum sesquipedale* has a floral spur 12 inches (30 cm) long and is considered by many orchidologists as the outstanding member of the genus.

The column is short, being almost as broad as long. The stigmatic surface is separated from the pollinia by an entire or bilobed rostellum. Two yellow, almost-elliptical pollinia are present, each with a distinct broad or narrow stipe.

CULTURE: Temperature, 60–70°F (15–21°C); light, 2400–3600 footcandles; humidity, 40–70%; media, tree fern, osmunda, bark; fertilization, monthly, ratio depends on medium.

COLOR PLATE: *Angraecum sesquipedale*

SPECIES	FLOWERING SEASON	GENERAL LOCALE
bicallosum	W–S–SS–F	Madagascar
birrinense	F	Ghana
compactum	S–SS	Madagascar
didieri	S–SS	Madagascar
distichum	F–W	Sierra Leone to Cameroon and Congo; tropical western Africa
eburneum	F–W	Mascarene Islands, Seychelles
eichlerianum	SS	Tropical western Africa
erectum	F–W–S–SS	Uganda, Kenya, Tanzania, Zambia
germinyanum	S	Madagascar, Mascarene Islands
infundibulare	F–W	Tropical western Africa, Uganda, Nigeria, Cameroon, Congo basin
leonis	W	Madagascar, Comoro Islands
magdalenae	S–SS–F	Madagascar
montanum	S	Kenya
ramosum	S–SS	Madagascar, Comoro Islands
scottianum	F	Comoro Islands
sesquipedale	W–S	Madagascar
superbum	S–SS–F	Madagascar, Comoro Islands, Seychelles

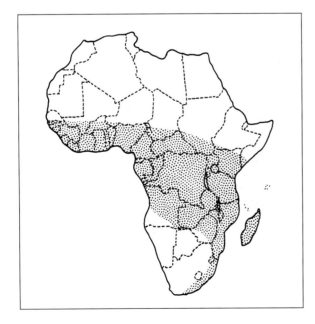

Angraecum sesquipedale
A: Plant in flower, × ¼.
B: Flower, face view, × ½.
C: Flower, side view, × ½.
D: Lip, × ½.
E: Flower, vertical section, × ½.
F: Column, ventral view, × 3.
G: Column, end view, × 3.
H: Column, side view, × 3.
I: Column, vertical section, × 3.
J: Column, end view, anther
   cap lifted, × 3.
K, L: Pollinia, × 5.

49

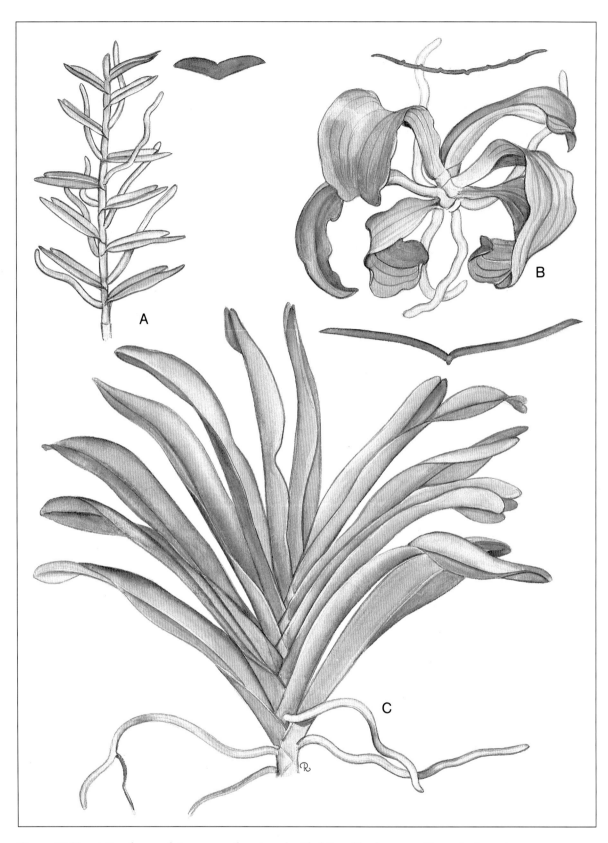

Figure 16. Vegetative forms of *Angraecum* showing plant habit and leaf cross sections. A: *A. erectum*. B: *A. kotschyi*. C: *A. superbum*.

Angraecum

Anguloa

GENUS: *Anguloa* Ruiz & Pavón (an-gyew-LOH-uh)

TRIBE: Maxillarieae   SUBTRIBE: Lycastinae

IDENTIFICATION CHARACTERISTICS: Affectionately called "tulip orchids" by the hobbyist, *Anguloa* species have extremely attractive flowers. Spanish botanists Hipólito Ruiz Lopez and José Antonio Pavón founded the genus in the late 1770s when they discovered *A. uniflora*. They dedicated the genus to Don Francisco de Angulo, who was then in charge of Peruvian mines. Unfortunately, the genus was lost to culture for approximately 50 years. It was not until 1844 that plants (collected by Jean Jules Linden in 1842) flowered in George Barker's collection in Birmingham, England.

The 10 known sympodial species of *Anguloa* may be terrestrial or epiphytic. Vegetatively, the plants are robust with large, soft, lanceolate leaves resembling the leaves of *Lycaste*. Each folded leaf may be up to 2 feet (60 cm) long. The oblong pseudobulbs are tightly clustered, up to 7 inches (17.5 cm) long, and become furrowed with age. The large flowers, 3 to 4 inches (7.5–10 cm) wide, are borne singly atop a short stem that is partially covered with green, leafy bracts. Several inflorescences may arise from a single pseudobulb.

The unusual flowers, which may be yellow, brown, or white, depending on the species, are easy to identify. The three sepals and two petals, which are almost identical and of the same color, are concave and form a cuplike flower, somewhat resembling a tulip in shape. The lip and other floral segments are contained within the cup. The small three-lobed lip is hinged to the foot of the column. Any breeze or movement of the flower causes the lip to move.

The column is short with a comparatively large foot. Two earlike appendages near the apex of the column almost hide the stigmatic surface. The anther cap looks beaked due to the extended caudicle. Four yellowish pollinia are borne on a narrow stipe with a very small shield-shaped foot. Two pollinia are slightly larger than the others.

CULTURE: Temperature, 50–60°F (10–15°C); light, 2400–3600 footcandles; humidity, 40–60%; media, peat and perlite, fir bark for epiphytes; soil, tree fern, sphagnum for terrestrials; fertilization, every two weeks when in active growth, monthly at other times, with a 1–1–1 ratio.

COLOR PLATE: *Anguloa uniflora*

SPECIES	FLOWERING SEASON	GENERAL LOCALE
brevilabris	SS	Colombia
cliftonii	S–SS	Colombia
clowesii	S–SS	Colombia, Venezuela
ruckeri	S–SS	Colombia, Venezuela
uniflora	S	Colombia, Ecuador, Peru

Anguloa uniflora
A: Plant in flower, × ³⁄₈.
B: Flower, face view, × ¾.
C: Flower, side view, × ¾.
D: Lip, × 1½.
E: Flower, vertical section, × ¾.
F: Column, ventral view, × 1½.
G: Column, end view, × 1½.
H: Column, side view, × 1½.
I: Column, vertical section,
   × 1½.
J, K, L: Pollinia, × 3.

53

Ansellia ———————————————————————

GENUS: *Ansellia* Lindley (an-SELL-ee-uh)
TRIBE: Cymbidieae   SUBTRIBE: Cyrtopodiinae
IDENTIFICATION CHARACTERISTICS: Many taxonomists now believe that *Ansellia* consists of two highly variable species. In the past, however, some taxonomists described up to five species, although the variability among them was limited mainly to the flowers. The genus was named by John Lindley for John Ansell, who discovered the first plant on an expedition to Niger around 1840.

The stiff, upright pseudobulbs of these sympodial epiphytes are 1 inch (2.5 cm) in diameter at their widest point and may be up to 2 feet (60 cm) tall. Each bulb has five or more leathery leaves attached at the upper nodes. The lower portion of the pseudobulb is covered by papery, leaflike bracts attached at each node. Individual leaves are about 5 inches (12.5 cm) long and 1 inch (2.5 cm) wide. Branched inflorescences bearing many flowers arise from the apex of the pseudobulb, while smaller inflorescences arise from some of the pseudobulb's lower nodes.

The 1.5- to 2-inch (4- to 5-cm) wide flowers are yellow or yellowish green with varying degrees of brownish red marks. Some varieties are identified by the amount and intensity of floral marks. The three sepals and two petals are alike in size, shape, and color. The three-lobed lip is small and not very showy. Its pale cream-colored lateral lobes partially encircle the short column and may have brownish red lines on the inside. The apex lobe is bright yellow with a wavy margin and two or three longitudinal keels.

The column is short with a pronounced anther cap at the apex. The stigmatic surface, which is very narrow and almost as wide as the column, is slightly compressed near the middle. The pollinia resemble two pocketbook rolls. The pale lemon-yellow pollinium segments are fused together near the point of attachment to the stipe. The degree of fusion varies among plants.

CULTURE: Temperature, 60–70°F (15–21°C); light, 2400–3600 footcandles; humidity, 40–70%; media, tree fern, osmunda, bark; fertilization, monthly, ratio depends on medium.

COLOR PLATE: *Ansellia africana*

SPECIES	FLOWERING SEASON	GENERAL LOCALE
africana	W–S–SS	Tropical and southern Africa

Ansellia africana

A: Plant in flower, × ¼.
B: Flower, face view, × 1.
C: Flower, side view, × 1.
D: Lip, face view, × 2.
E: Lip, side view, × 2.
F: Flower, vertical section, × 1.
G: Column, ventral view, × 5.
H: Column, end view, × 5.
I: Column, side view, × 5.
J: Column, vertical section, × 5.
K: Anther cap and pollinia, × 8.
L, M, N: Pollinia, × 10.

Arachnis _____

GENUS: *Arachnis* Blume (uh-RAK-niss)
TRIBE: Vandeae   SUBTRIBE: Aeridinae
IDENTIFICATION CHARACTERISTICS: The genus *Arachnis* contains about 15 species of often very tall, leggy plants. The distinctive flowers, said by many to resemble a scorpion or a spider, inspired Carl Blume in 1825 to name the genus after the Greek word for spider (*arachne*). *Arachnis* is closely related to *Renanthera* and *Vanda*, but the lip differs in that it is not spurred, it has a keel, and it is hinged at its base.

Basically, these monopodial plants are epiphytes, but they often grow on rocks (lithophytes) or as terrestrials. Plant size varies greatly from less than 12 inches (30 cm) to 15 or more feet (450 cm) tall. The stiff, alternate, leathery leaves, up to 4 inches (10 cm) long and 0.75 inch (2 cm) wide, are usually spaced about 1 inch (2.5 cm) apart on the stem. Strap-shaped, they clasp the stem at their base. In native habitat, plants produce a new leaf every two weeks. The inflorescence arises from the stem just above the clasping leaf and from the side opposite the leaf blade. Basically, the flowers are creamy white or yellowish with brownish purple irregular blotches. Erect and up to 25 inches (62.5 cm) long, an inflorescence bears six to ten flowers, each 2 to 3 inches (5–7.5 cm) across.

The spiderlike flowers of *Arachnis* species are very similar to one another. The sepals and petals are almost alike in size, shape, and color, varying only somewhat in curvature between species. The lip is small and inconspicuous. Its two lateral lobes partially enclose the column. The base of the lip is hinged to the base of the column, and the midlobe is narrow to broad with either a high or low keel.

The short, straight column widens slightly near the somewhat kidney-shaped stigmatic surface. Two yellowish pollinia are attached almost perpendicular to the main axis of a nearly pyramid-shaped stipe. In some species (e.g., *Arachnis flos-aeris*) the caudicle is bent just above the midpoint.

CULTURE: Temperature, 65°F (18°C); light, 2400–3600 footcandles; humidity, 60–75%; media, tree fern, rich organic compost; fertilization, monthly, with a 1–1–1 ratio.

COLOR PLATE: *Arachnis flos-aeris*

SPECIES	FLOWERING SEASON	GENERAL LOCALE
cathcartii	S	Sikkim, Bhutan
flos-aeris	S–SS–F	Sumatra, Borneo, Malay Peninsula, Java
hookeriana	S–SS	Riouw Archipelago (Indonesia), Malay Peninsula, Borneo
× *maingayi*	SS–F	Singapore to Borneo

Arachnis flos-aeris
A: Plant in flower, × ⅓.
B: Flower, face view, × ¾.
C: Flower, side view, × ¾.
D: Lip, side view, × 1½.
E: Lip, face view, × 1½.
F: Flower, vertical section, × ¾.
G: Column, ventral view, × 3.
H: Column, end view, × 3.
I: Column, side view, × 3.
J: Column, vertical section, × 3.
K, L, M: Pollinia, × 5.

Arpophyllum

GENUS: *Arpophyllum* La Llave & Lexarza (ar-poh-FILL-um)

TRIBE: Epidendreae   SUBTRIBE: Arpophyllinae

IDENTIFICATION CHARACTERISTICS: *Arpophyllum* has long, cylindrical inflorescences made up of neat, prim, closely spaced rows of upside-down flowers. Multitudes of small pink-to-magenta flowers create a beautiful display, making this genus worth including in an orchid collection. The common name hyacinth orchid has been given to this plant by some authors because of its resemblance in color and shape to that bulb flower. Depending on the authority followed, there are two (Correll 1947) to five (Garay 1974, Cribb 1992) species in the genus. *Arpophyllum* was first identified in 1825 by Pablo de La Llave and Juan Jose Martinez de Lexarza, who coined the generic name from the Greek words *arpi* (sickle) and *phyllon* (leaf). Undoubtedly, the name referred to the leaves of the type specimen, *A. spicatum*.

Arpophyllum species vary vegetatively but exhibit similarities. They have tall, narrow stems topped by a single leaf, with plants up to 4 feet (120 cm) tall reported for *A. spicatum*. The solitary, leathery leaves, which may be 2 feet (60 cm) long and 1.5 inches (4 cm) wide, are often almost sickle-shaped. Each inflorescence, which arises from the top of the newest stem and may be up to 16 inches (40 cm) long, is subtended by a large, leafy bract and bears flowers 0.4 to 0.8 inch (1–2 cm) wide.

The basic flower color for this genus is pinkish purple. Diminutive sepals and petals vary in size, with the sepals larger. The petals, which are narrower than the sepals, have slightly jagged margins. The lip, which is the darkest colored segment of the flower, has a small, saclike projection at the base. The margin of the lip midlobe appears torn, leaving an irregular saw-tooth edge.

The small, erect column is slightly longer than broad, with a small, almost-oval stigmatic surface on the underside. In our plants, eight light gray pollinia are borne on small stipes slightly united at their bases.

CULTURE: Temperature, 60°F (15°C); light, 2400–3600 footcandles; humidity, 40–60%; media, fir bark, tree fern, osmunda; fertilization, monthly, ratio depends on medium.

COLOR PLATE: *Arpophyllum spicatum*

SPECIES	FLOWERING SEASON	GENERAL LOCALE
alpinum	S	Mexico, Guatemala, Honduras
giganteum	W–S	Mexico to Costa Rica, Jamaica, Colombia
spicatum	S	Mexico to Costa Rica, Jamaica, Colombia

Arpophyllum spicatum

A: Plant in flower, × ⅓.
B: Portion of flowering spike, × 1½.
C: Flower, face view, × 4.
D: Flower, side view, × 4.
E: Lip, face view, × 6.
F: Lip, side view, × 6.
G: Flower, vertical section, × 4.
H: Column, ventral view, × 10.
I: Column, end view, × 10.
J: Column, side view, × 10.
K: Column, vertical section, × 10.
L, M: Pollinia, × 20.

Arundina

GENUS: *Arundina* Blume (ar-un-DEE-nuh)
SUBTRIBE: Arundinae
IDENTIFICATION CHARACTERISTICS: In the landscape, *Arundina* forms a dense clump of reedlike growths up to 6 feet (180 cm) tall that resemble miniature bamboo, but the genus is easily recognized as an orchid by the showy, *Cattleya*-like flowers borne at the apex of each stem. Although some taxonomists claim the genus contains as many as eight species, Holttum (1953) presented valid arguments to support his belief that the genus consists of one highly variable species. Presuming only one species exists, the oldest name, *A. graminifolia*, is the valid name for all variants of the species. Carl Blume first described the genus in 1825 based on plants collected in Java. He derived the generic name from the Greek word *arundo* (reed), a reference to the plant's reedy growth.

Vegetatively, these sympodial terrestrials produce thick clusters of erect stems with two-ranked (distichous) leaves. The semirigid, grasslike leaves may be up to 1 foot (30 cm) long and 1 inch (2.5 cm) wide, with the leaf base clasping the stem. The close arrangement of the clasping leaves virtually hides the main stem. An erect inflorescence arises from the tip of each mature stem, elongating as the flowers develop. Flowering continues for several months, with each flower remaining open for approximately three days. As the inflorescences develop, they may produce one or more lateral branches. Towards the end of the flowering cycle, vegetative offsets often form near the base of the flower stalk. Once a bulblike growth develops at the base of the offset, it can be removed and rooted in a moist medium.

The 2.5-inch (6-cm) wide flowers are white, pale lavender or medium lavender with darker purple lips. Usually one but occasionally two flowers are open at the same time on a given stem. The sepals and petals are alike in color, but the petals are usually a little broader. Although very similar to flowers of *Cattleya*, flowers of *Arundina* can be separated easily because of their two lateral sepals arranged close together and almost hidden beneath the lip. The showy, flaring lip is slightly three-lobed with two smaller lateral lobes folded over the column. The larger midlobe has three long, narrow keels and a wavy margin, making the lip the most attractive portion of the flower.

The long, narrow column is almost straight-sided with a slight broadening near the stigmatic surface. Eight yellow pollinia, somewhat compressed, are arranged in four pairs. The caudicle, with a basal viscidium, is usually covered with pollen granules.

CULTURE: Temperature, 60°F (15°C); light, tolerates full sun, can be grown as *Cattleya* in the greenhouse; humidity, 40–60%; media, any well-drained potting mixture containing at least 50% organic matter; fertilization, monthly, with a 1–1–1 ratio.

COLOR PLATE: *Arundina graminifolia*

SPECIES	FLOWERING SEASON	GENERAL LOCALE
graminifolia	All year	Java, Malaya, Thailand, northwest to tropical Nepal

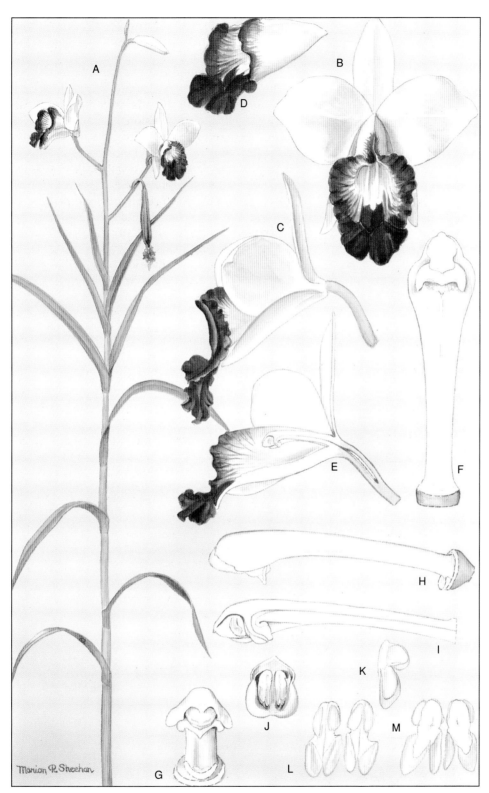

Arundina graminifolia
A: Plant in flower, × ⅜.
B: Flower, face view, × 1.
C: Flower, side view, × 1.
D: Lip, × 1.
E: Flower, vertical section, × 1.
F: Column, ventral view, × 3.
G: Column, end view, × 3.
H: Column, side view, × 3.
I: Column, vertical section, × 3.
J: Anther cap with pollinia, × 5.
K, L, M: Pollinia, × 10.

Ascocentrum

GENUS: *Ascocentrum* Schlechter (ass-koh-SEN-trum)

TRIBE: Vandeae   SUBTRIBE: Aeridinae

IDENTIFICATION CHARACTERISTICS: This small genus of miniature *Vanda*-like plants has dense inflorescences of diminutive yellow, rose, or red flowers. The genus's popularity has increased immensely since the 1960s due to the advent of *Ascocenda* hybrids (*Ascocentrum* crossed with *Vanda*, a combination that has produced some delightful hybrids). When the plants were first discovered in the 1840s, they were assigned to the genus *Saccolabium*, but later were transferred to *Ascocentrum* by Rudolf Schlechter, who used the Greek words *ascos* (bag) and *kentron* (spur) to denote the large spur on the lip. Presently the genus consists of five to ten species.

The monopodial growth habit of *Ascocentrum* resembles that of a very compact *Vanda* species with closely spaced leaves. The small, narrow, strap-shaped leaves, up to 10 inches (25 cm) long, may be thick and stiff (e.g., *A. miniatum*) or soft and recurved (e.g., *A. curvifolium*). Each leaf has an irregular apex. The leaf blade may be covered with brownish purple dots in some species. The axillary flower spikes are seldom more than 8 inches (20 cm) tall and are covered with many closely spaced flowers 0.5 to 0.75 inch (1–2 cm) wide.

The flowers of *Ascocentrum* species vary little. The three sepals are slightly larger than the two petals and are uniform in color. The three-lobed lip is distinctly spurred with the spur representing a large portion of the lip. The midlobe is the largest of the three lobes and is often pointed.

The column is small and erect. The stigmatic area covers much of the underside of the column. Two round pollinia are borne on a very thin stipe ending in a small shield-shaped foot.

CULTURE: Temperature, 65°F (18°C); light, 2400–3600 footcandles; humidity, 40–60%; media, tree fern, osmunda, bark; fertilization, monthly, ratio depends on medium.

COLOR PLATE: *Ascocentrum ampullaceum*

SPECIES	FLOWERING SEASON	GENERAL LOCALE
ampullaceum	S–SS	Myanmar, Himalayas, China
curvifolium	S–SS	Himalayas to Java
hendersonianum	S–SS	Borneo
miniatum	W–S–SS–F	Malaysia to Himalayas, Java, Borneo, Philippines

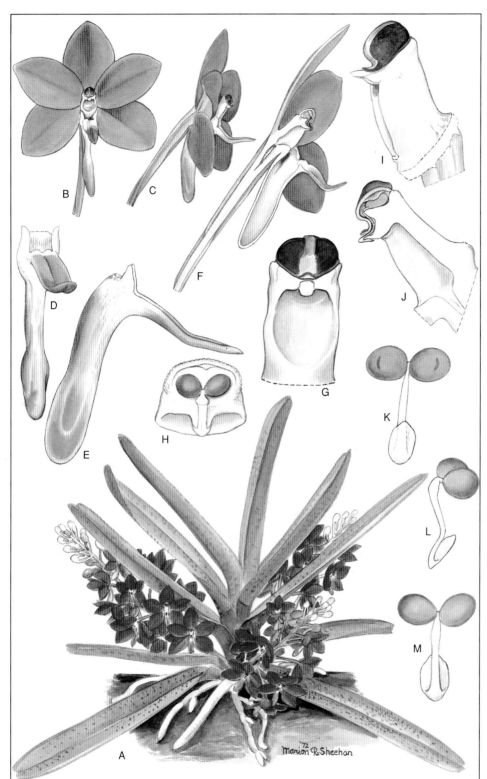

Ascocentrum ampullaceum
A: Plant in flower, × ½.
B: Flower, face view, × 2.
C: Flower, side view, × 2.
D: Lip, face view, × 5.
E: Lip, side view, × 5.
F: Flower, vertical section, × 3.
G: Column, ventral view, × 10.
H: Column, end view, anther
  cap removed, × 10.
I: Column, side view, × 10.
J: Column, vertical section, × 10.
K, L, M: Pollinia, × 15.

63

Ascoglossum

GENUS: *Ascoglossum* Schlechter (ass-koh-GLOSS-um)

TRIBE: Vandeae   SUBTRIBE: Aeridinae

IDENTIFICATION CHARACTERISTICS: The flowers of *Ascoglossum* may be small and average for orchids, but their color is striking. The large number of vividly colored blossoms borne on branched inflorescences make this plant stand out, and the very deep magenta stems add to the overall floral attractiveness. According to most taxonomists, this Pacific islands genus consists of a single species, while other taxonomists feel there may be two species. The genus was first described by Rudolf Schlechter in 1913 when he segregated *Ascoglossum* from *Saccolabium*. Schlechter coined the new generic name from the Greek words *askos* (bag) and *glossa* (tongue), a reference to the distinctly spurred lip. *Ascoglossum* is closely related to *Ascocentrum*, but differs in floral characteristics and in having a branched inflorescence.

Vegetatively, *Ascoglossum* species resemble *Ascocentrum* species when small, but tend to become more leggy with age as the stems rarely branch. The obtuse leaves, up to 10 inches (25 cm) long and 1 inch (2.5 cm) wide, have clasping leaf bases and unequally lobed apices. The dark green stiff leaves are often reddish purple on the underside. The branching inflorescences arise from the leaf axils and may be 2 feet (60 cm) long. The small deep rose-purple flowers, seldom more than 0.75 inch (2 cm) wide, are borne 10 or more to a branchlet.

The flowers seem much smaller than they are because the lateral sepals and petals are deeply reflexed when fully open. The sepals and petals are alike in color but differ in size, with the sepals larger than the petals and with the apices of the petals more acute. At first glance, the lip looks almost bootlike, but it is actually three-lobed with the major portion of the lip being the large saccate spur. The two small lateral lobes of the lip are erect, and the pointed midlobe is very small.

The column, which is the same color as the floral segments, is widest at the base and narrowest at its midpoint. It has a very small stigmatic surface. The reddish purple anther cap and pollinia are darker than the rest of the floral segments. Four pollinia, in two pairs, are attached to a single stipe with a large viscidium at its base.

CULTURE: Temperature, 60–65°F (15–18°C); light, 3600–4000 footcandles; humidity, 40–60%; medium, any coarse mix for epiphytes, grow in baskets or mounted on plaques; fertilization, monthly, ratio depends on medium.

COLOR PLATE: *Ascoglossum calopterum*

SPECIES	FLOWERING SEASON	GENERAL LOCALE
calopterum	S–SS	Philippines, New Guinea, Solomon Islands, Moluccas

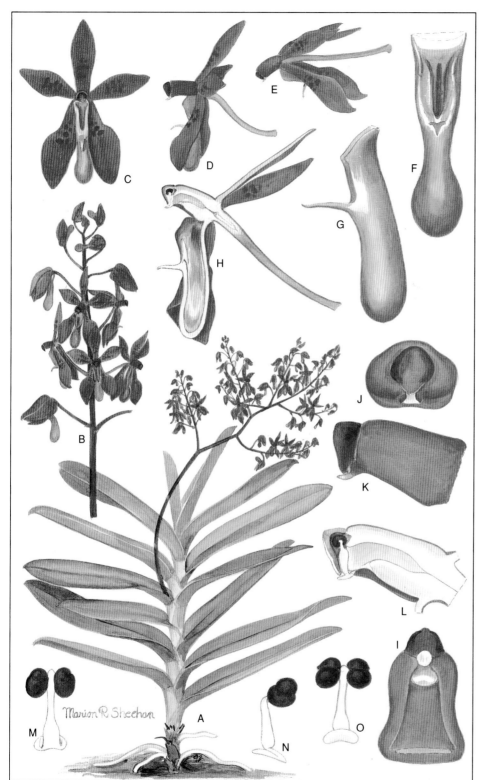

Ascoglossum calopterum

A: Plant in flower, × ⅓.
B: Portion of inflorescence, × 1.
C: Flower, face view, × 2.
D: Flower, newly opened, side view, × 2.
E: Flower, petals and sepals reflexed, × 2.
F: Lip, face view, × 5.
G: Lip, side view, × 5.
H: Flower, vertical section, × 3.
I: Column, ventral view, × 8.
J: Column, end view, × 8.
K: Column, side view, × 8.
L: Column, vertical section, × 8.
M, N, O: Pollinia, × 15.

Aspasia

GENUS: *Aspasia* Lindley (ass-PAY-zee-uh)
TRIBE: Maxillarieae   SUBTRIBE: Oncidiinae
IDENTIFICATION CHARACTERISTICS: *Aspasia* is a small genus of probably no more than 10 species of medium-sized plants with attractive, long-lasting flowers. Vegetatively, these species resemble *Oncidium* species to which they are closely allied. The genus was first described by John Lindley in 1833, but the derivation of the generic name is not clear. Lindley used either the Greek word *aspasios* (beautiful), or he may have named the genus after Aspasia, the beautiful wife of Pericles. Since both words denote beauty, either is apropos.

These sympodial epiphytes (sometimes lithophytes) have flattened and usually grooved pseudobulbs, which may be sessile or borne on a short stalk. Each pseudobulb has four or more clasping leaves (which hide the stalk) at its base and one or two leaves at the apex. The soft, leathery, lancelike leaves are up to 12 inches (30 cm) long and 2 inches (5 cm) wide. One or more inflorescences, which may be up to 10 inches (25 cm) tall, arise from the axils of the leaves attached at the base of the pseudobulb.

Dominant flower colors are white, lavender, and brown. Individual flowers are longer than wide and range from 1.5 to 3 inches (4–7.5 cm) long. The three sepals are alike in size, shape, and color, often with transverse bands of brown. In general, the two petals are shorter than the sepals, are curved towards the column, and are a different color from the sepals. The flaring, three-lobed lip is attached at the midpoint and fused to the base of the column. Two yellow, sometimes hairy calli are often found on the lip at the point where it is attached to the column.

The long, narrow column is widest at the anther cap, has a broad stigmatic area, and may be white or the same color as the lateral petals. The two yellow pollinia are borne on a single-footed stipe and, when viewed from the side, are almost kidney-shaped.

CULTURE: Temperature, 60–65°F (15–18°C); light, 2400–3600 footcandles; humidity, 40–60%; media, tree fern, osmunda, bark; fertilization, monthly, ratio depends on medium.

COLOR PLATE: *Aspasia epidendroides*

SPECIES	FLOWERING SEASON	GENERAL LOCALE
epidendroides	W–S	Guatemala to northern South America
lunata	S–SS–F	Brazil
principissa	W–S	Costa Rica, Panama
variegata	W–S	Trinidad, Guyana to Brazil

Aspasia epidendroides
A: Plant in flower, × ½.
B: Flower, face view, × 1½.
C: Flower, side view, × 1½.
D: Lip, × 4.
E: Flower, vertical section, × 1½.
F: Column, ventral view, × 2½.
G: Column, end view, × 2½.
H: Column, side view, × 2½.
I: Column, vertical section,
   × 2½.
J, K, L: Pollinia, × 5.

Baptistonia

GENUS: *Baptistonia* Barbosa-Rodrigues (bap-tiss-TONE-ee-uh)

TRIBE: Maxillarieae SUBTRIBE: Oncidiinae

IDENTIFICATION CHARACTERISTICS: This attractive, eye-catching genus is rare and has only one species, a sympodial epiphyte. Over the years this species has been a controversial subject among taxonomists. Célestin Alfred Cogniaux first described it as an *Oncidium* in 1877, but João Barbosa-Rodrigues separated it from that genus in 1882. The latter's views were ignored by many taxonomists until Leslie Garay in 1970 established a separate genus for the species. Unfortunately, not all taxonomists accept the finding of Barbosa-Rodrigues and Garay, although there are enough differences in floral characteristics, such as the column shape, callus, and mode of flower opening, to warrant separating this plant from *Oncidium*. As far as is known, only one species of this Brazilian genus has been found.

When Barbosa-Rodrigues founded the genus, he named it in honor of Baptista Caetano d'A. Nogueira, a well-known Brazilian ethnologist. Although still considered somewhat of a rarity, *Baptistonia* is being grown from seed and, to the delight of orchidologists, plants are becoming more evident in shows in late winter and early spring.

Vegetatively, *Baptistonia* resembles *Oncidium* with its tightly clustered, elongate pseudobulbs, each topped by two leaves and subtended by small papery bracts. The thick, medium green leaves are usually widest near the middle and approximately 6 inches (15 cm) long and 1 inch (2.5 cm) wide. The pendent inflorescence arises from the base of the pseudobulb.

Each flower is subtended by a minute leafy bract. The base colors of the flowers are pale green and bright yellow, with reddish maroon marks on the lip. Although the flowers are small (only 1 inch [2.5 cm] wide), they are borne in relatively large numbers and are very colorful, making the plants delightfully attractive. The flowers may open very slowly and look almost tubular before the floral segments unfurl and recurve. Open flowers look like a flock of tiny yellow birds. The sepals and petals are similar in color and shape, although the petals usually are larger than the sepals. The bright yellow lip with deep reddish maroon midlobe is the most attractive segment of the flower. The golden yellow side lobes accentuate the outstanding marks on the rest of the lip.

The interesting column has unusual surface features on the underside, which can be seen readily. Two yellow pollinia are borne on a single stipe with a small reddish foot.

CULTURE: Temperature, 60°F (15°C); light, 2400–3600 footcandles; humidity, 40–60%; medium, grows best on tree fern plaques; fertilization, monthly, with a 1–1–1 ratio.

COLOR PLATE: *Baptistonia echinata*

SPECIES	FLOWERING SEASON	GENERAL LOCALE
echinata	W–S	Brazil

Baptistonia echinata

A: Plant in flower, × ½.
B: Flower, face view, × 2.
C: Flower, side view, × 2.
D: Lip, side view, × 3.
E: Lip, face view, × 3.
F: Flower, vertical section, × 3.
G: Column, ventral view, × 6.
H: Column, end view, × 6.
I: Column, side view, × 6.
J: Column, vertical section, × 6.
K, L, M: Pollinia, × 12.

69

Barkeria

GENUS: *Barkeria* Knowles & Westcott (bar-KARE-ee-uh)

TRIBE: Epidendreae SUBTRIBE: Laeliinae

IDENTIFICATION CHARACTERISTICS: Dainty, colorful flowers on slender stems are one of the fine attributes of the small genus *Barkeria*, which comprises approximately a dozen species. The genus was first described in 1838 by Fredric Westcott and George Knowles and named in honor of George Barker, a British horticulturist who imported the plant on which the genus was founded. *Barkeria* closely resembles *Epidendrum* and is considered by some taxonomists to be a subsection of that genus. Small variations, however, separate the two genera. The lip of *Barkeria* is not attached to the column, or is attached only near the base of the column, and the stems are often swollen at the base.

Vegetatively, these sympodial epiphytes resemble reed-type *Epidendrum* species; however, the leaves usually are clustered near the top of the stem and fall off during the winter season. The lanceolate leaves often are gently recurved and may have warty margins. The inflorescence arises from the tip of stem and may be several times the length of the leafy stem. Each spike bears from a few to 20 flowers.

The delicate flowers range in size from 1 to 3 inches (2.5–7.5 cm) in diameter, depending on the species. Flower color varies, with red, lavender, and yellow the main colors. The sepals and petals are alike in shape and color, sometimes with slight variations in size and sometimes curved or slightly twisted. The lip, which is narrow at the base, broadest near the middle, and sometimes sharp-pointed at the apex, often has three to five distinct keels.

The long column is broadest near the stigmatic area and often the same base color as the flower. Four yellow pollinia on caudicles are found in each flower.

CULTURE: Temperature, 60°F (15°C); light, 2400–3600 footcandles; humidity, 40–60%; media, tree fern, fir bark; fertilization, monthly, ratio depends on medium.

COLOR PLATE: *Barkeria spectabilis*

SPECIES ·	FLOWERING SEASON	GENERAL LOCALE
chinensis	W	Mexico
cyclotella	SS–F	Mexico
elegans	F–W	Mexico
lindleyana	F	Mexico to Costa Rica
skinneri	F–W	Guatemala
spectabilis	S–SS	Mexico to El Salvador

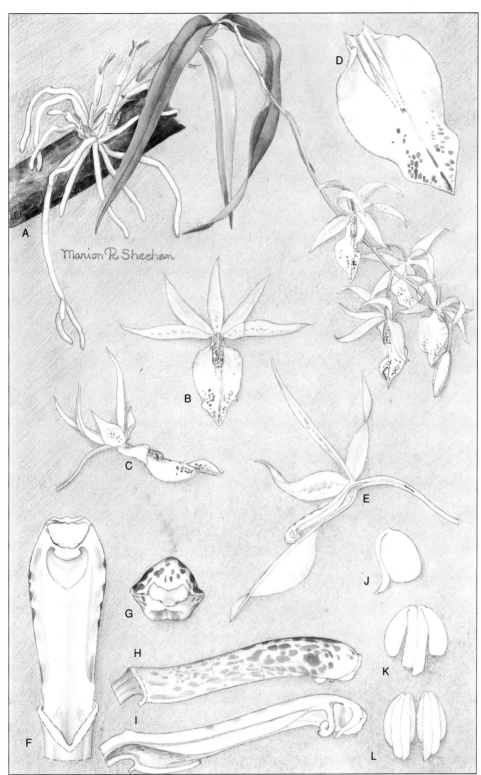

Barkeria spectabilis
A: Plant in flower, × ½.
B: Flower, face view, × ¾.
C: Flower, side view, × ¾.
D: Lip, × 1½.
E: Flower, vertical section, × 1½.
F: Column, ventral view, × 4.
G: Column, end view, × 4.
H: Column, side view, × 4.
I: Column, vertical section, × 4.
J, K, L: Pollinia, × 12.

Batemannia

GENUS: *Batemannia* Lindley (bayt-MAN-ee-uh)
TRIBE: Maxillarieae SUBTRIBE: Zygopetalinae
IDENTIFICATION CHARACTERISTICS: Although found over a broad area in tropical South America, *Batemannia* (sometimes spelled *Batemania*) has not been a common component of most collections. This small genus has showy, attractive flowers, which makes it well worth cultivating. Perhaps one reason *Batemannia* has not been appreciated by growers is the mild fragrance of the flower, which is typical of the genus. This fragrance has been characterized by some as "the smell of a sweet stink bug," not a very flattering description.

The genus was first identified in 1834 by John Lindley, who named it in honor of James Bateman, an English orchid enthusiast and writer. Bateman's book, *Orchids of Mexico and Guatemala* (1843), still stands as one of the classic orchid books. Taxonomists disagree about the number of species in this genus, with the number varying from three to nine species, three being the most common number. *Batemannia colleyi* is probably the best-known species.

Vegetatively, these sympodial epiphytes are recognized by their closely clumped, angular pseudobulbs, topped by up to three leaves and subtended by a number of large leafy bracts. The latter are short-lived and soon fall, exposing the pseudobulbs. Each leaf may be up to 12 inches (30 cm) long and 2 inches (5 cm) wide. The arched or pendent inflorescence arises from the base of the pseudobulb and averages three to six flowers.

The flowers, which may be up to 3 inches (7.5 cm) wide, are easy to distinguish. The dorsal sepal and two petals are alike in size, shape, and color. The flaring lateral sepals vary, being longer and narrower and very concave on the basal third. The lip is distinctly three-lobed with the side lobes small and often very erect. The middle lobe is often slightly reflexed at the apex. The margin of the lip is often denticulate. The base color of the sepals and petals is light green, often with a variable flush of maroon, giving the flowers a reddish brown appearance. The lip is white or white with reddish purple marks.

The footed column, a distinguishing characteristic of this genus, is long and narrow with a very small, slitlike stigmatic surface. Four light yellow pollinia, of two sizes, are borne on a short, almost-shield-shaped stipe.

CULTURE: Temperature, 60°F (15°C); light, 2400–3600 footcandles; humidity, 40–60%; media, tree fern, fir bark, peat and perlite, sphagnum moss; fertilization, monthly, ratio depends on medium.

COLOR PLATE: *Batemannia colleyi*

SPECIES	FLOWERING SEASON	GENERAL LOCALE
armillata	S–SS	Colombia
colleyi	F–W	Trinidad, Guyana to Brazil

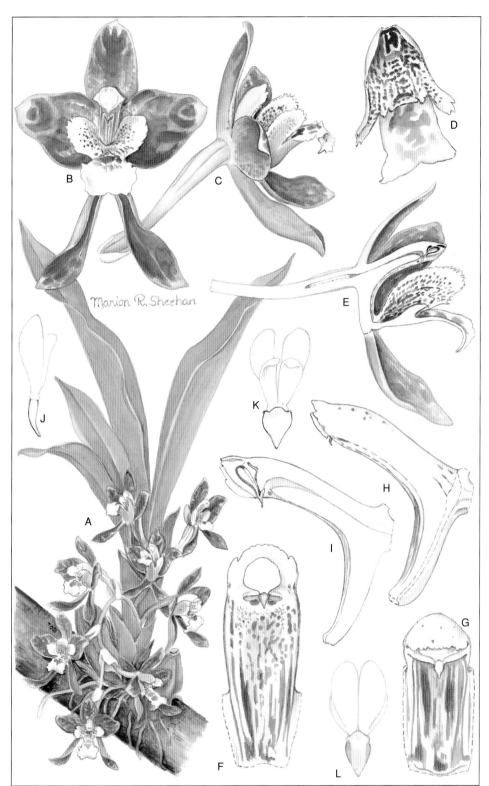

Marion R. Sheehan

Batemannia colleyi
A: Plant in flower, × ½.
B: Flower, face view, × 1½.
C: Flower, side view, × 1½.
D: Lip, face view, × 2.
E: Flower, vertical section, × 1½.
F: Column, ventral view, × 3.
G: Column, end view, × 3.
H: Column, side view, × 3.
I: Column, vertical section, × 3.
J, K, L: Pollinia, × 8.

Bifrenaria

GENUS: *Bifrenaria* Lindley (bye-fren-AIR-ee-uh)
TRIBE: Maxillarieae   SUBTRIBE: Lycastinae
IDENTIFICATION CHARACTERISTICS: This small genus consisting of 11 species was founded by John Lindley in 1832 on the basis of specimens of *Bifrenaria atropurpurea* imported by Conrad and George Loddiges from Brazil in 1828. The generic name was coined from the Greek words *bi* (two) and *frenum* (strap), referring to the two-stalked pollinia. Once more popular, bifrenarias are not found often in collections today, yet they are easy to grow, have excellent flowers, and should be more widely grown.

Vegetatively, these sympodial epiphytes are very much alike. The tightly clustered pseudobulbs are almost egg-shaped, 2 to 4 inches (5–10 cm) high, and four-angled. Each pseudobulb has one leathery leaf at its apex. Leaves are oblong to lanceolate and up to 18 inches (45 cm) long and 5 inches (12.5 cm) wide. The inflorescence arises from the base of the pseudobulb and bears one to three flowers. The genus is very similar to *Maxillaria* except that the latter always has one flower per inflorescence and only one caudicle.

The 2- to 3-inch (5- to 7.5-cm) wide flowers are fleshy and long-lasting. Flower color is highly variable and includes yellow-greens and wine reds. The sepals are alike in size, shape, and color. Two lateral sepals are attached at right angles to the dorsal sepal, as in *Maxillaria*, and are fused to the foot of the column where they form a short spur. The two petals are similar to the sepals in shape but may be slightly smaller and often have wavy margins. The three-lobed lip also is attached to the foot of the column and forms part of the spur. The two lateral lobes partially enclose the column. The midlobe of the lip is sometimes reflexed. The lip is covered with numerous hairs and has a hairy yellow crest.

The column, which is almost round, narrow, and usually widest near the stigmatic surface, has a foot at the base and is clothed in long hairs. The anther cap has a slightly roughened surface. The four tightly arranged yellow pollinia are borne on a two-stalked foot.

CULTURE: Temperature, 60–65°F (15–18°C); light, 2400–3600 footcandles; humidity, 40–60%; media, tree fern, bark, peat and perlite; fertilization, monthly, ratio depends on medium.

COLOR PLATE: *Bifrenaria harrisoniae*

SPECIES	FLOWERING SEASON	GENERAL LOCALE
atropurpurea	SS	Brazil
bicornaria	SS	Brazil
harrisoniae	S–SS	Brazil
inodora	W–S–SS	Brazil
longicornis	SS	Colombia, Venezuela, Guyana, Brazil, Peru, Suriname, Amazonas
minuta	SS	Venezuela
tetragona	SS	Brazil
tyrianthina	S–SS	Brazil
vitellina	SS	Brazil

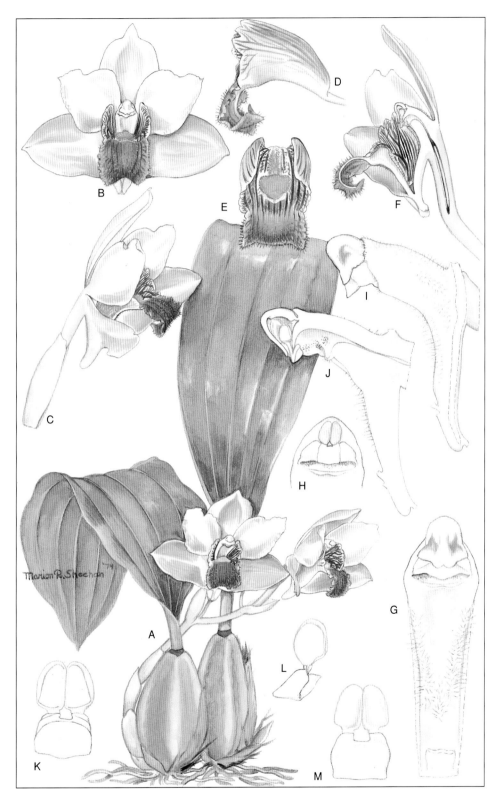

Bifrenaria harrisoniae

A: Plant in flower, × ½.
B: Flower, face view, × ¾.
C: Flower, side view, × ¾.
D: Lip, side view, × 1.
E: Lip, face view, × 1.
F: Flower, vertical section, × ¾.
G: Column, ventral view, × 2.
H: Column, end view, × 2.
I: Column, side view, × 2.
J: Column, vertical section, × 2.
K, L, M: Pollinia, × 5.

Bletilla

GENUS: *Bletilla* Reichenbach f. (bleh-TILL-uh)
TRIBE: Arethuseae SUBTRIBE: Bletiinae
IDENTIFICATION CHARACTERISTICS: *Bletilla* is a small genus of not more than six species, of which only one, *B. striata*, is commonly found in the trade, where it is widely sold as a hardy orchid for outdoor landscaping. The genus was first described by H. G. Reichenbach in 1853, who saw in it a resemblance to *Bletia* and thus used the diminutive form *Bletilla* as the generic name. (*Bletia* was named after Spanish botanist Don Luis Blet.) Both genera are terrestrial and have cormlike pseudobulbs but differ in floral and flowering characteristics.

These sympodial plants produce new corms and new sets of leaves annually. The new leaves arise from the underground corm in the spring and, before the new leaves can unfold, the inflorescence arises from the center of the new growth. Each stem has three or more soft, pleated leaves. Each leaf base encircles the stem, completely covering it. The almost-lancelike leaves may be 12 to 24 inches (30–60 cm) long. Each inflorescence bears six to twelve flowers.

The lavender or white flowers are 1.5 to 2 inches (4–5 cm) wide. The sepals and two petals are alike in shape and color, but the petals are usually a little larger. The lip is three-lobed. The two smaller lateral lobes partially enclose the column. The large midlobe is deeply keeled and has a wavy margin.

The column is long and narrow with a very slight bulge at the midpoint and has a minuscule stigmatic surface. Four yellow pollinia, looking almost like rice grains, are found in each flower.

CULTURE: Temperature, 60°F (15°C), survives outdoors if the ground does not freeze; light, 2400–3600 footcandles; humidity, 40–60%; medium, a mixture of 2 peat : 1 sand; fertilization, monthly, with a 1–1–1 ratio.

COLOR PLATE: *Bletilla striata*

SPECIES	FLOWERING SEASON	GENERAL LOCALE
striata	S–SS	China, Japan, Taiwan

Bletilla striata
A: Plant in flower, × ½.
B: Flower, face view, × 1.
C: Flower, side view, × 1.
D: Lip, face view, × 2.
E: Lip, side view, × 2.
F: Flower, vertical section, × 1½.
G: Column, ventral view, × 3.
H: Column, end view, × 3.
I: Column, side view, × 3.
J: Column, vertical section, × 3.
K, L, M: Pollinia, × 8.

Bollea

GENUS: *Bollea* Reichenbach f. (BOH-lee-uh)

TRIBE: Maxillarieae SUBTRIBE: Zygopetalinae

IDENTIFICATION CHARACTERISTICS: The delightful patterns of bluish and reddish purples found in the genus *Bollea* add another dimension to the wide range of colors found in the Orchidaceae. Unfortunately, flowers of this genus are borne close to the base of the leaves and may go undetected in a crowded greenhouse.

There are, according to most taxonomists, six showy-flowered species in the genus. *Bollea* is closely related to both *Huntleya* and *Pescatorea*, but is easily distinguished from them by the large hooded column that is hollow beneath and covers most of the base of the lip. It was mainly due to the lip characteristics that H. G. Reichenbach established the genus in 1852, when he removed *B. violacea* from *Huntleya*, where John Lindley originally had placed it. Reichenbach named the genus in honor of German horticulturist Carl Boll.

Vegetatively, these sympodial epiphytes are very attractive, with fans of six to ten shiny, medium green leaves. A well-grown plant has many fans because individual leaves persist for a number of years. The generally lanceolate, pointed leaves may be up to 12 inches (30 cm) long and 2 inches (5 cm) wide. The solitary-flowered inflorescences arise from the lower leaf axils, with one to several inflorescences per fan.

The fleshy flowers may be up to 4 inches (10 cm) in diameter, and their base color may be white, bluish purple, or reddish purple. They vary slightly among the six species but in basic characteristics are very much alike. The sepals and petals are alike in color and shape, with the petals often a little smaller. Their margins may be entire or undulate. The attractive lips have a very pronounced callus with, in some species, warts and hairs. *Bollea violacea* has teeth at the apex of the callus. The lip color pattern is often similar to that of the sepals and petals.

The column is very large and has a distinct hood, the hallmark of this genus. The hood covers the entire base of the lip and callus. Four yellow pollinia are borne on a distinct stipe with a viscidium.

CULTURE: Temperature, varies (*B. coelestis*, 55–60°F [12–15°C]; *B. violacea*, 60–65°F [15–18°C]); light, 2400–3600 footcandles; humidity, 40–60%; medium, any good mix for epiphytes; fertilization, monthly, ratio depends on medium.

COLOR PLATE: *Bollea violacea*

SPECIES	FLOWERING SEASON	GENERAL LOCALE
coelestis	SS–F	Colombia
lalindei	SS–F	Colombia
lawrenceana	S–SS	Colombia
patinii	SS	Colombia
violacea	SS	Guyana

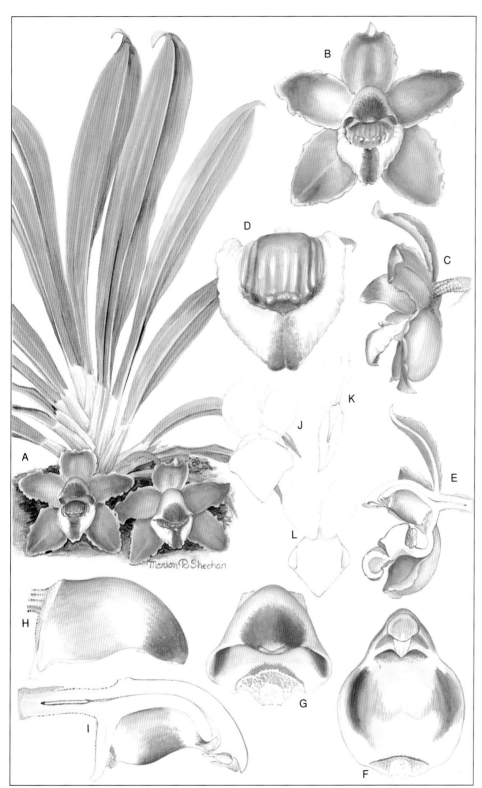

Bollea violacea

A: Plant in flower, × ½.
B: Flower, face view, × ¾.
C: Flower, side view, × ¾.
D: Lip, face view, × 1½.
E: Flower, vertical section, × ¾.
F: Column, ventral view, × 1½.
G: Column, end view, × 1½.
H: Column, side view, × 1½.
I: Column, vertical section,
   × 1½.
J, K, L: Pollinia, × 4.

Bothriochilus _____

GENUS: *Bothriochilus* Lemaire (bah-three-oh-KYE-luss)

TRIBE: Arethuseae   SUBTRIBE: Bletiinae

IDENTIFICATION CHARACTERISTICS: The four known species of *Bothriochilus* bear their small and delicate, brightly colored flowers on erect inflorescences that have anywhere from a few (e.g., *B. bellus*) to over 200 (e.g., *B. densiflorus*) flowers each, making these easy-to-grow species an attractive addition to any greenhouse. The genus was first recognized in 1852 by Charles Lemaire, who formed the name from two Greek words meaning little pit and lip. Undoubtedly, Lemaire was referring to the saccate nature of the lips of some species.

These sympodial epiphytes have tight clusters of almost-egg-shaped pseudobulbs with three or more linear-to-lancelike leaves at their apices. Each pseudobulb has two papery bracts at its base, the remains of two leaves that were shed earlier. The soft, folded leaves, up to 3 feet (90 cm) long and 0.5 inch (1 cm) wide, may be shiny or, in the case of *Bothriochilus guatemalensis*, somewhat fleshy. The erect inflorescence arises from the base of the pseudobulb and is ensheathed with leafy bracts. In some species, the inflorescence is just a few inches tall, but in others it may be up to 2 feet (60 cm) tall.

Basic colors for the flowers, up to 2 inches (5 cm) wide, are pink and white. The sepals and petals are almost the same size, but the sepals are more concave and often slightly darker in color. Some species (e.g., *Bothriochilus macrostachyus*) have small, spar-

kling, wartlike protuberances scattered on the dorsal side, giving the flower a crystalline look. The lip is narrow and indistinctly three-lobed, with the midlobe long, narrow, and often recurved. The lip may be almost saccate to almost spurred at the base.

The small column is widest at the apex and tapers slightly towards the base. The anther cap at the apex is very pronounced. Eight yellow pollinia are attached to a minute, almost-triangular caudicle.

CULTURE: Temperature, 60–65°F (15–18°C); light, 2400–3600 footcandles; humidity, 40–60%; media, tree fern, bark; fertilization, monthly, ratio depends on medium.

COLOR PLATE: *Bothriochilus macrostachyus*

SPECIES	FLOWERING SEASON	GENERAL LOCALE
bellus	Variable	Mexico, Guatemala, Honduras
densiflorus	S	Honduras, Guatemala
guatemalensis	S	Guatemala
macrostachyus	SS–F	Mexico to Panama

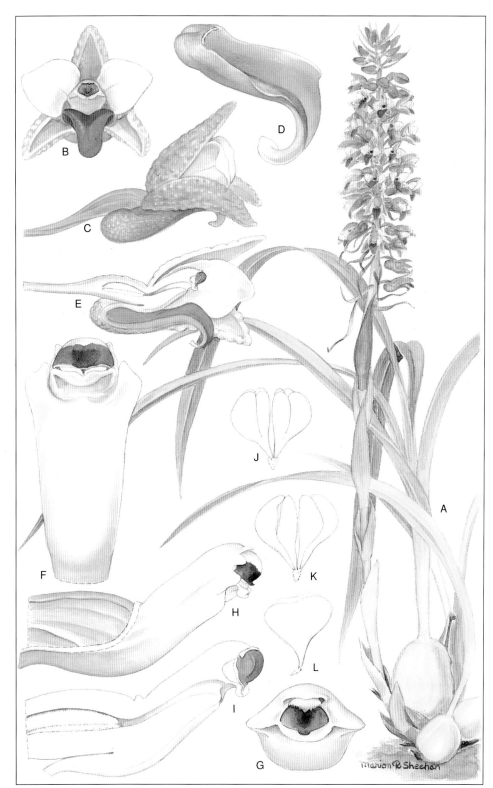

Bothriochilus macrostachyus
A: Plant in flower, × ½.
B: Flower, face view, × 3.
C: Flower, side view, × 3.
D: Lip, × 4.
E: Flower, vertical section, × 3.
F: Column, ventral view, × 8.
G: Column, end view, × 8.
H: Column, side view, × 8.
I: Column, vertical section, × 8.
J, K, L: Pollinia, × 18.

Brassavola

GENUS: *Brassavola* R. Brown (bra-sah-VOH-luh)
TRIBE: Epidendreae   SUBTRIBE: Laeliinae
IDENTIFICATION CHARACTERISTICS: Approximately 15 species of *Brassavola* are known today. *Brassavola glauca* and *B. digbyana*, two of the better-known original species, have been transferred to *Rhyncholaelia*.

Brassavola was named in the early 1800s by Robert Brown, who described *B. cucullata*. The genus was named in honor of Venetian botanist Antonio Musa Brassavola and contains sympodial epiphytes that are closely related to *Laelia* and *Cattleya* species.

The round, stemlike pseudobulbs range from 1 to 7 inches (2.5–17.5 cm) in length and are slender or club-shaped. Each pseudobulb is topped by a single, fleshy, deep green terete leaf up to 2 feet (60 cm) long. Except for *Brassavola acaulis*, flowers are borne at the apex of the pseudobulb, either singly (e.g., *B. cucullata*) or on a simple inflorescence with up to 12 flowers (e.g., *B. cordata*).

The fragrant, long-lasting flowers range in size from slightly less than 2 to 7 inches (5–17.5 cm) across. The base color of the flowers is white, with some flowers having cream and greenish segments. The sepals are long, narrow, and usually sharp-pointed at the apex. The petals are similar to the sepals, except slightly narrower. The base of the lip almost encircles the column and flares out into a broad, almost-heart-shaped apex lobe, which may have an entire margin or be fringed.

The short column terminates in three sharp lobes that partially cover the anther cap. The stigmatic area is irregular in outline and has two small projections on the distal end. Although in general the genus has eight yellow pollinia, *Brassavola cucullata* has twelve. Two pollinia, one large and one small, are borne on each caudicle. Each flat caudicle has irregular margins and a number of small tubercles.

CULTURE: Temperature, 60–65°F (15–18°C); light, 2400–3600 footcandles; humidity, 40–70%; media, tree fern, peat and perlite, bark; fertilization, monthly, ratio depends on medium.

COLOR PLATE: *Brassavola nodosa*

SPECIES	FLOWERING SEASON	GENERAL LOCALE
acaulis	SS–F	Guatemala to Panama
amazonica	S	Amazonas, Peru
cebolleta	S	Brazil, Peru, Argentina, Paraguay
cordata	SS–F	West Indies, Trinidad
cucullata	S	West Indies, Mexico to northern South America
flagellaris	S–SS	Brazil
gardneri	SS	Brazil
marliana	S	Northern Brazil, Guyana, Suriname, French Guiana, Amazonas, Venezuela
nodosa	F–W–S–SS	West Indies, Mexico to Peru
tuberculata	SS	Brazil

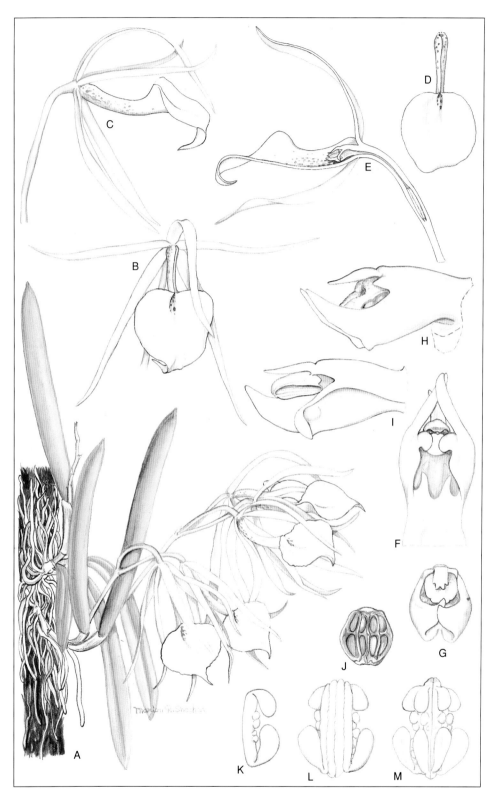

Brassavola nodosa

A: Plant in flower, × ½.
B: Flower, face view, × ¾.
C: Flower, side view, × ¾.
D: Lip, × ¾.
E: Flower, vertical section, × ¾.
F: Column, ventral view, × 5.
G: Column, end view, × 5.
H: Column, side view, × 5.
I: Column, vertical section, × 5.
J: Anther cap, × 5.
K, L, M: Pollinia, × 10.

Brassia

GENUS: *Brassia* R. Brown (BRASS-ee-uh)
TRIBE: Maxillarieae   SUBTRIBE: Oncidiinae
IDENTIFICATION CHARACTERISTICS: The approximately 30 species of *Brassia* are readily recognized by their elongate sepals. Named by Robert Brown for William Brass, a botanical enthusiast and collector, the genus was founded when *B. maculata* flowered in the Royal Botanic Gardens, Kew, England, in 1814. The plants had been collected in Jamaica by Joseph Banks.

Brassia species are sympodial epiphytes. Their large, flattened pseudobulbs can be up to 6 inches (15 cm) long and 1 to 1.5 inches (2.5–4 cm) wide. Each pseudobulb is topped by one to three green leathery leaves, which may be up to 16 inches (40 cm) long, and is subtended by one or more leafy bracts. The inflorescence, bearing up to 12 flowers, arises from the base of the pseudobulbs.

From tip to tip, flowers measure 2 inches (5 cm) (e.g., *Brassia chlorops*) to 21 inches (53 cm) (e.g., *B. arcuigera*, according to some reports); most average 5 to 6 inches (12.5–15 cm) in length. The base color is pale yellow-green with spots or areas of brownish red, brown, or blackish brown. The sepals are alike in size, shape, and color and often are very long and narrow. The two petals are similar to the sepals in color and shape but are much shorter and a little narrower. The lip varies from ovate to almost shield-shaped, may have sharp apices, and is the same length as the petals but broader. The margins of the lip also vary; some are rolled under, others are flat, slightly toothed, or plain. All lips have small calli.

The column is very short, without any pronounced wings or lobes, and is terminated by a smooth anther cap. The stigmatic surface is almost heart-shaped. Two teardrop-shaped yellow pollinia of uniform size are attached to the apex of a flat, curved, white stipe, which is attached to a brownish thickened foot.

CULTURE: Temperature, 60–70°F (15–21°C); light, 2400–3600 footcandles; humidity, 40–70%; media, peat and perlite, bark, plaques; fertilization, monthly, ratio depends on medium.

COLOR PLATE: *Brassia caudata*

SPECIES	FLOWERING SEASON	GENERAL LOCALE
alleni	F	Panama
arcuigera	S–SS	Costa Rica to Brazil, Peru
bidens	S–SS	Venezuela, Guyana, Peru, Brazil
caudata	F–W	South Florida, Cuba to northern South America
chlorops	SS	Costa Rica, Panama
forgetiana	S–SS	Venezuela, Peru
gireoudiana	S–SS	Costa Rica, Panama
keiliana	S–SS	Venezuela, Colombia
lanceana	F	Venezuela, Guyana, Suriname, French Guiana
macrostachya	S–SS	Venezuela, Guyana
maculata	F–W–S	Cuba, Jamaica, British Honduras, Guatemala
neglecta	S–SS	Venezuela
verrucosa	S–SS	Mexico, Guatemala, El Salvador, Honduras, Venezuela
wageneri	S–SS	Venezuela, Colombia

Brassia caudata

A: Plant in flower, × ¼.
B: Flower, face view, × ½.
C: Flower, side view, × ½.
D: Lip, × 1.
E: Flower, vertical section, × ½.
F: Column, ventral view, × 2½.
G: Column, end view, × 2½.
H: Column, side view, × 2½.
I: Column, vertical section,
   × 2½.
J, K, L: Pollinia, × 5.

Broughtonia

GENUS: *Broughtonia* R. Brown (brow-TOH-nee-uh)

TRIBE: Epidendreae SUBTRIBE: Laeliinae

IDENTIFICATION CHARACTERISTICS: *Broughtonia*, a small genus of only two or four species, was one of the earliest epiphytic orchids to be grown in the Royal Botanic Gardens, Kew, England, having been introduced in 1793. In 1813, Robert Brown named the genus to honor Arthur Broughton, a British botanist who worked in Jamaica. Plants of this very popular genus are small, pseudobulbous, and sympodial in growth habit. *Broughtonia* is closely related to *Epidendrum*, from which it differs in several taxonomic characteristics.

The pseudobulbs are borne in thick clusters, and the plants appear to be rhizomeless. Green and usually 1.5 to 2 inches (4–5 cm) long, some of the pseudobulbs are almost egg-shaped while others are narrow and elongate; all are fluted, have dark leaf-trace scars encircling the bulbs, and are topped with one or more (commonly two) leathery, pale green leaves up to 4 inches (10 cm) long. The very slender, dark brown inflorescences arise from the pseudobulb apex and may be erect or pendent. Each inflorescence is at least 1 foot (30 cm) long, is terminated by six or more flowers, and bears a papery bract at each node. Short lateral flowering branches may arise from some of the upper bracts, usually after the terminal cluster is spent.

The flowers, 1.5 inches (4 cm) in diameter, are greatly admired, primarily because of their color.

The most common color is crimson purple, although white and yellow forms of *Broughtonia sanguinea* are known. The three sepals are alike in shape and color. The two petals are broader than the sepals but identical in color. The free lip is three-lobed with the lateral lobes folded over the column. The terminal lobe is broad and flaring with a very finely toothed margin. The lip has a long slender spur at its base. The spur is adnate to the ovary and appears as a small swelling on the side of the ovary.

The very short column is broadest near the stigmatic surface and terminates in three lobes: one small sharp point over the anther cap and two broad lobes on either side which do not enclose the cap. The stigmatic surface, which is almost three times as wide as the anther cap, resembles a top with a blunt round base. The four cream-colored pollinia are uniform in size. Each one is attached to its own caudicle. The caudicles resemble those of *Cattleya* and have margins that are almost saw-toothed in appearance.

CULTURE: Temperature, 65–70°F (18–21°C); light, 2400–3600 footcandles; humidity, 40–70%; media, peat and perlite, tree fern, bark, excellent on tree fern slabs; fertilization, monthly, ratio depends on medium.

COLOR PLATE: *Broughtonia sanguinea*

SPECIES	FLOWERING SEASON	GENERAL LOCALE
negrilensis	F–W–S	West Indies
sanguinea	F–W–S	Jamaica

Broughtonia sanguinea
A: Plant in flower, × ½.
B: Flower, face view, × 1.
C: Flower, side view, × 1.
D: Lip, × 2.
E: Flower, vertical section, × 2.
F: Column, ventral view, × 6.
G: Column, end view, × 6.
H: Column, side view, × 6.
I: Column, vertical section, × 6.
J: Anther cap and pollinia, × 12.
K, L, M: Pollinia, × 12.

Bulbophyllum

GENUS: *Bulbophyllum* Thouars (bulb-oh-FILL-um)

TRIBE: Dendrobieae SUBTRIBE: Bulbophyllinae

IDENTIFICATION CHARACTERISTICS: This exceedingly large genus of most unusual flowering plants is deserving of a place in every collection. Even the small-flowered types are worthwhile when in flower, especially if they can be magnified while being viewed. Found in abundance worldwide in tropical areas, more than 2000 species have been classified by some taxonomists. The generic name, which was derived by Aubert Du Petit-Thouars in the early 1800s from the Greek words *bolbos* (bulb) and *phyllon* (leaf), is a descriptive name befitting most species in the genus.

Bulbophyllum species are sympodial epiphytes that are very similar vegetatively. The almost-egg-shaped pseudobulbs are topped by one thick, leathery leaf and vary greatly in size. Some have rhizomes up to 8 inches (20 cm) thick and leaves 2 feet (60 cm) long, though most species have smaller rhizomes and leaves. The pseudobulbs often are widely spaced on the rhizome and form a chainlike growth. Inflorescences arise from the apex or base of the pseudobulb and bear anywhere from a few to 100 flowers.

The unusual flowers, from 0.1 to 6 inches (0.2–15 cm) wide, come in a variety of colors, each with numerous shades and tints. Their wide diversity and extreme complexity make it almost impossible to describe this genus adequately within the confines of this text. The lateral sepals are often fused, are larger than the petals, and are often confused with the lip. The sepals and petals may have appendages. The lip is small, often partially enclosed by the fused lateral sepals, and weakly three-lobed.

The small column has a recurved basal foot and is broadest in the middle. The stigmatic surface is small and narrow. The two yellow pollinia are borne on a short, broad foot.

CULTURE: Temperature, 65°F (18°C); light, 2400–3600 footcandles; humidity, 40-60%; media, tree fern, bark; fertilization, monthly, ratio depends on medium.

COLOR PLATE: *Bulbophyllum collettii*

SPECIES	FLOWERING SEASON	GENERAL LOCALE
appendiculatum	SS	India, Myanmar
barbigerum	SS	Tropical Africa
collettii	S	Myanmar
crassipes	F–W	Himalayas
cylindracum	SS	India
falcatum	S–SS–F	West Africa
leopardinum	SS	India, Assam
medusae	W	Malay Peninsula, Thailand, Borneo
ornatissimum	SS	Himalayas, Philippines
pachyrhachis	SS	South Florida, West Indies, Mexico to Panama
picturatum	F–W–S	Myanmar
refractum	SS	Himalayas, Java
umbellatum	F	India, Nepal
uniflorum	SS	Java, Malay Peninsula

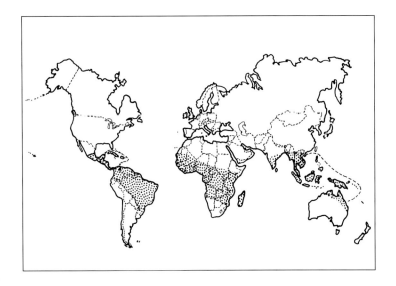

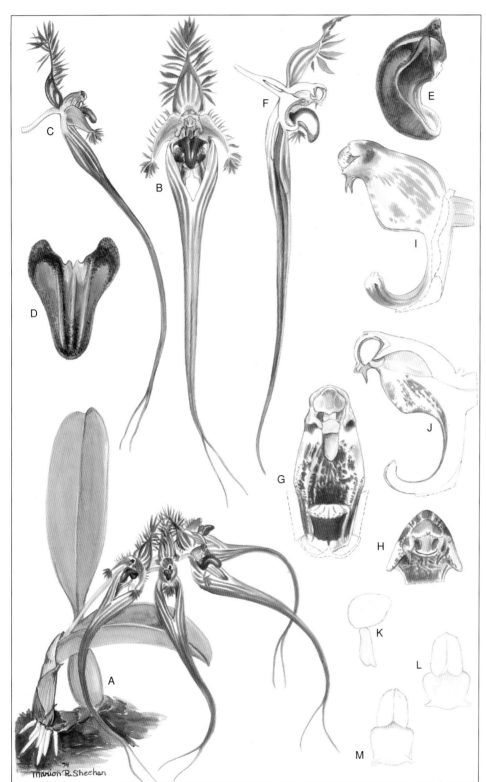

Bulbophyllum collettii
A: Plant in flower, × ¾.
B: Flower, face view, × 1½.
C: Flower, side view, × 1½.
D: Lip, face view, × 5.
E: Lip, side view, × 5.
F: Flower, vertical section, × 1½.
G: Column, ventral view, × 5.
H: Column, end view, × 5.
I: Column, side view, × 5.
J: Column, vertical section, × 5.
K, L, M: Pollinia, × 10.

89

Calanthe

GENUS: *Calanthe* R. Brown (kal-ANN-thee)
TRIBE: Arethuseae   SUBTRIBE: Bletiinae
IDENTIFICATION CHARACTERISTICS: When Robert Brown discovered and identified this genus during his Australian travels in 1821, he named it *Calanthe*. Coined from the Greek words *kalos* (beautiful) and *anthe* (flower), the generic name very aptly describes this fine group of winter-flowering orchids. More than 150 species are known today. The genus also is famous because J. Dominy used it in the early 1850s to make the first orchid hybrid. *Calanthe* Dominyi (*C. masuca* × *C. furcata* [*triplicata*]) flowered in 1856, thus starting the era of breeding which is so well entrenched in the orchid world.

The major vegetative differences among *Calanthe* species lie in the pseudobulbs. These sympodial terrestrials can be divided into two groups: evergreen and deciduous. The evergreen species have cormlike pseudobulbs that are not significant. The deciduous species have large, usually angular pseudobulbs that may be strongly constricted near the middle. Several soft, pleated leaves are attached to each pseudobulb. Leaves range from 1 to 4 feet (30–120 cm) long and 3 to 8 inches (7.5–20 cm) wide and may be stalked. Each inflorescence arises from the base of the pseudobulb and bears from a few to 20 flowers, which are subtended by leafy bracts.

The flowers are basically white, red, and mauve. The three sepals are alike in size, shape, and color. The lateral sepals are usually attached to the dorsal sepal at an angle of 90 degrees or less. The two petals may be identical to the sepals or shorter and broader. The three-lobed, spurred lip is one of the distinguishing characteristics of this genus. The claw of the lip is adnate to the column. The exterior parts of the flower and inflorescence are often covered with soft pubescence.

The short, straight column is covered with a distinct hood and is broadest near the stigmatic surface and often pubescent beneath. The hood is fused to the spur. Each flower contains eight elongate, yellow pollinia in two groups of four each.

CULTURE: Temperature, 55–60°F (12–15°C); light, 2400–3600 footcandles; humidity, 40–60%; medium, a mixture of 1 peat moss : 1 perlite : 1 soil; fertilization, monthly, with a 1–1–1 ratio.

COLOR PLATE: *Calanthe rosea*

SPECIES	FLOWERING SEASON	GENERAL LOCALE
alismaefolia	S–SS	Himalayas to Taiwan
biloba	F	Nepal
brevicornu	S	Himalayas
discolor	S–SS	Japan
elmeri	W–S	Philippines
gracilis	F	Sikkim
herbacea	SS	Sikkim
masuca	SS	Sikkim
mexicana	SS	Mexico to Panama, West Indies
nipponica	SS	Japan
puberula	SS	Himalayas
reflexa	SS	Japan
rosea	W	Thailand
rubens	W	Thailand, Malaysia
triplicata	S	India, Pacific islands, Australia
vestita	W	Myanmar, Malay Peninsula

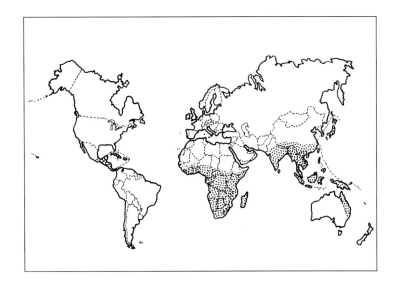

Calanthe rosea

A: Plant in flower, × ½.
B: Flower, face view, × 1½.
C: Flower, side view, × 1½.
D: Lip, × 1½.
E: Flower, vertical section, × 1½.
F: Column, ventral view, × 5.
G: Column, end view, × 5.
H: Column, side view, × 5.
I: Column, vertical section, × 5.
J, K, L: Pollinia, × 10.

Calopogon

GENUS: *Calopogon* R. Brown (kal-oh-POH-gon)
TRIBE: Arethuseae   SUBTRIBE: Bletiinae
IDENTIFICATION CHARACTERISTICS: The bright, colorful flowers of *Calopogon*, shimmering above the foliage in grassy meadows or along roadsides, are always a welcome sight in the late spring and summer. Despite human inroads on their native habitats, the calopogons have survived, possibly by becoming roadside weeds in many areas of eastern United States. The four known, sympodial, terrestrial species are not widely cultivated because of the difficulty in duplicating their native habitats. Although plants were first collected in the early 1700s, the present generic name was not coined until 1813, when Robert Brown restudied the genus. In Greek, the generic name signifies a beautiful beard, which is an apt description for the colorful hairs on the lip of the flower.

Calopogons produce a new set of leaves annually from the tip of an elongate, underground, cormlike structure. Each plant produces from one to five linear leaves up to 20 inches (50 cm) long and up to 1.5 inches (4 cm) wide. The grasslike leaves are erect and ribbed. The terminal inflorescence, up to 30 inches (75 cm) tall, bears anywhere from a few to 25 flowers, which open gradually over a period of time.

The nonresupinate, seemingly upside-down flowers are somewhat unusual among North American species. They are rose-pink to white and up to 1.5 inches (4 cm) in diameter. The petals and sepals are alike in shape and color, though the sepals occasionally are slightly wider than the petals. The three-lobed lip has two very small lateral lobes, which are almost obscure in some cases. The narrow midlobe flares out at the apex and is adorned with very colorful and attractive hairlike structures that often are yellow.

The slender column, the same color as the flower, is gently curved and winged near the apex. There are four yellow pollinia.

CULTURE: Temperature, tubers survive below-freezing temperatures in the northern part of the genus's native habitat; light, full sun to partial shade; humidity, grows best in moist situations; media, rich organic to sandy soils; fertilization, once or twice during growing season, with a 1–1–1 ratio.

COLOR PLATE: *Calopogon tuberosus*

SPECIES	FLOWERING SEASON	GENERAL LOCALE
barbatus	S	U.S. Coastal Plain, Louisiana to North Carolina
multiflorus	S	Florida
pallidus	S	U.S. Coastal Plain, Louisiana to Virginia
tuberosus	S–SS	Eastern United States, Canada, Cuba

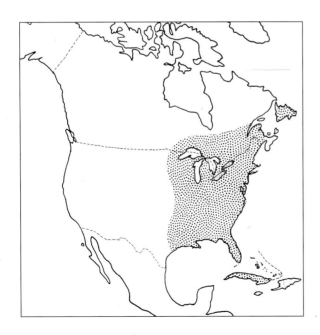

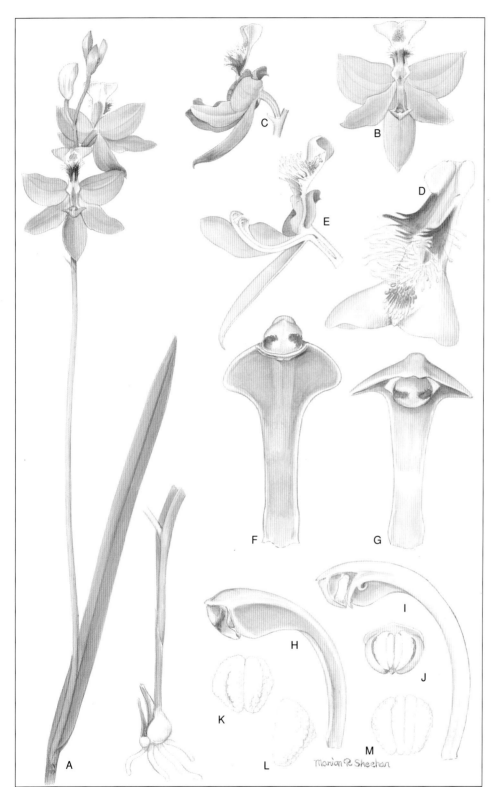

Calopogon tuberosus
A: Plant in flower, × ¾.
B: Flower, face view, × 1.
C: Flower, side view, × 1.
D: Lip, × 3.
E: Flower, vertical section, × 1½.
F: Column, ventral view, × 4.
G: Column, end view, × 4.
H: Column, side view, × 4.
I: Column, vertical section, × 4.
J: Anther cap with pollinia, × 6.
K, L, M: Pollinia, × 8.

Marion R. Sheehan

93

Catasetum

GENUS: *Catasetum* L. C. Richard ex Kunth (kat-uh-SEA-tum)

TRIBE: Cymbidieae   SUBTRIBE: Catasetinae

IDENTIFICATION CHARACTERISTICS: Dimorphic flowers of great variability have made *Catasetum* a very desirable genus to grow, but they also have caused some concern among early taxonomists who attempted to define the limits of the genus. Through time, however, taxonomists have sorted out the genus to its present complement of over 50 species. The dimorphic flowers often confuse novice growers when they first appear, and even longtime hobbyists may be surprised to find a different-looking flower on their plants when the other sex suddenly appears.

Carl Kunth first described this genus in 1820. He coined the generic name from the Greek words *kata* (down) and *seta* (bristle) to describe the two antenna-like projections on the column of male flowers. The base colors of these showy flowers are green and creamy yellow, with some maroons and browns, depending on the species.

Vegetatively, these sympodial epiphytes are most interesting. Sometimes found growing in small pockets of organic matter at the base of a tree, they are not terrestrials. The mostly conical pseudobulbs, up to 8 inches (20 cm) tall, are hidden by the clasping bases of up to seven leaves. When the leaves fall at the end of the growing season, the cluster of pseudobulbs becomes the plant's dominant feature. Plants often are leafless at flowering. The leaves, usually soft-pleated and lanceolate and sometimes prominently three-nerved, may be up to 24 inches (60 cm) long and 5 inches (12.5 cm) wide. The inflorescence arises from the base of the pseudobulb or one of the lower nodes. The male inflorescence usually bears more flowers than the female, and flowers range from 1.5 to 4 inches (4–10 cm) wide.

Male flowers are usually the most showy. Almost fleshy, their sepals and petals generally are alike in size, shape, and color. Depending on the species, the sepals and petals may be flat and erect, reflexed, or concave. The lips are highly variable, from broad and spreading to almost saccate. Their margins may be entire or heavily fringed. Many lips have a saclike pouch in the center; others have a velvety pubescence. The column is unique with two antenna-like appendages, part of the triggering mechanism that fires the pollinarium at the insect to ensure cross-pollination. Two yellow pollinia are borne on a single stipe with a basal viscidium.

Female flowers are usually fewer in number, less colorful, and more fleshy than their male counterparts. The sepals and petals are alike in size, shape, and color and are mostly reflexed. The thick, fleshy lips are saccate and surround the short, broad column. The column is the same color as the flower and has a narrow, almost-slitlike stigmatic area in some species.

CULTURE: Temperature, 60–65°F (15–18°C); light, 2400–3600 footcandles; humidity, 40–60%; medium, any good medium for epiphytes, grows well on palm trees among bases of old leaves in nature; fertilization, monthly, ratio depends on medium.

COLOR PLATE: *Catasetum expansum*

SPECIES	FLOWERING SEASON	GENERAL LOCALE
atratum	S	Brazil
barbatum	S–SS	Venezuela, Guyana, Brazil, Peru
discolor	F–W	Colombia, Venezuela to Brazil
expansum	SS	Ecuador, Colombia
fimbriatum	SS–F	Tropical South America
gnomus	SS–F–W	Brazil
integerrimum	SS–F–W	Guatemala
maculatum	F	Nicaragua to Panama, northern South America
pileatum	S–SS–F–W	Venezuela, Trinidad, Brazil
platyglossum	S–SS–F	Ecuador, Colombia
saccatum	S–SS–F–W	Peru, Brazil, Guyana
viridiflavum	S–SS	Panama

Catasetum expansum—with staminate inflorescence

Aa: Plant in flower, × ⅓.
Ab: Flower, face view, × ¾.
Ac: Flower, side view, × ¾.
Ad: Lip, × 1.
Ae: Flower, vertical section, × ¾.
Af: Column, ventral view, × 2.
Ag: Column, side view, × 2.
Ah, Ai, Aj: Pollinia, × 3.

95

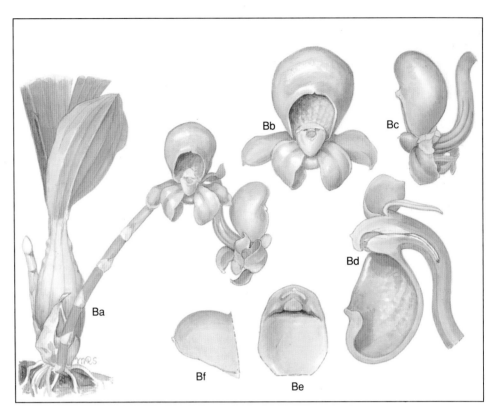

Catasetum expansum—with pistillate inflorescence

Ba: Plant in flower, × ½.
Bb: Flower, face view, × ¾.
Bc: Flower, side view, × ¾.
Bd: Flower, vertical section, × 1.
Be: Column, ventral view, × 1½.
Bf: Column, side view, × 1½.

Catasetum species

Cattleya

GENUS: *Cattleya* Lindley (KAT-lee-uh)

TRIBE: Epidendreae SUBTRIBE: Laeliinae

IDENTIFICATION CHARACTERISTICS: When members of the general public think of an orchid, they immediately picture the flower of a *Cattleya* species. Many people consider cattleyas to be the preeminent members of the orchid family. This is logical, for the genus *Cattleya*, containing around 65 species, is one of the most popular, widely grown genera in the family.

The first cattleyas were introduced into England in 1818 when the plants were used as a protective outer wrapping for some mosses and lichens shipped from Brazil. Fortunately, British horticulturist William Cattley noted the unusual plants and saved them from destruction. The first plant flowered in 1824, and after extensive study, renowned botanist John Lindley put it in a new genus, which he named in honor of Cattley. The first species identified was *Cattleya labiata* var. *autumnalis*.

Cattleyas are epiphytic species with pseudobulbs arising from a creeping rhizome. They have been widely used in breeding and have produced many fine hybrids. The genus is closely allied to *Laelia* and *Epidendrum*.

Cattleya can be divided readily into two main divisions based on the number of leaves surmounting the pseudobulb (Fig. 17). One section, called unifoliate and typified by *C. labiata*, is characterized by a single thick, fleshy leaf, up to 1 foot (30 cm) long, at the apex of a more or less cylindrical, fluted pseudobulb. The flowers are large, from 2 to 7 inches (5–17.5 cm) across (with hybrids often larger), showy, and borne singly or up to five per inflorescence. They arise from a sheath at the tip of the pseudobulb. The second section, called bifoliate and typified by *C. skinneri*, comprises species with two (occasionally one or three) thick leaves at the tip of a longer cylindrical pseudobulb, which is almost stemlike or reedlike on some plants. Bifoliate species have 2 to 25 flowers per inflorescence, which is smaller and often fleshier than the inflorescence of unifoliate species.

The flowers of both sections are similar. The three sepals are broad, spreading, and of the same color. The two petals are wider than the sepals and often have undulating margins. The lip is the largest segment of the flower and in many cattleyas is tubelike at the base and usually encloses the entire column in the tubular section. The apex or limb of the lip is broad and flaring with wavy margins. The limb usually is a darker color than the petals and sepals and is often highlighted with yellow or gold marks. Some bifoliate *Cattleya* species have "spade" lips. A spade lip has two indentations just behind the limb, so the lip resembles a three-lobed segment. Flower color is predominantly lavender, with white, yellow, green, and brown found in some species. Red-flowered cattleyas are usually the products of bigeneric crosses involving *Sophronitis*.

The elongate columns of *Cattleya* have three lobes at the apex. The two lateral lobes are broad, the middle lobe is narrow and pointed, and all three lobes are appressed to the anther cap. The stigmatic surface is on the underside of the column just behind the rostellum and resembles a top-shaped indentation. Two lobes are located at the basal portion of the stigmatic surface. There are four bright yellow, waxy pollinia of equal size in two pairs. Each pollinium is attached at the apex of a caudicle, and each pair of pollinia is either attached by fusion of the bases of the caudicles or separate with caudicle ends overlapping.

CULTURE: Temperature, 60–65°F (15–18°C); light, 2400–3600 footcandles; humidity, 40–70%; media, osmunda, tree fern, bark; fertilization, monthly, ratio depends on medium.

COLOR PLATE: *Cattleya percivaliana*

Cattleya percivaliana
A: Plant in flower, × ½.
B: Flower, face view, × ½.
C: Flower, side view, × ½.
D: Lip, × ¾.
E: Flower, vertical section, × ¾.
F: Column, ventral view, × 2.
G: Column, end view, × 2.
H: Column, side view, × 2.
I: Column, vertical section, × 2.
J: Anther cap and pollinia, × 5.
K, L: Pollinia, × 5.

CATTLEYA SPECIES	FLOWERING SEASON	GENERAL LOCALE
Bifoliates		
aclandiae	SS–F	Brazil
amethystoglossa	SS	Brazil
aurantiaca	SS–F	Mexico, northern Central America
bicolor	F–W	Brazil
bowringiana	F	Honduras, Guatemala
deckeri	F	Mexico to Panama
dormaniana	F	Brazil
elongata	SS	Brazil
forbesii	SS–F	Brazil
granulosa	SS–F–W	Brazil
guttata	F–W	Brazil
var. *alba*	F–W	Brazil
intermedia	S–SS	Southern Brazil, Paraguay, Uruguay
var. *aquinii*	S–SS	Brazil
leopoldii	SS	Brazil
loddigesii	SS–F	Brazil, Paraguay
var. *harrisoniana*	F	Brazil
nobilior	W–S	Brazil
schilleriana	SS–F	Brazil
skinneri	S–SS	Mexico to Colombia & Venezuela, Trinidad
velutina	S–SS	Brazil
violacea	SS	Northern South America
walkeriana	W–S	Brazil
Unifoliates (Labiatas)		
dowiana	SS–F	Costa Rica
var. *aurea*	SS–F	Colombia
eldorado	SS	Brazil
gaskelliana	SS	Venezuela
jenmanii	S	Venezuela, Guyana, Suriname, French Guiana
labiata	F	Brazil
lawrenceana	S–SS	Venezuela, Guyana, Suriname, French Guiana
lueddemanniana	F	Venezuela
luteola	F–W	Brazil, Peru
maxima	F–W	Colombia to Peru
mendelii	S	Colombia
mossiae	S	Venezuela
percivaliana	W	Venezuela
quadricolor	W	Colombia
rex	W	Brazil, Peru
schroederae	S	Colombia
trianaei	W	Colombia
warneri	SS	Brazil
warscewiczii (gigas)	SS	Colombia

Figure 17. Vegetative forms of *Cattleya* showing plant habit and leaf and pseudobulb cross sections. Unifoliate *Cattleya* (left) and bifoliate *Cattleya* (right).

Unifoliate *Cattleya* species,
Plate 1
A: *C. lueddemanniana*
B: *C. lawrenceana*
C: *C. schroderae*
D: *C. gaskelliana*
E: *C. luteola*
F: *C. maxima*
G: *C. warneri*

Unifoliate *Cattleya* species,
Plate 2
A: *C. labiata*
B: *C. mossiae*
C: *C. trianaei*
D: *C. percivaliana* on plant
E: *C. warscewiczii*
F: *C. dowiana*

Bifoliate *Cattleya* species,
Plate 3
A: *C. granulosa*
B: *C. guttata*
C: *C. guttata* var. *alba*
D: *C. velutina*
E: *C. forbesii* on plant
F: *C. aurantiaca*
G: *C. aclandiae*
H: *C. schilleriana*
I: *C. leopoldii*
J: *C. bicolor*

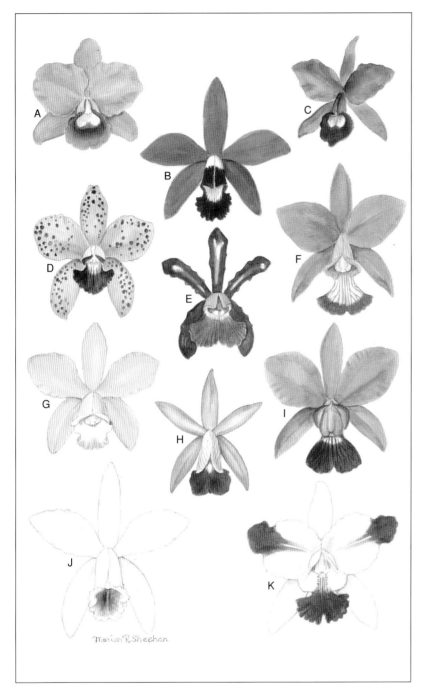

Bifoliate *Cattleya* species,
Plate 4

A: *C. bowringiana*
B: *C. violaceae*
C: *C. skinneri*
D: *C. amethystoglossa*
E: *C. elongata*
F: *C. nobilior*
G: *C. loddigesii* var. *harrisoniana*
H: *C. dormaniana*
I: *C. walkeriana*
J: *C. intermedia*
K: *C. intermedia* var. *aquinii*

Cattleyopsis

GENUS: *Cattleyopsis* Lemaire (kat-lee-OPP-siss)
TRIBE: Epidendreae   SUBTRIBE: Laeliinae
IDENTIFICATION CHARACTERISTICS: The delicately colored flowers of *Cattleyopsis* swaying on the ends of long, almost-wiry spikes make these plants very attractive. At most there are only three species in this miniature, epiphytic genus, which has not always survived taxonomic scrutinizing. Some taxonomists combine the genus with *Broughtonia*, while others feel there is sufficient variation in the floral structure to justify the separate genus *Cattleyopsis*. Since a number of intergeneric hybrids have been registered, it would seem wise from a horticultural standpoint to conserve the name. The genus was first described by Charles Lemaire in 1853, who felt the flowers had a fair resemblance to *Cattleya*, so he called the new genus *Cattleyopsis* (*Cattleya*-like).

The small- to medium-size, sympodial, epiphytic plants form tight clusters of pseudobulbs, making the plants very compact. The roundish-to-elongate pseudobulbs usually are less than 3 inches (7.5 cm) tall and are distinctly marked with rings. Two small leaves, up to 5 inches (12.5 cm) long, are borne on the apex of each pseudobulb. The gray-green, thick, leathery leaves have very fine, saw-toothed margins. The thin, wiry inflorescences, up to 3.5 feet (105 cm) long, bear up to 12 flowers near the apex.

The delicate, long-lasting flowers in various shades of rose-purple may be up to 2 inches (5 cm) across and are somewhat flattened. The sepals and petals are alike in shape and color, with the petals often slightly broader and having wavy margins. The lip, the showiest portion of the flower, almost encircles the column. A toothlike fringe on the margin of the lip and on the callus adds to the attractiveness of this delightful flower.

The column is almost straight, long, and narrow, with a slight broadening near the stigmatic surface. Eight yellow pollinia are borne, two to a short caudicle.

CULTURE: Temperature, 60–65°F (15–18°C); light, 2400–3600 footcandles; humidity, 40–60%; media, tree fern, osmunda, bark; fertilization, monthly, ratio depends on medium.

COLOR PLATE: *Cattleyopsis lindenii*

SPECIES	FLOWERING SEASON	GENERAL LOCALE
lindenii	W–S	Bahamas, Cuba
ortgesiana	W–S	Bahamas, Cuba, Jamaica

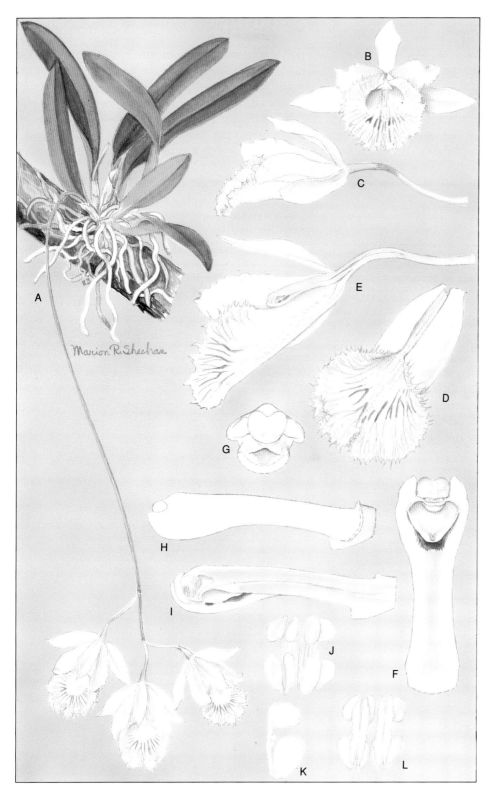

Cattleyopsis lindenii
A: Plant in flower, × ½.
B: Flower, face view, × 1.
C: Flower, side view, × 1.
D: Lip, × 1½.
E: Flower, vertical section, × 1½.
F: Column, ventral view, × 4.
G: Column, end view, × 4.
H: Column, side view, × 4.
I: Column, vertical section, × 4.
J, K, L: Pollinia, × 10.

Caularthron

GENUS: *Caularthron* Rafinesque (call-ARR-thron)
TRIBE: Epidendreae   SUBTRIBE: Laeliinae
IDENTIFICATION CHARACTERISTICS: According to the late Alex Hawkes (1965), *Caularthron bicornutum* "is often considered to be among the finest of all American orchids." At least two of the six possible species in the genus are commonly cultivated for their distinctive white flowers. The generic name, which was derived by Constantine S. Rafinesque in 1836 from the Greek words *kaulos* (stem) and *arthron* (joint), undoubtedly refers to the persistent leaf bases clasping the pseudobulb and giving it a jointed appearance. The genus is closely allied to *Epidendrum* and at one time was included in it. The two genera are now separated because of differences in lip characteristics.

Caularthron species are sympodial epiphytes with tightly clustered, hollow pseudobulbs. In their native habitat, plants are often found growing in ant nests and therefore are very difficult to collect. Each pseudobulb bears three stiff, leathery, 6- to 9-inch (15- to 22-cm) long, slightly stalked leaves. The lower portion of the pseudobulb is partially ensheathed by persistent leaf bases. A terminal inflorescence, up to 3 feet (90 cm) long and bearing as many as two dozen white flowers, arises from the apex of the pseudobulb.

The flowers are almost 3 inches (7.5 cm) wide. The sepals and two petals are generally alike in size, shape, and color. Some flowers have been observed in which the two petals are a little smaller than the sepals. The lip may be distinctly three-lobed, with the midlobe ending in a sharp point, or may have two very small, toothlike side lobes. The midlobe also has a pronounced callus just beneath the stigmatic surface.

The short, winged column is broadest near the stigmatic surface and has a very distinct anther cap at the apex. The four almost-elliptical yellow pollinia, each with a very simple caudicle, are very much like those of *Cattleya*.

CULTURE: Temperature, 60–65°F (15–18°C); light, 2400–3600 footcandles; humidity, 40–60%; media, tree fern, peat and perlite, fir bark; fertilization, monthly, with a 1–1–1 ratio for tree fern, peat and perlite, and with a 3–1–1 ratio for fir bark.

COLOR PLATE: *Caularthron bicornutum*

SPECIES	FLOWERING SEASON	GENERAL LOCALE
bicornutum	S	Colombia, Trinidad to Brazil
bilamellatum	S	Guatemala to Venezuela, Colombia

Caularthron bicornutum
A: Plant in flower, × ½.
B: Flower, face view, × 1½.
C: Flower, side view, × 1½.
D: Lip, × 2.
E: Flower, vertical section, × 1½.
F: Column, ventral view, × 3.
G: Column, end view, × 3.
H: Column, side view, × 3.
I: Column, vertical section, × 3.
J, K, L: Pollinia, × 10.

Ceratocentron

GENUS: *Ceratocentron* Senghas (sir-at-oh-SENT-ron)

TRIBE: Vandeae   SUBTRIBE: Aeridinae

IDENTIFICATION CHARACTERISTICS: It is amazing that this delightful jewel of a miniature orchid with its brilliantly colored flowers went undetected in the Philippines until the 1980s when the Javiers discovered plants on their property in Santa Fe, north of Manila, and named them "red angraecums." Taxonomists originally placed the species in the genus *Hymenorchis*, where it remained until 1989 when studies by K. Senghas determined it was a new monotypic genus which he called *Ceratocentron*. Senghas derived the generic name from the Greek words *kerato* (horn) and *kentron* (spur), presumably to depict the large spur and the hornlike projection on the midlobe of this species' unusual lip. Although closely related to *Hymenorchis*, *Ceratocentron* is separated on floral differences.

Vegetatively, *Ceratocentron* looks like miniature species of *Amesiella*. This monopodial epiphytic plant has up to five leaves with the leaf bases clasping the very short stem. At maximum growth an individual leaf may be up to 2 inches (5 cm) long and 0.75 inch (2 cm) wide. These plants tend to produce copious short roots. The short inflorescence arises from an axil of the lower leaves. Each erect to pendent inflorescence bears one to three flowers, up to 1 inch (2.5 cm) wide. The base flower color is orange. These plants are precocious, often flowering while still in the flask or soon after removal from the flask.

The flowers of *Ceratocentron* are large in comparison to the miniature plants which they almost completely hide, especially when very young plants are in flower. The sepals and petals are similar in shape and size, though the sepals are a little shorter and have blunt or rounded apices. As far as color is concerned, the sepals and petals are alike. The lip of *Ceratocentron* is very interesting. It lacks the usual insect landing platform so it might be assumed to be bird pollinated. There is a very large spur, which constitutes the major portion of the lip. The narrow apical midlobe contains a hornlike projection on the under side.

The column is short, almost globular, and widest near the middle, tapering toward both ends. The stigmatic surface is almost ovate. Two almost-round yellow pollinia are borne on a single narrow stipe with a shield-shaped viscidium at the base.

CULTURE: Temperature, 60°F (15°C); light, 2400–3600 footcandles; humidity, 40–60%; media, plaques of tree fern, cork, paperbark; fertilization, monthly, with a 1–1–1 ratio or a balanced fertilizer.

COLOR PLATE: *Ceratocentron fesselii*

SPECIES	FLOWERING SEASON	GENERAL LOCALE
fesselii	W–S	Philippines

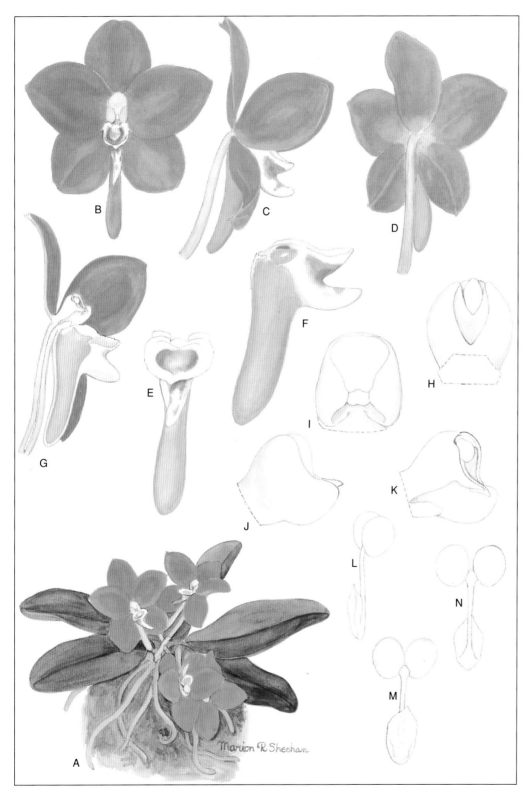

Ceratocentron fesselii

A: Plant in flower, × 2.
B: Flower, face view, × 4.
C: Flower, side view, × 4.
D: Flower, three-quarter back view, × 4.
E: Lip, front view, × 6.
F: Lip, side view, × 6.
G: Flower, vertical section, × 4.
H: Column, ventral view, × 12.
I: Column, end view, × 12.
J: Column, side view, × 12.
K: Column, vertical section, × 12.
L, M, N: Pollinia, × 25.

111

Ceratostylis _____

GENUS: *Ceratostylis* Blume (sir-at-oh-STY-liss)
TRIBE: Podochileae   SUBTRIBE: Eriinae

IDENTIFICATION CHARACTERISTICS: Anyone who has grown the plant long known as *Ceratostylis rubra* (and now correctly *C. retisquama*) has been enthralled by the bright orange-red to brick-red flowers often produced several times a year by these interesting, diminutive orchids. It is surprising that other species of this genus are not more widely grown. Even though the genus is composed of some 60 species and has been known for more than 150 years, it is still little known among orchid hobbyists. One probable reason is that many species resemble tufts of grass and are considered unorchidlike by some authors. Carl Blume described the genus in 1825, forming the generic name from the Greek words *kerato* (horn) and *stylis* (style), undoubtedly referring to the fleshy, hornlike column.

The species vary vegetatively from having fine, almost-terete leaves to having thicker, more fleshy leaves. The leaves of *Ceratostylis retisquama* may be 5 inches (12.5 cm) long and 0.5 to 0.75 inch (1–2 cm) wide. They are deeply grooved and not very grasslike. Although the short inflorescence is terminal, it appears to be axillary. Usually only one flower opens at a time, but an inflorescence can have several flowers opening in sequence.

The flowers, which are subtended by brown, papery bracts, may be up to 1.5 inches (4 cm) wide. The sepals and petals are alike in overall shape and color, with the petals slightly narrower. The very short, narrow, fleshy lip is attached to the base of the column and is entire.

The very short, broad column has two arms partially enclosing the stigmatic surface. Eight pale yellow pollinia are attached by a caudicle to a short, almost-flat viscidium.

CULTURE: Temperature, 60–65°F (15–18°C); light, 2400–3600 footcandles; humidity, 40–60%; media, tree fern plaques, baskets; fertilization, monthly, with a 1–1–1 ratio.

COLOR PLATE: *Ceratostylis retisquama*

SPECIES	FLOWERING SEASON	GENERAL LOCALE
retisquama	Variable	Philippines

Ceratostylis retisquama
A: Plant in flower, × 1.
B: Flower, face view, × 2.
C: Flower, side view, × 2.
D: Lip, face view, × 6.
E: Lip, three-quarter view, × 6.
F: Flower, vertical section, × 6.
G: Column, ventral view, × 10.
H: Column, end view, × 10.
I: Column, side view, × 10.
J: Column, vertical section, × 10.
K, L, M: Pollinia, × 16.

113

Chiloschista _____

GENUS: *Chiloschista* Lindley (kye-loh-SHIS-tuh)
TRIBE: Vandeae   SUBTRIBE: Aeridinae
IDENTIFICATION CHARACTERISTICS: Upon seeing *Chiloschista* in flower for the first time, the observer immediately marvels at how this leafless plant can produce such a multitude of flowers. In many texts, this genus is listed as a leafless epiphyte. In reality, however, some species produce leaves, although the leaves are caducous. Appearing in early spring, the green leaves usually are gone before flowering.

This small genus, which consists of probably no more than seven species, was first named by John Lindley in 1832. The generic name, derived from the Greek words *cheilos* (lip) and *schistos* (cleft), describes the cleft lip found on the flowers. The genus is closely allied to *Sarcochilus* but separated by periodical leaflessness and differences in the lip.

For a portion of the year, these monopodial epiphytes consist of a massive root system emanating from a small, compact stem and nothing else. When leaves are present, usually two to four, they arise from the very compressed stem and grow to 1 to 2 inches (2.5–5 cm) long and around 0.5 inch (1 cm) wide. They remain for several months then gradually die back when the inflorescences start to elongate. By flowering time, the leaves usually are gone, but occasionally the youngest leaves may remain. The inflorescences are usually pendent and bear a few to many flowers.

The small flowers, approximately 0.5 inch (1 cm) wide, are most attractive, and flower color varies from creamy white to greenish to deep brown-red. The three sepals and two petals are generally alike in size, shape, and color, but the petals are slightly reflexed and appear to be smaller. The slightly cupped lip is small and not a dominant portion of the flower. The flower and its pedicel are pubescent on the outside.

The footed column is very short and of equal width along its length. The small stigmatic surface is adjacent to the anther cap. Two deeply grooved, yellow pollinia are borne on a stipe with a waxy viscidium.

CULTURE: Temperature, 60–65°F (15–18°C); light, 2400–3600 footcandles; humidity, 40–60%; media, tree limbs, tree fern plaques; fertilization, monthly, with a 1–1–1 ratio.

COLOR PLATE: *Chiloschista usneoides*

SPECIES	FLOWERING SEASON	GENERAL LOCALE
lunifera	S	Myanmar, Thailand, Laos
usneoides	S	Southeast Asia

114

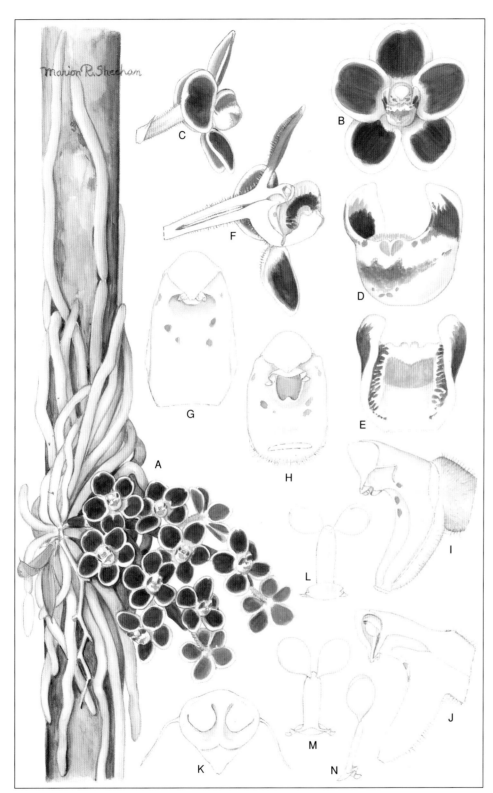

Chiloschista usneoides
A: Plant in flower, × 1.
B: Flower, face view, × 2½.
C: Flower, side view, × 2½.
D: Lip, three-quarter face view,
 × 8.
E: Lip, face view, × 8.
F: Flower, vertical section, × 4.
G: Column, ventral view, × 10.
H: Column, end view, × 10.
I: Column, side view, × 10.
J: Column, vertical section, × 10.
K: Anther cap, ventral view,
 × 15.
L, M, N: Pollinia, × 20.

115

Chysis

GENUS: *Chysis* Lindley (KYE-siss)
TRIBE: Arethuseae   SUBTRIBE: Chysinae
IDENTIFICATION CHARACTERISTICS: *Chysis* is a small genus not widely grown, yet one that deserves more consideration. Authorities disagree on the number of species in the genus, the number varying between two and four. The genus was first described in 1834 by John Lindley when a plant collected by John Henchman in Venezuela flowered. Lindley named the plant *C. aurea*, deriving the generic name from the Greek word *chysis* (to melt), thus describing the fusion of the pollinia when self-fertilization occurs.

Chysis is a genus of sympodial epiphytes distinguished by pendent, fleshy pseudobulbs 6 to 12 inches (15–30 cm) long that are covered by papery bracts and topped by five or more soft, pleated leaves. The deciduous leaves are up to 18 inches (45 cm) long and 4 to 6 inches (10–15 cm) wide. Showy flowers are borne on short inflorescences that develop when the new growth commences in the spring.

The flowers, up to 3 inches (7.5 cm) across, are white, cream, or yellowish with brown or pink marks. They are long-lived and subtended by green leafy bracts. The three sepals and two petals are alike in shape and color. The two petals are often a little narrower than the sepals and slightly reflexed. The two lateral lobes of the three-lobed lip almost encircle the column; they are light yellow on the outside and brownish purple inside. The midlobe has a wavy margin and brownish purple marks on the upper side. A prominent callus marks the center of the lip under the column.

The column has a pronounced foot that extends into a short spur at the base of the lip. The short column has a distinct beaklike rostellum separating the anther cap and stigmatic surface. There are eight narrow, almost-elliptical, yellow pollinia attached in pairs to a caudicle. They may be fused or partially fused at the time the flower opens.

CULTURE: Temperature, 60–70°F (15–21°C); light, 2400–3600 footcandles; humidity, 40–70%; media, tree fern, peat and perlite, bark; fertilization, monthly, ratio depends on medium.

COLOR PLATE: *Chysis bractescens*

SPECIES	FLOWERING SEASON	GENERAL LOCALE
aurea	SS	Mexico to Venezuela, Peru
bractescens	SS	Mexico, British Honduras, Guatemala
laevis	S–SS	Mexico to Costa Rica

Chysis bractescens
A: Plant in flower, × ¼.
B: Flower, face view, × ½.
C: Flower, side view, × ½.
D: Lip, side view, × 1.
E: Lip, face view, × 1.
F: Flower, vertical section, × 1.
G: Column, ventral view, × 2.
H: Column, side view, × 2.
I: Column, vertical section, × 2.
J: Anther cap and pollinia, × 5.
K, L, M: Pollinia, × 6.

Clowesia

GENUS: *Clowesia* Lindley (klo-ESS-ee-uh)
TRIBE: Cymbidieae   SUBTRIBE: Catasetinae
IDENTIFICATION CHARACTERISTICS: The attractive, highly fragrant, pendent inflorescence of *Clowesia russelliana* is a good example of why *Clowesia* has long been cultivated. This small, easy-to-grow genus contains mostly Central American natives that often have been included in *Catasetum* because of their similar vegetative characteristics. Although *Clowesia* was first defined by John Lindley in 1843 and named in honor of horticulturist Rev. Clowes, it was generally considered a section of *Catasetum* by most taxonomists. In 1975 Calaway Dodson restored the genus to its proper rank, and it now consists of five species. Although *Clowesia* resembles *Catasetum*, it differs in having bisexual flowers and a different pollinating mechanism.

Vegetatively, these sympodial, mostly epiphytic species produce tight clusters of pseudobulbs. Each bulb has several nodes and longitudinal grooves, and is topped and ensheathed by up to five soft, pleated leaves up to 18 inches (45 cm) long and 3 inches (7.5 cm) wide. The plants are deciduous; hence, the leaves are shed annually, after which the pseudobulbs are ensheathed by the dry, papery leaf bases. The multiflowered inflorescences arise from the base of the pseudobulb and may have as many as 25 flowers per stem.

Clowesia species have very similar flowers that are 2.5 inches (6 cm) wide and generally light green or rose. The petals and sepals are alike in size, shape, and color; often both are concave. The lip is a very interesting structure. It may be saccate or spurred with a long limb or midlobe. The limb is variable with margins that range from fringed to entire. The callus is also very distinct, often having dentate margins.

The column varies in length depending on the species. Although in general the column is similar to its counterpart in *Catasetum*, it lacks the two antennae found in *Catasetum*. The two large, yellow pollinia are borne on a single broad stipe with a distinctive viscidium.

CULTURE: Temperature, 60–65°F (15–18°C); light, 2400–3600 footcandles; humidity, 40–60%; medium, any good mix for epiphytes; fertilization, monthly, ratio depends on medium.

COLOR PLATE: *Clowesia russelliana*

SPECIES	FLOWERING SEASON	GENERAL LOCALE
rosea	W	Mexico
russelliana	SS–F	Mexico to Panama, Venezuela
warscewiczii	F–W	Costa Rica to Colombia, Venezuela

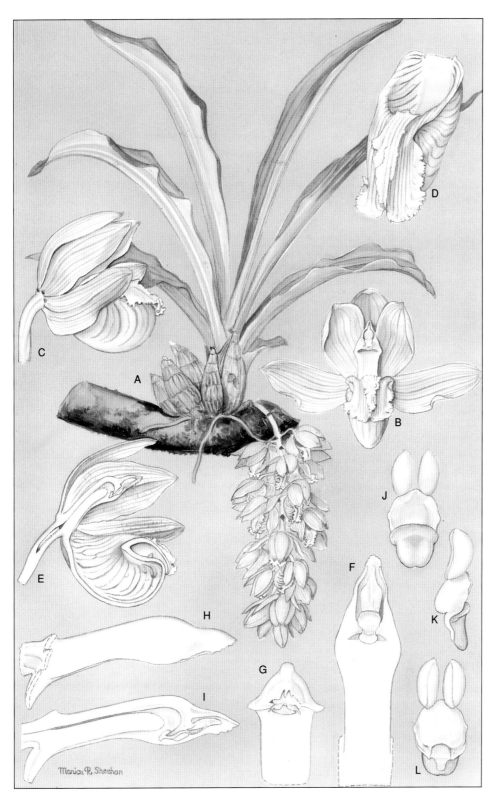

Clowesia russelliana
A: Plant in flower, × ¼.
B: Flower, face view, × 1.
C: Flower, side view, × 1.
D: Lip, × 1½.
E: Flower, vertical section, × 1.
F: Column, ventral view, × 2.
G: Column, end view, × 2.
H: Column, side view, × 2.
I: Column, vertical section, × 2.
J, K, L: Pollinia, × 5.

Cochleanthes

GENUS: *Cochleanthes* Rafinesque (kok-lee-ANN-theez)

TRIBE: Maxillarieae SUBTRIBE: Zygopetalinae

IDENTIFICATION CHARACTERISTICS: *Cochleanthes* is a small genus of approximately 12 easy-to-grow species. Unfortunately, when the plants form large clumps, the showy flowers are often hidden among the leaves, which is possibly why the plants have not enjoyed the popularity they deserve.

The genus was first described in 1838 by Constantine S. Rafinesque, who derived the generic name from the Greek word *cochlos* (shell), undoubtedly referring to the shell-like characteristics of the flowers. This genus has often been confused with *Zygopetalum*, *Chondrorhyncha*, and *Warscewiczella*, to which it is closely allied. Although very similar, the four genera can be separated by differences in pseudobulb and lip characteristics.

The pseudobulbless, sympodial, epiphytic plants are composed of fans of up to six soft leaves with clasping leaf bases. The 8- to 10-inch (20- to 25-cm) long, narrow, almost-lanceolate leaves are usually jointed 1 or 2 inches (2.5–5 cm) above the base. Because the fans of leaves are closely arranged, the plants form dense clumps. Each inflorescence arises from the axil of a leaf and consists of a naked peduncle with one terminal flower.

The single flower, up to 2 inches (5 cm) across, is subtended by a small, papery bract. The sepals and two petals are alike in size and color. The two petals have wavy margins and may partially encircle the lip and the column or they may be reflexed. The inner side of the petals may be the same color as the three-lobed lip, which has a very large midlobe and two small lateral lobes. The lateral lobes partially encircle the column. There is a very distinct callus on the basal portion of the lip.

The short column is broadest at the middle and pubescent on the underside. The stigmatic surface appears as a narrow slit just behind the anther cap. Four light yellowish pollinia of two different sizes are borne on an almost-shield-shaped stipe.

CULTURE: Temperature, 60–65°F (15–18°C); light, 2400–3600 footcandles; humidity, 40–60%; media, tree fern, peat and perlite, bark; fertilization, monthly, ratio depends on medium.

COLOR PLATE: *Cochleanthes discolor*

SPECIES	FLOWERING SEASON	GENERAL LOCALE
aromatica	S–SS–F	Costa Rica, Panama, Honduras, Venezuela
discolor	S–SS–F	Cuba, Costa Rica, Panama
flabelliformis	S–SS–F	Central to South America
marginata	S–SS–F	Colombia, Venezuela, Ecuador

Cochleanthes discolor
A: Plant in flower, × ½.
B: Flower, face view, × 1.
C: Flower, side view, × 1.
D: Lip, face view, × 1½.
E: Lip, top view, × 1½.
F: Flower, vertical section, × 1.
G: Column, ventral view, × 4.
H: Column, end view, × 4.
I: Column, side view, × 4.
J: Column, vertical section, × 4.
K, L, M: Pollinia, × 6.

Cochlioda

GENUS: *Cochlioda* Lindley (kok-lee-OH-duh)
TRIBE: Maxillarieae   SUBTRIBE: Oncidiinae
IDENTIFICATION CHARACTERISTICS: The small- to medium-size, compact plants of *Cochlioda*, with their graceful sprays of brightly colored flowers, are ideal candidates for orchidists interested in cultivating cool-growing miniature plants. The genus, with possibly no more than five or six species, is native to a limited area of the Andes in South America. It thrives best in areas where summer temperatures are seldom above 75°F (25°C) and night temperatures are near 50°F (10°C).

The genus was established by John Lindley in 1853. The generic name is derived from the Greek word *kochliodes* (spiral or snail shell) and probably refers to the callus tissue on the lip, which is somewhat snaillike in appearance. Although the genus is closely related to *Odontoglossum* and *Symphyglossum*, it is readily distinguished by the column with two stigmatic cavities and by the lip, which is partially adnate to the column at its base.

Vegetatively, these sympodial epiphytes are very similar to many other members of the Oncidiinae. The pseudobulbs, which are tightly clustered on short rhizomes and topped by one or two leaves, range from ovoid to ellipsoid and are up to 2.5 inches (6 cm) tall. The leaves are linear to oblong, often folded at the base, and may be up to 10 inches (25 cm) long. Inflorescences arise from the base of the pseudobulbs, may be erect or pendent, and may bear a few to many flowers.

The flowers are 2 inches (5 cm) in diameter and range in color from scarlet to magenta. The sepals and petals, with their spreading segments, are similar in shape and color, although the petals frequently are slightly broader. The three-lobed lip is partially fused to the column, with the degree of fusion ranging from one-third the length of the column in *Cochlioda rosea* to almost the entire length of the column in *C. noezliana*. The apex of the midlobe also differs from species to species; sometimes it is entire, other times it is bilobed.

The column may be long and slender or stout, and usually is slightly curved, with a fringed or pointed apex. There are two distinct stigmatic areas on the underside of the column. The two yellow pollinia are borne on a single stipe with a viscidium.

CULTURE: Temperature, 50–55°F (10–12°C) at night; light, 2400–3600 footcandles; humidity, 40–60%; medium, any good mix for epiphytes; fertilization, monthly, ratio depends on medium.

COLOR PLATE: *Cochlioda rosea*

SPECIES	FLOWERING SEASON	GENERAL LOCALE
noezliana	S–SS	Peru, Bolivia
rosea	W–S–SS	Ecuador, Peru
vulcanica	W–S–SS–F	Ecuador, Peru

Cochlioda rosea

A: Plant in flower, × ½.
B: Flower, face view, × 1½.
C: Flower, face view (second showing floral variation within a species), × 1½.
D: Flower, side view, × 1½.
E: Lip, × 3.
F: Flower, vertical section, × 2.
G: Column, ventral view, × 4.
H: Column, end view, × 4.
I: Column, side view, × 4.
J: Column, vertical section, × 4.
K, L, M: Pollinia, × 15.

Coelogyne

GENUS: *Coelogyne* Lindley (see-LOJ-in-ee)
TRIBE: Coelogyneae   SUBTRIBE: Coelogyninae
IDENTIFICATION CHARACTERISTICS: Approximately 125 species are found in the popular genus *Coelogyne*, which John Lindley founded in 1825 when he described a plant collected by Dr. N. Wallich in Nepal in 1824 as *C. cristata*. Lindley derived the generic name from two Greek words, *koilos* (hollow) and *gyne* (female), to describe the hollow stigmatic area on the column. Although the genus is composed of both epiphytic and terrestrial species, the most popular members are the epiphytes.

Pseudobulbs of these sympodial orchids vary in size and arrangement on the rhizome. Most are ovoid-shaped and spaced either closely or far apart on the rhizome. Each medium to dark green slightly fluted pseudobulb is topped by usually two but sometimes as many as four leaves. The leaves, which usually persist two years, vary considerably, from soft and pleated to thick and leathery, with some having pronounced stalks. Individual leaf blades may be up to 15 inches (38 cm) long and half as wide. Inflorescences appear with the new growth and may bear from one to many flowers, each one subtended by a papery bract.

The flowers range from 1 to 5 inches (2.5–12.5 cm) in diameter and basically are very similar. The basic flower color is white with yellow marks on the lip, while some flowers are creamy white or yellowish green with darker patterns. The three sepals and two petals are alike in shape and color, with the sepals generally larger in size. In some species (e.g., *Coelogyne parishii*), the petals are almost linear. The three-lobed lip varies in shape from almost saclike to almost fiddle-shaped. It is attached to the base of the column and is marked with from two to five raised lines that are sometimes fringed. The apex lobe of the lip often has a very wavy margin.

The long, narrow column flares near the apex, giving it a winglike appearance. The anther cap lies below the apex and almost adjacent to the stigmatic surface from whence the generic name was derived. The four yellow pollinia are almost flat and rectangular and are borne in pairs on broad caudicles.

CULTURE: Temperature, 50–70°F (10–21°C); light, 2400–3600 footcandles; humidity, 40–70%; media, tree fern, peat and perlite, bark, or a terrestrial mix, depending on the species; fertilization, monthly, ratio depends on medium.

COLOR PLATE: *Coelogyne asperata*

SPECIES	FLOWERING SEASON	GENERAL LOCALE
asperata	W	Vietnam
cinnamomea	S	Thailand, Malay Peninsula
cristata	W–S	Himalayas
elata	W–S	Himalayas
fimbriata	SS–F	China, northern India, Thailand, Vietnam
flaccida	W–S	Himalayas
foerstermannii	F–W–S–SS	Malay Peninsula, Sumatra, Borneo
fuliginosa	SS–F	Himalayas, Myanmar, Java
lactea	S–SS	Myanmar, Thailand
lawrenceana	S	Vietnam
massangeana	S–SS–F	Assam, Sumatra, Java, Borneo, Thailand, Malay Peninsula
mooreana	SS	Vietnam
nervosa	SS–F	India
nitida	S–SS–F	Himalayas (high elevations), Thailand
ovalis	SS–F	Himalayas, Thailand
pandurata	W–S–SS	Sumatra, Borneo, Malay Peninsula
parishii	S–SS	Myanmar
rhodeana	F	Myanmar, Thailand, Cambodia
sanderiana	SS–F	Borneo
sparsa	SS–F	Philippines
speciosa	W–S–SS–F	Sumatra, Java, Lesser Sunda Islands

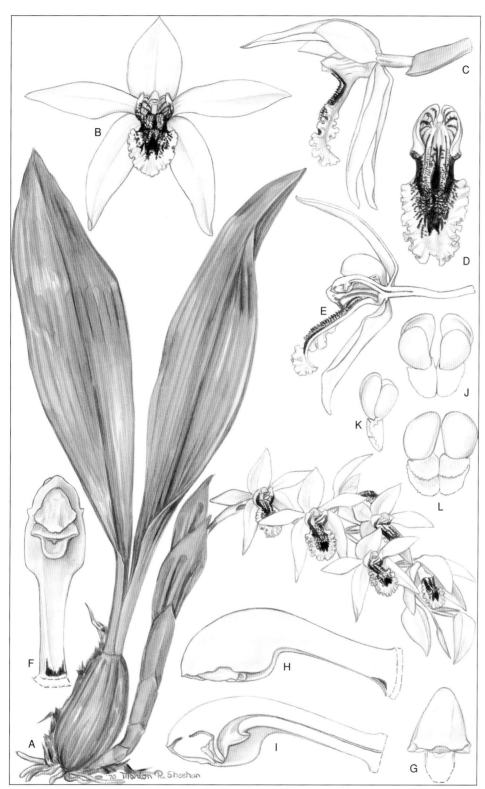

Coelogyne asperata

A: Plant in flower, × ⅓.
B: Flower, face view, × ¾.
C: Flower, side view, × ¾.
D: Lip, × 1.
E: Flower, vertical section, × ¾.
F: Column, ventral view, × 3.
G: Column, end view, × 3.
H: Column, side view, × 3.
I: Column, vertical section, × 3.
J, K, L: Pollinia, × 10.

Comparettia _____

GENUS: *Comparettia* Poeppig & Endlicher (kom-puh-RET-ee-uh)

TRIBE: Maxillarieae   SUBTRIBE: Oncidiinae

IDENTIFICATION CHARACTERISTICS: *Comparettia* is a genus of small plants bearing showy but delicate flowers. Consisting of up to 12 species, the genus was discovered in Ecuador and described around 1835 by Eduard Poeppig and Stephen L. Endlicher. It was named in honor of well-known plant physiologist Andreas Comparetti, who was working at Padua as a professor. The genus was first flowered in 1840 in England by Conrad and George Loddiges. *Comparettia* species are distinguished readily from other closely allied genera in the subtribe by the slender spurs on their flowers.

The plants have small, almost-pencil-shaped pseudobulbs that are not much more than 1 inch (2.5 cm) tall. The developing bulbs are covered with scales, which become papery and are shed at maturity. Each pseudobulb is topped by one to three leathery, lanceolate leaves up to 5 inches (12.5 cm) long and half as wide. In some species, the underside of the leaf is purplish. The slender arching inflorescence arises from the base of the pseudobulb and has five to seven flowers that are rose-purple, red, orange, or yellow. Some flowers are spotted or marked with magenta or white. The inflorescences are usually twice as long as the leaves so all the flowers are visible.

The 1-inch (2.5-cm) wide spurred flowers are unique in that they bear three spurs while appearing to have only one per flower. The dorsal sepal is erect and the two lateral sepals are fused to form the long external spur of the flower. The two petals are equal to or slightly larger than the dorsal sepal, and all three are in a fanlike arrangement. The petals are similar to the lip in color. The lip has a very broad midlobe and two small lateral lobes that are attenuated into spurs at the point of attachment. These two hairy spurs are hidden inside the spur formed by the lateral sepals.

The short column is narrow at the base and becomes very broad at the stigmatic area, which has a very large surface. The column narrows again in the vicinity of the anther cap. Two yellow pollinia are borne on a short stipe that is slightly concave on one side, almost like the handle on a teaspoon. There is a small foot at the base of the stipe.

CULTURE: Temperature, 50–60°F (10–15°C); light, 2400–3600 footcandles; humidity, 60–80%; media, tree fern, fir bark; fertilization, monthly, with a 1–1–1 ratio for tree fern or a 3–1–1 ratio for bark.

COLOR PLATE: *Comparettia macroplectron*

SPECIES	FLOWERING SEASON	GENERAL LOCALE
coccinea	F–W	Brazil, Mexico
falcata	F–W	West Indies, Peru, Mexico to northern South America
macroplectron	SS–F	Colombia
speciosa	F–W	Ecuador

Comparettia macroplectron
A: Plant in flower, × ½.
B: Flower, face view, × 1.
C: Flower, side view, × 1.
D: Lip, × 1½.
E: Flower, vertical section, × 1½.
F: Column, ventral view, × 5.
G: Column, end view, × 5.
H: Column, side view, × 5.
I: Column, vertical section, × 5.
J, K, L: Pollinia, × 10.

Coryanthes

GENUS: *Coryanthes* Hooker (kor-ee-ANN-theez)
TRIBE: Maxillarieae   SUBTRIBE: Stanhopeinae
IDENTIFICATION CHARACTERISTICS: *Coryanthes*, the bucket orchid, has one of the most unusual and complex flowers in the entire orchid family. Each bizarre flower has the ability to produce a considerable amount of a watery substance from two glands, partially filling a bucket formed by the lip. Bees unfortunate to fall into this bucket must swim to the proper exit to escape. This exit goes under the anther, where the pollinia adhere to the insect's underside and, on a subsequent visit to another flower of the same genus, are deposited on the stigma.

Usually only one or two flowers (but sometimes more) are produced per inflorescence and remain open only three or four days. Therefore, *Coryanthes* species are not frequently seen in shows or public displays. In nature, they grow in ant nests in areas of very high relative humidity. Thus in greenhouse culture, high humidity and an acid medium rich in nutrients are essential for good growth. Despite these difficulties, these close relatives of *Gongora* and *Stanhopea* are a fascinating addition to an orchid collection.

This unusual genus of approximately 15 species of sympodial epiphytes was first described by William Hooker in 1831. The generic name was derived from the Greek words *korys* (helmet) and *anthos* (flower) and referred to the helmetlike hypochile of the genus's very distinctive lip.

Vegetatively, *Coryanthes* resembles *Gongora*. The tight clusters of grooved, almost-pear-shaped to spindle-shaped pseudobulbs are topped by two soft, pleated leaves up to 2 feet (60 cm) long and 4 inches (10 cm) wide. The pendent inflorescence arises from the base of the pseudobulb.

The flowers are variable in color, often with a cream-colored base overlaid with reddish spots. In some species (e.g., *Coryanthes macrantha*), they are highly fragrant and 4 to 5 inches (10–12.5 cm) across. The flowers are hard to describe because they change constantly during anthesis. As they develop, the two lateral sepals open out and fold back, eventually resembling bat wings, hence a common name, bat orchid. The dorsal sepal opens and then may fold down accordion-fashion. The petals, which are narrower than the sepals and have undulate margins, are almost hidden by the massive sepals and lip. The lip is a highly modified structure and the most prominent feature of the flower. The two most pronounced parts are the hypochile (helmet), where euglosine bees land seeking fragrances, and the epichile (bucket), which contains the watery solution. The projections below the hypochile discourage insects from trying to enter the bucket from the wrong side.

The column is also different from most other orchid columns because it has two glands, one on either side. These supply the fluid to the bucket. The typical column is broadest near the stigmatic surface and slightly recurved near the tip. Two yellow pollinia are borne on a very intricate stipe, which is united to the column by an interesting flaplike attachment.

CULTURE: Temperature, 60–65°F (15–18°C); light, 2400–3600 footcandles; humidity, 60–80%; medium, acid organic, tree fern; fertilization, every two weeks, with a 1–1–1 ratio.

COLOR PLATE: *Coryanthes maculata*

SPECIES	FLOWERING SEASON	GENERAL LOCALE
biflora	F	Venezuela
macrantha	W–S–SS	Peru to Trinidad
maculata	S	Panama to Brazil
speciosa	S–SS	Brazil to Venezuela

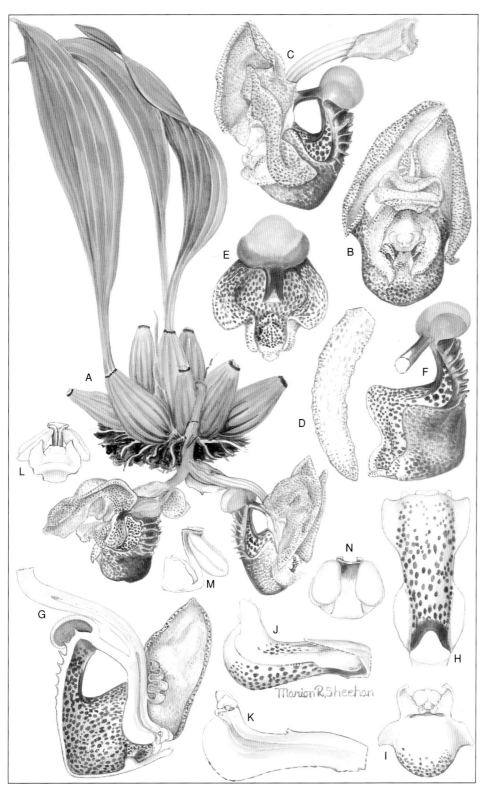

Coryanthes maculata

A: Plant in flower, × ⅓.
B: Flower, face view, × ½.
C: Flower, side view, × ½.
D: Petal, × 1.
E: Lip, face view, × ½.
F: Lip, side view, × ½.
G: Flower, vertical section, × ½.
H: Column, ventral view, × 1.
I: Column, end view, × 1.
J: Column, side view, × 1.
K: Column, vertical section, × 1.
L, M, N: Pollinia, × 4.

MarionR.Sheehan

Cycnoches

GENUS: *Cycnoches* Lindley (sik-NOH-cheez)
TRIBE: Cymbidieae   SUBTRIBE: Catasetinae
Identification Characteristics: The genus Cycnoches is often confused and misunderstood. In the early days, due to the distinctively dissimilar male and female flowers, different specific names were given to the same species. The swan orchids were aptly named by John Lindley in 1838 when he coined the generic name from the Greek words *kyknos* (swan) and *auchen* (neck). There are 12 recognized species in the genus.

The wide diversity of floral forms does not continue to the vegetative structures, which are very much alike. These sympodial epiphytes often have large pseudobulbs, up to 18 inches (45 cm) long, some resembling a club. Each pseudobulb has anywhere from a few to many soft, pleated leaves, up to 18 inches (45 cm) long and 4 to 6 inches (10–15 cm) wide. Because they are deciduous, the long, green pseudobulbs often are completely leafless and partially covered by papery bracts. The inflorescences, which develop from the upper portion of the pseudobulb, may have from a few to many flowers.

The greenish, yellowish, or brownish flowers, often with purple-brown dots, may be up to 7 inches (17.5 cm) in diameter. In some species (e.g., *Cycnoches chlorochilon*), there is little difference between the male and female flowers, whereas in others (e.g., *C. pentadactylon*) the flowers differ in size and other characteristics. In both groups, the female flowers are very much alike. Where the male flowers differ, the major differences are found in the lips. Inflorescences usually bear only one sex of flower, and male inflorescences have more flowers than their female counterparts. The sepals and petals in both male and female flowers are similar in size and color. The lips, which are a little more complex than those of other genera, vary between and among species. Female flowers and the occasional flower with both sexes (perfect) have the largest lips. The lip of the male flower is greatly reduced and almost disclike. The large lips are often concave and may have a basal claw.

Despite the variability of these flowers, they are easily recognized by their distinct columns, which in all three types of flowers, are much alike and resemble the neck and head of a swan. Long and narrow, the column curves gracefully above the lip, enlarging near the anther cap. An almost-elliptical stigmatic area is located under the broadest part of the column. Two yellow pollinia are borne on a broad stipe, which arises from an inverted helmet-like foot that may have a fringed margin.

CULTURE: Temperature, 60°F (15°C) minimum for best growth; light, 2400–3600 footcandles; humidity, 60–80%, can be critical; media, tree fern, any well-drained mix for epiphytes; fertilization, monthly when in active growth, with a 1–1–1 ratio.

COLOR PLATE: *Cycnoches chlorochilon*

SPECIES	FLOWERING SEASON	GENERAL LOCALE
chlorochilon	S–SS	Panama, Venezuela, Colombia, Guyana, Suriname, French Guiana
egertonianum	F–W	Mexico, Guatemala to Colombia, Peru, Brazil
* var. *aureum*	SS–F	Costa Rica, Panama
* var. *dianae*	SS–F	Panama
haagii	SS	Brazil, Colombia, Venezuela, Peru, Bolivia
lehmanii	SS	Ecuador
loddigesii	F–W	Guyana, Suriname, Brazil, Venezuela, Colombia
maculatum	F	Venezuela
pentadactylon	S–SS	Brazil, Peru
ventricosum	SS–F	Mexico, Guatemala, Honduras, Panama
* var. *warscewiczii*	S–SS	Costa Rica, Panama

* Some authors (e.g., Pridgeon 1992) elevate these varieties to species status.

Cycnoches chlorochilon
A: Plant in flower, × ³⁄₈.
B: Flower, face view, × ½.
C: Flower, side view, × ½.
D: Lip, × 1.
E: Flower, vertical section, × ½.
F: Column, ventral view, × 4.
G: Column, side view, × 4.
H: Column, vertical section, × 4.
I: Pollinia in anther cap, × 5.
J, K, L: Pollinia, × 5.

Cymbidiella

GENUS: *Cymbidiella* Rolfe (sym-bid-ee-ELL-uh)
TRIBE: Cymbidieae   SUBTRIBE: Cyrtopodiinae
IDENTIFICATION CHARACTERISTICS: *Cymbidiella pardalina* "is well worth trying for, since the flowers are absolutely spectacular with eye-catching, contrasting colors" (Hillerman and Holst 1986). This small genus of only three species confined to the island of Madagascar is closely allied to *Cymbidium*, *Eulophia* and *Eulophiella*, differing slightly in floral characteristics. The genus was established in 1918 by R. A. Rolfe, who named it *Cymbidiella*, the diminutive form of *Cymbidium*, because he saw a resemblance between the two genera. Due to the difficulties encountered in culture and seed germination, this genus is not common, an unfortunate situation. In its native habitat, *Cymbidiella pardalina* grows in association with a staghorn fern (*Platycerium madagascariense*) on trees of *Albizia*; *C. flabellata* grows terrestrially under heathlike shrubs; and *C. falcigera* grows only on the trunks of *Raphia ruffia* (palm), thus indicating that each species has very precise cultural requirements.

Vegetatively, these sympodial species are similar to *Cymbidium* species but have pseudobulbs that are more elongate, up to 1 foot (30 cm) long, and borne in clumps that are more open. Each pseudobulb may be topped by as many as 40 persistent, distichous leaves up to 39 inches (100 cm) long and arranged in the shape of a fan. The many-flowered inflorescence, either racemose or paniculate, arises from the base of the pseudobulb.

The large showy flower, 1.75 to 2.5 inches (4–6 cm) wide, is subtended by a narrow bract, a distinguishing characteristic of this genus. Yellowish green to pale green in color, the flowers have either green or orange-to-red lips with various dark reddish brown spots. The sepals are similar to the petals in shape and color but usually a little broader and with differing amounts of dark reddish brown spots. The spurless lip may be three- to four-lobed with a small basal callus. The two erect lateral lobes and the basal portion of the midlobe are adorned with varying amounts of dark spots.

The very short footed column, 0.4 inch (1 cm) long, may have a dull purple anther cap (e.g., *Cymbidiella falcigera*). Two yellow pollinia are attached to a stipe with a rectangular- to trapezoidal-shaped viscidium.

CULTURE: Temperature, 60°F (15°C); light, up to 2000 footcandles; humidity, 40–60%; media, fir bark or husky fiber are suggested; fertilization, monthly, ratio depends on medium.

COLOR PLATE: *Cymbidiella pardalina*

SPECIES	FLOWERING SEASON	GENERAL LOCALE
falcigera	S–SS	Madagascar
flabellata	S–SS	Madagascar
pardalina	S–SS	Madagascar

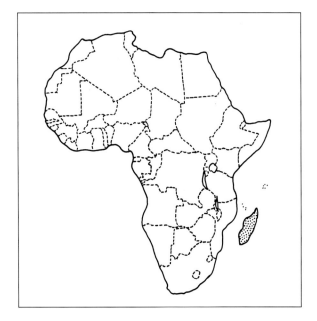

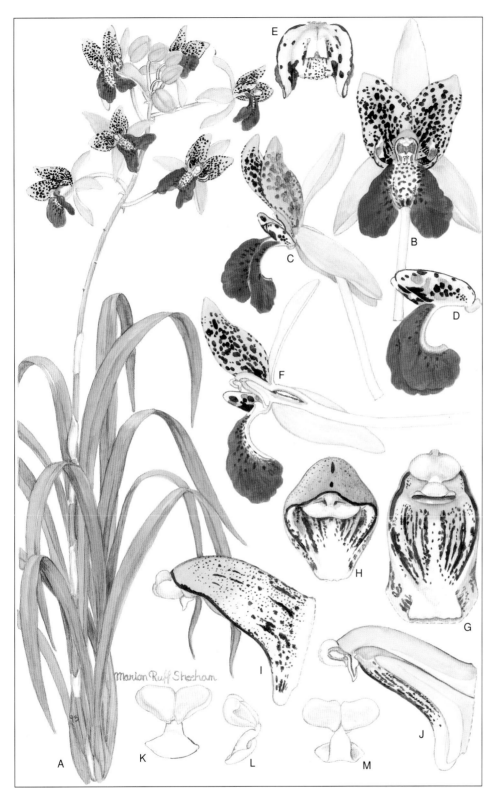

Cymbidiella pardalina

A: Plant in flower, × ¼.
B: Flower, face view, × ¾.
C: Flower, side view, × ¾.
D: Lip, side view, × 1.
E: Lip, face view of inner end, × 1.
F: Flower, vertical section, × 1.
G: Column, ventral view, × 3.
H: Column, end view, × 3.
I: Column, side view, × 3.
J: Column, vertical section, × 3.
K, L, M: Pollinia, × 6.

133

Cymbidium _____

GENUS: *Cymbidium* Swartz (sym-BlD-ee-um)
TRIBE: Cymbidieae SUBTRIBE: Cyrtopodiinae
IDENTIFICATION CHARACTERISTICS: Swedish botanist Olof Swartz founded the genus *Cymbidium* around 1800, and the genus now contains approximately 70 species of both terrestrial and epiphytic, sympodial orchids. The generic name was derived from the Greek word *cymbid* (boat) and probably refers to the lip, which resembles a boat in some species.

There is very little variation of vegetative characteristics among *Cymbidium* species. Short, stout pseudobulbs are often ensheathed by encircling leaf bases. The lanceolate leaves, often up to 2 feet (60 cm) long, may be either soft or leathery and remain green for several years. Inflorescences arise from the base of the pseudobulb and may be pendulous or erect. Depending on the species, the inflorescence may bear 12 or more flowers.

The flowers, which are 0.5 to 5 inches (1–12.5 cm) in diameter, vary more in size than in shape. The three sepals and two petals are almost equal and usually free and erect. The three-lobed lip is attached to the base of the column. The smaller, lateral lobes are erect and partially encircle the column. The central lobe of the lip is the largest and may have a wavy margin. Two ridges are often found on the disc of the lip. Colors include most of the soft pastel tints.

The column is long, narrow, and widest near the stigmatic surface. The anther cap may be one- or two-celled. Depending on the species, there are either two or four pollinia, the former deeply grooved. The yellow pollinia are often arranged in the form of a pyramid on a short stipe with a broad base.

CULTURE: Temperature, 50–70°F (10–21°C); light, partial shade to full sun; humidity, 40–70%; media, tree fern, bark, peat and perlite for epiphytes; any well-drained medium containing at least 40% organic matter for terrestrials; fertilization, monthly, ratio depends on medium.

COLOR PLATE: *Cymbidium finlaysonianum*

SPECIES	FLOWERING SEASON	GENERAL LOCALE
atropurpureum	SS	Philippines
canaliculatum	S	Australia
cochleare	F	Sikkim, Assam
devonianum	S–SS	Himalayas
eburneum	S–SS	Himalayas, Indochina
elegans	F	Northern India
ensifolium	F–W–S–SS	India, Southeast Asia to China, Japan
finlaysonianum	S–SS–F	Southeast Asia to Philippines
floribundum	S	China
giganteum	F–W	Himalayas, China, Indochina
grandiflorum	F–W	Himalayas, China
insigne	W	Indochina
lancifolium	F–W	Indonesia, Japan
longifolium	F	Himalayas
lowianum	W–S–SS	Myanmar
roseum	S	Java
schroederi	S	Vietnam
suave	S	Australia
tigrinum	S	Myanmar, Indochina
tracyanum	F	Myanmar, Indochina
virescens	S	China, Japan

Cymbidium finlaysonianum
A: Plant in flower, × ¼.
B: Flower, face view, × 1.
C: Flower, side view, × 1.
D: Lip, side view, × 2.
E: Lip, face view, × 2.
F: Flower, vertical section, × 1.
G: Column, ventral view, × 4.
H: Column, end view, × 4.
I: Column, side view, × 4.
J: Column, vertical section, × 4.
K: Column, anther cap lifted, × 4.
L: Anther cap and pollinia, × 6.
M, N, O: Pollinia, × 10.

Cynorkis

GENUS: *Cynorkis* Thouars (sin-OR-kiss)
TRIBE: Orchideae   SUBTRIBE: Habenariinae
IDENTIFICATION CHARACTERISTICS: *Cynorkis* is one of many very attractive orchid genera seldom seen in cultivation. The flowers are as pretty as and showier than those of many cultivated orchids. Because *Cynorkis* species are deciduous and dormant for more than half the year, growers are discouraged from growing these species; the dormant plant is completely out of sight, making its container appear to be an empty pot of soil. These delightful plants are well worth growing and enjoying, however, as they go through a complete cycle—from emergence of the first leaf to the dispersal of seeds—in about five months.

Cynorkis contains about 125 species of tuberous-rooted, mostly terrestrial plants, with an occasional epiphyte. The genus was first described in 1822 by Aubert Du Petit-Thouars, who coined the name from two Greek words, *kynosa* (dog) and *orchis* (testicle), to describe the small testiculate tubers of this genus.

During their active growing period, these plants produce one to several large leaves, often dark shiny green above and pale beneath or sometimes purplish on the underside. The large leaves are subtended by one or more leafy bracts, and the leaf blades sometimes spread out and lie flat on the ground. Some plants have one large leaf, 5 to 6 inches (12–15 cm) long and 3 inches (7.5 cm) wide, and a second greatly reduced leaf hidden in the rolled basal portion of the large leaf. This causes the plant to appear as if it has a single leaf. The inflorescence, which arises from the center of the encircling bracts and leaf blades, bears one to many flowers, depending on the species.

The basic colors of these 0.5- to 1.5-inch (1- to 4-cm) wide flowers are mauve and pink. The flowers are interesting because at first glance they appear to have only four segments rather than the usual six. Actually, six segments are present but two narrow petals are hard to distinguish because they appear to be almost fused to the hooded dorsal sepal. The two lateral sepals are similar in size and color, slightly cup-shaped, and reflexed. The highly variable lip, ranging from entire to five-lobed, is spurred and showy. It is the largest floral segment in many species.

The column is very complex, with a bilobed stigma and caudicles of the pollinia in channels. The two pollinia often are borne on long, slender caudicles with a minute viscidium at the base.

CULTURE: Temperature, 60–65°F (15–18°C) while growing, 43–50°F (6–10°C) while dormant; light, 2400–3600 footcandles; humidity, 40–60%; medium, any good mix for terrestrials, do not allow potting mixture to become excessively dry during dormant period but water sparingly; fertilization, monthly, when in active growth, with a 1–1–1 ratio.

COLOR PLATE: *Cynorkis* species

SPECIES	FLOWERING SEASON	GENERAL LOCALE
kassnerana	SS	Tropical Africa
lowiana	S–SS	Madagascar
purpurascens	S–SS–F	Madagascar
purpurea	SS–F	Madagascar
uniflora	SS–F	Madagascar

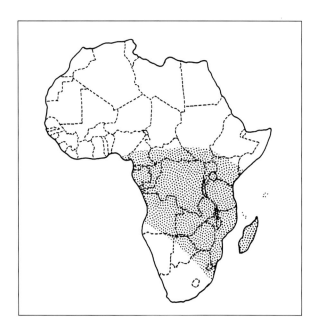

Cynorkis species
A: Plant in flower, × ½.
B: Flower, face view, × 1½.
C: Flower, side view, × 1½.
D: Petal, × 5.
E: Flower, vertical section, × 1½.
F: Column, ventral view, × 6.
G: Column, end view, × 6.
H: Column, side view, × 6.
I: Column, vertical section, × 6.
J, K: Pollinia, × 8.

Marion R. Sheehan

Cypripedium

GENUS: *Cypripedium* Linnaeus (sip-rih-PEE-dee-um)

Subfamily: Cypripedioideae

IDENTIFICATION CHARACTERISTICS: Cypripediums are extremely popular garden subjects throughout their range and are considered by some as the most famous of all orchids. This popularity has led to the demise of native populations in some areas in the attempt to satisfy the appetites of gardeners. Laws have been enacted to protect cypripediums still growing in the wild.

When Carl Linnaeus first described the genus in 1753, based on specimens of *Cypripedium calceolus*, he could not have selected a more appropriate generic name. In combining the Greek words *Kypris* (Venus) and *pedilon* (sandal), he very adequately described the soft, delicate, colorful, slipperlike lips that are the genus's prominent characteristic. Today cypripediums are affectionately dubbed lady's-slippers. Taxonomists recognize at least 25 species, the exact number depending on how many are classified as natural hybrids or varieties.

These sympodial, deciduous, terrestrial orchids have short underground rhizomes with fibrous roots. The vegetative growth, which is highly variable, may consist of a stemless growth with two basal leaves and a single-flowered scape (e.g., *Cypripedium acaule*) or a leafy stem with one or more terminal flowers (e.g., *C. reginae*). The soft leaves, often pleated and pubescent, may be up to 11 inches (28 cm) long and 4 inches (10 cm) wide. The inflorescences are solitary to multiflowered.

The flowers are up to 5 inches (12.5 cm) across and come in a wide variety of colors including pink, yellow, white, and brown, usually with two or more colors on the same flower, sometimes appearing as spots or other patterns. Every flower is a delightful entity in itself. The sepals and petals are often the same color, but that may be the only common characteristic. The dorsal sepal is usually larger than the lateral sepals and may be erect or arched forward. The two lateral sepals are fused to form a slightly smaller structure (synsepal). The petals are narrow and twisted or broad and flat. The bootlike (saccate) lip is the showiest and most colorful portion of most flowers. It has inrolled margins and appears to be inflated.

The short column has a staminode and two anthers with pollen masses on either side of the column. Although the pollen is arranged in two pollinia-like bodies, these masses of pollen disintegrate. Usually, only a part of the pollinia-like body is removed by the insect pollinator.

CULTURE: Temperature, rhizome withstands temperatures well below freezing; light, moderate to heavy shade, less than 1800 footcandles; humidity, variable; media, rich organic soil, forest humus; fertilization, once in spring, with a 1–1–1 ratio.

COLOR PLATE: *Cypripedium acaule*

SPECIES	FLOWERING SEASON	GENERAL LOCALE
acaule	S	Canada, Great Lakes to Georgia
calceolus	S	Temperate regions of North America, Europe, Asia
californicum	S	Northwestern California
candidum	S	Nebraska to western New York
guttatum	S	Alaska, Russia
irapeanum	S	Central & southern Mexico
japonicum	S	China, Japan
montanum	S	Montana to northern British Columbia
reginae	S	Southern Canada, northern United States

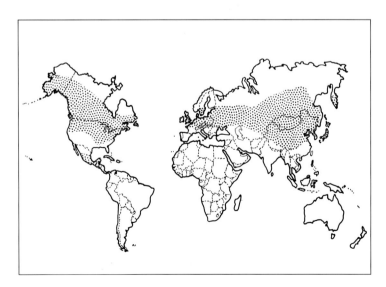

138

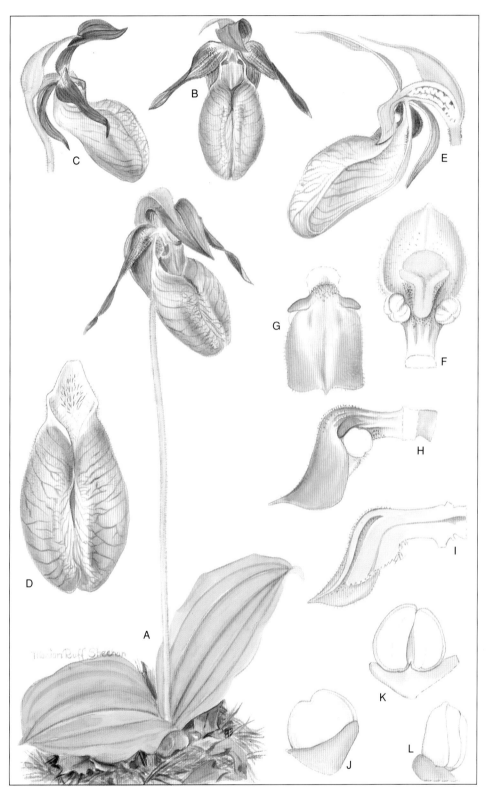

Cypripedium acaule
A: Plant in flower, × ½.
B: Flower, face view, × ½.
C: Flower, side view, × ½.
D: Lip, × 1.
E: Flower, vertical section, × ¾.
F: Column, ventral view, × 2.
G: Column, end view, × 2.
H: Column, side view, × 2.
I: Column, vertical section, × 2.
J, K, L: Pollinia, × 4.

Cyrtopodium

GENUS: *Cyrtopodium* R. Brown (sir-toh-POH-dee-um)

TRIBE: Cymbidieae   SUBTRIBE: Cyrtopodiinae

IDENTIFICATION CHARACTERISTICS: The genus *Cyrtopodium* was founded in 1813 when a plant collected by Alexander Anderson on the island of St. Vincent in the West Indies flowered for Thomas Evans in England. Robert Brown derived the generic name from two Greek words, *kyrtos* (curved) and *podion* (foot), to describe the distinct curve on the foot of the column. The original species, *C. andersonii*, was named after its discoverer. Today 30 species and one hybrid are known.

The genus includes both terrestrial and epiphytic, sympodial species. Pseudobulbs vary slightly, being either long and tapered (e.g., *Cyrtopodium punctatum*), or short and stubby (e.g., *C. virescens*). The former may be 3 or more feet (90 or more cm) long and usually are covered by persistent leaf bases that terminate with spinelike projections. Florida natives refer to *C. punctatum* as the cow-horn orchid due to the shape and color of the pseudobulbs. In general, each pseudobulb terminates with five to seven soft, pleated leaves up to 2 feet (60 cm) long. The leaves often have three prominent veins. The inflorescences arising from the base of the pseudobulb often are branched, up to 3 or 4 feet (90–120 cm) long, and many flowered. They have leafy bracts at each node and subtending each flower. On some species, (e.g., *C. punctatum*), the bracts subtending the flowers are so large and colorful that they are difficult to separate from the flowers. These convoluted bracts make the inflorescences very showy.

The 1- to 1.5-inch (2.5- to 4-cm) wide flowers are basically yellow or yellow-green, often with reddish brown blotches. The three sepals are alike in size and color and are often twisted or with undulating margins. The two petals are sometimes shorter and broader than the sepals and are often reflexed. They may or may not be the same color as the sepals. The three-lobed lip is a unique feature of the flower. The two lateral lobes are reflexed and almost encircle the column, while the middle lobe is short and broad, and has a wavy margin. The lip has a distinct callus with a number of round tubercles at the apex.

The short column has a pronounced foot and is broadest near the stigmatic surface. The base of the caudicle is triangular and partially covers the stigmatic surface. The two or four pollinia are usually yellow, almost elliptical, and compressed.

CULTURE: Temperature, 50–70°F (10–21°C) (*Cyrtopodium punctatum* survives temperatures to 30°F [–1°C]); light, 2400–3600 footcandles (some grow in full sun); humidity, 40–70%; media, bark, tree fern, osmunda; fertilization, monthly, ratio depends on medium.

COLOR PLATE: *Cyrtopodium punctatum*

SPECIES	FLOWERING SEASON	GENERAL LOCALE
aliciae	F	Brazil, Paraguay, Uruguay, Argentina
andersonii	S	West Indies to Brazil
cristatum	S–SS	Venezuela, Colombia, Guyana, Suriname, French Guiana
gigas	F	Central Brazil
palmifrons	F–W	Central & south Brazil
paniculatum	S–SS	Venezuela, Colombia, Peru
paranaense	F–W	Southern coast of Brazil
parviflorum	W	Guyana, Suriname, French Guiana, Brazil, Bolivia, Trinidad
punctatum	S–SS	South Florida, Mexico to Argentina
virescens	S	Brazil, Paraguay, Uruguay

Cyrtopodium punctatum

A: Plant in flower, × ¼.
B: Flower, face view, × 1.
C: Flower, side view, × 1.
D: Lip, three-quarter view, × 2.
E: Lip, face view, × 2.
F: Flower, vertical section, × 1½.
G: Column, ventral view, × 5.
H: Column, end view, × 5.
I: Column, side view, × 5.
J: Column, vertical section, × 5.
K: Anther cap with pollinia, × 10.
L, M, N: Pollinia, × 10.

141

Cyrtorchis

GENUS: *Cyrtorchis* Schlechter (sirt-OR-kiss)
TRIBE: Vandeae SUBTRIBE: Aerangidinae
IDENTIFICATION CHARACTERISTICS: *Cyrtorchis* is a very attractive genus with delicate, white, almost-star-shaped flowers that emit a pleasant fragrance day and night. There are about 15 species of easy-to-grow, miniature, *Vanda*-like species in this genus that was founded by Rudolf Schlechter in 1914 on the basis of *C. arcuata*. The generic name was derived from the Greek words *kyrtos* (swelling) and *orchis* (testicle), perhaps referring to the fleshy nature of the floral segments.

Vegetatively, these monopodial epiphytes usually have 8 to 12 stiff, leathery leaves. The dark green leaves, up to 10 inches (25 cm) long, are deeply bilobed at the apex. Coarse, aerial roots are produced from the lower nodes. The inflorescences, which arise from the axils of the leaves, may be stiff and erect or curve gently downward. Each node and flower bud is subtended by a leafy bract that dries and turns brown before the flower opens. The inflorescences bear up to 20 flowers.

In some species, the 3-inch (7.5-cm) wide white flowers turn yellowish pink as they age. The sepals and petals are alike in shape and color, with the petals slightly smaller in size. The apical lobe of the lip is similar in size and shape to the petals; but the lip, with its large, tapered spur, is slightly broader than the sepals. The spur may be straight or curved once or twice.

The column is very short, blunt, and topped by a most unusual anther cap and caudicle arrangement. The viscidium and rostellum actually extend a short distance into the spur. Some taxonomists divide the genus into two sections based on differences in the viscidium. There are two yellow, almost-round pollinia attached to a complex stipe.

CULTURE: Temperature, 55–65°F (12–18°C); light, 2400–3600 footcandles; humidity, 40–60%; media, tree fern, bark; fertilization, monthly, ratio depends on medium.

COLOR PLATE: *Cyrtorchis arcuata*

SPECIES	FLOWERING SEASON	GENERAL LOCALE
arcuata	S–SS–F	South Africa
chailluana	F	Tropical West Africa
hamata	W	Tropical West Africa
monteiroae	S	Tropical West Africa

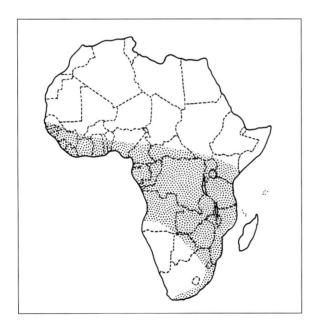

Cyrtorchis arcuata
A: Plant in flower, × ⅓.
B: Flower, face view, × 1.
C: Flower, side view, × 1.
D: Lip, side view, × 1½.
E: Lip, detail, × 1½.
F: Flower, vertical section, × 1.
G: Column, ventral view, × 8.
H: Column, end view, × 8.
I: Column, side view, × 8.
J: Column, vertical section, × 8.
K: Column, end view, anther
   cap removed, × 8.
L, M, N: Pollinia, × 6.
O: Lower portion of caudicle
   and viscidium, × 8.

143

Dendrobium

GENUS: *Dendrobium* Swartz (den-DROH-bee-um)
TRIBE: Dendrobieae   SUBTRIBE: Dendrobiinae
IDENTIFICATION CHARACTERISTICS: This very complex and extremely large genus is very popular. People in any climate can grow dendrobiums by selecting species native to similar climates. In its native habitat, the genus ranges from the often snow-covered slopes of mountains in Japan to the warm tropics. Most authorities now consider *Dendrobium* to be comprised of a number of distinct groups and more than 1500 valid species. Olof Swartz, who was the first to describe the genus when he described all the orchid plants known to him in 1800, derived the generic name from the Greek words *dendron* (tree) and *bios* (life).

Dendrobium is a genus of sympodial epiphytes varying immensely in vegetative characteristics (Fig. 18). Pseudobulbs range from small, roundish, and 1 inch (2.5 cm) tall to canelike bulbs 5 feet (150 cm) tall. They may be deciduous or evergreen. There are immense variations in leaves, as well, which may be flat, thin, thick, leathery, or even terete, and from 1 to 15 inches (2.5–38 cm) long. Inflorescences are either terminal or axillary and bear from one to many flowers, which may last only a day (e.g., *D. crumenatum*) or be long-lived (e.g., *D. cuthbertsonii*).

The flowers of *Dendrobium* species are highly variable. There is a wide range of color, and size varies from approximately 0.5 to 6 inches (1–15 cm) in diameter. The three sepals are generally alike in size, shape, and color. The two petals may be equal to or broader than the sepals; they may be flat and broad or narrow and elongate with undulate margins. Some petals are twisted like corkscrews, others are almost grotesque in appearance because of undulations, twists, or unusual color patterns. The three-lobed lip exhibits variability among species. The two lateral lobes are smaller than the terminal lobe and partially encircle the column. The apex lobe is constricted and attached to the spurlike foot on the column. Some species have fringed margins on the lip and some have distinct calli.

The short column has a pronounced spurlike foot below the point of attachment between the column and ovary, and is widest near the stigmatic surface. *Dendrobium* species have four, usually yellow, oval pollinia in two pairs, each tightly compressed. The pollinia have no caudicle and resemble small rice grains.

CULTURE: Temperature, 50–70°F (10–21°C), depending on species, some tolerate lower temperature; light, 2400–3600 footcandles; humidity, 40–70%; media, bark, tree fern, combinations of the two; fertilization, monthly, ratio depends on medium.

COLOR PLATE: *Dendrobium phalaenopsis*

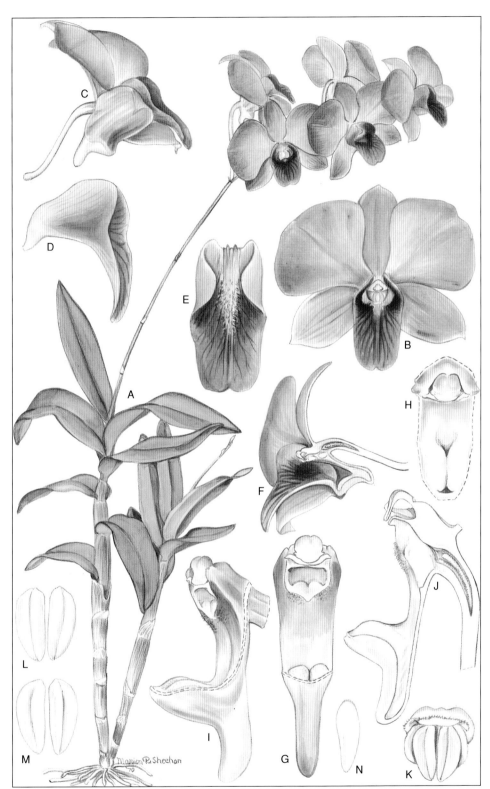

Dendrobium phalaenopsis
A: Plant in flower, × ½.
B: Flower, face view, × 1.
C: Flower, side view, × 1.
D: Lip, side view, × 1½.
E: Lip, face view, × 1½.
F: Flower, vertical section, × 1.
G: Column, ventral view, show-
   ing spurlike foot, × 3.
H: Column, end view, × 3.
I: Column, side view, × 3.
J: Column, vertical section, × 3.
K: Anther cap with pollinia, × 8.
L, M, N: Pollinia, × 10.

145

DENDROBIUM SPECIES	FLOWERING SEASON	GENERAL LOCALE
aduncum	SS	Himalayas
anosmum	W–S–SS	Borneo, Celebes, Philippines
aphrodite	SS	Myanmar
aphyllum	F–W–S–SS	Himalayas to Myanmar, Vietnam
atroviolaceum	W–S–SS	New Guinea
aureum	F–W–S–SS	Himalayas to Philippines, Sri Lanka, Java
bigibbum	F	Northern Australia
brymerianum	F–W–S	Myanmar to Vietnam
canaliculatum	F–W	Northern Australia
chrysanthum	F–W–S–SS	Himalayas to China
chrysotoxum	S–SS	Myanmar to China, Vietnam
crumenatum	F–W–S–SS	Myanmar to Philippines, Malay Peninsula
crystallinum	S–SS	Himalayas to Vietnam
cuthbertsonii	F–W–S–SS	New Guinea
dearei	SS	Philippines
discolor	SS–F	Australia
draconis	S–SS	Myanmar to Vietnam
falconeri	S–SS	Himalayas to Myanmar
farmeri	S–SS	Himalayas to Myanmar
fimbriatum	S	Himalayas to Myanmar
formosum	W–S	Himalayas to Myanmar
hookerianum	F–W–S–SS	Sikkim, Assam
johannis	SS	Northern Australia
kingianum	S	Australia
lindleyi	S	Himalayas to Vietnam
loddigesii	S	China
lowii	SS–F	Borneo
moniliforme	S	Korea, China, Japan
moschatum	S–SS	Himalayas to Myanmar
nobile	W–S–SS	Himalayas to Myanmar, China
parishii	S–SS	Thailand
phalaenopsis	F	Northern Australia
primulinum	W–S	Himalayas to Myanmar, China
pulchellum	S	Himalayas to Myanmar, Vietnam
secundum	F–W–S–SS	Myanmar to Vietnam, Pacific Islands
speciosum	W	Australia
spectabile	W–S	New Guinea, Solomon Islands
tetragonum	S	Australia
tortile	SS	Myanmar
victoriae-reginae	S–SS–F	Philippines
williamsonii	S–SS	Himalayas

Figure 18. Vegetative forms of *Dendrobium* showing plant habit and leaf and pseudobulb cross sections.
A: *Dendrobium barreyii*. B: *D. tetragonum*. C: *D. phalaenopsis* var. *compactum*. D: *D. speciosum*. E: *D. agristophyllum*.
F: *D. aggregatum*. G: *D. arcinaciforme*.

Dendrochilum

GENUS: *Dendrochilum* Blume (den-droh-KYE-lum)

TRIBE: Coelogyneae SUBTRIBE: Coelogyninae

IDENTIFICATION CHARACTERISTICS: This genus of over 100 species is known for long, graceful, arching inflorescences of dainty flowers. Although the flowers are small, they are borne in large numbers with upwards to 50 flowers per inflorescence.

When Carl Blume first described the genus in 1825, he coined the generic name from the Greek words *dendron* (tree) and *cheilos* (lip). Undoubtedly, he was referring to the epiphytic nature of the genus and the variability of the lips. Some references apply the common name necklace orchid to the members of this genus, likening the chains of small flowers to necklaces. Although closely related to *Coelogyne* and *Pholidota*, *Dendrochilum* is readily separated by vegetative and floral characteristics.

These sympodial epiphytes have two distinct vegetative habits. One group, *Platyclinis*, has closely arranged pseudobulbs that are usually ovoid, erect, and with one terminal leaf. The inflorescence appears with the young developing leaves. The second group, *Eu-Dendrochilum*, has similar pseudobulbs that are more widely separated on a branched rhizome. The inflorescence is borne on a separate flowering branch. The terminal leaves are borne on stalks up to several inches long. The medium green, leathery leaf blades are up to 15 inches (38 cm) long and 2.5 inches (6 cm) wide. The ovoid pseudobulbs, which are up to 3 inches (7.5 cm) tall, are covered by leafy bracts in the early stages of growth. As the pseudobulbs mature, the bracts become dry and fall off.

The small flowers, seldom over 0.75 inch (2 cm) in diameter, are arranged in chains, are sometimes twisted (e.g., *Dendrochilum cobbianum*), and are basically cream to yellowish cream in color. The sepals and petals are similar in shape and color with the sepals slightly larger. The lips may be three-lobed or entire. The former have a large midlobe and two small side lobes. The lip may have two or three very weak keels.

The column is very interesting and distinct with two lateral arms. Short and slightly curved, the column also has a shield over the anther cap. The small stigmatic surface is located near the point of attachment of the two arms. Four yellowish pollinia are borne on a short caudicle on the underside of the column just forward of the stigmatic surface.

CULTURE: Temperature, 60–70°F (15–21°C); light, 2400–3600 footcandles; humidity, 40–60%; media, tree fern, osmunda, bark; fertilization, monthly, ratio depends on medium.

COLOR PLATE: *Dendrochilum cobbianum*

SPECIES	FLOWERING SEASON	GENERAL LOCALE
album	SS	Malay Peninsula
angustifolium	SS	Malay Peninsula
cobbianum	F	Philippines
crassum	SS	Malay Peninsula
ellipticum	SS	Malay Peninsula
filiforme	S–SS	Philippines
glumaceum	S	Philippines
latifolium	S	Philippines
longifolium	S–SS	Sumatra, Java
uncatum	SS–F	Philippines

Dendrochilum cobbianum
A: Plant in flower, × ½.
B: Flower, face view, × 4.
C: Flower, side view, × 4.
D: Lip, × 5.
E: Flower, vertical section, × 4.
F: Column, ventral view, × 10.
G: Column, end view, × 10.
H: Column, side view, × 10.
I: Column, vertical section, × 10.
J, K, L: Pollinia, × 30.

149

Diaphananthe

GENUS: *Diaphananthe* Schlechter (dye-uh-fa-NAN-thee)

TRIBE: Vandeae   SUBTRIBE: Aerangidinae

IDENTIFICATION CHARACTERISTICS: An abundance of small, dainty flowers is a distinctive characteristic of the tropical genus *Diaphananthe*, which has between 25 and 40 species, depending on which classification is accepted. In 1960 V. S. Summerhayes, for example, combined *Rhipidoglossum* with *Diaphananthe*, bringing the total number of species to more than 40. As originally described by Rudolf Schlechter in 1914, the genus was based partially on the almost-transparent floral segments. Schlechter combined two Greek words, *diaphanes* (transparent) and *anthos* (flower), to form the generic name.

Although species of this genus vary considerably in size, they are easily recognized in the vegetative state. The erect, monopodial growth habit of these epiphytes is similar to the habit of *Vanda*, but often the long, leathery leaves, up to 18 inches (45 cm) long, are greatly recurved, so their tips touch the leaves below. The pendulous, many-flowered inflorescences arise from the axils of the leaves. Each plant produces a multitude of spikes with delicate, lacy, highly fragrant, greenish white flowers.

The small flowers, approximately 0.5 inch (1 cm) wide, are almost translucent. The three sepals and two petals are alike in size and color but easily separated, as the petals have lacerated (torn) margins. The three-lobed, spurred lip (where the lobes are sometimes not very distinct) also has a fringed or lacerated margin. In some cases, the midlobe also ends in a very distinct spur.

The short, erect column is distinctive and looks almost like an insect emerging from the flower because of a large anther cap with protruding stipes below it. This resemblance to the mouth of an insect attracts real insects, which seek nectar from the spur, resulting in pollination of the flower. The two almost-elliptical, yellow pollinia are borne on separate stipes that are joined near the shield-shaped foot.

CULTURE: Temperature, 60–65°F (15–18°C); light, 2400–3600 footcandles; humidity, 40–60%; medium, tree fern plaques; fertilization, monthly, with a 1–1–1 ratio.

COLOR PLATE: *Diaphananthe pellucida*

SPECIES	FLOWERING SEASON	GENERAL LOCALE
bidens	SS	Sierra Leone
fragrantissima	S	Kenya, Uganda, Tanzania
lorifolia	W–S	Sudan to Kenya, Uganda, Tanzania
pellucida	W	Sierra Leone to Zaire
pulchella	F–W	Kenya, Uganda, Tanzania
rutila	F	Tropical West Africa

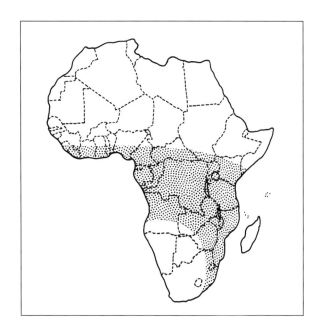

150

Diaphananthe pellucida
A: Plant in flower, × ½.
B: Flower, face view, × 2.
C: Flower, side view, × 2.
D: Lip, × 3.
E: Flower, vertical section,
× 3.
F: Column, ventral view,
× 10.
G: Column, end view, × 10.
H: Column, side view, × 10.
I: Column, vertical section,
× 10.
J, K, L: Pollinia, × 20.

Marion R. Sheehan

151

Disa

GENUS: *Disa* Bergius (DEE-suh)
TRIBE: Diseae   SUBTRIBE: Disinae

IDENTIFICATION CHARACTERISTICS: *Disa* is a very apt name for this spectacular group of terrestrial orchids. The genus was first described by Peter Bergius in 1767 from specimens of *D. uniflora* collected during an expedition to the Cape of Good Hope. The generic name probably was derived from the Latin *dis* (rich), undoubtedly a reference to the intense orange-red flowers of *D. uniflora*. There are approximately 100 species in this genus, which was last revised taxonomically in 1913. The vivid colors and outstanding, showy flowers of many *Disa* species have made the genus much sought after. *Disa uniflora*, certainly one of the most spectacular terrestrial orchids, is the best-known *Disa* species and represents a cultural challenge to many orchid growers.

This sympodial, terrestrial genus has fleshy, tuberous roots. Vegetatively, some species have both leafy, sterile (flowerless) shoots and leafy, fertile (flowering) shoots. Leaf size varies with the species; larger leaves usually are found on sterile shoots, while leaves on flowering stems may be reduced to leafy bracts (e.g., *Disa similis*). Leaves up to 12 inches (30 cm) long and 4 inches (10 cm) wide are produced by some species (e.g., *D. eminii*). Depending on the species, the terminal inflorescences bear anywhere from one to many flowers. Flower size is also variable for the genus, with the fewest-flowered species (e.g., *D. uniflora*) having the largest blooms (4 inches [10 cm] wide). There is a wide range of flower colors, including orange-red, lavender, blue, and white.

The flowers of this genus are most interesting. Each bud is subtended by a leafy bract. The sepals are the dominant and showiest portion of the flower. The spurred dorsal sepal, the largest floral segment, forms a hood over the column, lip, and petals. The two sometimes-bilobed petals are much smaller than the sepals, and are often curved and hidden under the hood. In general, the sepals and petals have the same color scheme. The lips of the flowers are highly variable and usually about the same size as the petals; they may be entire, long, and narrow or broad with fringed margins.

The column is unique, with the anther held behind the stigmatic surface. Two elongate, yellow pollinia are divided into many small packets of pollen (massulae). Each pollinium has a basal stipe and one or two viscidia at the base.

CULTURE: Temperature, varies with the species, from cool to warm; light, tolerates full sun to partial shade, as for *Cattleya*; humidity, 40–60%; media, bog-type soils, top-dress with live sphagnum moss; *Disa uniflora* is often found growing in running water; fertilization, bimonthly, with a 1–1–1 ratio.

COLOR PLATE: *Disa uniflora*

SPECIES	FLOWERING SEASON	GENERAL LOCALE
capricornis	W	South Africa
crassicornis	F–W	South Africa
draconis	W	South Africa
eminii	S	Zambia, Uganda, Tanzania
laeta	W	South Africa
longicornu	W	South Africa
porrecta	F–W–S	South Africa
racemosa	W	South Africa
sanguinea	W	South Africa
similis	S–SS	Angola, South Africa
stolzii	SS	Tanzania, Malawi, Zambia
tripetaloides	W–S–SS	South Africa
uniflora	S	South Africa

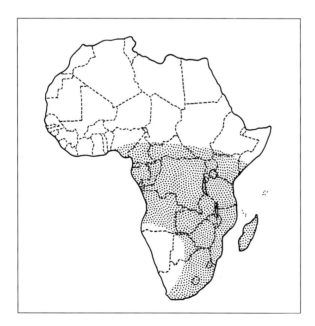

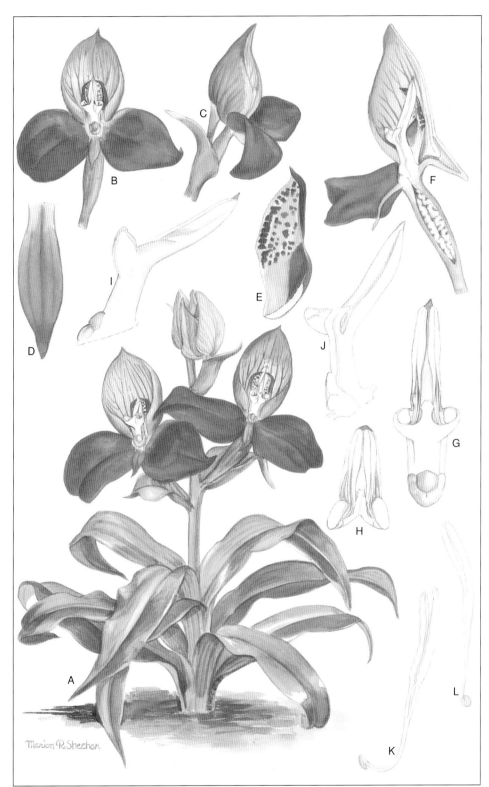

Disa uniflora

A: Plant in flower, × ½.
B: Flower, face view, × ½.
C: Flower, side view, × ½.
D: Lip, × 2¼.
E: Petal, × 1½.
F: Flower, vertical section, × ¾.
G: Column, ventral view, × 1½.
H: Column, end view, × 1½.
I: Column, side view, × 1½.
J: Column, vertical section, × 1½.
K, L: Pollinia, × 2¼.

Domingoa

GENUS: *Domingoa* Schlechter (doh-ming-GO-uh)
TRIBE: Coelogyneae   SUBTRIBE: Laeliinae
IDENTIFICATION CHARACTERISTICS: Dainty and delicate are two very descriptive terms to aptly portray *Domingoa* species. These miniatures are very pleasing and, when well established, are in flower most of the year with "rather oddly attractive flowers" (Hawkes 1965). This small genus of perhaps four species was established in 1913 by Rudolf Schlechter and named for Santa Domingo, now the Dominican Republic, where the type specimen was found. The genus is closely allied to *Epidendrum* but differs in floral characteristics, especially the lip, which is free and entire.

Vegetatively, *Domingoa* resembles *Pleurothallis*, but when in flower, the difference between the two genera is evident. The elongate pseudobulbs of these sympodial epiphytes are tightly clustered on the short, creeping rhizome. Each narrow pseudobulb is ensheathed by papery bracts and topped by one fleshy, almost-linear leaf up to 1.5 inches (4 cm) long and 0.25 inch (0.5 cm) wide. The slender terminal inflorescences are also ensheathed by light tan papery bracts and bear several flowers. Because buds open one at a time, the plant is in flower over a long period of time.

The 1-inch (2.5-cm) wide flowers in this genus are very similar. The base flower color is creamy yellow with red-purple marks. The sepals and petals are alike in size, shape, and color. The two petals are bent forward on either side of the column so they are not readily seen in face view. The simple lip has weakly reflexed margins and is slightly bilobed at the apex. There are two long, linear calli on the lip.

The slender, slightly curved column may be either three-lobed or three-winged at the apex and is broadest in the vicinity of the almost-round stigmatic surface. There are four elongate yellow pollinia, each with its own narrow caudicle, similar to those of *Cattleya*.

CULTURE: Temperature, 60–65°F (15–18°C); light, 2400–3600 footcandles; humidity, 40–60%; medium, excellent on cork or bark plaques; fertilization, monthly, with a 1–1–1 ratio.

COLOR PLATE: *Domingoa hymenodes*

SPECIES	FLOWERING SEASON	GENERAL LOCALE
hymenodes	W–S–SS–F	Cuba, Hispaniola
nodosa	W	Hispaniola

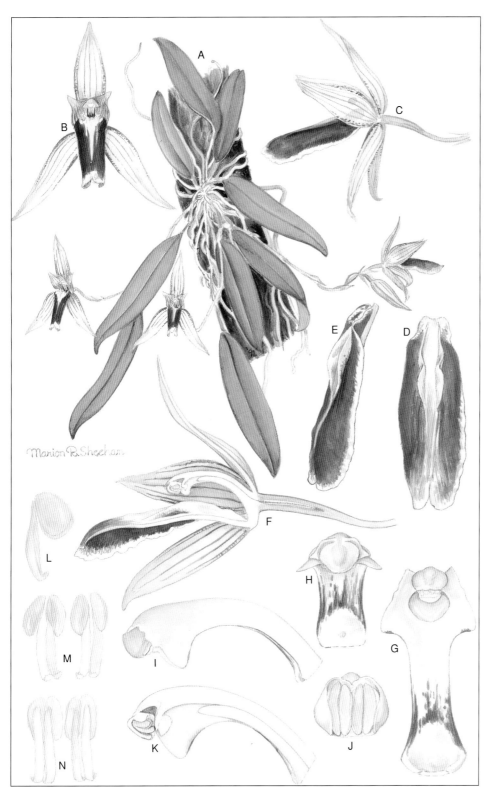

Domingoa hymenodes
A: Plant in flower, × 1.
B: Flower, face view, × 2.
C: Flower, side view, × 2.
D: Lip, face view, × 3.
E: Lip, side view, × 3.
F: Flower, vertical section, × 3.
G: Column, ventral view, × 6.
H: Column, end view, × 6.
I: Column, side view, × 6.
J: Anther cap and pollinia, × 10.
K: Column, vertical section, × 6.
L, M, N: Pollinia, × 15.

Doritis _____

GENUS: *Doritis* Lindley (doh-RYE-tiss)

TRIBE: Vandeae   SUBTRIBE: Aeridinae

IDENTIFICATION CHARACTERISTICS: When these lovely plants were first discovered, they were classified as *Phalaenopsis esmeralda* Reichenbach f. or *P. buyssoniana* Reichenbach f. but later were transferred to *Doritis* by John Lindley in 1833. Although *D. pulcherrima*, the only species in the genus, shows a great deal of variation, most taxonomists recognize the variations as belonging to one species. *Doritis* is from the Greek word *dory* (spear) and also is one of the names applied to Aphrodite. Some believe the generic name applies to the spear-shaped lip, whereas others believe it is associated with the beauty of the flowers.

This small, stemless, monopodial epiphyte closely resembles *Phalaenopsis* species when not in flower, although *Doritis* often forms dense clumps unlike most monopodials. Plants may have 12 to 15 stiff, leathery leaves with clasping leaf bases. The oblong-to-elliptical leaves, 5 to 8 inches (12.5–20 cm) long, are dark green, often with purplish brown mottling. The underside may be purple. The flowers are borne on stiff, erect inflorescences, a characteristics that readily distinguishes *Doritis* from *Phalaenopsis*. Each inflorescence bears up to 25 flowers.

The mostly pale to dark lavender flowers range from 0.5 to 1.5 inches (1–4 cm) in diameter. The dorsal sepal and two petals are equal in size, shape, and color. In some flowers the petals may be reflexed. The two lateral sepals are much broader than the dorsal sepal and are fused to a spurlike projection on the base of the column. The lip also has a distinguishing characteristic that helps to separate *Doritis* from *Phalaenopsis*. Distinctly three-lobed, the lip has two almost-erect, lateral lobes and a larger midlobe sometimes with a slightly undulate margin. There are two antennae behind the lateral lobes at the base of the lip, while in *Phalaenopsis* the antennae are at the apex of the lip.

The short column is sometimes constricted at the midpoint and ends in a long reflexed beak, which causes the column, when viewed below, to appear as if it had two stigmatic surfaces. The four yellowish pollinia are borne on a long, narrow stipe with an elliptical foot that is pointed at either end.

CULTURE: Temperature, 65–70°F (18–21°C); light, 1500–1800 footcandles; humidity, 40–60%; media, tree fern, fir bark; fertilization, monthly, ratio depends on medium.

COLOR PLATE: *Doritis pulcherrima*

SPECIES	FLOWERING SEASON	GENERAL LOCALE
pulcherrima	F–W	Myanmar, Thailand, Laos, Cambodia, Vietnam, Malay Peninsula, Sumatra

Doritis pulcherrima
A: Plant in flower, × ½.
B: Flower, face view, × 1.
C: Flower, side view, × 1.
D: Lip, × 3.
E: Flower, vertical section, × 2.
F: Column, ventral view, × 4.
G: Column, end view, anther
   cap removed, × 4.
H: Column, side view, × 4.
I: Column, vertical section, × 4.
J, K, L: Pollinia, × 10.

157

Encyclia

GENUS: *Encyclia* Hooker (en-SIK-lee-uh)

TRIBE: Epidendreae   SUBTRIBE: Laeliinae

IDENTIFICATION CHARACTERISTICS: The showy, sometimes fragrant flowers of *Encyclia* are often borne in large numbers making these plants very attractive and well worth cultivating. In 1828, Joseph Dalton Hooker first addressed dividing the genus *Epidendrum* by proposing that the pseudobulbous types be separated and called *Encyclia*. Even after Robert Dressler's comprehensive study in 1961 agreed with Hooker's thesis, many taxonomists still were reluctant to accept the change. Today the majority of growers and taxonomists accept the genus *Encyclia* as a valid one based on Hooker's and Dressler's studies.

The basic difference between *Epidendrum* and *Encyclia* is the presence of pseudobulbs in *Encyclia* and a lip that is partially adnate to the column. Hooker based the generic name on the Greek word *enkyklein* (to encircle), undoubtedly referring to the partial enclosure of the column by the two lateral lobes of the lip. As originally founded, the genus included approximately 150 species located mainly in Mexico and the West Indies with a scattering of species from Florida to tropical northern South America. Taxonomists have transferred some of the West Indian species to other genera, hence the number of species attributed to *Encyclia* has dwindled slightly.

The sympodial, epiphytic species of this genus are for the most part similar vegetatively (Fig. 19). The tightly clustered pseudobulbs are mostly pyriform, although a few species have slender, elongate pseudobulbs (e.g., *Encyclia cochleata*). Generally two to three leaves are borne close to or on top of the pseudobulb. The leaves vary from lanceolate to elliptic to strap-shaped and may be up to 18 inches (45 cm) long. Some leaves are coriaceous or fleshy. The inflorescence arises from the apex of the pseudobulb. The many-flowered racemes or panicles are highly variable and may be up to 3 feet (90 cm) in length (e.g., *E. alata*).

Flower color is highly variable among species, as is flower size and fragrance, but floral characteristics readily tie the genus together. The sepals and petals are generally alike in size, shape, and color. They may be flat or curved when the flowers are fully open. The lips of these attractive flowers are also variable, often large and showy (e.g., *Encyclia mariae*) and in some species relatively small (e.g., *E. calamaria*). The three-lobed lip is free from or partially adnate to the column. The two lateral lobes of the lip fold over and encircle the column. It was this characteristic of the group that Hooker used to derive the generic name.

The column is generally long and narrow or may be slightly swollen near the midpoint. In some species, the column is winged (e.g., *Encyclia fragrans*). The stigmatic surface is almost elliptical in shape and may have two toothlike projections at the distal end. Four yellow-orange pollinia, either round or flattened, are attached singly to flat, pale yellow caudicles. The margins of the caudicles are often ragged on one side as if they were torn apart. Two pollinia are found in each anther cell.

CULTURE: Temperature, 50–70°F (10–21°C); light, 2400–3600 footcandles; humidity, 40–60%; media, bark, tree fern, plaques; fertilization, monthly, ratio depends on medium.

Color Plate: *Encyclia cordigera*

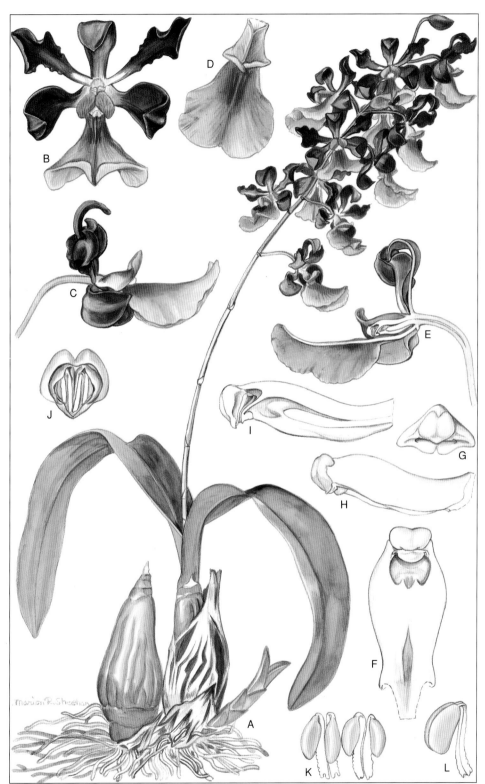

Encyclia cordigera
A: Plant in flower, × ⅓.
B: Flower, face view, × ½.
C: Flower, side view, × ½.
D: Lip, × ½.
E: Flower, vertical section, × ½.
F: Column, ventral view, × 1.
G: Column, end view, × 1
H: Column, side view, × 1.
I: Column, vertical section, × 1
J: Anther cap and pollinia, × 2.
K, L: Pollinia, × 4.

ENCYCLIA SPECIES	FLOWERING SEASON	GENERAL LOCALE
adenocarpum	S–SS	Mexico to Nicaragua
adenocaula	S–SS	Mexico
alata	S–SS	Mexico to Costa Rica
aromatica	S–SS	Mexico to Guatemala
baculus	S–SS	Mexico to Brazil
belizensis	S–SS	Mexico, Honduras, Belize
boothiana	F	Florida, West Indies, Mexico, Honduras
brachiata	S	Mexico
bractescens	W–S–SS	Mexico, Guatemala, Honduras
brassavolae	SS–F	Mexico to Panama
calamaria	SS–F	Brazil, Venezuela
chacaoensis	S–SS–F	Mexico to Venezuela
citrina	S–SS–F	Mexico
cochleata	W–S–SS–F	Florida, West Indies, Mexico to Colombia, Venezuela
concolor	SS	Mexico
cordigera	W–S–SS	Mexico to Colombia
diota	W–S–SS	Mexico to Nicaragua
fragrans	S–SS–F	Greater Antilles, central & northern South America
ghiesbreghtiana	S–SS	Mexico
guatemalensis	S–SS	Mexico to Nicaragua
hanburyi	S–SS	Mexico
livida	S–SS	Mexico to Colombia, Venezuela
lorata	S	Mexico
luteorosea	S	Mexico to Peru
maculosa	S–SS	Mexico
mariae	S–SS–F	Mexico
meliosma	S–SS	Mexico
nematocaulon	S–SS	Mexico to Guatemala, Cuba, Bahamas
ochracea	W–S–SS–F	Mexico to Costa Rica
phoenicea	S–SS	Florida, tropical America
pseudopygmaea	F–W	Mexico to Panama
pygmaea	F–W	Tropical America
radiata	S–SS–F	Mexico, Guatemala, Honduras
selligera	S–SS	Mexico, Guatemala
suaveolens	S	Mexico
tampensis	S–SS	Florida, Bahamas, Mexico
trachycarpa	S–SS	Mexico
vagans	S–SS	Guatemala to Costa Rica
venosa	S–SS–F	Mexico
vespa	S–SS–F	Tropical America
vitellina	W–S–SS–F	Mexico, Guatemala

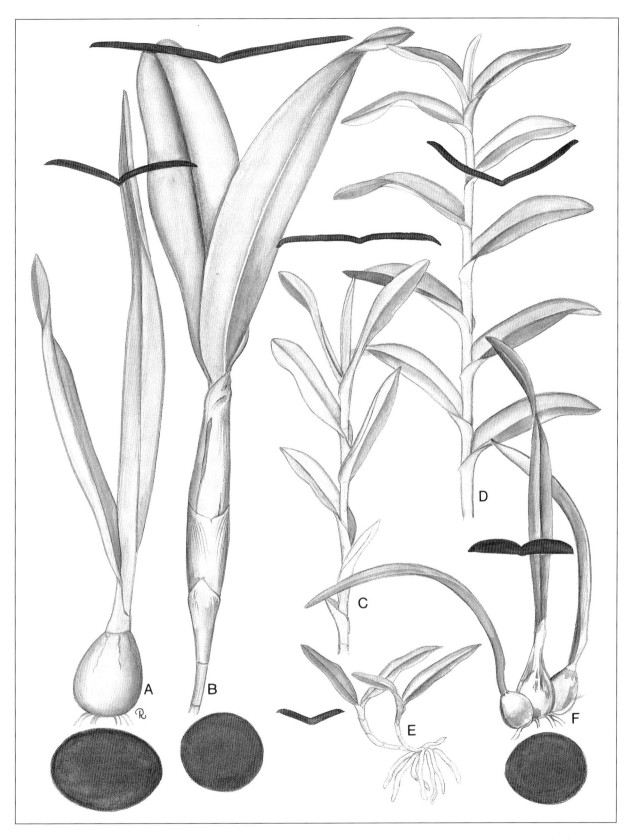

Figure 19. Vegetative forms of *Encyclia* and *Epidendrum*. A: *Encyclia cordigera*. B: *Epidendrum ciliare*. C: *Epidendrum anceps*. D: *Epidendrum cinnabarinum*. E: *Epidendrum conopseum*. F: *Encyclia tampensis*.

Epidendrum

GENUS: *Epidendrum* Linnaeus (ep-ih-DEN-drum)
TRIBE: Epidendreae SUBTRIBE: Laeliinae
IDENTIFICATION CHARACTERISTICS: The brightly colored clusters of flowers borne on many *Epidendrum* species have long made these plants an integral part of almost every orchid collection. The genus has to be considered the oldest American genus taxonomically because it was the first to be named. In 1753 Carl Linnaeus used this genus initially as a catchall for all epiphytic orchid plants from the New World. He coined the generic name from two Greek words, *epi* (upon) and *dendron* (trees), a good descriptive term for these mostly epiphytic orchids.

Over the years taxonomists have been, and still are, dividing this extremely large genus. Probably the most notable split was the removal of most of the mainly pseudobulbous species with the lip only slightly adnate to the column to form the genus *Encyclia*, while those species with adnate lips remained in *Epidendrum*. This grouping was first proposed by Joseph Dalton Hooker in 1828 and resurrected by Robert Dressler in 1961, although not all taxonomists accept it. Despite the removal of a large block of species to *Encyclia*, *Epidendrum* is still one of the largest genera in the New World. There are several hundred species in the genus, the exact number depending on how many generic splits are accepted (*Encyclia, Barkeria, Oerstedella, Jacquiniella*, etc.).

Even with the removal of many species from *Epidendrum*, there is still a great deal of variability in the vegetative characteristics of this widespread genus (Fig. 19). Stems are either reedlike in growth, often with many leaves (e.g., *E. cinnabarinum*), or pseudobulbous, with one or two leaves at the apex

(e.g., *E. stamfordianum*). Plants range in height from 3 to 4 inches (7.5–10 cm) (e.g., *E. porpax*) to more than 3 feet (90 cm) (e.g., *E. pseudepidendrum*). Leaves are also highly variable, ranging from almost linear to ovate, thin or fleshy, with some almost terete. Sometimes the leaves clasp the stem. The inflorescences usually arise at the apex of the stem (there are exceptions) and bear from one to many flowers.

The flowers in this genus exhibit a wide variety of color, ranging from pastels to strong hues, and may be up to 6 inches (15 cm) in diameter. A typical flower has narrow sepals and petals, sometimes flat, sometimes curved or reflexed, depending on the species. Although, the sepals and petals are very much alike in shape and color, they often vary slightly in size. The three-lobed lip is adnate to the column for its entire length. The midlobe ranges from broad with a fringed margin (e.g., *E. medusae*) to almost lancelike (e.g., *E. nocturnum*).

The column of most species is mostly narrow but length varies, being very short in some species (e.g., *Epidendrum porpax*) and either winged or wingless. Often the column is the same color as the lip and usually it is broadest near the stigmatic surface, which in this genus is small and reached by a small opening on the underside of the column. There are four yellow pollinia attached to small caudicles, often compressed, either equal or of two sizes.

CULTURE: Temperature, variable, depends on habitat of species; light, 2400–3600 footcandles; humidity, 40–60%; media, depends on species—tree fern, peat and perlite, bark for epiphytes, any well-drained potting mix having 40% or more organic matter for terrestrials; fertilization, monthly, ratio depends on medium.

COLOR PLATE: *Epidendrum pseudepidendrum*

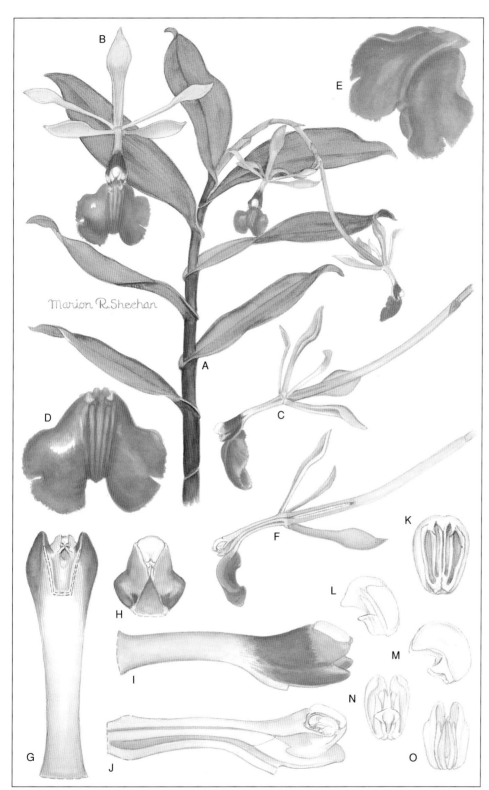

Epidendrum pseudepidendrum
A: Plant in flower, × ½.
B: Flower, face view, × 1.
C: Flower, side view, × 1.
D: Lip, face view, × 2.
E: Lip, back view, × 2.
F: Flower, vertical section, × 1.
G: Column, ventral view, × 3.
H: Column, end view, × 3.
I: Column, side view, × 3.
J: Column, vertical section, × 3.
K: Anther cap, × 6.
L, M, N, O: Pollinia, × 6.

163

EPIDENDRUM SPECIES	FLOWERING SEASON	GENERAL LOCALE
anceps	S–SS–F	Florida, Mexico to northern South America
ciliare	F–W–S–SS	Mexico to South America
cinnabarinum	S–SS	Brazil, Venezuela
conopseum	W–S–SS	Southern United States to Mexico
difforme	S–SS	Southern Florida through tropical America
eburneum	SS–F	Panama
ibaguense	F–W–S–SS	Central & South America
lindleyanum	F	Central America
medusae	S–SS	Ecuador
nocturnum	F–W–S–SS	Florida through tropical America
paniculatum	SS	Tropical America
parkinsonianum	SS	Central America
porpax	S–SS	Mexico to Peru
pseudepidendrum	S–SS	Costa Rica, Panama
rigidum	F–W–S–SS	Tropical America
schlechterianum	S–SS	Central & South America
secundum	F–W–S–SS	Tropical America
skinneri	F–W	Guatemala
stamfordianum	F–W–S–SS	Central America, Colombia, Venezuela
strobiliferum	S–SS	Tropical America

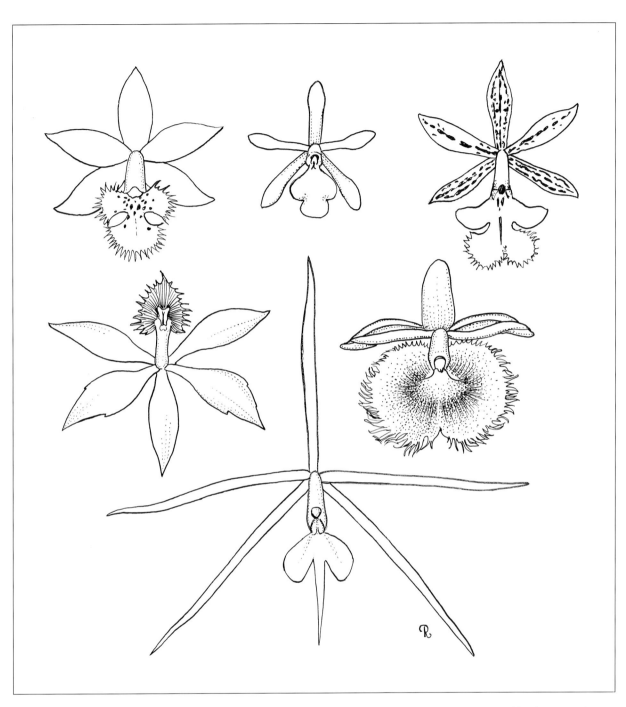

Epidendrum species

Epigeneium

GENUS: *Epigeneium* Gagnepain (eh-pih-JEEN-ee-um)

TRIBE: Dendrobieae SUBTRIBE: Dendrobiinae

IDENTIFICATION CHARACTERISTICS: The large, bright purplish red, almost-star-shaped flowers of *Epigeneium lyonii* make this species a delightful addition to any orchid collection. Approximately 35 species belong to the genus that was established in 1932 by François Gagnepain, who believed the taxonomic differences were sufficient to warrant separating these species from *Dendrobium* and establishing a new genus. He called the genus *Epigeneium*, deriving the name from two Greek words, *epi* (upon) and *geneion* (chin), to describe the method by which the sepals and petals are attached to the column foot.

Vegetatively, these sympodial, epiphytic species are similar. The ovoid pseudobulbs may be enclosed or almost covered by dry leafy sheaths at maturity. The rhizomes are distinct, and the pseudobulbs may be spaced as much as 2 inches (5 cm) apart on creeping rhizomes (e.g., *Epigeneium coelogyne*). Each pseudobulb is topped by one or two elliptical-to-oblong leaves, either sessile or with a short petiole. The somewhat-fleshy leaves are up to 7 inches (17.5 cm) long and minutely lobed at the apex. The often-pendent inflorescence arises from the top of the pseudobulb and, depending on the species, may have anywhere from 1 (e.g., *E. coelogyne*) to 20 (e.g., *E. acuminatum*) flowers.

The attractive flowers are white, yellow, or magenta. The sepals and petals are very similar in size, shape, and color with the petals usually slightly narrower than the sepals, which are almost triangular in arrangement. The lip is three-lobed with the midlobe often broader than long and slightly reflexed.

The column is short, often slightly curved, and usually the same color as the sepals and petals. The column sides are almost straight, and a small stigmatic surface is centered just behind the anther cap. The two or four yellow pollinia, the latter in two pairs, have no stipe or caudicle.

CULTURE: Temperature, 55–60°F (12–15°C) at night; light, 2400–3600 footcandles; humidity, 40–60%; media, any good mix for epiphytes, grows well on plaques; fertilization, monthly, ratio depends on medium.

COLOR PLATE: *Epigeneium lyonii*

SPECIES	FLOWERING SEASON	GENERAL LOCALE
acuminatum	S	Philippines
amplum	W	India
coelogyne	F	Myanmar, Thailand
cymbidioides	S	Java, Philippines
lyonii	S	Philippines
stella-silvae	W–S	Philippines

Epigeneium lyonii
A: Plant in flower, × ⅜.
B: Flower, face view, × 1.
C: Flower, side view, × 1.
D: Lip, face view, × 1½.
E: Flower, vertical section, × 1.
F: Column, ventral view, × 3.
G: Column, end view, × 3.
H: Column, side view, × 3.
I: Column, vertical section, × 3.
J, K, L: Pollinia, × 10.

Eria

GENUS: *Eria* Lindley (EHR-ee-uh)

TRIBE: Podochileae   SUBTRIBE: Eriinae

IDENTIFICATION CHARACTERISTICS: The delightfully fragrant flowers of this large and highly variable genus deserve a place in all collections. *Eria* also can be interesting because inflorescences of some species (e.g., *E. cylindrostachya*) appear to burst through the sides of the pseudobulb, leaving a sizable hole when the bloom spike falls away. Some taxonomists estimate that there are as many as 550 species in this genus, but 350 seems to be a more reasonable figure. The genus, which may be related to *Dendrobium* and is found in much of the same natural range, is easily separated from it by the number of pollinia: *Eria* has eight pollinia, *Dendrobium* has four. *Eria* was first described by John Lindley in 1825, who coined the generic name from the Greek word *erion* (wool), undoubtedly referring to the very heavy pubescence on many species.

The variety of vegetative forms within *Eria* is so great that taxonomists divide the genus into 15 sections, based mainly on pseudobulb and leaf characteristics. Some species are covered with hairs (e.g., *E. dasyphylla*), others have leaves and sheaths without hairs (e.g., *E. javanica*). Pseudobulbs range from short and stubby (2 inches [5 cm] tall) to reed types up to 12 to 16 inches (30–40 cm) tall. Each pseudobulb may have from one to many leaves, often clustered near the apex. Individual leaves range from less than 3 to almost 18 inches (7.5–45 cm) long and 2 inches (5 cm) wide. They can be thin or leathery in texture, depending on the species. Inflorescences arise from different points on the pseudobulbs and may be terminal, basal, or lateral. They may be erect or pendent and may carry few to many flowers.

The flowers, which are often hairy and up to 2 inches (5 cm) wide, are predominantly white, but creamy yellow and pink-striped variations are found. The flower shape of *Eria javanica* is typical of many species, although flowers of other species (e.g., *E. truncata*) scarcely open. In many species, the sepals and petals are alike in shape and color, but the lateral sepals often are larger than the petals. The floral segments and peduncle are usually hairy on the outside. The three-lobed lip varies in size and shape from species to species and sometimes is shorter than the sepals and petals. The lip is attached to the column foot and may have a variety of discs or keels.

The footed column is very short and narrow but slightly wider near the stigmatic surface. The heavy anther cap protects the eight yellow pollinia. Each group of four pollinia shares one very small viscidium, but if the pollinia are not removed carefully, there may appear to be eight pollinia.

CULTURE: Temperature, 50–60°F (10–15°C) at night, depending on species; light, 2400–3600 footcandles; humidity, 40–60%; media, tree fern, peat and perlite; fertilization, monthly, ratio depends on medium.

COLOR PLATE: *Eria javanica*

SPECIES	FLOWERING SEASON	GENERAL LOCALE
aliciae	F–W	Philippines
bractescens	W–S	Thailand to Philippines
carinata	W–S	India to Thailand
coronaria	F–W–S	India
cylindrostachya	S–SS	Thailand
dasyphylla	S–SS	Himalayas to Laos
javanica	S–SS–F	Himalayas to Philippines south to New Guinea
longissima	S–SS–F	Philippines
nudicaulis	S–SS	Taiwan
spicata	S	Nepal to Thailand
truncata	S–SS	Myanmar to Laos
velutina	SS	Myanmar to Borneo

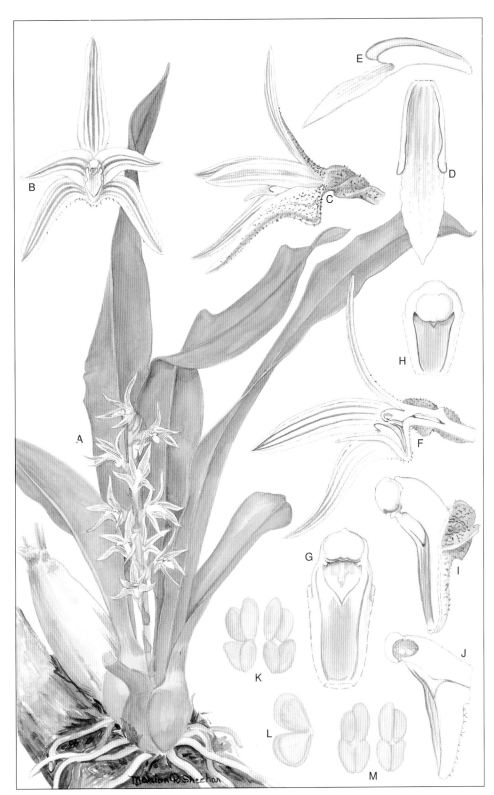

Eria javanica
A: Plant in flower, × ½.
B: Flower, face view, × 2.
C: Flower, side view, × 2.
D: Lip, face view, × 4.
E: Lip, side view, × 4.
F: Flower, vertical section, × 2.
G: Column, ventral view, × 6.
H: Column, end view, × 6.
I: Column, side view, × 6.
J: Column, vertical section, × 6.
K, L, M: Pollinia, × 15.

Erycina

GENUS: *Erycina* Lindley (eh-rih-SYE-nuh)
TRIBE: Maxillarieae   SUBTRIBE: Oncidiinae
IDENTIFICATION CHARACTERISTICS: There are only two known species in this fascinating genus. Although somewhat rare in cultivation, these miniatures are delightful plants. *Erycina* resembles *Oncidium* but is easily distinguished from it by the distinctly three-lobed lip, which is the only showy portion of the flower. The genus was identified in 1853 by John Lindley, who used the Latin word *Erycina* (the name attributed to Aphrodite of Mount Eryx) to symbolize the beauty of the delicate flowers.

Vegetatively, these sympodial epiphytes resemble petite oncidiums, having small, round, somewhat-compressed pseudobulbs up to 1 inch (2.5 cm) tall. Usually there is one small, leathery leaf at the apex of the pseudobulb and two to four leaflike bracts subtending it. By contrast, the apical leaf of *Erycina echinata* is often reduced to a small stub. Plants may grow in an ascending or descending manner. The inflorescence arises from the base of the pseudobulb and bears up to 15 flowers. The often-arching inflorescence also may be branched with one or two lateral branches (e.g., *E. echinata*).

The flowers are brilliant yellow in color and 0.75 inch (2 cm) in diameter. They are easily recognized by their large, three-lobed lip. The midlobe is often kidney-shaped (e.g., *Erycina echinata*), and the lateral lobes may have smooth or ruffled margins. The crests on the lip vary between the two species. The small, narrow sepals and lateral petals are greatly reflexed and are often overlooked due to the dominant characteristics of the lip.

Another striking feature of this genus is the column. The apex of the column, which is slightly reflexed, is dominated by a large anther cap and a greatly extended rostellum. The two round, yellow pollinia are attached to a single, long, narrow stipe with a small, viscid foot.

CULTURE: Temperature, 60–65°F (15–18°C); light, 2400–3600 footcandles; humidity, 40–60%; media, tree fern plaques, tree branches; fertilization, monthly, with a 1–1–1 ratio.

COLOR PLATE: *Erycina echinata*

SPECIES	FLOWERING SEASON	GENERAL LOCALE
diaphana	S–SS	Mexico
echinata	S–SS	Mexico

Erycina echinata
A: Plant in flower, × 1.
B: Flower, face view, × 3.
C: Flower, side view, × 3.
D: Lip, × 3.
E: Flower, vertical section, × 3.
F: Flower, lip and petals
    removed, × 5.
G: Column, ventral view, × 10.
H: Column, end view, × 10.
I: Column, side view, × 10.
J: Column, vertical section, × 10.
K, L, M: Pollinia, × 10.

Euanthe

GENUS: *Euanthe* Schlechter (yew-ANN-thee)
TRIBE: Vandeae SUBTRIBE: Aeridinae
IDENTIFICATION CHARACTERISTICS: The large, showy flowers of *Euanthe sanderiana* have endeared this species to many orchid growers the world over. Beautiful in its natural form, the species also has made spectacular contributions to a myriad of colorful hybrids resulting from crosses with other vandaceous orchids. Its quality is readily attested to by the many, many awards the species and its hybrid offspring have received.

Euanthe sanderiana was originally discovered by Carl Robelin in 1882 and was described in the same year by H. G. Reichenbach as *Vanda sanderiana*. Later, however, in 1914, Rudolf Schlechter transferred it to the monotypic genus *Euanthe*. Although the species is closely related to *Vanda* species, Schlechter felt that the distinctly different lip was reason enough to transfer the species to the new genus. The generic name was taken from the Greek word *euanthes* (blooming), undoubtedly a reference to the distinct, showy flowers. Although *Euanthe sanderiana* is considered by some taxonomists to be the correct botanical name, *Vanda sanderiana* is retained as the horticultural name for hybrid registration purposes.

Vegetatively, this robust, monopodial epiphyte resembles *Vanda* species in growth habit. The strap-shaped, leathery leaves, which grow to 18 inches (45 cm) long, have unevenly lobed apices, and the bases clasp the stem. The axillary inflorescences may be erect or suberect and are usually shorter than the leaves. Each inflorescence bears up to 10 flowers, which are 3.5 to 4.5 inches (8–11 cm) in diameter.

The large, flat flowers are creamy to rose in color, with tawny yellow and reddish brown spots and reticulations. The color varies, depending on which floral segment is observed. The sepals and petals, which are similar in shape although the sepals are slightly larger, vary greatly in color and color patterns. In typically colored forms, the petals and dorsal sepal are usually some shade of pink, with brownish spotting at the base of each segment. The lateral sepals are heavily tessellated reddish brown. The waxy lip is sharply constricted between the broad midlobe and the cuplike rear portion.

The short, broad column has no distinctive marks and is slightly curved at the apex. Two bright yellow pollinia are borne on a single stipe with an almost-rectangular, shield-shaped viscidium at the base.

CULTURE: Temperature, 60°F (15°C) at night; light, 3600 footcandles; humidity, 40–60%; medium, any coarse, well-drained mix for epiphytes; fertilization, monthly, ratio depends on medium.

COLOR PLATE: *Euanthe sanderiana*

SPECIES	FLOWERING SEASON	GENERAL LOCALE
sanderiana	SS–F	Philippines

Euanthe sanderiana
A: Plant in flower, × ¼.
B: Flower, face view, × ½.
C: Flower, side view, × ½.
D: Lip, face view, × 1½.
E: Lip, side view, × 1½.
F: Flower, vertical section, × ¾.
G: Column, ventral view, × 3.
H: Column, end view, × 3.
I: Column, side view, × 3.
J: Column, vertical section, × 3.
K: Anther cap removed to show
   pollinia, × 3.
L, M, N: Pollinia, × 6.

Eulophia _____

GENUS: *Eulophia* R. Brown (you-LOH-fee-uh)
TRIBE: Cymbidieae   SUBTRIBE: Eulophiinae
IDENTIFICATION CHARACTERISTICS: *Eulophia*, as the genus is now envisioned, contains almost 300 species of outstanding sympodial, mostly terrestrial plants and is found on most continents. Robert Brown founded the genus in 1822 when he described *E. guineensis*, which was introduced from Sierra Leone by George Don in 1821. The generic name was derived from the Greek word meaning handsomely crested; undoubtedly, Brown was referring to the crests on the lip.

The species vary vegetatively with some having subterranean pseudobulbs (e.g., *Eulophia bicarinata*), while others have exposed pseudobulbs (e.g., *E. guineensis*). Each pseudobulb, whether above ground or cormlike, is topped by three to five linear-to-lanceolate leaves, which may be leathery or soft, pleated, and up to 6 feet (180 cm) tall and 4 to 5 inches (10–12.5 cm) wide. The clasping leaf bases cause the plant to appear as if it has stems. Inflorescences arise from the base of the pseudobulbs, are usually not branched, and are up to 7 feet (210 cm) tall. Individual flowers open from the base upwards. Plants remain in flower for long periods due to the slow opening of the flowers and the large number of flowers present on each spike.

Basically, the 1- to 3-inch (2.5- to 7.5-cm) wide flowers are yellowish or greenish with some brown and purplish marks. The petals may be broader and larger than the sepals (e.g., *Eulophia krebsii*) or smaller (e.g., *E. alta*). The three sepals are alike in size and color and are the same color as the petals (e.g., *E. squalida*) or different (e.g., *E. krebsii*). The three-lobed lip may be equal in size to the petals and the same color. The two lateral lobes partially enclose the column. The midlobe often has a wavy margin and a crest just below the column. In some species the lip is entire rather than three-lobed. The lip is usually attached to the footed column and may be spurred.

The length of the column varies among species, but all columns have a basal foot and are attached to the lip. The anther cap often bears an almost-horn-like projection. A very narrow stigmatic area lies just below and behind the anther cap. Two yellow, almost-triangular pollinia are attached to the apex of a triangular-footed stipe.

CULTURE: Temperature, some species withstand mild frost, 60°F (15°C) minimum for tropical species; light, full sun to partial shade, 3,000–10,000 footcandles; media, a mixture of 1 peat : 1 perlite : 1 sand or 2 peat : 1 sand for terrestrials, any good mix for epiphytes; fertilization, monthly during growing season, ratio depends on medium.

COLOR PLATE: *Eulophia alta*

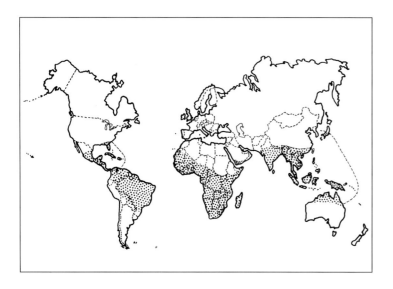

Eulophia alta

A: Plant in flower, × ⅙.
B: Flower, face view, × 1½.
C: Flower, side view, × 1½.
D: Lip, × 2½.
E: Flower, vertical section, × 1½.
F: Column, ventral view, × 5.
G: Column, end view, × 5.
H: Column, side view, × 5.
I: Column, vertical section, × 5.
J, K, L: Pollinia, × 10.

175

EULOPHIA SPECIES	FLOWERING SEASON	GENERAL LOCALE
alta	F–W	Southern Florida to northern South America, tropical Africa
angolensis	S	Tropical & southern Africa
bicarinata	SS	India to Australia
ecristata	SS–F	Southern United States, Cuba
ensata	S	Southern Africa
epidendroides	S–SS	Sri Lanka, India, Myanmar
euglossa	S–SS	Tropical western Africa
gigantea	SS	Zaire, Angola
graminea	S	Malay Peninsula, Java, Philippines, India, Myanmar, Thailand, Vietnam
guineensis	F–W	Tropical western Africa
horsfallii	S–SS	Tropical western Africa
keithii	F	Malay Peninsula, Kedah State & Langkawi Islands (Malaysia), Thailand
krebsii	W–S	Natal, Transvaal
macrostachya	W	Malaysia, Philippines to Australia, Mascarene Islands, India, Sri Lanka
mahoni	S–SS	Uganda
nuda	S	Nepal, southern China, Cambodia, India to Thailand
porphyroglossa	SS	Congo, Uganda, Kenya
pulchra	S	Madagascar, Mauritius
purpurata	S	Tropical Africa
rosea	W–S	Sierra Leone
sanguinea	S	Himalayas
squalida	S	Indonesia to New Guinea, India, Sumatra, Malay Peninsula
streptopetala	S	Southern Africa
stricta	S	Philippines, Java, Celebes
stylites	SS	Tropical Africa
zeyheri	S–SS	South Africa, Natal, Transvaal
zollingeri	W	India through Malaysia to New Guinea

Eulophia

Eurychone

GENUS: *Eurychone* Schlechter (your-ee-KONE-ee)
TRIBE: Vandeae SUBTRIBE: Aerangidinae
IDENTIFICATION CHARACTERISTICS: Two species are recognized in this tropical African genus and only one of them is generally found in cultivation. The unique flowers with their distinctive funnel-shaped lips and interesting coloration make this genus a standout. The commonly grown species, *Eurychone rothschildiana*, has white flowers with central bands of green on the sepals and petals, and green and purplish brown coloration in the throat of the lip. The rarer and elusive *E. galaendrae* has pink flowers.

The genus was originally classified as part of *Angraecum* by Robert Brown in 1903 and later transferred to *Eurychone* by Rudolf Schlechter in 1918. Schlechter made the separation based on differences in floral characteristics of the lip and column, deriving the generic name from two Greek words, *eurys* (broad) and *chone* (funnel), to describe the genus's unusual, funnel-shaped lip.

These monopodial, epiphytic species, somewhat resembling *Phalaenopsis* species, have a very short stem and bear five to seven obovate leathery leaves with unequally lobed apices. Leaves may be up to 8 inches (20 cm) long and 3 inches (7.5 cm) wide but usually are somewhat smaller in size. The lax axillary inflorescence arises from the lower leaves, is usually no longer than the leaf length, and bears up to seven flowers.

The sharp-tipped sepals and petals are very similar in size, shape, and color and are displayed in an almost-fan-shaped arrangement. The lip is the most distinctive and interesting segment of the flower.

Weakly three-lobed, the lip is almost funnel-shaped, and the very large flaring midlobe has a wavy margin. There is a noticeable constriction near the base of the funnel-shaped lip, after which the tip turns upward slightly.

The short, broad column has a large almost-elliptical stigmatic area covering most of its underside. The anther cap on the plant illustrated in the color plate (which see) had an array of small protuberances on either side of the upper half of the cap and adjoining area. Two yellow elliptical pollinia are borne on a long slender stipe with a small shield-shaped viscidium at the base.

CULTURE: Temperature, 60°F (15°C); light, 2400–3000 footcandles; humidity, 40–60%; media, tree fern, peat and perlite; fertilization, monthly, with a 1–1–1 ratio.

COLOR PLATE: *Eurychone rothschildiana*

SPECIES	FLOWERING SEASON	GENERAL LOCALE
galaendrae	F–W	Cameroon, Gabon, Central Africa Republic
rothschildiana	F–W	Tropical Central & West Africa

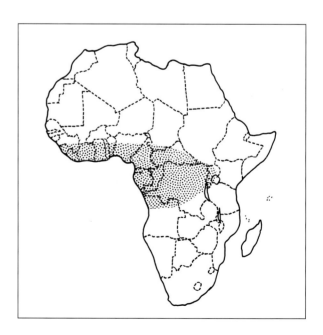

Eurychone rothschildiana
A: Plant in flower, × ½.
B: Flower, face view, × 1.
C: Flower, side view, × 1.
D: Lip, three-quarter view, × 1½.
E: Flower, vertical section, × 1½.
F: Column, ventral view, × 4.
G: Column, end view, × 4.
H: Column, side view, × 4.
I: Column, vertical section, × 4.
J, K, L: Pollinia, × 6.

179

Galeandra

GENUS: *Galeandra* Lindley (gal-ee-ANN-druh)
TRIBE: Cymbidieae SUBTRIBE: Cyrtopodiinae
IDENTIFICATION CHARACTERISTICS: Approximately 25 species of this delightful genus are scattered from Mexico to Brazil. The genus was founded by John Lindley around 1830 when he described *Galeandra baueri*, which had been collected in French Guiana. The generic name, which was coined from two Greek words meaning helmet and anther, refers to the anther cap, which resembles helmets of old. The genus is closely allied to *Eulophia* but easily separated by its funnel-shaped spur and the arrangement of the pollinia.

These sympodial epiphytes have tight clusters of approximately 12-inch (30-cm) long spindle-shaped pseudobulbs that are ensheathed by the clasping leaf bases. Each pseudobulb has six or more soft, lancelike leaves near the apex. The gently arching leaves are up to 12 inches (30 cm) long and seldom more than 1 inch (2.5 cm) wide. The short, curving inflorescence arises from the tip of the pseudobulb and may bear up to 12 flowers 1 to 3 inches (2.5–7.5 cm) wide. Many times a secondary or even a tertiary inflorescence develops from the original inflorescence, thus greatly prolonging the flowering period.

The three sepals and two petals are alike in size, shape, and color and are arranged fanlike behind the lip, which is the largest and most distinct segment of the flower. The three-lobed lip is almost funnel-shaped and tapers into a long spur but has a flaring midlobe. The two lateral lobes form the funnel around the column.

The short column is broadest just below the stigmatic surface and is terminated by a hooded anther cap. The two nearly round pollinia are attached to a single almost-triangular stipe with two small projections at the base.

CULTURE: Temperature, 60–65°F (15–18°C); light, 2400–3600 footcandles; humidity, 40–60%; media, tree fern, osmunda, fir bark; fertilization, monthly, with a 1–1–1 ratio for tree fern and osmunda, and a 3–1–1 ratio for bark.

COLOR PLATE: *Galeandra baueri*

SPECIES	FLOWERING SEASON	GENERAL LOCALE
baueri	F–W–S–SS	Mexico to Panama
beyrichii	F	Tropical America
claesiana	S	Brazil
devoniana	SS	Venezuela to Brazil
lucustris	W	Venezuela, Brazil
pubicentrum	W	Peru

Galeandra baueri

A: Plant in flower, × ½.
B: Flower, face view, × 1.
C: Flower, side view, × 1.
D: Lip, × 1½.
E: Flower, vertical section, × 1½.
F: Column, ventral view, × 5.
G: Column, end view, × 5.
H: Column, side view, × 5.
I: Column, vertical section, × 5.
J: Anther cap, × 10.
K, L, M: Pollinia, × 10.

Gastrochilus

GENUS: *Gastrochilus* D. Don (gas-troh-KYE-luss)
TRIBE: Vandeae   SUBTRIBE: Aeridinae
IDENTIFICATION CHARACTERISTICS: This very delightful group of mostly dwarf, monopodial epiphytes was assembled into the genus *Gastrochilus* by David Don in the early 1800s. The generic name, a combination of the Greek words *gaster* (stomach, belly) and *cheilos* (lip), refers to the unusual lips. As known today, the genus consists of approximately 15 species.

Vegetatively, *Gastrochilus* species resemble small *Phalaenopsis* species with longer, narrower leaves. The thick, leathery, fairly stiff leaves are almost lance-shaped and up to 7 inches (17.5 cm) long. The very short stems usually bear six to ten closely spaced leaves. The leaf blade clasps the stem, making the plant appear to have a taller stem. One or more inflorescences arise from the axil of the lower leaves. The short, densely flowered inflorescence has a few to 20 flowers and may be erect or pendent.

The sepals and petals are arranged in the shape of a fan and vary from 0.5 to 1.5 inches (1–4 cm) across. They are alike in color, which ranges from a clear yellow (e.g., *Gastrochilus dasypogon*) to blotched with large brownish purple spots (e.g., *G. bellinus*), but may vary in size, with sepals sometimes slightly larger. The complex lip, which is the unique portion of the flower, is composed of a stomach-shaped sac and a broad, fringed midlobe. The lip is generally white with small reddish dots and a yellow blotch on the midlobe.

The very small column terminates just above the opening of the sac in the lip. A smooth anther cap covers the column apex, and most of the underside is devoted to the stigmatic surface. A pair of light yellow somewhat-elliptical pollinia are borne on the top of a narrow-footed stipe. The stipe and foot look like a two-tined fork from several views.

CULTURE: Temperature, 60–65°F (15–18°C); light, 1800–2400 footcandles, grows with *Cattleya* or *Phalaenopsis*; humidity, 40–60%; media, fir bark, tree fern; fertilization, monthly, ratio depends on medium.

COLOR PLATE: *Gastrochilus dasypogon*

SPECIES	FLOWERING SEASON	GENERAL LOCALE
bellinus	W–S	Myanmar, Thailand
bigibbus	F	Myanmar
calceolaris	F	Thailand, Sumatra, Java, Assam, Myanmar, Malaysia
dalzellianus	S	India (Bombay)
dasypogon	F	Thailand to Sikkim, Java, Nepal, India, Sumatra
formosanus	S–SS	Taiwan
intermedius	S	Himalayas to Thailand
japonicus	F	Taiwan
maculatus	S	India
monticolus	S	Thailand to China
patinatus	S	Sumatra, Borneo
sutepensis	S	Thailand

Gastrochilus dasypogon

A: Plant in flower, × ½.
B: Flower, face view, × 2.
C: Flower, side view, × 2.
D: Lip, three-quarter view, × 3.
E: Lip, face view, × 3.
F: Flower, vertical section, × 2.
G: Column, ventral view, × 6.
H: Column, end view, × 6.
I: Column, side view, × 6.
J: Column, vertical section, × 6.
K, L, M: Pollinia, × 15.

183

Gomesa

GENUS: *Gomesa* R. Brown (go-MEE-suh)
TRIBE: Maxillarieae SUBTRIBE: Oncidiinae
IDENTIFICATION CHARACTERISTICS: *Gomesa* is a genus of small plants with pale yellow-green fragrant flowers. Consisting of about 13 species, the genus is closely allied to *Oncidium* and often confused by the amateur. Taxonomically, the two genera can be separated on flower characteristics, especially in the lip. Due to the unusual shape of the lip and floral segments in *Gomesa*, the plants have been affectionately called "little man orchids."

Robert Brown first described the genus in 1815, basing his description on a plant introduced from Brazil that flowered at Chelsea Botanic Garden, London, England. Brown called the plant *Gomesa recurva* in honor of Bernardino Antonio Gomes, a well-known Portuguese physician and botanist.

The pseudobulbs are almost elliptical and flattened, up to 4 inches (10 cm) long, and closely arranged on the rhizome. Each pseudobulb is subtended by several leafy bracts and has two leaves at its apex. The soft, arching leaves may be up to 12 inches (30 cm) long and 2 inches (5 cm) wide. The short, curved inflorescence arises from the base of the pseudobulb and bears up to 25 flowers subtended by small leafy bracts.

The small flowers, up to 1 inch (2.5 cm) wide, are fragrant. The three sepals are alike in size and color. The dorsal sepal is erect and free, while the two lateral sepals are fused for almost half their length and form an inverted Y beneath the lip. The two petals are similar to the sepals in size and color. The short, three-lobed lip is curved and almost U-shaped when viewed in vertical section. There are small protuberances on the disc of the lip.

The short, narrow column adds much to the attractiveness of these flowers. Basically, the column is white, but it may have an orange-red ring around the stigmatic area. Two yellow teardrop-shaped pollinia are attached to a single stipe with a sometimes brown shield-shaped foot.

CULTURE: Temperature, 60°F (15°C); light, 2400–3600 footcandles; humidity, 40–60%; media, tree fern, fir bark; fertilization, monthly, with a 3–1–1 ratio for bark and a 1–1–1 ratio for tree fern.

COLOR PLATE: *Gomesa crispa*

SPECIES	FLOWERING SEASON	GENERAL LOCALE
crispa	S–SS	Brazil
glaziovii	S–SS	Brazil
laxiflora	S–SS	Brazil
planifolia	SS	Brazil
recurva	S–SS–F	Brazil
sessilis	S–SS	Brazil
verboonenii	S–SS	Brazil

Gomesa crispa

A: Plant in flower, × ½.
B: Flower, face view, × 2.
C: Flower, side view, × 2.
D: Lip, back view, × 4.
E: Lip, face view, × 4.
F: Flower, vertical section, × 3.
G: Column, ventral view, × 8.
H: Column, end view, × 8.
I: Column, side view, × 8.
J: Column, vertical section, × 8.
K, L, M: Pollinia, × 12.

185

Gongora

GENUS: *Gongora* Ruiz & Pavón (gon-GOR-uh)
TRIBE: Maxillarieae   SUBTRIBE: Stanhopeinae
IDENTIFICATION CHARACTERISTICS: This small genus of a dozen species and a number of variants was described by Hipólito Ruiz Lopez and José Antonio Pavón in the late 1700s. They named the genus in honor of the Bishop of Cordoba, Don Antonio Cabballero y Gongora. Some taxonomists divide the genus into two groups, *Eugongora* (e.g., *Gongora quinquenervis*) and *Acropera* (e.g., *Gongora armeniaca* var. *bicornuta*), separated by floral shape. These sympodial epiphytes are grown primarily for their unique flowers. The genus has not been widely hybridized.

Gongora is typified by short, stout pseudobulbs with pronounced perpendicular ridges. Each pseudobulb is topped by two, sometimes three, soft, pleated, broad leaves up to 10 inches (25 cm) long and 3 inches (7.5 cm) wide. Pendent inflorescences arise from the pseudobulb bases and bear from a few to many flowers.

The 2-inch (5-cm) wide flowers are usually fragrant and colorful. Although strange and unlike the typical orchid, they are both fragrant and visually enjoyable. The three sepals with reflexed margins are alike in size and color. The dorsal sepal is attached to the column for one-half its length. The two petals, which are much reduced and attached to the column, appear as wings that end in sharp points at the apex. The apex of each petal may be reflexed toward the column. *Gongora* species have very complex, fleshy, two-parted lips, sometimes with earlike lobes and/or antennae. The lip is usually lighter in color than the sepals.

The long, narrow column is slightly curved and topped with a very distinct anther cap. The beaklike projection in the center of the rostellum partially obscures its narrow stigmatic surface. *Gongora* species have two narrow, elongate, yellow pollinia resembling rabbit ears in profile. They are attached to a single shield-shaped stipe.

CULTURE: Temperature, 60–70°F (15–21°C); light, 2400–3600 footcandles; humidity, 40–70%; media, bark, osmunda, tree fern; fertilization, monthly, ratio depends on medium.

COLOR PLATE: *Gongora quinquenervis*

SPECIES	FLOWERING SEASON	GENERAL LOCALE
armeniaca var. *bicornuta*	SS–F	Nicaragua, Costa Rica, Panama
cassidea	F	Mexico, Guatemala, Honduras, Nicaragua
galeata	SS–F	Mexico
portentosa	S	Colombia
quinquenervis	F	Colombia, Venezuela, Peru, Guyana, Trinidad, Ecuador
truncata	F–W–S	Mexico

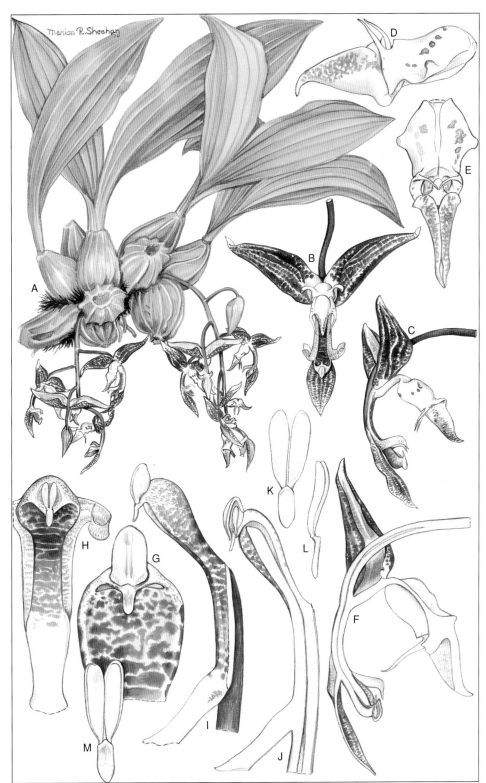

Gongora quinquenervis

A: Plant in flower, × ½.

B: Flower, face view, × 1.

C: Flower, side view, × 1.

D: Lip, side view, × 2.

E: Lip, face view, × 2.

F: Flower, vertical section, × 1.

G: Column, upper portion only, ventral view, × 5.

H: Column, ventral view, anther cap removed, × 3.

I: Column, side view, × 3.

J: Column, vertical section, × 3.

K, L, M: Pollinia, × 8.

187

Grammatophyllum

GENUS: *Grammatophyllum* Blume (grah-mat-oh-FILL-um)

TRIBE: Cymbidieae SUBTRIBE: Cyrtopodiinae

IDENTIFICATION CHARACTERISTICS: This small genus of sympodial epiphytes comprises five to eight species of extremely large plants that consequently are not commonly grown in small greenhouses. For example, *Grammatophyllum speciosum* has been recorded as large as 42.5 feet (12.75 m) in circumference.

The genus probably was first discovered by G. E. Rumphius in Malaysia during the mid-1700s and was classified as *Grammatophyllum* by Carl Blume in 1825. The generic name is derived from two Greek words meaning marked leaf and probably refers to the marks on the sepals and petals.

Vegetative characteristics vary widely from the short, stout pseudobulbs (8 × 3 inches [20 × 7.5 cm]) of *Grammatophyllum scriptum* with two to five leaves at the apex to the long, thick pseudobulbs of *G. speciosum* (7 feet × 3 inches [210 × 7.5 cm]) with leaves attached to the upper third of the pseudobulb. The leaves, which may be 24 inches (60 cm) long, have a very pronounced midrib on the underside. The inflorescences, which are as thick as an adult's finger and up to 8 feet (240 cm) long, arise from the base of the pseudobulbs and may bear 50 to 100 flowers.

The very distinctive flowers of this genus are greenish yellow with purplish spots and range from 1.5 to 6 inches (4–15 cm) in diameter. The sepals and petals are similar in color, but the petals are narrower than the sepals. The lip is very small and distinctly three-lobed. The two lateral lobes partially enclose the column. The apical lobe of the lip is small, with brownish purple lines, and often with small hairs near the midpoint. Many plants bear abnormal flowers near the base of the inflorescence.

The very small column is slightly curved with a pronounced anther cap at the apex and a small foot-like projection at the base. A very narrow stigmatic area lies just below and behind the anther cap. Two yellow, rounded pollinia are borne on a stipe that is almost U-shaped.

CULTURE: Temperature, 70°F (21°C); light, 2400–3600 footcandles, grows in full sun in native habitat as well as partial shade; media, tree fern, fir bark, osmunda; fertilization, monthly, ratio depends on medium.

COLOR PLATE: *Grammatophyllum scriptum*

SPECIES	FLOWERING SEASON	GENERAL LOCALE
measuresianum	S	Philippines
scriptum	S	Borneo, Solomon Islands, Moluccas, Philippines, New Guinea, Celebes
speciosum	SS–F	Myanmar, Thailand, Laos, Vietnam, Malay Peninsula, Sumatra, Java, Borneo, Philippines, Moluccas, New Guinea

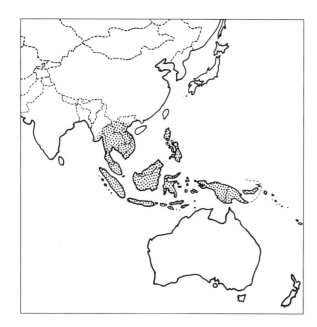

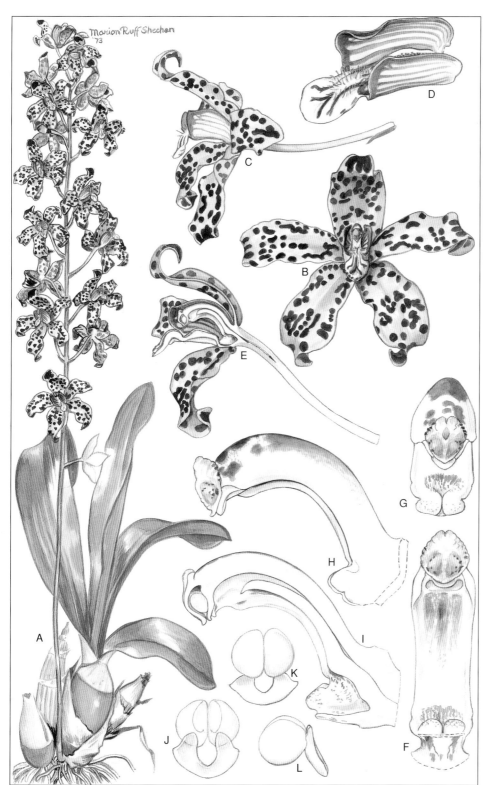

Grammatophyllum scriptum
A: Plant in flower, × ¼.
B: Flower, face view, × 1.
C: Flower, side view, × 1.
D: Lip, × 2.
E: Flower, vertical section, × 1.
F: Column, ventral view, × 4.
G: Column, end view, × 4.
H: Column, side view, × 4.
I: Column, vertical section, × 4.
J, K, L: Pollinia, × 10.

189

Habenaria

GENUS: *Habenaria* C. L. Willdenow (hab-in-AIR-ee-uh)

TRIBE: Orchideae SUBTRIBE: Habenariinae

IDENTIFICATION CHARACTERISTICS: *Habenaria*, the largest genus of terrestrial plants distributed throughout the world, consists of over 500 species, many with colorful flowers, but is not widely grown. The fact that these perennial herbs die back after flowering and are dormant six to eight months of the year is an important aspect in determining whether or where they are grown. Most orchid growers do not like to see empty pots sitting on the greenhouse bench, so they usually opt to grow the evergreen genera. There is no doubt that when *H. rhodocheila* flowers, it is most attractive and well worth waiting for. Even some of the green-flowered species (e.g., *H. splendens*) are rewarding to grow. The genus was first described by C. L. Willdenow in 1805, who derived the generic name from the Latin word *habena* (reins) to describe the long strap shapes of some petals and lips.

Vegetatively, *Habenaria* species are typical perennial herbs. They produce a new growth in late spring or early summer, flower in mid- to late summer, set seed, and then die back in early fall. They have simple tubers with fleshy roots that sustain the plants while dormant. The leafy stems attain heights of 30 inches (75 cm) and have a few to many soft, smooth leaves with the leaf bases clasping the stem. Leaf color varies even within a species. For example, leaves of *H. rhodocheila* are light green when grown in shade but purplish gray-green when grown in bright light. The terminal inflorescence arises above the leaves and is a spike or raceme bearing a few to many 1- to 2-inch (2.5- to 5.0-cm) wide flowers. Flower color is variable with green and white dominant.

The showy flowers really highlight *Habenaria* species. The dorsal sepal is usually shorter than the two lateral sepals. It can be erect, reflexed, or deflexed. The two petals are smaller than the lateral sepals and may be adnate to the dorsal sepal, thus appearing to be absent. The lip has a long slender spur and may be three- or four-lobed. In some species the lip is densely pubescent beneath (e.g., *H. splendens*) or reflexed.

The column is very short and complex compared to the columns of most other orchids. The small rostellum has two lateral lobes and lies between the two anther cells. The two yellow glandular-looking pollinia are in separate anther cells and are attached to a very elongate caudicle with a small, often colorful viscidium, which is exserted and may appear as two dots on the side of the column.

CULTURE: Temperature, variable, depends on species; light, 3000 footcandles to full sun; humidity, 40–60%; medium, any good terrestrial mix; fertilization, monthly, with a balanced fertilizer.

COLOR PLATE: *Habenaria rhodocheila*

SPECIES	FLOWERING SEASON	GENERAL LOCALE
carnea	SS	Malaya to Thailand
dentata	S–SS	India east to Thailand & Vietnam
rhodocheila	SS	Southern China to Malaya
splendens	S–SS	East Africa, Ethiopia, Zambia, Malawi

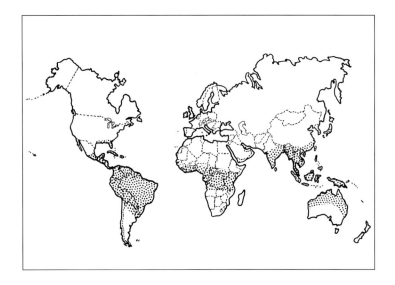

Habenaria rhodocheila
A: Plant in flower, × ½.
B: Flower, face view, × 2.
C: Flower, side view, × 2.
D: Lip, three-quarter view, × 2.
E: Flower, vertical section, × 2.
F: Column, ventral view, × 6.
G: Column, end view, × 6.
H: Column, side view, × 6.
I: Column, vertical section, × 6.
J, K, L: Pollinia, × 8.

Haraella

GENUS: *Haraella* Kudo (har-ee-ELL-uh)
TRIBE: Vandeae SUBTRIBE: Aeridinae
IDENTIFICATION CHARACTERISTICS: Endemic to Taiwan, this truly miniature genus contains only one enchanting species, *Haraella odorata*, which has long been popular among growers. The novel flowers are almost as large as the plants themselves. Yushun Kudo named the genus in 1930 in honor of Yoshie Hara, a Taiwanese orchid collector who found the specimen upon which the genus description was based.

Vegetatively, these monopodial epiphytes closely resemble seedlings of *Phalaenopsis* and bear four to six leaves. The fleshy green leaves are seldom over 2 inches (5 cm) long. The short inflorescence is usually pendent and consists of up to three flower buds, only one flower opening at a time.

The 1-inch (2.5-cm) wide flowers are yellowish green with a large, velvety purple blotch on the lip. On close observation, they are an interesting study in textures, especially in the large lip. The sepals and petals are alike in shape and color, but the petals are slightly smaller than the sepals. The large, lobed lip is densely covered with hairs and has banded hairlike structures on the margin. The lip is by far the most outstanding and colorful feature of the flower.

The very short column is almost as broad as it is long, with the stigmatic surface covering a major portion of the underside. Two almost-spherical pollinia are borne on a recurved stipe with a horseshoe-shaped foot at the base.

CULTURE: Temperature, 60°F (15°C); light, 2400–3600 footcandles; humidity, 40–70%; medium, tree fern plaques; fertilization, monthly, with a 1–1–1 ratio.

COLOR PLATE: *Haraella odorata*

SPECIES	FLOWERING SEASON	GENERAL LOCALE
odorata	SS–F	Taiwan

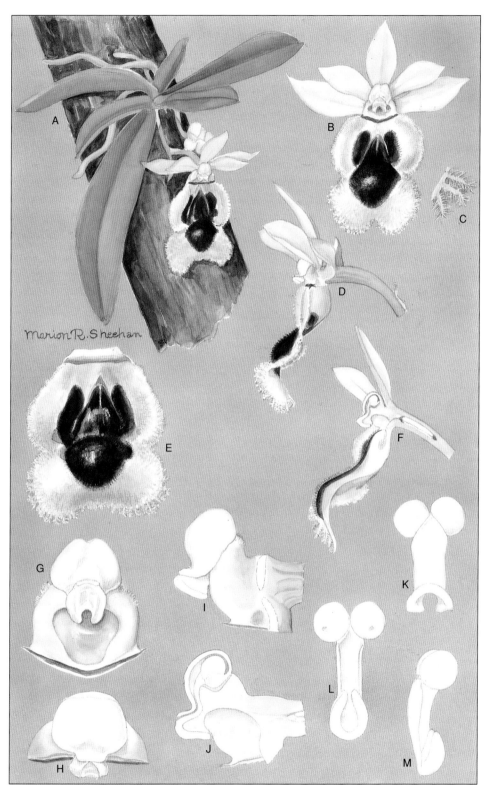

Haraella odorata

A: Plant in flower, × 2.
B: Flower, face view, × 3.
C: Flower detail, lip edge much enlarged.
D: Flower, side view, × 3.
E: Lip, × 4.
F: Flower, vertical section, × 3.
G: Column, ventral view, × 8.
H: Column, end view, × 8.
I: Column, side view, × 8.
J: Column, vertical section, × 8.
K, L, M: Pollinia, × 10.

Hexisea

GENUS: *Hexisea* Lindley (hex-ISS-ee-uh)
TRIBE: Epidendreae   SUBTRIBE: Laeliinae
IDENTIFICATION CHARACTERISTICS: *Hexisea* is a small but very interesting genus containing not more than a half-dozen valid species. John Lindley first described the genus in 1834 and coined the generic name *Hexisea* from the Greek words *hex* (six) and *isos* (equal). Undoubtedly, he was referring to the six outer floral segments, which are almost equal in size and shape. The genus is also unique in that the pseudobulbs grow in a chainlike fashion. The delightful flowers are borne in small clusters at the apex of each maturing pseudobulb. Shortly after flowering, a new pseudobulb arises from the apex of the mature pseudobulb.

These sympodial epiphytes have thickened and often three-sided pseudobulbs. Each segment averages 3 to 4 inches (7.5–10 cm) in length and is topped by one or two leaves at maturity. The leaves, which often drop when the next growth matures, are leathery, almost lanceolate, and up to 6 inches (15 cm) long and 0.5 inch (1 cm) wide. The new growths and inflorescences are ensheathed by small, leafy bracts that become dry and papery as the pseudobulbs or inflorescences mature.

Although flowers are small, seldom an inch (2.5 cm) in diameter, they are a brilliant reddish orange or yellow. From a distance, the flower appears to have six almost-equal segments. The sepals and two petals are alike in shape and color; however, the two petals are slightly smaller than the sepals. The apex of the lip is similar to the sepals in size, shape, and color, but the base of the lip is different. The basal one-fourth of the lip is yellow and sharply curved just before the point of attachment at the base of the column.

The short, broad column is concave in the middle and corresponds to the curvature of the lip. The apex of the column has two toothlike projections, one on either side of the anther cap. Two whitish elliptical pollinia are borne on narrow caudicles, which are covered with small roundish bumps and which are slightly footed at the base.

CULTURE: Temperature, 60–65°F (15–18°C); light, 2400–3600 footcandles; humidity, 40–60%; media, tree fern, peat and perlite, fir bark; fertilization, monthly, ratio depends on medium.

COLOR PLATE: *Hexisea bidentata*

SPECIES	FLOWERING SEASON	GENERAL LOCALE
bidentata	F–W–S–SS	Mexico to northern South America, Venezuela
dunstevilleorum	F–W–S–SS	Venezuela
imbricata	F–W–S–SS	Peru

Hexisea bidentata
A: Plant in flower, × ½.
B: Flower, face view, × 2.
C: Flower, side view, × 2.
D: Lip, face view, × 4.
E: Lip, side view, × 4.
F: Flower, vertical section, × 3.
G: Column, ventral view, × 8.
H: Column, end view, × 8.
I: Column, side view, × 8.
J: Column, vertical section, × 8.
K, L, M: Pollinia, × 20.

Holcoglossum

GENUS: *Holcoglossum* Schlechter (hole-koh-GLOSS-um)

TRIBE: Vandeae   SUBTRIBE: Aeridinae

IDENTIFICATION CHARACTERISTICS: *Holcoglossum* has been called "a collector's delight," "a rarity seldom grown," and "a favorite miniature," but while plants are easy to grow, they are slow to bloom. When the inflorescence emerges from between the leaves, it may be six months later before the first flower opens. The delightful flowers, however, are well worth the wait. Each one opens very slowly and may not be fully open for two weeks or more.

In Taiwan, this miniature *Vanda*-like genus is called the pine needle orchid because the terete leaves of *Holcoglossum quasipinifolium* are not much larger than pine needles. In certain characteristics the flower closely resembles the flower of *Amesiella* from the Philippines, and scientists indicate that *Holcoglossum* is close taxonomically to *Angraecum*. Most taxonomists believe *Holcoglossum* has only one valid species. Rudolf Schlechter first described the genus in 1919 and formed the generic name by combining two Greek words meaning strap and tongue to describe the beautiful spurred lip on these attractive flowers.

Vegetatively, this monopodial epiphyte averages six to ten needlelike leaves, usually less than 0.15 inch (2 mm) in diameter and around 6 inches (15 cm) long. The dark green leaves taper toward the apex into a point. The one- to several-flowered, slender, purplish brown inflorescences usually arise from between two leaves but also can arise from the base of the plant. Usually they are pendent.

The 1-inch (2.5-cm) wide flowers are white to pinkish purple. Slow to open, they are most attractive when fully expanded. The sepals and petals are alike in size and color and have wavy margins. The three-lobed, spurred lip is the last segment of the flower to unfold and is the most fascinating. The two upright lateral lobes almost encompass the column and vary in color among clones. The midlobe is the least colorful portion of the flower, even with its sharply curved spur. A very dominant feature, the spur is usually the same color as the midlobe of the lip but may have an apple-green tip.

The short, erect column has a proportionally large stigmatic surface, which is the broadest area of the column. A pair of deeply cleft squarish yellow pollinia are borne on a single stipe with an almost-diamond-shaped viscidium.

CULTURE: Temperature, 60°F (15°C); light, 2400–3600 footcandles; humidity, 40–60%; media, tree fern, bark, osmunda; fertilization, monthly, ratio depends on medium.

COLOR PLATE: *Holcoglossum quasipinifolium*

SPECIES	FLOWERING SEASON	GENERAL LOCALE
amesianum	S	Myanmar, Thailand, Indochina
kimballianum	S	Myanmar, Thailand, southern China
quasipinifolium	S	Taiwan

Holcoglossum quasipinifolium

A: Plant in flower, × ½.
B: Flower, face view, × 1½.
C: Flower, side view, × 1½.
D: Lip, three-quarter view, × 2.
E: Lip, back view, × 2.
F: Flower, vertical section, × 1½.
G: Column, ventral view, × 5.
H: Column, end view, × 5.
I: Column, side view, × 5.
J: Column, vertical section, × 5.
K, L, M: Pollinia, × 8.

Huntleya

GENUS: *Huntleya* Bateman ex Lindley (HUNT-lee-uh)

TRIBE: Maxillarieae   SUBTRIBE: Zygopetalinae

IDENTIFICATION CHARACTERISTICS: Although four species are known to exist in this delightful genus, only one is commonly grown, namely, *Huntleya meleagris*. The genus was named by John Lindley to honor the Rev. J. T. Huntley in 1837 and the name was retained by James Bateman in his revision of the genus in 1839. The genus is closely related to *Batemannia* and *Zygopetalum* and species were often confused in the early 1800s. Huntleyas lack pseudobulbs and are found in cool, moist situations in their native habitats; hence, they are not the easiest plants to cultivate.

These sympodial epiphytes have fans of six to eight leaves each up to 12 inches (30 cm) long. The lanceolate leaves have a distinct mark about one-quarter to one-third the way up the leaf. Soft and leathery, the leaves tend to reflex, leaving a somewhat open fan. The inflorescences, each with a single flower bud, arise from the axils of the leaves.

The flowers may be up to 5 inches (12.5 cm) in diameter, and flower color is very variable, with brown dominating. The very fragrant flower is most interesting in the pattern of its coloration, which gives the flower a somewhat checkerboard appearance. The two lateral sepals are attached at right angles to the dorsal sepal. The three sepals and two petals are alike in size, shape, and color, often being brightly colored on the upper extremities and becoming almost white at the base. The lip of the flower is unique. The large midlobe is prominent, being very colorful at the apex and white at the base. The base of the lip is very narrow and attached to the foot of the column. In the center of the lip is a raised callus layer that has a pronounced fringe on three sides.

The short, curved, footed column has a very distinct hood partially covering the anther cap and stigmatic area. The column is broadest in the stigmatic region. The four almost-tear-shaped pollinia are borne on a shield-shaped stipe.

CULTURE: Temperature, 60–65°F (15–18°C); light, 2400–3600 footcandles; humidity, 60–80%; media, tree fern, sphagnum moss; fertilization, monthly, with a 1–1–1 ratio.

COLOR PLATE: *Huntleya meleagris*

SPECIES	FLOWERING SEASON	GENERAL LOCALE
meleagris	S–F	Costa Rica, Panama, Colombia, Brazil, Trinidad

Huntleya meleagris
A: Plant in flower, × ¼.
B: Flower, face view, × ½.
C: Flower, side view, × ½.
D: Lip, three-quarter view, × 1½.
E: Lip, face view, × 1½.
F: Flower, vertical section, × ½.
G: Column, ventral view, × 2.
H: Column, end view, × 2.
I: Column, side view, × 2.
J: Column, vertical section, × 2.
K, L, M: Pollinia, × 5.

Ionopsis

GENUS: *Ionopsis* Humboldt, Bonpland, & Kunth (eye-oh-NOPP-siss)

TRIBE: Maxillarieae SUBTRIBE: Oncidiinae

IDENTIFICATION CHARACTERISTICS: Although there are around 10 species in this genus, which was first discovered by Alexander von Humboldt, Alexandre Bonpland, and Carl Kunth in 1815, only *Ionopsis utricularioides* is widely recognized. According to some, the genus would be even more common if it were not so difficult to keep alive in greenhouse collections, but others claim the genus is easy to grow. Humboldt and his coworkers derived the generic name from two Greek words which mean appearing like a violet. Undoubtedly, they were referring to the violetlike characteristics of some of the dainty flowers in this genus.

These sympodial epiphytes appear to be pseudobulbless as the small, short pseudobulbs are hidden by the clasping leaf bases. The thick, leathery, green leaves, up to 6 inches (15 cm) long and 0.75 inch (2 cm) wide, are folded and have a distinct keel on the underside. On healthy plants there are usually up to six leaves per growth. Because the lateral growths are closely arranged along the rhizome, the plants form dense clumps. The wiry, flowering panicle arises from a leaf axil. Inflorescences up to 3 feet (90 cm) long have been reported, but generally anything 18 to 24 inches (45–60 cm) is a large inflorescence.

Flower colors are basically white, violet and white, or pale lavender-pink with violet stripes. The dainty flowers, 0.75 inch (2 cm) wide, are borne in large numbers and usually have three sepals and two petals alike in color, although the petals are often a little broader than the sepals and less pointed at the apex. The spreading, distinctly bilobed lip is the showiest portion of the flower. The two lobes may be rounded (e.g., *Ionopsis utricularioides*) or pointed (e.g., *I. satyrioides*). There are two yellow calli near the base of the lip and the throat may be slightly hairy.

The very short column is broadest near the stigmatic surface and has a slightly three-lobed anther cap at its apex. Two yellow pollinia, almost round with a slight groove, are attached to a single stipe, which has an elliptical foot.

CULTURE: Temperature, 60°F (15°C); light, 2400–3600 footcandles; humidity, 40–60%; media, tree fern, peat and perlite, bark; fertilization, monthly, ratio depends on medium.

COLOR PLATE: *Ionopsis utricularioides*

SPECIES	FLOWERING SEASON	GENERAL LOCALE
satyrioides	S–SS–F	Caribbean Islands
utricularioides	W–S	South Florida to Brazil & Bolivia

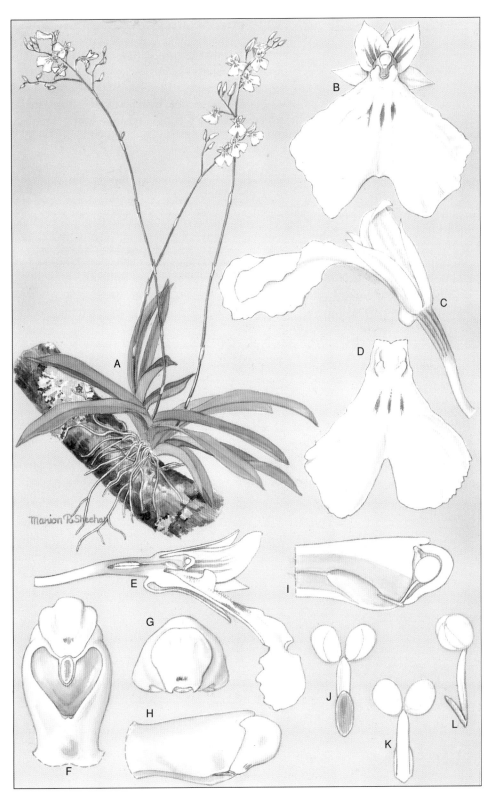

Ionopsis utricularioides
A: Plant in flower, × ½.
B: Flower, face view, × 5.
C: Flower, side view, × 5.
D: Lip, face view, × 5.
E: Flower, vertical section, × 5.
F: Column, ventral view, × 20.
G: Column, end view, × 20.
H: Column, side view, × 20.
I: Column, vertical section, × 20.
J, K, L: Pollinia, × 30.

Isochilus

GENUS: *Isochilus* R. Brown (eye-soh-KYE-luss)
TRIBE: Epidendreae SUBTRIBE: Laeliinae
IDENTIFICATION CHARACTERISTICS: This singular genus was first described by Robert Brown in 1813 and contains only two species. One species (*Isochilus major*) is unique, especially when in flower, as the leaves subtending the inflorescence turn pink, the same color as the flowers. This is a characteristic often found in bromeliads. Brown derived the generic name from the Greek words *isos* (equal) and *cheilos* (lip); he probably was trying to denote that the lip and sepals were equal in size.

Isochilus is also of interest from a vegetative standpoint. These sympodial epiphytes form dense masses. The wiry, reedlike stems are up to 2 feet (60 cm) tall with the upper two-thirds clothed in small, soft, flat, green leaves with clasping bases. The linear leaves are seldom over 2.5 inches (6 cm) long. The short inflorescences appear at the terminal of each reedlike growth and consist of one to several flowers. Basically, the flowers are pink or magenta. Plants often flower several times a year.

The small flowers, 0.3 inch (0.8 cm) across, do not open fully and look like five-pointed stars if viewed head on. The sepals and petals, which are alike in size, shape, and color, almost form a tube around the remaining floral segments. The small three-lobed lip often will be a different shade of pink from the petals and sepals and may have two very pronounced, dark purple dots near the lateral lobes.

The column is long and narrow, being widest near the anther cap and stigmatic area. Two distinct lateral lobes partially enclose the anther cap. Four very pale, almost-white pollinia are attached to an almost-heart-shaped caudicle.

CULTURE: Temperature, 55–60°F (12–15°C); light, 2400–3600 footcandles; humidity, 40–60%; media, tree fern, bark; fertilization, monthly, ratio depends on medium.

COLOR PLATE: *Isochilus major*

SPECIES	FLOWERING SEASON	GENERAL LOCALE
linearis	F–W–S–SS	Antilles, Mexico & Cuba to Argentina
major	F–W–S–SS	Mexico to Panama, Jamaica

202

Isochilus major

A: Plant in flower, × ½.
B: Inflorescence, × 1½.
C: Flower, face view, × 4.
D: Flower, side view, × 3.
E: Lip, face view, × 4.
F: Lip, side view, × 4.
G: Flower, vertical section, × 3.
H: Column, ventral view, × 8.
I: Column, end view, × 8.
J: Column, side view, × 8.
K: Column, vertical section, × 8.
L, M, N: Pollinia, × 25.

203

Jumellea

GENUS: *Jumellea* Schlechter (joo-MELL-ee-uh)
TRIBE: Vandeae SUBTRIBE: Angraecinae

IDENTIFICATION CHARACTERISTICS: The angraecoid orchids include many interesting species, and although their flowers are predominantly white, they sport a diversity of floral shapes, some with almost-unbelievable spurs. *Jumellea* is one genus of this group that is often overlooked, probably because some species may have only one bloom on each fan of leaves, but the flowers are delightful and long-lasting. *Jumellea* species are easy to grow and flower reliably each year. Consisting of more than 40 species, the genus was named by Rudolf Schlechter in honor of Henri Jumelle, a French botanist known for his studies of the flora of Madagascar. The genus is closely allied to *Angraecum*, but is separated on slightly differing floral characteristics.

Although basically a monopodial, epiphytic genus, some species are lithophyte-like, becoming established on mossy rocks. There are also considerable differences in their vegetative characteristics. Most species, however, have thin, leathery leaves, often folded, that clasp the base of the stem. Stems of most plants are completely enclosed within the leaf bases. The apex of each leaf is bilobed, with the lobing more pronounced on some species. The flowers appear singly on wiry green inflorescences that arise from the lower leaf axils.

The white, delicate, long-lasting flowers are 1.5 to 5 inches (4–12.5 cm) wide. The narrow sepals and petals, although similar in size and shape, are often reflexed, causing the flower to appear much narrower than it really is. The entire lip is the largest segment of the flower and terminates in a distinct basal spur, the length of which varies among the species. The spur generally is very slender and often light green at the base. In some species, sepal bases may be united slightly around the spur.

The short column is almost as broad as it is long, with the major portion of the underside being stigmatic surface. Two pollinia are borne either attached directly to the viscidium or on very short stipes.

CULTURE: Temperature, 60°F (15°C); light, 2400–3600 footcandles; humidity, 40–60%; medium, most epiphytic media; fertilization, monthly, ratio depends on medium.

COLOR PLATE: *Jumellea gracilipes*

SPECIES	FLOWERING SEASON	GENERAL LOCALE
fragrans	W	Mascarene Islands
gracilipes	W–S	Madagascar
sagittata	W–S	Madagascar

Jumellea gracilipes

A: Plant in flower, × ¼.
B: Flower, face view, × ¾.
C: Flower, side view, × ½.
D: Lip, face view, × 1½.
E: Lip, side view, × 1½.
F: Flower, vertical section, × 1.
G: Column, ventral view, × 6.
H: Column, end view, × 6.
I: Column, side view, × 6.
J: Column, vertical section, × 6.
K, L, M: Pollinia, × 20.

205

Kingidium

GENUS: *Kingidium* P. F. Hunt (king-ID-ee-um)
TRIBE: Vandeae   SUBTRIBE: Aeridinae
IDENTIFICATION CHARACTERISTICS: There are only a few (two to five) species in this fascinating genus. Their charm lies in the small, enchanting flowers, often borne on open panicles, the large number offsetting their diminutive size. Over the years, these species have been assigned to *Phalaenopsis*, *Doritis*, and *Kingiella*. Then in 1970 P. F. Hunt changed the name to *Kingidium* because the name *Kingiella* had been used already in the Loranthaceae (mistletoe family) prior to the naming of this orchid. Hunt selected *Kingidium* to honor the English botanist Sir George King, who is known for his studies of orchids, especially those of India. When *Kingidium* species are not in flower, they look like small *Phalaenopsis* species.

These monopodial epiphytes appear to be stemless when in fact they have a short stem that is up to 0.5 inch (1 cm) long and hidden by the clasping leaf bases. Most plants have three to five oblong-lanceolate or even obtuse leaves up to 8 inches (20 cm) long and about one-fourth as wide. These are usually bright, shiny green. The mostly branched inflorescence (panicle) arises from the axil of the leaves, and a well-grown plant may have two or more inflorescences in bloom at the same time.

Diminutive or dainty are good adjectives to describe the 0.6-inch (1.5-cm) wide flowers, which basically are cream-colored to white with bright purple and magenta marks. The sepals and petals are alike in shape and color, with the sepals often slightly larger in size. The lip, which is distinctly three-lobed and almost spurlike at the base, is in some plants the most colorful part of the flower. The two lateral lobes often have earlike appendages and are slightly curved upward. The midlobe, with an emarginate apex, is the largest segment. The callus is flat and toothlike.

The column is short, with a relatively large stigmatic area, and is constricted just below the stigma. The two rounded yellow pollinia, each with a pronounced cleft, are borne on a single curved stipe with a rounded viscidium.

CULTURE: Temperature, 70°F (21°C); light, 1500–2000 footcandles; humidity, 40–60%; media, tree fern, bark, peat and perlite; fertilization, monthly, ratio depends on medium.

COLOR PLATE: *Kingidium deliciosum*

SPECIES	FLOWERING SEASON	GENERAL LOCALE
deliciosum	S	India to Philippines
taenialis	S	India to China

Kingidium deliciosum
A: Plant in flower, × ½.
B: Flower, face view, × 3.
C: Flower, side view, × 3.
D: Lip, expanded, × 5.
E: Lip, three-quarter view, × 5.
F: Flower, vertical section, × 4.
G: Column, ventral view, × 5.
H: Column, upper ventral view,
   × 8.
I: Column, end view, × 8.
J: Column, side view, × 5.
K: Column, vertical section, × 5.
L, M, N: Pollinia, × 10.

Koellensteinia

GENUS: *Koellensteinia* Reichenbach f. (koal-en-STEIN-ee-uh)

TRIBE: Maxillarieae SUBTRIBE: Zygopetalinae

IDENTIFICATION CHARACTERISTICS: *Koellensteinia*, which is somewhat rare in cultivation, comprises about 10 epiphytic and terrestrial species widely distributed throughout northern South America. When *K. graminea* is not flowering, it looks like grass and can easily fool the novice. On close examination, however, the plant immediately is recognized as an orchid since typical epiphytic roots emerge from the base of the clump of leaves. When the species is in flower, which is most of the year in Florida, the diminutive, typical orchid flowers soon dispel any doubts as to what family the species belongs. The genus was first described by H. G. Reichenbach in 1854 and revised by Rudolf Schlechter in 1918. Reichenbach named the genus in honor of Kellner von Koellenstein, a captain in the Austrian army.

Vegetatively, these sympodial orchids appear to be comprised solely of tufts of leaves. Some species (e.g., *Koellensteinia graminea*) lack pseudobulbs, while others (e.g., *K. kellneriana*) possess small angular pseudobulbs that are hidden by the ensheathing leafy bracts and leaf bases. Each growth bears one to three leaves, with individual leaves varying from grassy linear (e.g., *K. graminea*) to stalked linear lanceolate (e.g., *K. kellneriana*), and may be up to 2 feet (60 cm) long. The lateral inflorescences are erect and bear from a few to 15 flowers.

The base flower color varies from greenish white to light yellow, and the flowers are highlighted with purplish bars and stripes. The star-shaped flowers vary in size from 0.5 to 1 inch (1–2.5 cm) in diameter, with size depending on species. The sepals and petals are generally alike in shape and color, with the two lateral petals usually smaller than the other perianth segments. The lip is distinctly three-lobed, with the two lateral lobes mostly erect. There is a distinct fleshy callus under the column and directly between the two lateral lobes of the lip.

The column is short and stout, almost-straight-sided, often winged and footed. There is confusion in the literature as to whether *Koellensteinia* has four pollinia or two deeply lobed pollinia. The material we examined readily separated into four distinct pollinia. The pollinia are attached in pairs to a single shield-shaped foot by two very short stipes.

CULTURE: Temperature, 60°F (15°C); light, 2400–3600 footcandles; humidity, 40–60%; medium, any good mix for epiphytes; fertilization, monthly, ratio depends on medium.

COLOR PLATE: *Koellensteinia graminea*

SPECIES	FLOWERING SEASON	GENERAL LOCALE
graminea	S	Venezuela, Colombia to Brazil
kellneriana	S–SS	Panama, Colombia southeast to Brazil
tricolor	S	Guyana, Suriname, French Guiana, Brazil

Koellensteinia graminea
A: Plant in flower, × ¾.
B: Flower, face view, × 4.
C: Flower, side view, × 4.
D: Lip, side view, × 6.
E: Lip, face view, × 6.
F: Flower, vertical section, × 4.
G: Column, ventral view, × 10.
H: Column, end view, × 10.
I: Column, side view, × 10.
J: Column, vertical section, × 10.
K, L, M: Pollinia, × 20.

Laelia

GENUS: *Laelia* Lindley (LAY-lee-uh)
TRIBE: Epidendreae   SUBTRIBE: Laeliinae
IDENTIFICATION CHARACTERISTICS: The number
of species attributed to the genus *Laelia* varies from
35 to 75. Some writers place a number of species in
the genera *Brassavola* and *Schomburgkia*, while others include them in the genus *Laelia*. The first plants
were introduced into England in the early 1800s.
John Lindley founded the genus in 1831 and, as far
as is known, did not name it for a specific purpose.
Laelia may have been selected because it was the
name given to the female members of the Roman
family Laelius. These sympodial, pseudobulbous
epiphytes are closely related to *Cattleya* species and
have played an important part in producing many
of the hybrids grown today.

Authors often divide the genus into four subdi-
visions based primarily on the size and shape of the
pseudobulbs (Fig. 20). These bulblike structures
vary considerably from the flat, rounded bulbs of
Laelia rubescens to the ovoid or egg-shaped forms in
L. anceps to the almost-reedlike bulbs in *L. harpophylla*. The leaves are thick, leathery, and entire,
varying in length from less than 2 inches (5 cm) to
10 inches (25 cm). Some species have one leaf per
pseudobulb, whereas others have two or more.
Laelia species are easy to separate by the variations
among pseudobulbs. The flowers are borne solitary
and close to the pseudobulb apex or in clusters of
up to 20 flowers per inflorescence. The inflorescences range from less than 1 inch to 6 feet (2.5
cm–180 cm) in length.

The flowers vary in size from 1 to 8 inches (2.5–20
cm) across. They also exhibit variations from
species to species, but in general are more similar
than dissimilar. The three sepals are narrow,
spreading, and usually of the same color. The two
petals are broader than the sepals and generally the
same color as the sepals. The lip is the showiest and
largest segment of the floral structure. Most species
have a very pronounced three-lobed lip. The two
lateral lobes are often folded toward the column;
they overlap and form a tube around the column.
The third, or apex lobe of the lip, is usually flat and
spreading. The lip of a few species is similar to that
of *Cattleya labiata*. In general, the lip of *Laelia* species
exhibits a darker color than that of the other floral
segments. Flower colors are predominantly lavender, with red, yellow, orange, white, brown, and
maroon appearing in some species.

The column is elongate and narrow, having three
lobes at the apex. Two lateral lobes are broad and
short. The midlobe is short, narrow, and blunt at the
apex. All three lobes are appressed to the anther
cap. The stigmatic surface on the underside of the
column lies just behind the rostellum, appears top-
shaped, and has two lobes at the basal end. There
are four pairs of uniform yellow pollinia, borne in
two groups of four; each pair is attached at opposite ends of a small yellow caudicle.

CULTURE: Temperature, 50–65°F (10–18°C),
varies with some species; light, 2400–3600 footcandles; humidity, 40–70%; media, peat and perlite,
tree fern, bark; fertilization, monthly, ratio depends
on medium.

COLOR PLATE: *Laelia anceps*

Laelia anceps

A: Plant in flower, × ¼.
B: Flower, face view, × ½.
C: Flower, side view, × ½.
D: Lip, × 1.
E: Flower, vertical section, × ¾.
F: Column, ventral view, × 2½.
G: Column, end view, × 2½.
H: Column, side view, × 2½.
I: Column, vertical section,
    × 2½.
J: Anther cap and pollinia, × 5.
K, L: Pollinia, × 5.

LAELIA SPECIES	FLOWERING SEASON	GENERAL LOCALE
albida	F–W	Mexico
anceps	F–W	Mexico, Honduras
angereri	S	Brazil
autumnalis	F–W–S	Mexico
bradei	F	Brazil
briegeri	S	Brazil
cinnabarina	S–SS–F	Brazil
crispa	SS–F–W	Brazil
crispata	W	Brazil
crispilabia	SS	Brazil
dayana	F–W	Brazil
endsfeldzii	W	Brazil
esalqueana	S–SS	Brazil
flava	SS–F–W	Brazil
ghillanyi	S–SS	Brazil
gouldiana	F–W	Brazil
grandis	S–SS	Brazil
harpophylla	W–S	Brazil
itambana	S	Brazil
jongheana	W	Brazil
lilliputana	W–S	Brazil
lobata	S	Brazil
longipes	SS–F–W	Brazil
lucasiana	F	Brazil
lundii	SS	Brazil
milleri	S–SS	Brazil
perrinii	F	Brazil
pumila	F	Brazil
purpurata	S	Brazil
rubescens	F	Mexico through Central America
sincorana	S	Brazil
speciosa	S	Mexico
tenebrosa	S–SS	Brazil
xanthina	S–SS–F	Brazil

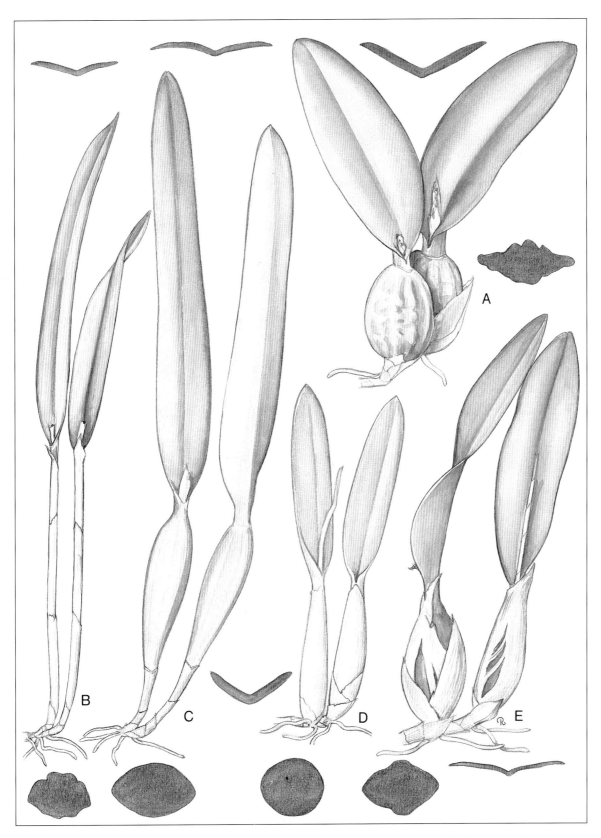

Figure 20. Vegetative forms of *Laelia*. A: *L. rubescens*. B: *L. harpophylla*. C: *L. purpurata*. D: *L. breigeri*. E: *L. anceps*.

Lemboglossum

GENUS: *Lemboglossum* Halbinger (lem-boh-GLOSS-um)

TRIBE: Maxillarieae SUBTRIBE: Oncidiinae

IDENTIFICATION CHARACTERISTICS: Crisp, colorful flowers borne on upright racemes are the hallmark of *Lemboglossum*, the versatile sympodial species of which are found growing in soil, on rocks, or as epiphytes on trees (e.g., *L. bictoniense*). Although a small genus of only 14 species, these cool- to intermediate-growing orchids have enjoyed a place in many collections and some have been widely used for breeding purposes.

The genus as presently recognized was established by Federico Halbinger in 1984 when he removed the Mexican and Central American species from *Odontoglossum*. His studies indicated sufficient differences in floral characteristics to warrant the separation. Not all taxonomists, however, have accepted this transfer. In naming the genus, Halbinger maintained the *glossum* root of the original generic name to designate the tonguelike lips often found in these species. The name also serves as a reference to the original genus, which encompassed a wide array of species.

Vegetatively, *Lemboglossum* resembles *Odontoglossum*, having similar, tightly clustered pseudobulbs. Each flattish, almost-oval pseudobulb is usually subtended by two leafy bracts and is topped by one to three ovate-to-lanceolate leaves up to 18 inches (45 cm) long and 2 inches (5 cm) wide. The leaves are conduplicate at the base. The tall (up to 36 inches [90 cm] high), mostly erect inflorescences arise from the base of the pseudobulb out of a leaf axil and may bear up to 20 delicate, 2-inch (5-cm) wide flowers.

The flowers may be white to light green with brown spots and/or bars. Some have rose to lavender lips. The sepals and petals are alike in size, shape, and color for any given species, but vary among species in shape of their tips. For example, the sepals and petals of *Lemboglossum bictoniense* are sharp-tipped and slightly curved, whereas those of *L. cordatum* are extremely attenuate and curled at the apex. The lips, which vary among species, are very sharp-pointed and almost arrowhead-like to very broad and showy.

The column, which is narrow and either slightly bulging or eared in the stigmatic region, may be almost white or the same color as the lip. The two yellow cleft pollinia are borne on a single stipe. Because of the way it is bent, the viscidium appears clawlike.

CULTURE: Temperature, 55–60°F (12–15°C); light, 2400–3600 footcandles; humidity, 40–60%; medium, any good mix for epiphytes; fertilization, monthly, ratio depends on medium.

COLOR PLATE: *Lemboglossum bictoniense*

SPECIES	FLOWERING SEASON	GENERAL LOCALE
bictoniense	W–S	Mexico to El Salvador
cervantesii	F–W–S	Mexico
cordatum	SS–F	Mexico to Costa Rica, Venezuela
maculatum	SS	Mexico to Costa Rica
rossii	S	Mexico to Nicaragua
uroskinneri	SS–F	Mexico to Guatemala

Lemboglossum bictoniense
A: Plant in flower, × ¼.
B: Flower, face view, × 1.
C: Flower, side view, × 1.
D: Lip, face view, × 2.
E: Flower, vertical section, × 1½.
F: Column, ventral view, × 4.
G: Column, end view, × 4.
H: Column, side view, × 4.
I: Column, vertical section, × 4.
J, K, L: Pollinia, × 10.

215

Leochilus

GENUS: *Leochilus* G. Knowles & F. Westcott (lee-oh-CHI-luss)

TRIBE: Maxillarieae   SUBTRIBE: Oncidiinae

IDENTIFICATION CHARACTERISTICS: *Leochilus* species are good examples of the many fine dwarf orchids. With their chainlike growth patterns and dainty flowers borne on delicate inflorescences, they also are some of the more likeable dwarfs. The approximately 15 species of *Leochilus* are mostly lowland plants. In their native habitat they are common inhabitants on guava, citrus, and coffee plants. The genus was first described by G. Knowles and F. Westcott in 1838. They derived the generic name from the Greek words *leios* (smooth) and *cheilos* (lip) to describe the smooth lips found in this genus. *Leochilus* is closely related to *Oncidium* but differs in anther characteristics.

Vegetatively *Leochilus* species resemble some *Oncidium* species. The ovoid, somewhat-flattened pseudobulbs are topped by one or two leaves and subtended by up to three leaf-bearing sheaths. The pseudobulbs may be spaced several inches apart on the thin, almost-wiry rhizome. Plants often grow in chainlike fashion along a tree limb. The lancelike leaf blades may be up to 6 inches (15 cm) long. The inflorescence arises from the axil of one of the lower sheaths, may be up to 12 inches (30 cm) tall, and bears several flowers. Inflorescences often have secondary lateral branches while the primary spike is still flowering. Flowers range in color from green to greenish yellow to yellow with a variety of brownish purple spots.

The small flowers, 0.5- to 0.75-inch (1.25- to 2-cm) wide, have three sepals alike in size and color, with the dorsal sepal slightly hooded and bent forward over the column. The two petals are slightly smaller than the sepals and are curved inward toward the column. The lip, which is adnate to the base of the column, may be entire or three-lobed. There is a disc with a fleshy callus on the lip under the column. The callus may be cup-shaped and lined with silky pubescence in some species (e.g., *Leochilus scriptus*).

The column is short but thick for its size. It has two projections (stelidia), one on each side near the middle. The rostellum is elongate and the stigmatic surface is small. There are two almost-elliptical yellow pollinia attached to an elongate caudicle, swollen at the apex and having a small viscidium at the base.

CULTURE: Temperature, 55–60°F (12–15°C) at night; light, 2400–3600 footcandles; humidity, 50–70%; media, tree fern plaques, citrus branches; fertilization, monthly, with a balanced fertilizer.

COLOR PLATE: *Leochilus carinatus*

SPECIES	FLOWERING SEASON	GENERAL LOCALE
ampliflorus	SS	Mexico
carinatus	SS–F	Mexico
labiatus	SS–F	Mexico & West Indies to Brazil
oncidioides	SS–F	Mexico, Honduras, Guatemala
scriptus	SS	Mexico to Panama, Cuba

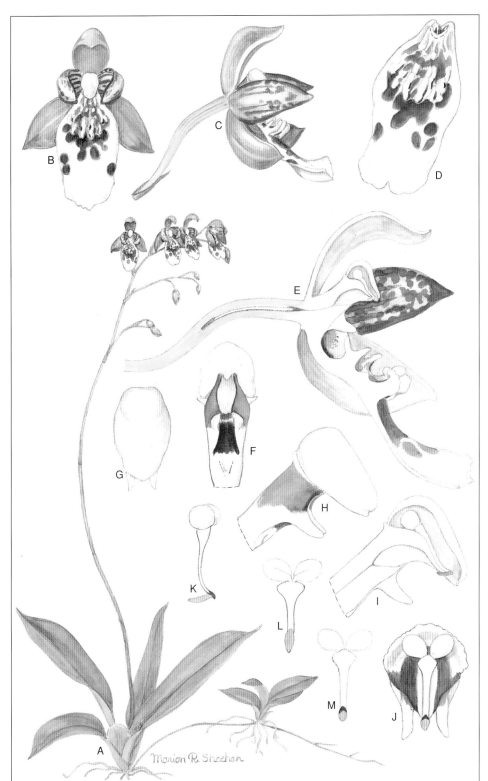

Leochilus carinatus

A: Plant in flower, × ¾.
B: Flower, face view, × 3.
C: Flower, side view, × 3.
D: Lip, top view, × 4.
E: Flower, vertical section, × 5.
F: Column, ventral view, × 8.
G: Column, end view, × 8.
H: Column, side view, × 8.
I: Column, vertical section, × 8.
J: Column end, anther cap removed to show pollinia in place, × 10.
K, L, M: Pollinia, × 10.

Marion R. Sheehan

217

Leptotes

GENUS: *Leptotes* Lindley (lep-TOH-teez)
TRIBE: Epidendreae   SUBTRIBE: Laeliinae
IDENTIFICATION CHARACTERISTICS: There are just five species in this attractive genus of miniature plants, which look like diminutive forms of *Brassavola*; however, when *Leptotes* species are in flower in winter and spring it is easy to distinguish the two genera. The genus was first described by John Lindley in 1833, based on flowering plants of *L. bicolor*. Lindley used the Greek word *leptotes* (delicateness) to depict these plants. The seed pods have a very high vanillin content and are used for flavoring in their native habitats.

Vegetatively, these sympodial epiphytes have many characteristics common to *Brassavola*. The tightly clustered pseudobulbs are stemlike and seldom more than 1 inch (2.5 cm) tall, with each stem topped by a single, terete leaf up to 5 inches (12.5 cm) long. The fleshy, grooved leaves are usually gray-green, but often have a purplish cast (e.g., *Leptotes unicolor*). The short inflorescences arise from the base of the leaves and typically have two to twelve flowers.

The rose or white flowers are about 1.5 inches (4 cm) across. The sepals and petals are alike in shape and color, but the two petals are usually a little narrower than the sepals. The floral segments project forward in some species (e.g., *Leptotes bicolor*), having strongly curved sepals and petals. The lip is three-lobed, with the midlobe being the largest segment. Each lateral lobe may also have small lobes near the column.

The column is very short, slightly longer than broad, and widest near the stigmatic surface. There are eight yellow pollinia, varying both in size and form on a single short caudicle.

CULTURE: Temperature, 60–65°F (15–18°C); light, 2400–3600 footcandles; humidity, 40–70%; media, osmunda, tree fern, bark; fertilization, monthly, ratio depends on medium.

COLOR PLATE: *Leptotes unicolor* and a flower of *L. bicolor*

SPECIES	FLOWERING SEASON	GENERAL LOCALE
bicolor	W–S	Brazil
unicolor	W–S	Brazil

218

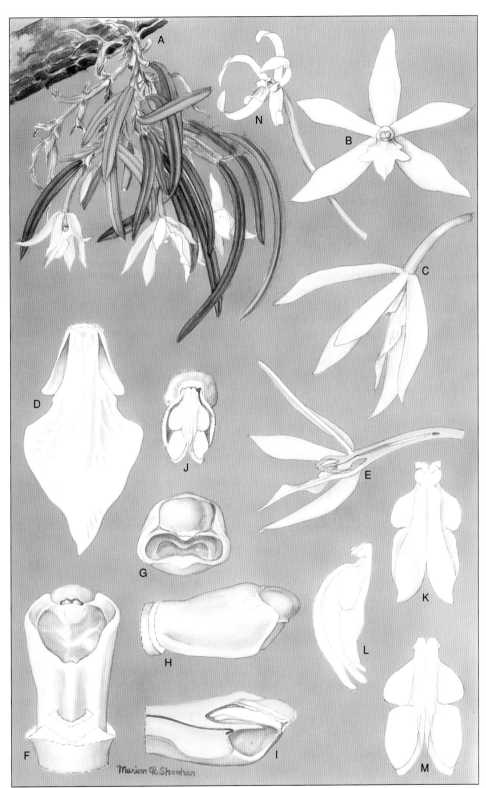

Leptotes unicolor

A: Plant in flower, × 1.
B: Flower, face view, × 2.
C: Flower, side view, × 2.
D: Lip, face view, × 4.
E: Flower, vertical section, × 2.
F: Column, ventral view, × 8.
G: Column, end view, × 8.
H: Column, side view, × 8.
I: Column, vertical section, × 8.
J: Anther cap with pollinia, × 8.
K, L, M: Pollinia, × 16.
N: Flower, *Leptotes bicolor*, three-quarter view, × 1.

Lockhartia

GENUS: *Lockhartia* Hooker (lok-HART-ee-uh)
TRIBE: Maxillarieae   SUBTRIBE: Oncidiinae
IDENTIFICATION CHARACTERISTICS: *Lockhartia* species have often been called braided orchids because of the neat arrangement of the two-ranked, imbricated leaves, which appear as though they were braided. Joseph D. Hooker named the genus in 1827 in honor of David Lockhart, superintendent of the Royal Botanical Gardens in Trinidad and an avid plant collector who sent many plants to England from South America. There are about 25 species of *Lockhartia* known today.

At first glance, these sympodial epiphytes almost resemble monopodial growers. Although flowering is axillary and the growths continue to elongate and flower for several years, the plants are sympodial growers. The clasping leaves are arranged in two ranks (distichous) and completely hide the stem. The small, leathery leaves are almost triangular-shaped. The small inflorescences arise from the upper leaf axils and usually have only one flower open at a time. The basic flower color is yellow.

The flowers have a slight resemblance to flowers of *Oncidium*, but are distinctly different. Most flowers are less than 0.7 inch (2 cm) wide. The sepals and petals are alike in size, shape, and color, with the two lateral sepals greatly reflexed and often hidden by the lip in face view. The three-lobed lip is the showiest portion of the flower. The two lateral, ear-like lobes partially enclose the column.

The very short column has pronounced wings extended straight out from each side and a very small stigmatic surface centered between the two wings. The two almost-elliptical, light yellow pollinia are borne on a very short stipe and are united by a very small foot at the base of the stipe.

CULTURE: Temperature, 60°F (15°C); light, 2400–3600 footcandles; humidity, 30–40%; media, tree fern, osmunda, fir bark; fertilization, monthly, ratio depends on medium.

COLOR PLATE: *Lockhartia oerstedii*

SPECIES	FLOWERING SEASON	GENERAL LOCALE
acuta	S–SS	Panama, Colombia, Venezuela, Trinidad
elegans	SS–F	Brazil
lunifera	S–SS–F	Brazil
micrantha	W–S	Nicaragua to Brazil
oerstedii	S–SS–F–W	Mexico to Panama
serra	F–W	Ecuador

Lockhartia oerstedii
A: Plant in flower, × ½.
B: Flower, face view, × 3.
C: Flower, side view, × 3.
D: Lip, × 4.
E: Flower, vertical section, × 3.
F: Column, ventral view, × 10.
G: Column, end view, × 10.
H: Column, side view, × 10.
I: Column, vertical section, × 10.
J, K, L: Pollinia, × 20.

Ludisia

GENUS: *Ludisia* A. Richard (loo-DISS-ee-uh)
TRIBE: Cranichideae   SUBTRIBE: Goodyerinae
IDENTIFICATION CHARACTERISTICS: Ludisias belong to that collective group of terrestrial orchids called the jewel orchids. By jewels, it is meant that the plants are equally attractive as foliage or flowering plants. In the early 1800s John Lindley named the genus *Haemaria*, deriving the name from the Greek word for blood red; undoubtedly, he was referring to the deep red undersides of the leaves and the often blackish red stems. In 1825, Achille Richard transferred this group to *Ludisia*. The origin of this name is unknown and is possibly derived from a personal name. At one time some taxonomists claimed there were four species in the genus, but today most believe that there is only one species and one more distinctly colored variety.

The short, brittle stems are usually red in color and may be erect or procumbent, the latter type rooting readily at the nodes. A cluster of four to six tightly arranged leaves appears at the apex of the stem. Each leaf blade may be up to 3 inches (7.5 cm) long and half as broad. The leaves, which are dark green above and blood red beneath, may have pronounced red or yellow venation above (e.g., *Ludisia discolor* var. *dawsoniana*) or dull red venation. A very hairy inflorescence bearing up to 12 white flowers with yellow anther caps arises from the branch apex.

The small, 0.75-inch (2-cm) wide flowers are subtended by small brownish purple leafy bracts. The sepals and lateral petals are similar in size, shape, and color. The uniqueness of the flowers lies in the lip and anther cap. The lip has a saclike structure and a wide claw at its base. There are two twisted lobes at the apex. Actually, the whole apex of the lip is twisted to the right when the flower is viewed face on.

The short column is almost-sphere-shaped at the apex. The apical anther cap is twisted to the left. Two elongate, almost-granular, light yellow pollinia are attached to a small, almost-semicircular foot.

CULTURE: Temperature, 60–65°F (15–18°C); light, 2400–3600 footcandles; humidity, 40–60%; medium, a mixture of 1 peat moss : 1 perlite : 1 soil; fertilization, monthly, with a 1–1–1 ratio.

COLOR PLATE: *Ludisia discolor*

SPECIES	FLOWERING SEASON	GENERAL LOCALE
discolor	F–W	Southern China & Myanmar to Indonesia
var. *dawsoniana*	F–W	Myanmar

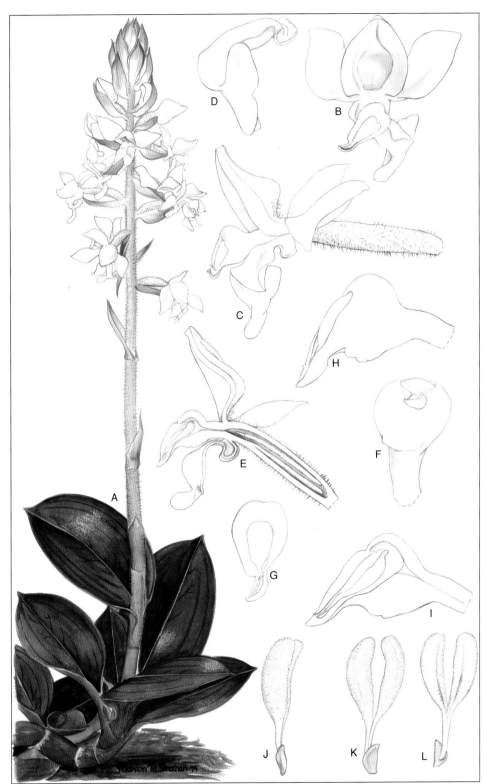

Ludisia discolor
A: Plant in flower, × 1.
B: Flower, face view, × 3.
C: Flower, side view, × 3.
D: Lip, × 4.
E: Flower, vertical section, × 3.
F: Column, ventral view, × 6.
G: Column, end view, × 6.
H: Column, side view, × 6.
I: Column, vertical section, × 6.
J, K, L: Pollinia, × 8.

223

Lycaste

GENUS: *Lycaste* Lindley (lye-KASS-tee)
TRIBE: Maxillarieae   SUBTRIBE: Lycastinae
IDENTIFICATION CHARACTERISTICS: John Lindley first described this genus of most interesting plants in the early 1800s and gave it the name *Lycaste*. The derivation of the generic name is not clear: Lindley may have been comparing these showy flowers to Lycaste, the lovely daughter of Priam, king of Troy; he also may have derived the name from the Greek word for nymph. The genus contains approximately 35 species of sympodial epiphytes that are fine flowering plants. Although closely related to *Maxillaria* species, they differ in foliage and flower characteristics.

Vegetatively, *Lycaste* species are very similar to each other. The oval pseudobulbs are often furrowed and have one to three leaves at the apex. The leaves, which remain on the bulbs for slightly more than a year, are soft, thin, and lanceolate, and up to 2.5 feet (75 cm) long and 6 inches (15 cm) wide. The inflorescence arises from the base of the pseudobulb.

The showy flowers may be as much as 4.3 inches (11 cm) across. Color varies considerably, with yellow, pink, pale green, olive green, and brownish green flowers. The three sepals are alike in size and color, and the dorsal sepal is perpendicular to the lateral sepals. The two petals, which are slightly smaller than the sepals, are usually the same color and lie parallel to the column, almost enclosing it. The three-lobed lip, usually hinged to the foot of the column, is not much larger than the petals and is mostly hidden by them. In many flowers, only the apical lobe of the lip is visible.

The column is long and narrow with a short basal foot. The underside of the column may be hairy. The stigmatic surface is almost hidden. The anther cap is large with a slightly rough surface. The four yellow pollinia are borne on a single, narrow stipe with a peltate foot.

CULTURE: Temperature, 60–65°F (15–18°C); light, 2400–3600 footcandles; humidity, 40–60%; media, tree fern, bark; fertilization, monthly, ratio depends on medium.

COLOR PLATE: *Lycaste skinneri*

SPECIES	FLOWERING SEASON	GENERAL LOCALE
aromatica	S	Mexico to Honduras
bradeorum	S–F	Nicaragua, Honduras, Costa Rica
barringtoniae	S–SS	Cuba, Jamaica
brevispatha	S	Costa Rica, Panama, Nicaragua
campbellii	W	Panama
ciliata	S	Peru
cochleata	S	Guatemala, Honduras
consobrina	S–SS	Mexico
crinita	SS	Mexico
cruenta	S	Mexico to Costa Rica
denningiana	W–S	Ecuador
deppei	S–F	Mexico, Guatemala
dowiana	SS	Nicaragua to Panama
fulvescens	SS	Colombia
lasioglossa	S	Guatemala, Honduras
leucantha	F–W	Costa Rica
locusta	S	Peru
longiscapa	F	Ecuador, Peru
longipetala	W–S	Venezuela, Colombia
macrobulbon	S–SS	Colombia
macrophylla	S–SS	Costa Rica to Bolivia
mesochlaena	S–SS	Peru, Ecuador
powelli	SS–F	Panama
schilleriana	S	Colombia
skinneri	F–W.	Mexico to Honduras
tricolor	S–SS	Guatemala, Costa Rica, Panama
xytriophora	S–SS	Costa Rica, Ecuador

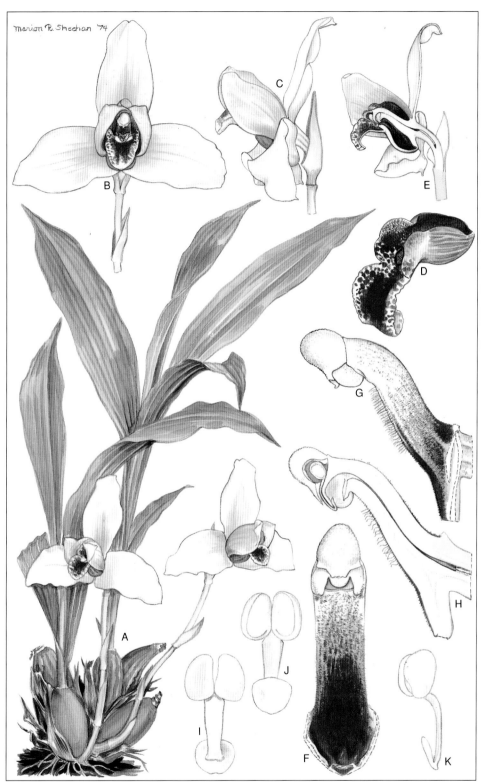

Lycaste skinneri
A: Plant in flower, × ⅜.
B: Flower, face view, × ½.
C: Flower, side view, × ½.
D: Lip, × 1.
E: Flower, vertical section, × ½.
F: Column, ventral view, × 2.
G: Column, side view, × 2.
H: Column, vertical section,
    × 2.
I, J, K: Pollinia, × 5.

225

Masdevallia

GENUS: *Masdevallia* Ruiz & Pavón (maz-deh-VAL-ee-uh)

TRIBE: Epidendreae SUBTRIBE: Pleurothallidinae

IDENTIFICATION CHARACTERISTICS: The unusual flowers and vivid colors have long made *Masdevallia* popular. Hipólito Ruiz Lopez and José Antonio Pavón founded the genus on plants obtained during an expedition to Peru in 1777. The genus was based on *M. uniflora* and named for Spanish botanist José Masdeval. *Masdevallia* was widely collected in the early 1800s, and by the mid-1800s over 50 species were known. Today more than 300 species are classified.

Vegetatively, *Masdevallia* species are very similar. Whether epiphytic or terrestrial, the plants are composed of tight clusters of leathery leaves without pseudobulbs. The short, lateral branches of these sympodial plants bear a single leaf, which usually is lanceolate to elliptical and up to 12 inches (30 cm) long. Some leaves are broadest above the base. The ramicaul (leaf stalk) may be sheathed by bracts or have small bracts at each node. Inflorescences arise from the terminal of the short ramicaul. Each inflorescence has one to three flowers.

The flowers range from less than 1 inch to 12 inches (2.5–30 cm) across. Flower color varies, with various combinations of white, red, and purple common in many flowers. The sepals are the largest and showiest portions of the flower and are usually the same color. The sepals form a tube at their bases, then flare out into three free, broad segments, many with a long, attenuated apex. The dorsal sepal is often the smallest of the three. The two petals are small, narrow, and parallel to the column. The lip is very small and varies in shape, sometimes having earlike appendages near the base. The petals and lip are often the same color, hidden in the tube formed by the sepals.

The short column, again hidden in the tube, may be winged or with a narrow margin around it. Some species have a small foot at the column base. Two yellow teardrop-shaped pollinia are found in each flower. The pollinia do not have caudicles.

CULTURE: Temperature, 50–60°F (10–15°C); light, 1800–2400 footcandles; humidity, 40–60%; media, tree fern, osmunda for epiphytes; a mixture of 1 peat moss : 1 perlite : 1 sand for terrestrials; fertilization, monthly, with a 1–1–1 ratio.

COLOR PLATE: *Masdevallia coccinea*

SPECIES	FLOWERING SEASON	GENERAL LOCALE
abbreviata	F–W	Peru
amabilis	W	Peru
attenuata	W–S	Costa Rica, Panama
barleana	S–SS	Peru
bicolor	S	Venezuela, Colombia, Ecuador, Peru, Bolivia
caloptera	SS	Colombia, Peru
carderi	SS–F	Colombia
caudata	F–W	Colombia, Venezuela, Ecuador, Peru
chestertonii	SS–F	Colombia
civilis	S–SS	Venezuela, Peru
coccinea	S	Colombia
coriacea	S–SS	Colombia
corniculata	SS–F	Colombia
davisii	S	Peru
elephanticeps	S–SS	Colombia
estradae	S	Colombia
infracta	S–SS	Brazil
macrura	W–S	Colombia
maculata	SS–F	Venezuela, Colombia
militaris	S	Colombia
mooreana	S	Colombia
peristeria	S–SS	Colombia
platyglossa	S–SS	Colombia
racemosa	S–SS–F	Colombia
radiosa	S–SS	Colombia
reichenbachiana	S–SS	Costa Rica
rosea	S–SS	Ecuador
schlimii	S	Venezuela
schroederiana	W–S	Peru
tovarensis	W	Venezuela
triangularis	SS	Venezuela, Colombia
triaristella	SS–F	Colombia, Nicaragua, Costa Rica
uniflora	S–SS	Peru
veitchiana	S–SS	Peru

Masdevallia coccinea

A: Plant in flower, × ½.
B: Flower, face view, × 1.
C: Flower, side view, × 1.
D: Petals and column, × 5.
E: Lip, × 8.
F: Flower, vertical section, × 1.
G: Column, ventral view, × 7.
H: Column, end view, × 7.
I: Column, side view, × 7.
J: Column, vertical section, × 7.
K, L: Pollinia, × 20.

Maxillaria

GENUS: *Maxillaria* Ruiz & Pavón (max-ih-LARE-ee-uh)

TRIBE: Maxillarieae   SUBTRIBE: Maxillariinae

IDENTIFICATION CHARACTERISTICS: The genus *Maxillaria* was named by Spanish botanists Hipólito Ruiz Lopez and José Antonio Pavón, based on plants they collected in Peru in 1777–1778. The generic name was derived from the Latin word *maxilla* (jawbone), since the lips and columns reminded Ruiz and Pavón of the jaws of insects. The number of species attributed to this genus is approximately 100, but some authors estimate the size at 300.

Maxillarias are sympodial epiphytes and can be classified into one of two major groups according to the arrangement of the pseudobulbs. One group contains species with short internodes on the rhizomes and tight clusters of pseudobulbs (e.g., *Maxillaria cucullata*). The contrasting group has internodes that are longer and pseudobulbs that are spread out in a chainlike arrangement (e.g., *M. tenuifolia*). Pseudobulbs are flattened, smooth, or fluted with one or more leafy bracts sheathing the bulb. Leaves vary both in number per bulb and size, but are generally dark green, leathery, and persistent. The flower scapes arise from the base of the pseudobulb and have solitary flowers. In some species, three or four scapes may arise from the same pseudobulb. Each scape is ensheathed by four or more green, leafy bracts, which often turn brown as the open flower matures.

The flowers range from 0.5 inch to over 6 inches (1–15 cm) in diameter, but all have the distinct characteristics of the genus. The three sepals are alike in size and color with the dorsal sepal perpendicular to the two lateral sepals. The two petals are much smaller than the sepals but of similar color. The petals are held close to the column. The three-lobed lip is attached to the base of the column by a small claw. The small lateral lobes of the curved lip almost touch the column. The predominant base colors are white, yellow, and red, but many flowers are overlaid with red, brown, or purple spots. Some are extremely fragrant (e.g., *Maxillaria tenuifolia*).

The short, slightly curved column is rounded at the apex and widest in the vicinity of the rostellum. Four pollinia are borne on a single, almost-round stipe; they are divided into two pairs, with one large and one small pollinium in each pair. The smaller pollinium is appressed to the larger one so that at first glance the flower appears to have only two large pollinia.

CULTURE: Temperature, 60–70°F (15–21°C); light, 2400–3600 footcandles; humidity, 40–70%; media, peat and perlite, tree fern, bark; fertilization, monthly, ratio depends on medium.

COLOR PLATE: *Maxillaria cucullata*

SPECIES	FLOWERING SEASON	GENERAL LOCALE
acuminata	SS	Colombia to Peru
camaridii	F–W–S–SS	Tropical America
crassifolia	SS	Florida, West Indies, Mexico to northern South America
cucullata	SS	Mexico, Guatemala, Costa Rica
curtipes	W–S	Mexico, Guatemala, Costa Rica
densa	S–SS	Mexico, Honduras, Guatemala, Belize
elatior	S–SS	Mexico, Guatemala, Honduras, Costa Rica
endresii	S–SS	Costa Rica
friedrichsthallii	S–SS	Central America
grandiflora	S–SS	South America
lepidota	S–SS	Venezuela to Ecuador
luteoalba	SS	Costa Rica to Ecuador
neglecta	SS	Nicaragua to Panama
nigrescens	SS	Colombia, Venezuela
reichenheimiana	SS	Costa Rica to Venezuela
sanderiana	SS	Peru, Ecuador
sanguinea	SS	Costa Rica, Panama
tenuifolia	SS	Central America
valenzuelana	SS	Tropical America
venusta	SS	Venezuela, Colombia

Maxillaria cucullata

A: Plant in flower, × ½.
B: Flower, face view, × 2.
C: Flower, side view, × 2.
D: Lip, × 6.
E: Flower, vertical section, × 3.
F: Column, ventral view, × 6.
G: Column, ventral view, anther
   cap removed, × 6.
H: Column, end view, × 6.
I: Column, side view, × 6.
J: Column, vertical section, × 6.
K, L: Pollinia, × 24.

229

Meiracyllium

GENUS: *Meiracyllium* Reichenbach f. (my-rah-SILL-ee-um)

TRIBE: Epidendreae SUBTRIBE: Meiracylliinae

IDENTIFICATION CHARACTERISTICS: Dainty, diminutive, and delightful describe this truly miniature genus of orchids. A well-grown specimen in full bloom seldom is 2 inches (5 cm) tall, because its leaves almost clasp the surface upon which the plant is growing. It is unfortunate that there are only two known species in this sympodial, epiphytic genus, and that it is not as widely cultivated as it should be. Even H. G. Reichenbach was impressed when he first identified the genus in 1864 and used the Greek word *meirakyllion* (little fellow) to describe the low, creeping habit of the plants.

The creeping rhizome, which branches rather freely, soon produces large plant clumps. The rhizomes and short lateral stems are enclosed in papery, leafy bracts. A single thick, fleshy, almost-rounded leaf tops each lateral stem. The leaves are not much more than 1 inch (2.5 cm) long and a little over half as wide. The slender inflorescence arises from the apex of the stem and bears a few bright, purplish to rose-colored flowers, each about 1 inch (2.5 cm) wide.

The flowers are delicate and seem almost a little too large for the size of the plant. The sepals and petals are similar in shape and color and are almost the same size. Most descriptions of the genus give the sepals the edge in size, but usually by only a few millimeters, so it takes a keen eye to see the difference in most cases. The lip of *M. trinasutum* is sessile, somewhat fleshy, and almost boat-shaped, but that of *M. wendlandii* is shallower.

The column is unique, and because of the beaklike rostellum, Robert Dressler set up a separate subtribe for this genus to distinguish it from the genera of Laeliinae. *Meiracyllium* has eight elongate, yellow pollinia attached to a single viscidium.

CULTURE: Temperature, 60–70°F (15–21°C); light, 2400–3600 footcandles; humidity, 40–60%; media, tree fern plaques, tree branches; fertilization, monthly, with a 1–1–1 ratio.

COLOR PLATE: *Meiracyllium trinasutum*

SPECIES	FLOWERING SEASON	GENERAL LOCALE
trinasutum	S	Mexico, Guatemala
wendlandii	S	Mexico, Guatemala

Meiracyllium trinasutum
A: Plant in flower, ×2.
B: Flower, face view, ×3.
C: Flower, side view, ×3.
D: Lip, ×5.
E: Flower, vertical section, ×3.
F: Column, ventral view, ×10.
G: Column, end view, ×10.
H: Column, side view, ×10.
I: Column, vertical section, ×10.
J, K, L: Pollinia, ×20.

Mendoncella

GENUS: *Mendoncella* A. D. Hawkes (men-don-SELL-uh)

TRIBE: Maxillarieae   SUBTRIBE: Zygopetalinae

IDENTIFICATION CHARACTERISTICS: *Mendoncella*, with its unique, showy flowers, is deserving of much greater recognition among orchid growers. This relatively new genus, formerly *Galeottia*, consists of 11 species and was formed by Alex Hawkes in 1963. Hawkes's studies indicated that Franz J. Ruprecht named a grass *Galeottia* one year before Achille Richard named an orchid by the same name and thus Richard's name was invalid. In 1973, Leslie Garay did some further uniting to make *Mendoncella* a more coherent genus. Alec Pridgeon (1993) included *Galeottia* as a valid genus, thus these plants can be found listed under both generic names. The genus *Mendoncella* was named by Hawkes in honor of Luys de Mendonca e Silva, founder and editor of the Brazilian orchid publication *Orquidea*.

These robust, sympodial epiphytes form tight clusters of ovoid, ribbed pseudobulbs, up to 3 inches (7.5 cm) long and 1 inch (2.5 cm) in diameter. Each pseudobulb is topped by two or three soft, pleated leaves up to 18 inches (45 cm) long and 3 inches (7.5 cm) wide. The new growth is protected by large, leafy, green sheaths that turn brown as the pseudobulbs mature. The inflorescences, which emerge while the new growth develops, may be up to 12 inches (30 cm) tall and bear a few to eight flowers.

Almost 3.5 inches (8 cm) across, the long-lived flowers are basically yellowish green with brown, maroon, or red marks. The sepals and petals are alike in size, shape, and color, but the lateral sepals have more undulations. The complex, three-lobed lip has a toothed or fimbriate margin and a distinct keel at the base. The midlobe is often reflexed.

The column is an interesting structure. It has a small, spurlike projection near the base. The apex is almost enshrouded by small, winglike appendages that partially obscure the anther cap. Four creamy-yellow pollinia of two distinct sizes are borne on an unusual, shield-shaped stipe.

CULTURE: Temperature, 55–60°F (12–15°C); light, 2400–3600 footcandles; humidity, 40–60%; media, tree fern, peat and perlite; fertilization, monthly, with a 1–1–1 ratio.

COLOR PLATE: *Mendoncella fimbriata*

SPECIES	FLOWERING SEASON	GENERAL LOCALE
burkei	S–SS	Venezuela to Amazonas
fimbriata	S–SS	Colombia, Venezuela
grandiflora	S–SS	Mexico to Costa Rica
jorisiana	S–SS	Venezuela

Mendoncella fimbriata

A: Plant in flower, × ⅓.
B: Flower, face view, × ¾.
C: Flower, side view, × ¾.
D: Lip, face view, × 1.
E: Lip, side view, × 1.
F: Flower, vertical section, × ¾.
G: Column, ventral view, × 2.
H: Column, side view, × 2.
I: Column, vertical section, × 2.
J, K, L: Pollinia, × 5.

233

Mexicoa

GENUS: *Mexicoa* Garay (mex-ee-KOH-uh)
TRIBE: Maxillarieae   SUBTRIBE: Oncidiinae
IDENTIFICATION CHARACTERISTICS: There are many ways to describe *Mexicoa ghiesbrechtiana*, an elegant miniature, but Rebecca Northen (*American Orchid Society Bulletin*, vol. 49, July 1980, p. 746) summed it up best: "What more can you ask of any species than to give a multitude of perky, brightly colored flowers to delight the eye for almost half a year each year." This species, which was first collected by Belgian geologist and botanical patron M. Ghiesbrecht in Mexico, was assigned to the genus *Oncidium* in 1845 by Achille Richard and Henri Galeotti, who honored the collector in the species epithet. It was known as an *Oncidium* species until 1974 when Leslie A. Garay noted the porrect petals and variations in column structure. He removed the species into its own monotypic genus, which he named *Mexicoa* after the home of the species, retaining the specific name *ghiesbrechtiana* (spelled *ghiesbreghtiana* in some texts). Not all taxonomists accept Garay's separation.

Vegetatively, these sympodial epiphytes are miniatures because even a well-grown plant seldom reaches 6 inches (15 cm) high. Each compressed, slightly ridged, ovoid pseudobulb is about 1 to 1.25 inches (2.5–3 cm) high, 1 inch (2.5 cm) in diameter, and topped by two or three leaves. The leathery leaves are narrow, lance-shaped, and up to 4.5 to 5 (10–12 cm) long and about 0.5 inch (1 cm) wide. The few-flowered inflorescence arises as the new growth is developing and bears up to six colorful flowers.

The flowers appear to be waxy and are 1 inch (2.5 cm) wide and usually slightly longer. The base color is yellow with various amounts of red to rosy-red coloration on the sepals and petals. The sepals and petals are very similar in size, shape, and color, with the two petals bending slightly forward. The petals often are pointed at the apex. The lip, the largest and brightest colored segment of the flower, is clear yellow with an orange crest. At first glance, the lip appears four-lobed because the median lobe is divided at the apex.

The curved column is slender and has a very pronounced yellow projection at the base. The almost-purplish base of the stipe looks like an eye protruding over the stigmatic surface. Two yellow pollinia are borne on a relatively long, narrow stipe.

CULTURE: Temperature, 50–60°F (10–15°C); light, 2400–3600 footcandles; humidity, 40–60%; media, tree fern plaques, cork bark; fertilization, monthly, with a 1–1–1 ratio.

COLOR PLATE: *Mexicoa ghiesbrechtiana*

SPECIES	FLOWERING SEASON	GENERAL LOCALE
ghiesbrechtiana	S–SS	Mexico

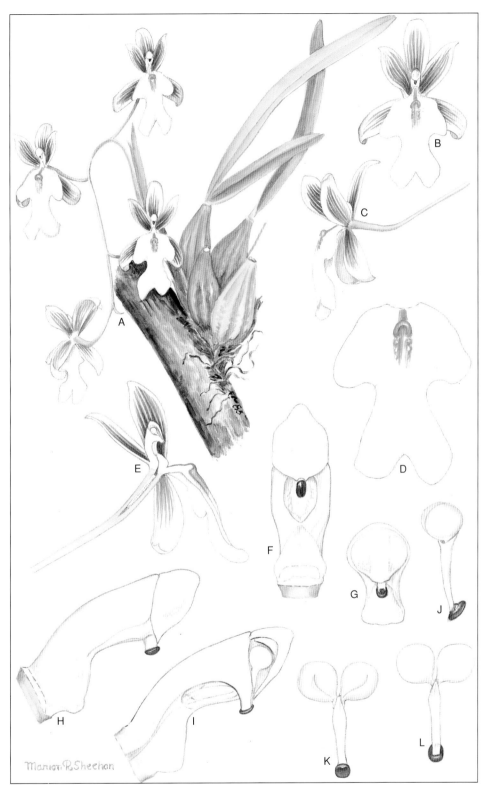

Mexicoa ghiesbrechtiana
A: Plant in flower, × 1.
B: Flower, face view, × 1½.
C: Flower, side view, × 1½.
D: Lip, × 3.
E: Flower, vertical section, × 2.
F: Column, ventral view, × 8.
G: Column, end view, × 8.
H: Column, side view, × 8.
I: Column, vertical section, × 8.
J, K, L: Pollinia, × 15.

235

Miltonia

GENUS: *Miltonia* Lindley (mill-TONE-ee-uh)
TRIBE: Maxillarieae   SUBTRIBE: Oncidiinae
IDENTIFICATION CHARACTERISTICS: In 1976, G. C. K. Dunsterville and Leslie Garay reviewed the genus *Miltonia* originally established by John Lindley in 1838 to honor Earl Fitz Williams, then Viscount Milton. They concluded that the work of Alexandre Godefroy-Lebeuf in 1899 was valid and that most of the Andean *Miltonia* species belonged in *Miltoniopsis* while the Brazilian species should remain in *Miltonia*. The four species now recognized as belonging to *Miltonia* have two light green leaves per pseudobulb and ears on the column, while *Miltoniopsis* has only one blue-green leaf per pseudobulb. *Miltonia* resembles and is closely related to *Oncidium* and *Odontoglossum*.

These sympodial epiphytes have a climbing, scaly rhizome with the pseudobulbs often spaced 1 to 1.5 inches (2.5–4 cm) apart. The flattened pseudobulbs, 3 to 4 inches (7.5–10 cm) tall, have two lancelike, light green to yellowish green leaves, up to 7 inches (17.5 cm) long at their apex. The leaves are folded at the base. The inflorescences, clothed with leafy bracts, arise from the base of the most recently matured pseudobulb and bear from one to many open flowers at a time.

The flowers are 3 inches (7.5 cm) wide. The basic flower colors are white, purple, and yellow. The three sepals and two petals are alike in size, shape, and color. In some species, the margins are reflexed. The apices are either blunt or pointed. The lip is the showiest portion of the flower having a very broad, almost-flat midlobe.

Differences in the column separate this genus from closely related genera. The column is short with two distinct, earlike appendages near the stigmatic surface; it is erect, is often at a right angle to the midlobe of the lip, and is terminated by a distinct anther cap. The lip is attached to the base of the column. Two light yellow pollinia are borne on a single broad stipe with a small foot.

CULTURE: Temperature, 60°F (15°C); light, 2400–3600 footcandles; humidity, 40–60%; media, tree fern, bark; fertilization, monthly, ratio depends on medium.

COLOR PLATE: *Miltonia spectabilis* var. *moreliana*

SPECIES	FLOWERING SEASON	GENERAL LOCALE
clowesii	SS–F	Brazil
flavescens	S	Brazil
regnellii	SS–F	Brazil
spectabilis	SS–F	Brazil

Miltonia spectabilis var.
moreliana
A: Plant in flower, × ½.
B: Flower, face view, × ½.
C: Flower, side view, × ½.
D: Lip, × 1.
E: Flower, vertical section, × 1.
F: Column, ventral view, × 3.
G: Column, end view, × 3.
H: Column, side view, × 3.
I: Column, vertical section, × 3.
J, K, L: Pollinia, × 6.

237

Miltoniopsis

GENUS: *Miltoniopsis* Godefroy-Lebeuf (mil-toh-nee-OPP-siss)

TRIBE: Maxillarieae   SUBTRIBE: Oncidiinae

IDENTIFICATION CHARACTERISTICS: The large flat, attractive flowers of *Miltoniopsis* were first recognized as being distinctive and worthy of generic recognition by Alexandre Godefroy-Lebeuf in 1889, when he described *M. vexillaria*. Godefroy-Lebeuf called the genus *Miltoniopsis* because of its close resemblance to *Miltonia*. Unfortunately, most botanists did not support the distinction between the two genera and continued to lump the four species of *Miltoniopsis* with *Miltonia*. In 1976 G. C. K. Dunsterville and Leslie Garay revisited the genus while describing a fifth member, *Miltoniopsis santanae*, and reestablished the genus.

Miltoniopsis species differ from *Miltonia* species in that they have only one leaf at the apex of the pseudobulb, the pseudobulbs are tightly clustered, and the columns lack the earlike appendages found in *Miltonia*. The five species now recognized in the genus *Miltoniopsis* range from Costa Rica to Ecuador and Venezuela. The genus is closely related to *Brassia*, *Oncidium*, and *Odontoglossum*, and the four genera are often hard to distinguish vegetatively, although there is no confusion when they flower.

Vegetatively, these sympodial, epiphytic, sometimes lithophytic plants have flattened pseudobulbs that form dense clumps. Each pseudobulb is topped by one linear leaf, up to 15 inches (38 cm) long, and subtended by several leaf-bearing distichous sheathes. The soft, mostly pale green leaves are usually less than 0.75 inch (2 cm) wide. The inflorescence arises from the base of the pseudobulb or lower leaf axils. The erect inflorescence, up to 15 inches (38 cm) long, bears from one to five showy 2-inch (5-cm) wide flowers. The base color is white with red or pink blotches.

The flowers are basically flat and pansylike, with the two lateral sepals borne at right angles to the dorsal sepal. The sepals and petals are alike in size and shape, although the two petals may be slightly broader or of a different color. The large flat lip is eared at the base and united to the base of the column. The small callus on the lip is either three-ribbed or three-toothed.

The column is short, lacks wings, and terminates in a pronounced anther cap. The stigmatic surface is large for the column size. Two somewhat-elliptical yellow pollinia are borne on a single short, curved stipe attached to an almost-shield-shaped foot.

CULTURE: Temperature, 50–60°F (10–15°C); light, 2400–3600 footcandles; humidity, 40–60%; media, fir bark, peat and perlite, sphagnum moss; fertilization, monthly, ratio depends on medium.

COLOR PLATE: *Miltoniopsis roezlii*

SPECIES	FLOWERING SEASON	GENERAL LOCALE
phalaenopsis	S–SS–F	Colombia
roezlii	S–SS–F	Panama, Colombia
santanae	S–SS–F	Venezuela, Colombia, Ecuador
vexillaria	S–SS	Colombia, Northern Ecuador
warscewiczii	S–SS–F	Costa Rica, Panama, Colombia, Ecuador, Peru

Miltoniopsis roezlii
A: Plant in flower, × ½.
B: Flower, face view, × 1.
C: Flower, side view, × 1.
D: Lip, face view, × 1.
E: Flower, vertical section, × 1.
F: Column, ventral view, × 4.
G: Column, end view, × 4.
H: Column, side view, × 4.
I: Column, vertical section, × 4.
J, K, L: Pollinia, × 8.

Mormodes

GENUS: *Mormodes* Lindley (mor-MOH-dees)
TRIBE: Cymbidieae   SUBTRIBE: Catasetinae
IDENTIFICATION CHARACTERISTICS: The fanciful flowers of this genus were somewhat of a puzzle to John Lindley when he first saw a plant in flower in 1836. He was amazed by their "astonishing deviations from ordinary structures" (Veitch 1894), undoubtedly referring to the unusual twists in the column and lip. The uniqueness of the flowers was so impressive that Lindley coined the generic name from the Greek word *mormo* (phantom, frightful object). Approximately 35 species with these most interesting flowers are known today. *Mormodes* is very closely related to *Catasetum* and *Cycnoches*. The three genera are very difficult to separate when not in flower, but once in flower they fall into very distinct groups.

These sympodial, deciduous epiphytes have their pseudobulbs arranged in tight clusters. Each pseudobulb, whether cylindrical or spindle-shaped, may be up to 15 inches (38 cm) tall and 2 inches (5 cm) in diameter. As the pseudobulb matures it produces 6 to 15 soft leaves up to 24 inches (60 cm) long that last less than one year. The old pseudobulbs are covered with tan, papery bracts. The short, usually erect inflorescences arise from just below the middle of the pseudobulb. Each inflorescence bears up to 12 flowers.

The fragrant, colorful, 2-inch (5-cm) wide flowers are often greatly speckled or spotted. They are fascinating. The three sepals and two petals are alike in size, shape, and color. The dorsal sepal and two petals often form a hood over the column and lip. The large, flaring lip is always twisted to one side and may be almost round (if straightened out) or pointed at the apex.

The short column, which is easily recognized by its twisted appearance, varies little in width, being slightly wider near the anther cap. The two pollinia are borne on a unique, sculptured stipe.

CULTURE: Temperature, 60°F (15°C); light, 2400–3600 footcandles; humidity, 40–60%; media, tree fern, peat and perlite, bark; fertilization, monthly, ratio depends on medium.

COLOR PLATE: *Mormodes rolfeanum*

SPECIES	FLOWERING SEASON	GENERAL LOCALE
atropurpureum	W	Costa Rica to Colombia
colossus	S	Costa Rica, Panama
hookeri	W	Costa Rica, Panama
maculatum	F–W	Mexico
rolfeanum	W	Peru

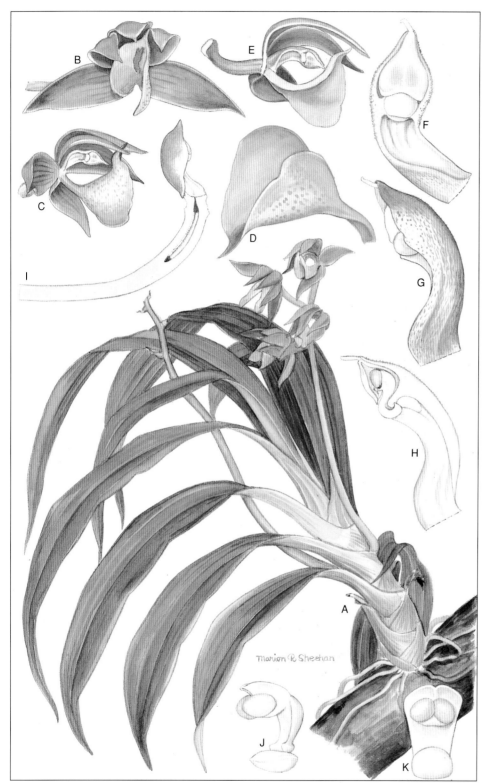

Mormodes rolfeanum
A: Plant in flower, × ½.
B: Flower, face view, × 1.
C: Flower, side view, × 1.
D: Lip, × 2.
E: Flower, cut away to show
   column, × 1.
F: Column, ventral view, × 3.
G: Column, side view, × 3.
H: Column, vertical section, × 3.
I: Ovary, vertical section, × 1½.
J, K: Pollinia, × 5.

Marion R Sheehan

Mormolyca

GENUS: *Mormolyca* Fenzl (more-moh-LYE-kuh)
TRIBE: Maxillarieae SUBTRIBE: Maxillariinae
IDENTIFICATION CHARACTERISTICS: Orchid hobbyists are always looking for orchid plants that are a little different to add more spice and charm to their collections. *Mormolyca* is one such oddity. According to some authors, the uniquely shaped and colored flowers of this genus are "odd rather than attractive" (Hawkes 1965) and have a "grotesque appearance" (Bechtel et al. 1992). When Eduard Fenzl first described the genus in 1850, he derived the generic name from the Greek word *mormolyca* (hobgoblin), undoubtedly referring to the unusual coloration and bizarre appearance of the flowers when viewed from the side.

Despite all the negative adjectives used to describe its appearance, this small genus of up to six species is worthy of inclusion in a collection. The plants do well in cultivation, providing interesting, colorful flowers to enjoy. This genus is closely related to *Maxillaria* and *Trigonidium*, but is taxonomically different from the former in the viscidium and inflorescence and from the latter by the absence of a sepaline tube.

Vegetatively, the sympodial, epiphytic species of this genus are very similar. The tightly clustered, generally ellipsoid pseudobulbs often form dense clumps. Each pseudobulb is topped by one leaf and subtended by one or more persistent leafy bracts. The linear to narrowly lanceolate, almost-leathery leaves are up to 14 inches (35 cm) long and 1.5 inches (4 cm) wide. The single-flowered inflorescences arise from the base of the pseudobulb.

The basic flower color is creamy yellow, highlighted with lavender or maroon lines on the sepals and petals and with some lips almost purple or maroon. The 0.5-inch (1-cm) wide flowers are by far the most interesting aspect of the plants. Overall, the sepals and petals are very much alike in size, shape, and color. The two petals are often slightly curved; with the dorsal sepal, they form a shallow hood. The lateral sepals are also slightly curved, especially in *Mormolyca ringens*, giving a bowlegged look. The three-lobed lip (lateral lobes are minute), which is often erect and lies parallel to the column, is usually the most colorful part of the flower.

The short, erect column tapers slightly near the apex and has a very small stigmatic surface. The four yellow pollinia, two of which are diminutive, are borne on an almost-wishbone-shaped stipe.

CULTURE: Temperature, 60–65°F (15–18°C); light, 2400–3600 footcandles; humidity, 40–60%; media, tree fern plaques, cork bark, peat and perlite; fertilization, monthly, ratio depends on medium.

COLOR PLATE: *Mormolyca ringens*

SPECIES	FLOWERING SEASON	GENERAL LOCALE
gracilipes	S	Colombia, Ecuador, Peru
peruviana	W	Peru
ringens	S–SS	Mexico to Costa Rica

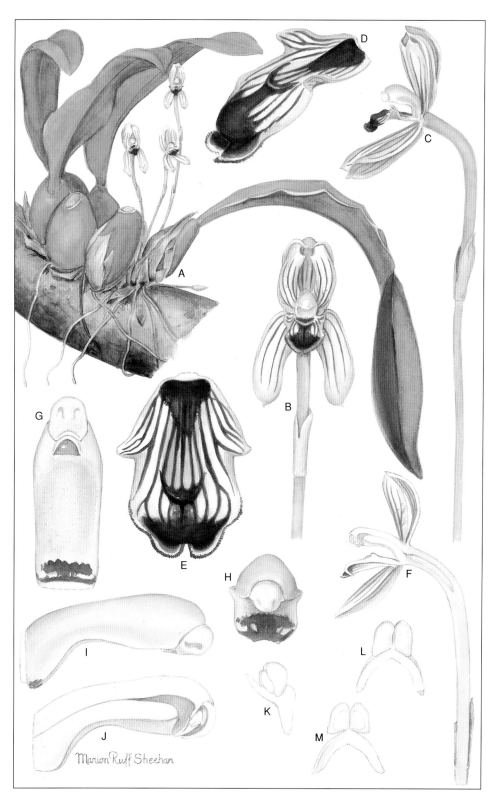

Mormolyca ringens

A: Plant in flower, × ½.
B: Flower, face view, × 2.
C: Flower, side view, × 2.
D: Lip, three-quarter view, × 6.
E: Lip, top view, × 6.
F: Flower, vertical section, × 2.
G: Column, ventral view, × 6.
H: Column, end view, × 6.
I: Column, side view, × 6.
J: Column, vertical section, × 6.
K, L, M: Pollinia, × 10.

Marion Ruff Sheehan

243

Nageliella

GENUS: *Nageliella* L. O. Williams (nah-gell-ee-ELL-uh)

TRIBE: Epidendreae   SUBTRIBE: Laeliinae

IDENTIFICATION CHARACTERISTICS: *Nageliella* is a very small genus of diminutive, easy-to-grow plants that produce an array of delicate flowers over several months. Originally known as (and still sometimes sold as) *Hartwegia*, the generic name was changed in 1940 by Louis O. Williams because *Hartwegia* had been used earlier for a genus in the lily family so was misnamed by John Lindley. Williams chose *Nageliella* to honor Otto Nagel, a much-traveled botanist who collected orchids in Mexico. Today, most taxonomists feel there are at least two species and possibly more in the genus.

These sympodial epiphytes are characterized by very similar vegetative features. The thick, fleshy, stiff leaves, up to 4 inches (10 cm) long, are borne on short, thin, slightly ridged stems (ramicauls). Almost lanceolate in shape, the leaves are variegated with dark green spots on a lighter green base. Sometimes the long-lived leaves have purplish marks. The thin, wiry inflorescence arises from the apex of the leaf-bearing stem and may be up to 18 inches (45 cm) long. Each inflorescence bears ten or more flowers clustered at the end of the stem, with usually only one or two flowers open at a time. The flowers open in succession, with each inflorescence in flower for several weeks. After the terminal flower cluster finishes blooming, a lateral inflorescence may develop on the same flower stem, thus prolonging the bloom period.

The 0.5-inch (1-cm) wide pinkish lavender flowers are similar among the species but vary in degrees of opening; *Nageliella angustifolia*, for example, opens fully, whereas *N. purpurea* opens only partially. The sepals are larger than the petals, with the petals a little more pointed on some species (see B on color plate). The lips also vary, with some more bulging at the base (A), and may be almost flat or with inrolled margins (B).

The small purplish column is slightly winged near the stigmatic area. It may or may not be rounded above. Four yellow pollinia are present, each with its own light yellow caudicle.

CULTURE: Temperature, 60°F (15°C); light, 2400–3600 footcandles; humidity, 40–60%; media, tree fern plaques, cork bark; fertilization, monthly, with a 1–1–1 ratio.

COLOR PLATE: *Nageliella purpurea* and *N. gemma*

SPECIES	FLOWERING SEASON	GENERAL LOCALE
angustifolia	SS	Guatemala
gemma	S–SS	Central America
purpurea	SS	Mexico to Nicaragua

244

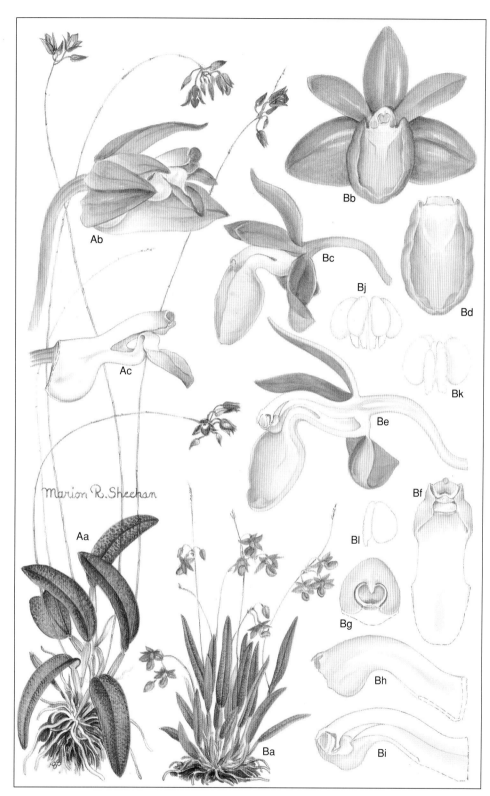

Nageliella purpurea
Aa: Plant in flower, × ½.
Ab: Flower, three-quarter view,
  × 4.
Ac: Column and lip, side view,
  × 4.

Nageliella gemma
Ba: Plant in flower, × ½.
Bb: Flower, face view, × 4.
Bc: Flower, side view, × 4.
Bd: Lip, face view, × 5.
Be: Flower, vertical section, × 5.
Bf: Column, ventral view, × 8.
Bg: Column, end view, × 8.
Bh: Column, side view, × 8.
Bi: Column, vertical section,
  × 8.
Bj, Bk, Bl: Pollinia, × 20.

245

Neobenthamia

GENUS: *Neobenthamia* Rolfe (nee-oh-ben-THAME-ee-uh)

TRIBE: Epidendreae SUBTRIBE: Polystachyinae

IDENTIFICATION CHARACTERISTICS: Clusters of long-lived, snowy white flowers atop each cane are the hallmark of this lovely African terrestrial orchid. Growing in its native habitat amid tall grasses, individual canes attain heights of 6 feet (180 cm). A plant isolated in a pot, however, produces tall canes that are weak and tend to sprawl or even break. This lax, untidy habit is one reason the species is not as popular as it should be. Grown cool (50–55°F [10–12°C]) in winter with bright light, new growths will be less than 2 feet (60 cm) tall but will flower well in summer.

The genus has but one known species and is closely related to *Polystachya* but differs slightly in floral characteristics. Robert Allen Rolfe described the genus in 1891, naming it in honor of George Bentham. Because Bentham already had been so honored, Rolfe added the *Neo-* (new) to designate it as the new Bentham genus.

The tall, straggly canes of this sympodial orchid have alternate leaves that are long, soft, and clasping. The leaves may have blades to 10 inches (25 cm) long and less than 1 inch (2.5 cm) wide, making them appear almost-grasslike. The bracted inflorescence arises from the top of each cane and forms round to almost-flat clusters of 25 or more dainty, waxy, white flowers with small red-to-magenta spots on the lips.

The 0.5-inch (1-cm) wide flowers of *Neobenthamia gracilis*, although not showy individually, compensate by the large number of flowers produced on each inflorescence. The white sepals and petals are almost equal in size. The petals, however, are tapered at the base and tend to be more recurved at the apex. There may be scattered hairs on both surfaces of the sepals and petals. The lip is the most colorful floral segment. It has a yellow mark in the center beneath the column and reddish dots on either side. The lines of reddish spots stop at the point where the apex of the lip recurves. The lip also is slightly pubescent.

The smooth, short column has a relatively large stigmatic area. The anther cap is almost helmet-shaped. Most anther caps are white with a maroon rim; the entire cap of the plant we examined was maroon. Pollinia are borne on a very short stipe with a distinct viscidium; in the plant we examined, the pollinia were the same color as the anther cap.

CULTURE: Temperature, 50–55°F (10–12°C) winter; light, 3600 footcandles; humidity, 80%; medium, acid organic; fertilization, weekly with a 1–1–1 ratio.

COLOR PLATE: *Neobenthamia gracilis*

SPECIES	FLOWERING SEASON	GENERAL LOCALE
gracilis	S–SS	Tanzania, Zanzibar

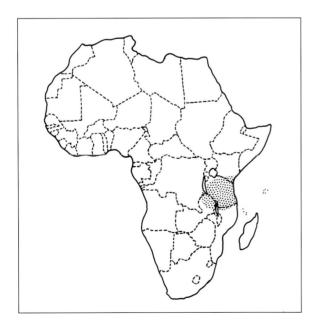

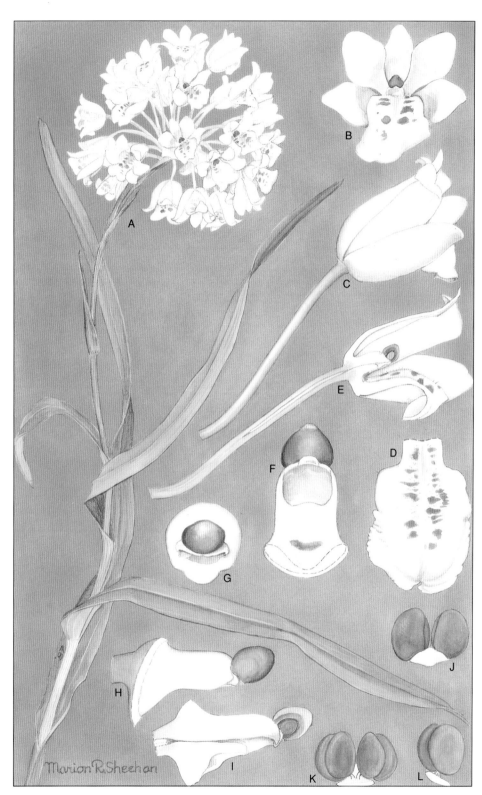

Neobenthamia gracilis
A: Plant in flower, × 1.
B: Flower, face view, × 3.
C: Flower, side view, × 3.
D: Lip, face view, × 4.
E: Flower, vertical section, × 4.
F: Column, ventral view, × 8.
G: Column, end view, × 8.
H: Column, side view, × 8.
I: Column, vertical section, × 8.
J, K, L: Pollinia, × 20.

Neofinetia

GENUS: *Neofinetia* Hu (nee-oh-fin-NET-ee-uh)
TRIBE: Vandeae SUBTRIBE: Aeridinae
IDENTIFICATION CHARACTERISTICS: There is only one species in this miniature genus, but it is a charming one: *Neofinetia falcata*. Its showy, white, long-spurred flowers are borne in great abundance on well-grown plants. A miniature species, it is ideal for growing in small, decorative Japanese pots. The genus was first discovered in 1784, but was given its present name by Professor Hu in 1925. The generic name *Neofinetia* was coined to honor the French botanist M. A. Finet, who worked with the orchids of China and Japan. Since Rudolf Schlechter had already named a genus for Finet in 1918, Hu added the prefix *Neo-* (new) to designate it as the new Finet genus.

Vegetatively, these monopodial epiphytes resemble vandas in miniature. They branch freely just above the base of the stem, soon forming dense clumps. Each stem is only 2 to 3 inches (5–7.5 cm) high and is hidden by the clasping leaves. The leaves, often gently curving and keeled, are up to 3 inches (7.5 cm) long, with four to eight leaves clasping the average stem. The inflorescences arise from the lower leaf axils and bear a few white flowers 1 to 1.5 inches (2.5–4 cm) wide during summer and fall. Although the inflorescences are short in length, the flowers stand above the leaves, showing off their airy delicacy.

The crystalline-white flowers of *Neofinetia falcata* are refreshingly fragrant in the evening. Although small in stature and resembling flowers of *Angraecum* in some aspects, flowers of *Neofinetia* are showy. The sepals and petals are similar in size, shape, and color. The margins of these segments are often wavy and their apices recurved. The lip is three-lobed, with two erect lateral lobes and a strap-like midlobe. A large, gently curving, 2-inch (5-cm) long spur projects from the base of the midlobe. The lip often appears to be shorter than it is because the midlobe is recurved.

The white, winged column of *Neofinetia falcata* is small, short, and fleshy, with a relatively large stigmatic area near the apex. The two rounded, yellow pollinia are borne on an interestingly footed stipe.

CULTURE: Temperature, 60–70°F (15–21°C); light, 2400–3600 footcandles; humidity, 40–60%; media, tree fern, bark, peat and perlite; fertilization, monthly, ratio depends on medium.

COLOR PLATE: *Neofinetia falcata*

SPECIES	FLOWERING SEASON	GENERAL LOCALE
falcata	SS–F	Japan, Korea, Ryukyu Islands

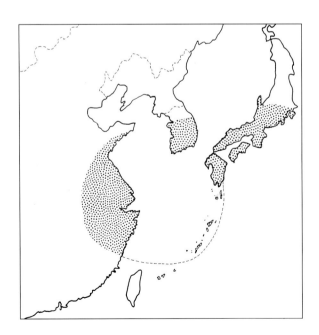

Neofinetia falcata
A: Plant in flower, × 1.
B: Flower, face view, × 2.
C: Flower, side view, × 2.
D: Lip, × 2.
E: Flower, vertical section, × 2.
F: Column, ventral view, × 9.
G: Column, end view, × 9.
H: Column, side view, × 9.
I: Column, vertical section, × 9.
J, K, L: Pollinia, × 12.

249

*Neomoorea*_____

GENUS: *Neomoorea* Rolfe (nee-oh-MOOR-ee-uh)
TRIBE: Maxillarieae SUBTRIBE: Lycastinae
IDENTIFICATION CHARACTERISTICS: When not in flower, *Neomoorea wallisii* at first glance looks like a palm seedling rather than an orchid, but closer examination verifies the presence of a pseudobulb, confirming immediately that this species is an orchid. The genus *Neomoorea*, which has only a single species, was originally described by Robert Rolfe in 1890 as *Moorea*. After discovering in 1904 that *Moorea* had already been used as a generic name, Rolfe changed the name to *Neomoorea*, the new *Moorea*. In this way Rolfe was still able to honor F. W. Moore, curator of Glasnevin Botanical Gardens, Dublin, Ireland, who first flowered this species in a greenhouse, and whose plant became the type specimen for the genus. The unusual characteristics of the lip separate this genus from other members of the tribe (e.g., *Lycaste*).

Vegetatively, this sympodial, sometimes epiphytic, sometimes terrestrial species is very distinctive. The almost-egg-shaped, furrowed pseudobulbs, often light green in color, can be up to 5 inches (12.5 cm) high and are topped by two often massive leaves. Each soft, pleated leaf may be up to 3 feet (90 cm) long and 6 inches (15 cm) wide. The erect inflorescence arises from the base of the pseudobulb and ranges up to 2 feet (60 cm) tall, bearing up to 20 flowers.

The flowers, around 2.5 inches (6 cm) across, are basically tan or brownish red (brick red) in color, fading to almost white in the center of the flower. The sepals and petals are alike in size, shape, and color, with the sepals a little more cup-shaped. The three-lobed lip is unique, having two large, broad lobes comprising the major portion of the lip. The smaller midlobe is very narrow and lance-shaped on the outer two-thirds, and terminates in a sharp point.

The short column, which is slightly curved and has a relatively small stigmatic surface, is broadest near the short, wide foot. There are four yellow pollinia, in two pairs of unequal size. All four pollinia are attached to a single stipe.

CULTURE: Temperature, 60–65°F (15–18°C); light, 2400–3600 footcandles; humidity, 40–60%; media, bark, tree fern, peat and perlite; fertilization, monthly, ratio depends on medium.

COLOR PLATE: *Neomoorea wallisii*

SPECIES	FLOWERING SEASON	GENERAL LOCALE
wallisii	S	Colombia, Panama

Neomoorea wallisii
A: Plant in flower, × ⅓.
B: Flower, face view, × 1.
C: Flower, side view, × 1.
D: Lip, × 2.
E: Flower, vertical section, × 1½.
F: Column, ventral view, × 4.
G: Column, end view, × 4.
H: Column, side view, × 4.
I: Column, vertical section, × 4.
J, K, L: Pollinia, × 8.

Notylia

GENUS: *Notylia* Lindley (no-TILL-ee-uh)
TRIBE: Maxillarieae   SUBTRIBE: Oncidiinae

IDENTIFICATION CHARACTERISTICS: *Notylia* is a captivating genus of some 40 species of miniature orchids that more than make up for their size with their abundant sprays of many delicate, diminutive flowers. The genus was first described in 1825 by John Lindley, who was so impressed by the unusual arrangement of the column in these flowers that he combined the Greek words *noton* (back) and *tylon* (hump) to form the generic name *Notylia*.

This sympodial, epiphytic genus can be divided into two distinct groups according to vegetative characteristics. One group (e.g., *Notylia barkeri*) has small pseudobulbs with single, flat leaves, while the other group has equitant leaves. The latter usually clasp a very small, short, recognizable pseudobulb. The somewhat-leathery leaves grow up to 6 inches (15 cm) long and range in color from vivid green to dark red depending on the species. The pendent inflorescences, which arise from the axils of the leaves, are from 1 to 4 inches (2.5–10 cm) long and bear from two to one hundred flowers, again depending on the species.

The flowers range in size from 0.1 to 0.3 inch (2–8 mm) in diameter. The basic flower color is white, but species with violet flowers or yellow- or purple-spotted flowers are available. The sepals in many species are slightly larger than the petals, and the two lateral sepals may be fused, in some cases almost to the apex, giving the appearance of only two sepals per flower. The color of the sepals and petals is usually the same, but some petals are marked with one or more dots. The three-lobed lip, which is typically spade-shaped, may be slightly concave near the tip of the midlobe.

The column and anther cap arrangement are unusual and interesting. The small column is narrowest near the middle but appears to be almost-straight-sided. The large anther cap hides the pair of slightly compressed yellow pollinia, borne on a long, slender stipe with a small viscidium at the base.

CULTURE: Temperature, 60°F (15°C); light, 2400–3600 footcandles; humidity, 40–60%; medium, tree fern plaques; fertilization, monthly, with a 1–1–1 ratio.

COLOR PLATE: *Notylia barkeri*

SPECIES	FLOWERING SEASON	GENERAL LOCALE
barkeri	S	Mexico to Panama
bicolor	S–SS–F	Mexico to Costa Rica
carnosiflora	S–SS	Peru
platyglossa	S–SS	Venezuela
punctata	S–SS	Trinidad, Venezuela

Notylia barkeri

A: Plant in flower, × ½.
B: Flower, face view, × 5.
C: Flower, side view, × 5.
D: Lip, three-quarter view, × 10.
E: Lip, face view, × 10.
F: Flower, vertical section, × 7.
G: Column, ventral view, × 12.
H: Column, end view, × 12.
I: Column, anther cap removed, × 12.
J: Anther cap, × 12.
K: Column, side view, × 12.
L: Column, vertical section, × 12.
M, N, O: Pollinia, × 20.

Odontoglossum

GENUS: *Odontoglossum* Humboldt, Bonpland, & Kunth (oh-dont-oh-GLOSS-um)

TRIBE: Maxillarieae   SUBTRIBE: Oncidiinae

IDENTIFICATION CHARACTERISTICS: The lofty, cool-growing *Odontoglossum* species with their crisp flowers have long been favorites of temperate-zone orchidists. Revisions of the genus by taxonomists have reduced the number of species to around 150, but the number varies depending on whether "splits" such as *Rossioglossum* are accepted. *Odontoglossum* was first described in 1815 from plants collected in Peru. Alexander von Humboldt and his co-workers derived the generic name from the Greek words *odonto* (tooth) and *glossa* (tongue), undoubtedly referring to the toothlike projection on the callus of the lip.

Vegetatively, the sympodial, epiphytic species of this genus are very similar, with ovoid, flattened pseudobulbs generally borne in tight clusters that completely obscure the rhizome. As each new pseudobulb develops, it has four to six leaves, the lower ones clasping the pseudobulb. These lower leaves are short-lived and die off, leaving only one to three leaves attached to the apex of the pseudobulb. The linear-to-lanceolate leaves, often folded, are either soft or leathery. The inflorescences arise from the base of the pseudobulb and bear up to 24 flowers.

The dominant flower colors are white, brown, and yellow. The sepals and petals are alike in shape and color. In some species the petals are larger than the sepals (e.g., *Odontoglossum crispum*) or may have more wavy and toothlike margins (e.g., *O. luteopurpureum*). The entire to three-lobed lip has a distinct, toothed callus on the midlobe under the column. The base of the lip is adnate to the column or parallel to it.

The column is very short and white or often the same color as the base color of the flowers. There are two pronounced, winglike appendages just behind the anther cap. Two light yellow pollinia are attached to a single stipe with a small viscid foot.

CULTURE: Temperature, 50–55°F (10–12°C); light, 2400–3600 footcandles; humidity, 40–60%; media, tree fern, fir bark, peat and perlite; fertilization, monthly, ratio depends on medium.

COLOR PLATE: *Odontoglossum crispum*

SPECIES	FLOWERING SEASON	GENERAL LOCALE
cirrhosum	S	Southern Colombia, Ecuador, Peru
constrictum	F–W	Venezuela, Colombia, Ecuador
crispum	F–W	Colombia
hallii	S–SS	Ecuador
lindenii	F	Venezuela, Colombia, Ecuador
lindleyanum	S–F	Venezuela, Colombia, Ecuador
luteopurpureum	S–SS	Colombia
odoratum	S	Venezuela, Colombia
ramosissimum	S	Venezuela, Colombia, Ecuador

Odontoglossum crispum
A: Plant in flower, × ½.
B: Flower, face view, × 1.
C: Flower, side view, × 1.
D: Lip, × 2.
E: Flower, vertical section, × 2.
F: Column, ventral view, × 3.
G: Column, end view, × 3.
H: Column, side view, × 3.
I: Column, vertical section, × 3.
J, K, L: Pollinia, × 6.

Oeoniella

GENUS: *Oeoniella* Schlechter (ee-oh-nee-ELL-uh)
TRIBE: Vandeae   SUBTRIBE: Angraecinae
IDENTIFICATION CHARACTERISTICS: The white, almost-trumpet-shaped lips of flowers of *Oeoniella* coupled with fragrance easily distinguish this delicate beauty from other angraecoid orchids. This small Madagascan genus, comprising two or possibly three species, was first discovered and described by Aubert Du Petit-Thouars in Madagascar in 1822 as *Epidendrum polystachys*. In 1918 Rudolf Schlechter transferred the species to *Oeoniella*. The new generic name was based on the diminutive form of *Oeonia*, an angraecoid genus to which Schlechter saw a resemblance.

Vegetatively, the monopodial, epiphytic species of this genus are similar to others in the same tribe, so the misclassification as *Epidendrum* species is understandable. The erect, leafy stems can attain heights of 2 feet (60 cm). Closely spaced, oblong, fleshy leaves, up to 4 inches (10 cm) long and 2 inches (5 cm) wide, are borne alternately on the stem. The leaf bases clasp the stem. Aerial roots are produced all along the stem to within 2 inches (5 cm) of the apex. The axillary inflorescences are either arching or upright, up to 10 inches (25 cm) long, and bear up to 15 flowers. A tall, well-grown plant produces up to seven inflorescences, making it very attractive.

The dainty, white flowers often are tinged green. Only 1.25 inch (3 cm) wide, the distinctive flowers of this genus have narrow, pointed sepals and petals that are alike in size, shape, and color. The apical one-third of these segments often curves toward the almost-trumpet-shaped lip, which is the most noteworthy feature of the flower. The three-lobed lip has a short basal spur. The two lateral lobes are the largest parts of the lip, completely enclosing the column and flaring out to give the flower its trumpetlike form. The midlobe is long, narrow, and pointed at the apex, almost taillike.

The column, often very light green, is short with a small stigmatic surface. The two egg-shaped, yellow pollinia are borne on individual stipes, which are attached to a single, shield-shaped, flat viscidium.

CULTURE: Temperature, 60°F (15°C); light, 2400–3600 footcandles; humidity, 40–60%; media, plaques, logs, pot for small plants less than 8 inches (20 cm) tall; fertilization, monthly, with a 1–1–1 ratio.

COLOR PLATE: *Oeoniella polystachys*

SPECIES	FLOWERING SEASON	GENERAL LOCALE
polystachys	S	Madagascar, Seychelles, Comoro, Mascarene Islands
sarcanthoides	S	Madagascar

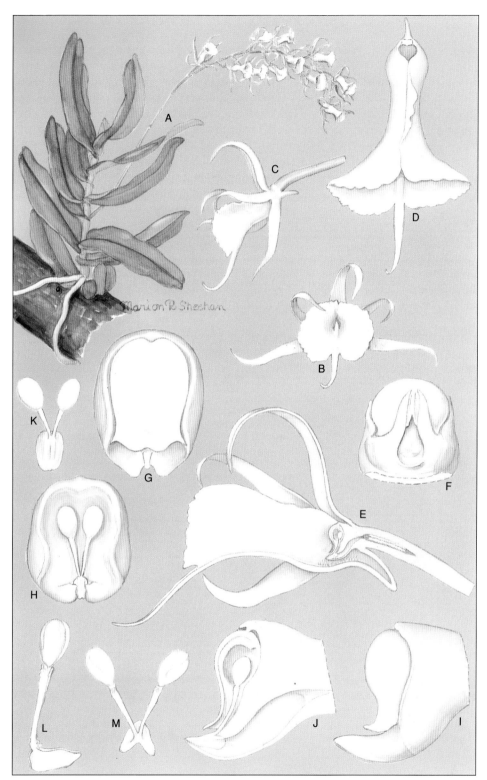

Oeoniella polystachys

A: Plant in flower, × ½.
B: Flower, face view, × 2.
C: Flower, side view, × 2.
D: Lip, face view, × 4.
E: Flower, vertical section, × 4.
F: Column, ventral view, × 15.
G: Column, end view, × 15.
H: Column, end view with
   anther cap removed, × 15.
I: Column, side view, × 15.
J: Column, vertical section, × 15.
K, L, M: Pollinia, × 20.

Oerstedella

GENUS: *Oerstedella* Reichenbach f. (er-ste-DELL-uh)

TRIBE: Epidendreae   SUBTRIBE: Laeliinae

IDENTIFICATION CHARACTERISTICS: *Oerstedella* is one of many interesting genera in the orchid family. It has approximately 40 species that are highly variable vegetatively. Some species are delicate and diminutive, only 6 inches (15 cm) tall, while others are more robust and grow to over 2 feet (60 cm). Despite this size differential, the species have flowers of equal size and number. Therefore, orchid growers can select the size plant that is best suited for a collection and receive the same satisfaction.

The genus was first described in 1852 by H. G. Reichenbach, who named it in honor of Anders Sandøe Ørsted, collector of the type material. Over the years the genus was intermingled with *Epidendrum* from which it differs in having a distinctive, large, flaplike projection on the column (clinandrium) and in lacking a viscidium.

The reed-type, sympodial, epiphytic species of this genus have short rhizomes so that tight clusters of stems are formed. The bases of the leaves, which are very warty in some species (e.g., *Oerstedella wallisii*), clasp the stem. Each reed may be up to 2 feet (60 cm) or more in height with approximately 10 narrow, lanceolate leaves up to 2 inches (5 cm) long. The terminal inflorescences bear from one to several attractive flowers.

The flowers are 0.5 × 1 inch (1 × 2.5 cm), and flower colors include lavender and yellow, although white forms with purple lips have been reported (e.g., *Oerstedella endresii*). The lip is the largest segment of the flower. The sepals and petals are almost alike in size and color but may vary slightly in shape, with the apex of the petals being more blunt in some species (e.g., *Oerstedella wallisii*). The three-lobed lip has a claw adnate to the column, which in vertical section appears as a spur. The bifid midlobe is much longer than the small, acute-tipped lateral lobes. The callus has papillae just below the tip of the column.

The very short column appears larger due to the extended folds covering the clawed anther cap. The four elongate, yellow pollinia are attached to two thin, narrow caudicles. There is no viscidium in *Oerstedella*.

CULTURE: Temperature, 55–60°F (12–15°C); light, 2400–3600 footcandles; humidity, 60%; medium, any good mix for epiphytes as plants often grow in clumps of moss on tree limbs in their native habitat; fertilization, monthly, ratio depends on medium.

COLOR PLATE: *Oerstedella centradenia*

SPECIES	FLOWERING SEASON	GENERAL LOCALE
centradenia	W	Central America
centropetala	W	Guatemala to Costa Rica, Panama
endresii	W	Costa Rica
wallisii	F–W	Colombia

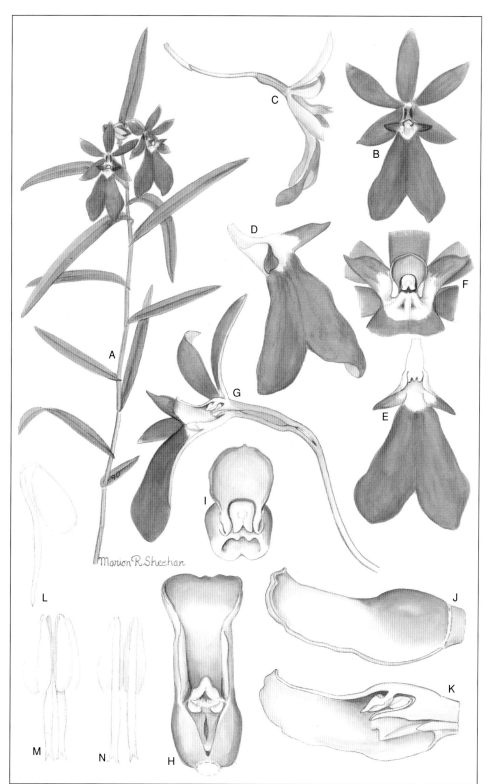

Oerstedella centradenia

A: Plant in flower, × 1.
B: Flower, face view, × 2.
C: Flower, side view, × 2.
D: Lip, three-quarter view, × 3.
E: Lip, face view, × 3.
F: Column and lip detail, face view, × 5.
G: Flower, vertical section, × 3.
H: Column, ventral view, × 10.
I: Column, end view, × 10.
J: Column, side view, × 10.
K: Column, vertical section, × 10.
L, M, N: Pollinia, × 30.

Oncidium

GENUS: *Oncidium* Swartz (on-SlD-ee-um)
TRIBE: Maxillarieae SUBTRIBE: Oncidiinae
IDENTIFICATION CHARACTERISTICS: Oncidiums were introduced into England in 1793 and have been favorite greenhouse subjects ever since. The genus is very large and divergent, containing over 300 species of sympodial epiphytes. Carl Linnaeus considered oncidiums as members of *Epidendrum*. His successor, Olof Swartz, separated the two genera and established the genus *Oncidium*. Swartz derived the generic name from the Greek word *onkos* (warty), referring to the wartlike growths on the lip. Vegetative characteristics of some *Oncidium* species closely resemble those of *Odontoglossum* species.

Plants in this genus may have pseudobulbs (e.g., *Oncidium splendidum*) or may be pseudobulbless and have equitant leaves (e.g., *O. variegatum*), yet the floral characteristics bind the species together (Fig. 21). Pseudobulbous species have large rounded bulbs which may be topped by one or more leaves, ranging from less than 2 inches (5 cm) to almost 2 feet (60 cm) in length. The texture of the leaves varies from flexible (e.g., *O. hastatum*), to pencillike (e.g., *O. cebolleta*), to very large, thick leathery leaves (e.g., *O. lanceanum*). The leaves may be bright light green, dark green, or overtoned with purple or brownish red stipples. Inflorescences arise from the base of the pseudobulbs or from the axils of the leaves, and range from less than 1 inch (2.5 cm) long with one flower (e.g., *O. crista-galli*) to branched inflorescences several feet long with hundreds of flowers (e.g., *O. sphacelatum*).

Although flowers of most species are yellow and brown, some species are red, pink, magenta, green, or white, and many are bicolored. The dainty flowers, often called "dancing girls," range from 0.5 to 5 inches (1–12.5 cm) in diameter. In general, the three sepals are alike in size, shape, and color but may vary. The two lateral petals are similar in size and shape to the dorsal sepal or may be larger. The lip is attached to the base of the column; the small side lobes are attached to the claw.

The very short column has petallike wings on either side of the stigma. A large projection lies beneath the wings. The stigmatic surface is broadest beneath the center of the wings. There is a single pair of pollinia, almost elliptical in shape. Both yellow pollinia are attached to a single stipe with two footlike projections at the base.

CULTURE: Temperature, 60–70°F (15–21°C); light, 2400–3600 footcandles; humidity, 40–70%; media, osmunda, tree fern, bark; fertilization, monthly, ratio depends on medium.

COLOR PLATE: *Oncidium splendidum*

SPECIES	FLOWERING SEASON	GENERAL LOCALE
altissimum	S–SS	West Indies
ampliatum	S	Mexico
barbatum	W–S	Brazil
batemannianum	W–S	Brazil, Bolivia, Peru
carthagenense	S	Tropical America
cavendishianum	S	Mexico, Guatemala
cebolleta	S	Tropical America
concolor	S	Brazil
crista-galli	F–W–S–SS	Mexico to Panama, Colombia, Peru, Ecuador
cucullatum	SS	Colombia, Ecuador
forbesii	S	Brazil
hastatum	SS	Mexico, Guatemala
incurvum	F	Mexico
lanceanum	SS	Venezuela to Brazil
leucochilum	SS	Mexico, Guatemala
longifolium	F–W–S	Tropical America
longipes	F	Brazil
luridum	W–S–SS	Tropical America
microchilum	SS	Mexico, Guatemala
ornithorhynchum	SS	Mexico to Venezuela, Peru
pumilum	SS	Brazil
reflexum	SS	Mexico
sarcodes	S	Brazil
sphacelatum	S–SS	Mexico
splendidum	S	Guatemala
stipitatum	SS	Panama
tetrapetalum	SS–F	West Indies
tigrinum	S–SS	Mexico
varicosum	SS	Brazil
variegatum	S–SS	West Indies

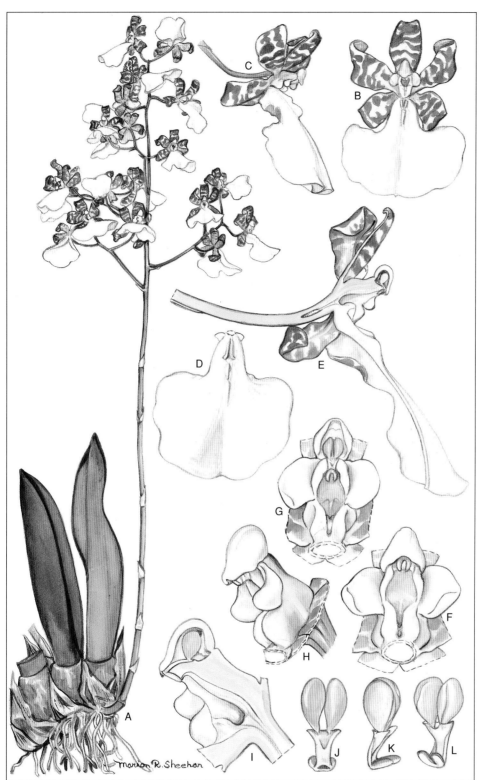

Oncidium splendidum

A: Plant in flower, × ½.
B: Flower, face view, × 1.
C: Flower, side view, × 1.
D: Lip, × 1.
E: Flower, vertical section, × 2.
F: Column, ventral view, × 6.
G: Column, ventral view, anther cap lifted, × 6.
H: Column, side view, × 6.
I: Column, vertical section, × 6.
J, K, L: Pollinia, × 12.

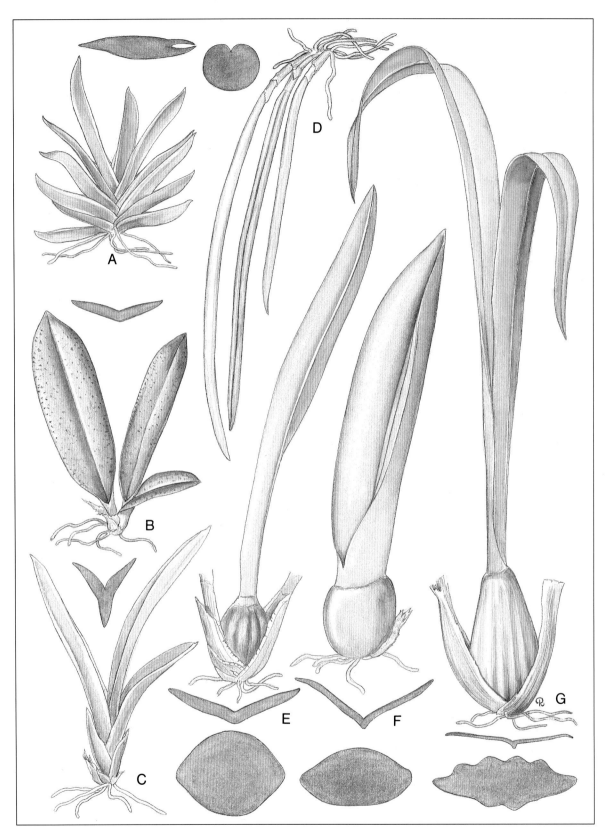

Figure 21. Vegetative forms of *Psygmorchis* and *Oncidium*. A: *Psygmorchis pusillum*. B: *Oncidium albaflorum*. C: *O. triquetrum*. D: *O. jonesianum*. E: *O. onustum*. F: *O. splendidum*. G: *O. sphacelatum*.

262

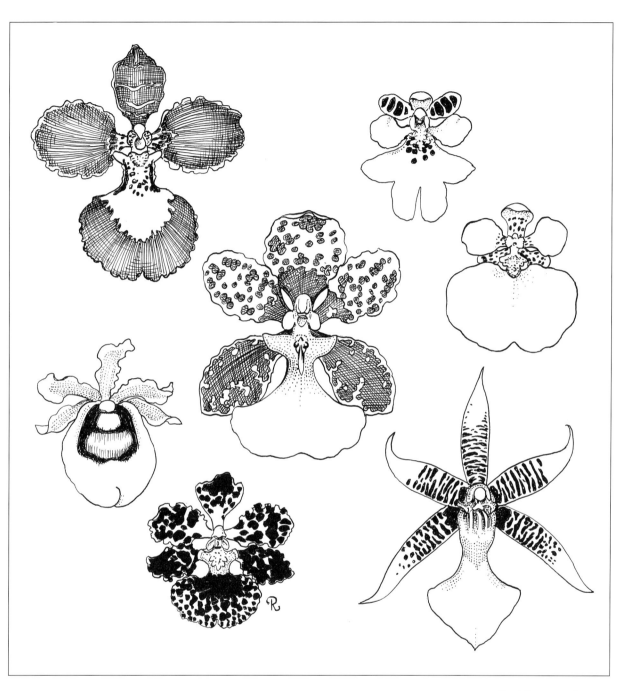

Oncidium species

Ophrys

GENUS: *Ophrys* Linnaeus (OH-frees)
TRIBE: Orchideae   SUBTRIBE: Orchidinae
IDENTIFICATION CHARACTERISTICS: The common names of *Ophrys* species read like a "Who's Who" of the insect world. There is the fly orchid (*O. insectifera*), the bee orchid (*O. apifera*), the early spider orchid (*O. sphegodes*), and the late spider orchid (*O. holoserica*). All the names are based on the shape and color of the fleshy, spurless lips, which greatly resemble the abdomens of the female pollinating insect. The species of this attractive Old World genus are highly variable in flower color and patterns, resulting in disagreement among taxonomists about species. The flowers of each of the 10 plants of *O. tenthredinifera* grown specifically for illustrating this genus differed slightly in shape and lip patterns. Someone unfamiliar with the genus could think there were different species in the group.

The genus was first described in 1753 by Carl Linnaeus, who named it *Ophrys*, which is Greek for eyebrow, perhaps alluding to two marks at the base of the lip or to a use of the plant to darken eyes. Today, more than 20 species are recognized.

Vegetatively, these terrestrial species are similar to many other temperate-climate orchids: primary growth and flowering of the genus is in winter and spring, with the plants going dormant during the hot, dry summers. The tuberoids survive these adverse conditions and produce a plant the following year. If the plants are dug while flowering, two tuberoids may be present, namely, the preceding year's shriveling tuberoid and the new, smooth tuberoid forming to carry the plant through to the next year. When growth commences, plants produce three or four soft, light to medium green leaves up to 4 inches (10 cm) long. As the inflorescence elongates in the center of the leaves, the new leaves on the stem become bractlike, terminating with a small bract subtending each flower. The inflorescence, up to 18 inches (45 cm) tall, may bear one to ten flowers, each flower opening successively. Frequently, the leaves start to turn brown at the tips while the plants are in flower. Flower color is variable.

The flowers are highly attractive, even though they are only 1 inch (2.5 cm) long. The three sepals are larger and broader than the petals. They may be the same color or different. The lip is the outstanding feature of the flower. Its shape, color, and patterns are highly variable from species to species. Often the lip is dark reddish purple to almost brown with the perimeter often lighter. Some lips are hairy and nearly feltlike while others are almost crystalline in appearance. The shape and color of the lip, plus the floral scent, usually attract one type of male insect, which, while attempting to copulate with the "female" on the flower, pollinates the orchid.

The column is short, with an unusual arrangement of the anther cap and pollinia at the apex. The pollinia are so positioned that the bending of the caudicle easily can bring about self-pollination. Four pollinia are borne in two pairs, with each pair having its own caudicle. When a pair of pollinia is removed, the narrow septum separating them stays behind and the two pollinia appear as a single club-shaped pollinium.

CULTURE: Difficult to cultivate. Temperature, 50–55°F (10–12°C); light, partial shade to full sun; humidity, variable; medium, well-drained (often found in soils that bake in summer); fertilization, minimal, with one-fourth the normal concentration.

COLOR PLATE: *Ophrys tenthredinifera*

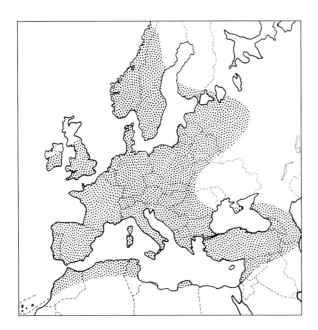

SPECIES	FLOWERING SEASON	GENERAL LOCALE
apifera	S–SS	Central Europe
arachnites	S–SS	Central & so. Europe
holoserica	S–SS	Great Britain, central & so. Europe
insectifera	S–SS	Europe
lutea	S	Mediterranean coast
muscifera	S–SS	Central & so. Europe
sphegodes	S–SS	Central & southern Europe
tenthredinifera	W	Mediterranean coast

Ophrys tenthredinifera
A: Plant in flower, × 1.
B: Flower, face view, × 2.
C: Flower, side view, × 2.
D: Flower, another color form, × 1.
E: Lip, similar to color form D, × 2½.
F: Flower, vertical section, × 2.
G: Column, ventral view, × 6.
H: Column, end view, × 6.
I: Column, side view, × 6.
J: Column, vertical section, × 6.
K, L: Pollinia, × 8.
M: Subterranean tuberoids, × 1.

Osmoglossum

GENUS: *Osmoglossum* Schlechter (oz-moh-GLOSS-um)

TRIBE: Maxillarieae SUBTRIBE: Oncidiinae

IDENTIFICATION CHARACTERISTICS: Waxy, pristine white flowers are the hallmark of the excellent species found in this delightful genus. *Osmoglossum* encompasses a very closely related group of approximately five species that often find themselves transferred into or out of *Odontoglossum*, a genus to which there is some resemblance. Rudolf Schlechter was the first to recognize the group as a distinct genus and named it in 1922. He derived the generic name from the Greek words *osme* (odor) and *glossa* (tongue), undoubtedly referring to the strong fragrance of the flowers. Later work by Edward S. Ayensu and Norris H. Williams indicated sufficient differences in both vegetative and floral characteristics, especially in the pollinaria, to support Schlechter's removing and maintaining *Osmoglossum* as distinct from *Odontoglossum*.

Vegetatively, the sympodial, epiphytic species of this genus are very much alike. The short, elliptical pseudobulbs are flattened and fluted, and form tight clumps. Each pseudobulb is topped by one or two leaves and subtended by up to five bracts that sheathe the pseudobulb. One or more of these bracts may be leaflike, giving the appearance of three or four leaves per pseudobulb. The leaves are linear to lanceolate and leathery with the blade deeply folded at the base. The unbranched inflorescence arises from the base of the pseudobulb and bears six or more flowers.

The nonresupinate flowers are basically white and 1 inch (2.5 cm) wide. In general, the sepals and petals are similar in size, shape, and color, although in a few cases petals may be slightly wider. The upright lip is indistinctly three-lobed, but due to the small size of the lateral lobes, this feature may escape the untrained eye; at first glance the lip may seem to be unlobed. The midlobe is reflexed, showing off to advantage the fleshy, ridged, yellow callus. On some flowers, the callus often is dotted with red, adding to the attractiveness of the lip.

The very short, waxy column is winged near the stigmatic surface and is widest at the base. Two yellow, grooved pollinia are borne on a single stipe with a small foot.

CULTURE: Temperature, 60°F (15°C); light, 2400–3600 footcandles; humidity, 40–60%; medium, tree fern, fir bark, plaques; fertilization, monthly, ratio depends on medium.

COLOR PLATE: *Osmoglossum pulchellum*

SPECIES	FLOWERING SEASON	GENERAL LOCALE
acuminatum	S	Mexico to Panama
convallarioides	S	Mexico to Costa Rica
pulchellum	F–W	Mexico to Costa Rica

Osmoglossum pulchellum
A: Plant in flower, × ½.
B: Flower, face view, × 1½.
C: Flower, side view, × 1½.
D: Lip, face view, × 4.
E: Flower, vertical section, × 1½.
F: Column, ventral view, × 6.
G: Column, end view, × 6.
H: Column, side view, × 6.
I: Column, vertical section, × 6.
J, K, L: Pollinia, × 12.

Panisea

GENUS: *Panisea* Lindley (pan-NISS-ee-uh)
TRIBE: Coelogyneae SUBTRIBE: Coelogyninae
IDENTIFICATION CHARACTERISTICS: *Panisea* may not be listed in many orchid books, except with the description, "rare and little-known genus of Southeast Asia." These delightful, miniature, intermediate- to cool-growing species, however, deserve better recognition. *Panisea* consists of three or possibly four species closely related to *Coelogyne* but easily separated by differences in floral characteristics. One unusual aspect of the genus is that the flowers of some species (e.g., *P. uniflora*) change color with age, often appearing to have two distinct colors of flowers on the same plant. The genus was first described by John Lindley in 1841, who combined the Greek words *pan* (all) and *isos* (equal). He undoubtedly was referring to the almost-similar floral segments of the type specimen.

The known species of this genus of sympodial epiphytes vary vegetatively. Although the pseudobulbs are similar and composed of one node, they are topped by one or two leaves, depending on the species, and subtended by one or two leafy bracts that turn brown and become papery, eventually falling off. The lance-shaped leaves are up to 6 inches (15 cm) long, although they may be less than 0.5 inch (1 cm) wide. An inflorescence bearing one or two flowers up to 2 inches (5 cm) wide appears to arise from the base of the pseudobulb. Some taxonomists, however, say that the inflorescence is actually formed at the apex of a yet-to-develop pseudobulb.

Flower color varies from light green to white to almost salmon pink. The lip is often salmon colored. Considering the size of the plant, flowers of this genus are showy and their crystalline nature creates an almost-iridescent effect. The three sepals and two petals are almost alike in shape and color, but the petals often are slightly smaller. The lip is not much larger than the dorsal sepal and is not obviously lobed. *Panisea uniflora*, however, has two distinct earlike projections near the base of the lip, giving this species pronounced lateral lobes. The lips of other species are less lobed. The lip callus marks vary from species to species.

The lower half of the stout, almost-erect column is narrower than the upper half. The stigmatic surface is very narrow. Four yellow pollinia are attached to prominent caudicles.

CULTURE: Temperature, 50–55°F (10–12°C); light, 1800–2400 footcandles; humidity, 40–60%; media, tree fern, tree fern plaques; fertilization, monthly, with a 1–1–1 ratio.

COLOR PLATE: *Panisea uniflora*

SPECIES	FLOWERING SEASON	GENERAL LOCALE
tricallosa	S	Himalayas to Thailand
uniflora	S	India to Vietnam

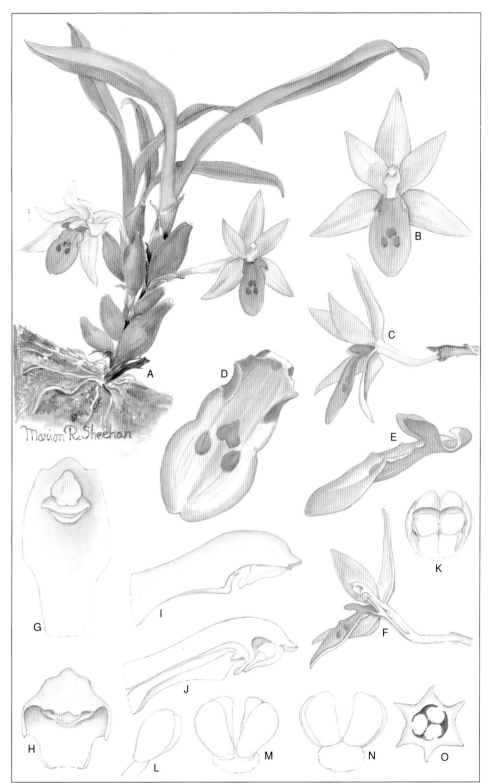

Panisea uniflora

A: Plant in flower, × 1.
B: Flower, face view, × 1½.
C: Flower, side view, × 1½.
D: Lip, face view, × 3.
E: Lip, side view, × 3.
F: Flower, vertical section, × 1½.
G: Column, ventral view, × 6.
H: Column, end view, × 6.
I: Column, side view, × 6.
J: Column, vertical section, × 6.
K: Anther cap and pollinia, × 12.
L, M, N: Pollinia, × 18.
O: Ovary, cross-section, × 12.

Paphinia

GENUS: *Paphinia* Lindley (pah-FINN-ee-uh)
TRIBE: Maxillarieae   SUBTRIBE: Stanhopeinae
IDENTIFICATION CHARACTERISTICS: *Paphinia*, a small genus of possibly five species with large colorful flowers, is native primarily to northern South America. Although considered somewhat rare, this genus is attractive and a worthwhile addition to any collection. In 1991 Mark Whitten and Norris Williams discovered a new species in Ecuador with larger flowers than those of the known species. This discovery should stimulate an even greater interest in the cultivation of this fine genus, which was first described by John Lindley in 1843 and named in honor of Paphia, the name of Aphrodite of Cyprus. The type specimen had originally been identified as a *Maxillaria*, but was transferred because it differed in pollinarium structure. *Paphinia* is also closely allied to *Houlletia* and *Lacaena*.

Vegetatively, these sympodial epiphytes are very similar to *Houlletia* species but can be distinguished readily because *Paphinia* has two or more leaves atop each pseudobulb. The ovoid, often slightly compressed pseudobulbs may form tight clusters and are subtended by small leafy bracts. The soft, broad, lanceolate leaves may be up to 10 inches (25 cm) long and 1.75 inches (4 cm) wide. The pendent inflorescence, bearing up to three colorful flowers, arises from the base of the pseudobulb.

The base flower color is white to yellowish with maroon to reddish brown spots, stripes, or blotches, depending on the species. The crisp, star-shaped, colorful flowers, often 3 inches (7.5 cm) in diameter, are very attractive. The sepals and petals are very similar in shape, and color although the petals tend to be slightly smaller and darker or more heavily marked. Some flowers have more stripes and spots while others have larger blotches of color. Although slightly smaller than the sepals and petals, the three-lobed lip is the most attractive floral segment. It has a variety of protuberances including glandular hairs and an angular, almost-sagittate midlobe.

The narrow, slightly curved column has two ears near the apex and a small foot at the base. Two cleft, yellow pollinia are borne on a long narrow stipe with a small viscidium at the base.

CULTURE: Temperature, 60°F (15°C); light, 2400–3600 footcandles; humidity, 40–60%; media, bark, tree fern, peat and perlite; fertilization, monthly, ratio depends on medium.

COLOR PLATE: *Paphinia cristata*

SPECIES	FLOWERING SEASON	GENERAL LOCALE
cristata	F–W	Colombia to Trinidad
grandiflora	F–W	Brazil
rugosa	F	Colombia

270

Paphinia cristata
A: Plant in flower, × 1.
B: Flower, face view, × 2.
C: Flower, side view, × 2.
D: Lip, face view, × 4.
E: Flower, vertical section, × 2.
F: Column, ventral view, × 6.
G: Column, end view, × 6.
H: Column, side view, × 6.
I: Column, vertical section, × 6.
J, K, L: Pollinia, × 16.

Marion R. Sheehan

Paphiopedilum

GENUS: *Paphiopedilum* Pfitzer (paff-ee-oh-PED-ih-lum)

TRIBE: Cypripedieae

IDENTIFICATION CHARACTERISTICS: Although many horticulturists commonly refer to all four genera of Cypripedieae (*Cypripedium, Paphiopedilum, Phragmipedium,* and *Selenipedium*) as "Cyps" and often sell them all as *Cypripedium,* the genera are distinct. The 60 to 65 known species of *Paphiopedilum,* as determined by Ernst H. H. Pfitzer (1886), originally were called *Cypripedium* or *Cordula.* Basically, these terrestrial (or sometimes epiphytic) species are native to tropical Asia. The generic name is derived from the Greek words *paphos* (Venus) and *pedilon* (sandal). Today most species are commonly called lady's-slipper orchids.

These stemless, pseudobulbless, sympodial species have fans of folded (conduplicate) leathery leaves (Fig. 22). Each fan consists of six or more leaves. Up to 15 inches (38 cm) long and 2 inches (5 cm) wide, the elliptical-to-lanceolate leaves clasp at the base and may be green or mottled green and white. The flowers, ranging from 2 to 6 inches (5–15 cm) in diameter, are borne singly or in few-flowered scapes. The terminal scapes may be up to 2 feet (60 cm) tall, often purplish brown in color, and covered with short hairs.

Because the flowers of this genus are unique compared to most orchids, some taxonomists suggest that this difference is sufficient to make the Cypripedieae a new family. The dorsal sepal is often one of the most showy segments of the flower and frequently has very distinct patterns. The two lateral sepals are fused to form a vertical sepal (synsepal), which may be almost hidden by the lip, causing the flower to appear to have only two sepals. The long and narrow petals, often with wavy margins and possibly with tufts of hairs on the margins, are usually borne at right angles to the sepals and often curve downward or forward towards the lip. The lip is shaped like a boot and may have an inrolled or an outrolled margin. Colors of the floral segments vary considerably, with browns, greens, whites, pinks, and mottled combinations of the aforementioned dominating.

The column is also unusual. It is broadest at the apex and is not terminated by an anther cap. Instead, the pollinia are attached to the sides of the column just behind the stigmatic surface. There are two roundish pollen masses or pollinia on short, broad stalks, one on either side of the column.

CULTURE: Temperature, 50–70°F (10–21°C); light, 1800–2400 footcandles; media, peat moss, tree fern, combination mixes; fertilization, monthly, ratio depends on medium.

COLOR PLATE: *Paphiopedilum insigne*

272

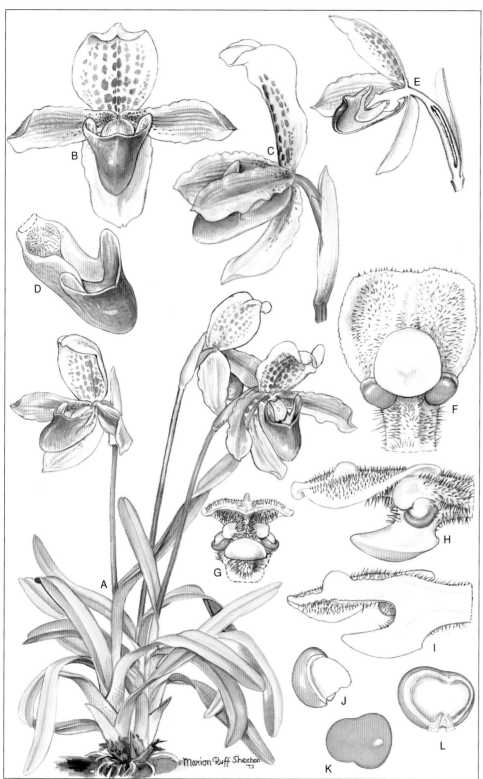

Paphiopedilum insigne
A: Plant in flower, × ½.
B: Flower, face view, × ¾.
C: Flower, side view, × ¾.
D: Lip, × 1.
E: Flower, vertical section, × ½.
F: Column, ventral view, × 3.
G: Column, end view, × 2.
H: Column, side view, × 3.
I: Column, vertical section,
   × 3.
J, K, L: Pollinia, × 8.

273

PAPHIOPEDILUM SPECIES	FLOWERING SEASON	GENERAL LOCALE
acmodontum	W–S	Philippines
appletonianum	SS	Thailand, Assam
argus	S–SS	Philippines
armeniacum	W–S	China
barbatum	W–S–SS	Java, Malaysia, Thailand
bellatulum	S	Myanmar, Thailand
bullenianum	S–SS	Borneo
callosum	W–S	Thailand, Indochina
charlesworthii	F	India, Myanmar, Bengal
concolor	F–S–SS	Myanmar to Vietnam
dayanum	W–S–SS	Borneo
delenatii	W–S–SS	Southeast Asia
druryi	S	India
emersonii	W–S	China
exul	SS	Thailand
fairrieanum	SS–F	Assam, Himalayas
glanduliferum	W	New Guinea
glaucophyllum	S–SS	New Guinea to Java
godefroyae	S–SS	Southeast Asia
haynaldianum	W–S	Philippines
hirsutissimum	S	Assam, Himalayas
insigne	F–W–S	Himalayas
lawrenceanum	S–SS	Borneo
lowii	S–SS	Malay Peninsula, Indonesia
malipoense	W–S	China
mastersianum	W–S–SS	Moluccas, New Guinea
micranthum	W–S	China
niveum	S–SS–F	Southeast Asia
parishii	F	Myanmar, Thailand
philippinense	S	Philippines
primulinum	S–SS	Sumatra
purpuratum	F–W	China
rothschildianum	W	Borneo
sanderianum	S	Borneo
spicerianum	F–W	Assam
sukhakulii	S	Thailand
tonsum	F	Sumatra
urbanianum	S	Philippines
venustum	W–S	Himalayas
villosum	W	Borneo

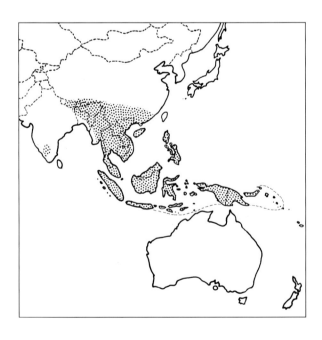

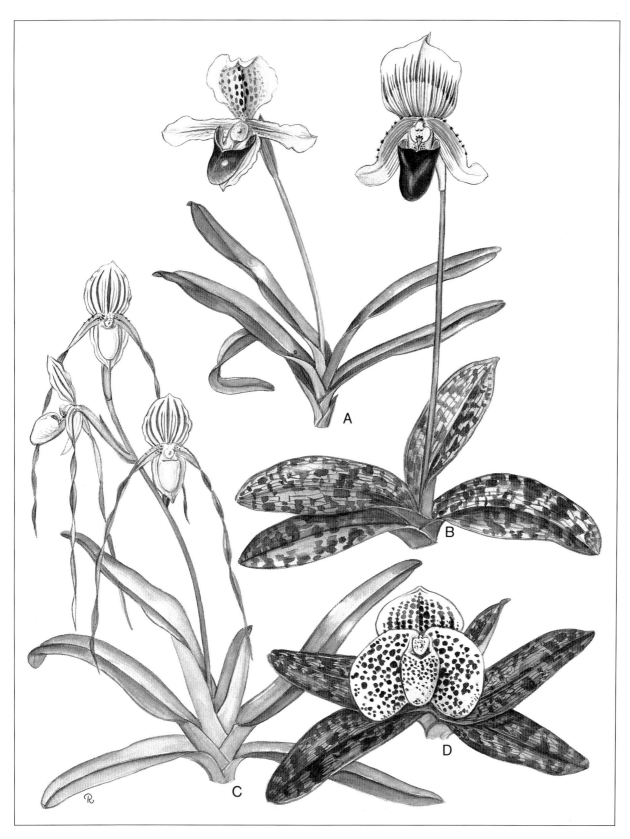

Figure 22. Vegetative forms of *Paphiopedilum* showing plants in flower. A: *P. insigne*. B: *P. callosum*. C: *P. philippinense*. D: *P. bellatulum*.

Paphiopedilum
species from
Thailand
A: *P. callosum.*
B: *P. concolor.*
C: *P. godefroyae.*
D: *P. bellatulum.*
E: *P. niveum.*
F: *P. sukhakulii.*
G: *P. barbatum.*

Paphiopedilum,
section
Parvisepalum

A: P. armeniacum.
B: P. delenatii.
C: P. emersonii.
D: P. micranthum.
E: P. malipoense.

Paraphalaenopsis

GENUS: *Paraphalaenopsis* A. D. Hawkes (par-uh-fal-en-OPP-siss)

TRIBE: Vandeae SUBTRIBE: Aeridinae

IDENTIFICATION CHARACTERISTICS: According to J. E. Zurowitz, "The plants flower freely, mostly three or four times a year. The flowers last about three weeks and exhale a very delicate perfume" (Sweet 1980). Despite this glowing description of *Paraphalaenopsis denevei* (then *Vanda denevei*) in 1933, the genus is rare in cultivation (see *Phalaenopsis* color plate 3). Seedlings are now being grown (e.g., *P. laycockii*) and plants should be available.

There are four species in the genus, which was established in 1963 by A. D. Hawkes when he separated the species from *Phalaenopsis* based on the long terete leaves and a number of differences in floral characteristics. Hawkes named the genus *Paraphalaenopsis* possibly to denote that these plants were derived from *Phalaenopsis*.

Vegetatively, the monopodial, epiphytic species of this genus more closely resemble terete-leaved vandas in some aspects than they do *Phalaenopsis* species (Fig. 23). The terete leaves of *Paraphalaenopsis* are much longer, sometimes up to 3 feet (90 cm), and are pendent, whereas those of *Vanda* are erect. The leaves are borne on very short stems. Each plant bears only a few leaves, usually up to six, but sometimes less. The axillary inflorescence usually is short, with the flowers often clustered near the apex. Each inflorescence bears five to seven flowers, although, a well-grown plant of *P. laycockii* may produce up to 15 flowers on a single inflorescence and plants often flower several times a year.

The faintly scented, long-lived flowers often have twisted or reflexed petals and sepals. The amount of reflexing or the waviness of the sepal and petal margins varies among the species. The sepals and petals are almost alike in size, shape, and color. The lip is distinctly three-lobed. The lateral lobes are narrow and stiffly erect. The midlobe is also long and narrow, and may be entire or forked at the apex, the latter appearing like a snake's forked tongue in one species (*Paraphalaenopsis serpentilingua*; see *Phalaenopsis* color plate 3). There is a very distinct disc and callus on the lip between the two lateral lobes.

The column, which is very short with an easily recognized anther cap, is widest near the stigmatic surface, tapers and then flares out near the point of attachment to the ovary. Two yellow pollinia are borne on a single stipe with a shield-shaped foot.

CULTURE: Temperature, 65°F (18°C) at night; light, 1800–2000 footcandles; humidity, 40–60%; media, tree fern, bark; fertilization, monthly, ratio depends on medium.

COLOR PLATE: *Paraphalaenopsis laycockii*

SPECIES	FLOWERING SEASON	GENERAL LOCALE
denevei	S–SS	West Borneo
labokensis	S–SS	Sabah
laycockii	SS	South Central Borneo
serpentilingua	S–SS	West Borneo

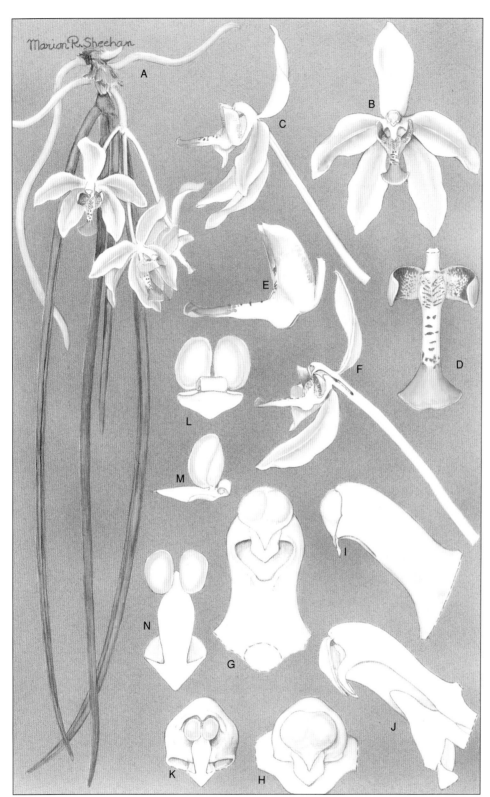

Paraphalaenopsis laycockii
A: Plant in flower, × ½.
B: Flower, face view, × ¾.
C: Flower, side view, × ¾.
D: Lip, face view, × 1½.
E: Lip, side view, × 1½.
F: Flower, vertical section, × ¾.
G: Column, ventral view, × 4.
H: Column, end view, × 4.
I: Column, side view, × 4.
J: Column, vertical section, × 4.
K: Column, end view, anther
    cap removed to show pollinia
    in place, × 4.
L, M, N: Pollinia, × 8.

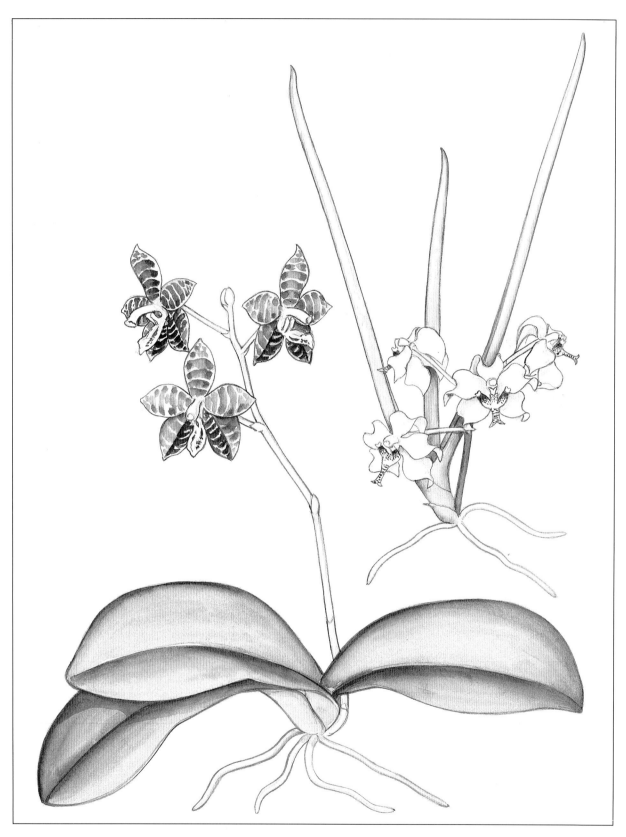

Figure 23. *Paraphalaenopsis* (right) was separated from *Phalaenopsis* (left) on the basis of its long, terete leaves and several floral characteristics.

Paraphalaenopsis species

Peristeria

GENUS: *Peristeria* Hooker (per-ih-STEER-ee-uh)
TRIBE: Maxillarieae SUBTRIBE: Stanhopeinae
IDENTIFICATION CHARACTERISTICS: The Holy Ghost or dove orchid (*Peristeria elata*) is the most widely known member of this small genus containing approximately six species. The first plants of *Peristeria* were sent to England in 1826 and were flowered by a Mr. Harrison in 1831. William J. Hooker, when describing the genus, named it *Peristeria* after the Greek word meaning dove, due to the likeness of a dove that appears in the flowers. *Peristeria elata* is the national flower of Panama.

This group of sympodial, terrestrial or epiphytic orchids has large, almost-teardrop-shaped pseudobulbs. The thickly clustered pseudobulbs are smooth, dark green, and often constricted at the point of attachment of old leaves. Four or five massive pleated leaves arise from the apex of each pseudobulb and an equal number of leafy bracts subtend the pseudobulb. A leaf may be 4 feet (120 cm) long and 6 or more inches (15+ cm) wide on *Peristeria elata*. The inflorescences arising from the base of the pseudobulb may be pendulous or erect and from 6 inches (15 cm) to 4 feet (120 cm) long, bearing 4 to 20 flowers. The base color of the flowers is white or yellowish with some pink or red spots.

The fleshy flowers, sometimes 1.5 to 2 inches (4–5 cm) across, are admired not for their color but primarily for the mimicry of the "dove." Three broad, concave sepals form a cup around the remaining floral segments. The two petals are similar in shape to the sepals but smaller in size and help to make the cup more pronounced in *Peristeria elata*. The fleshy lip is three-lobed with a broad central lobe. The two lateral lobes vary in size, depending on the species. In *P. elata* they are large and flare out on either side of the column, appearing as the wings of the dove.

The column is short and terminates in a round, smooth anther cap. At the base of the anther cap, a pointed projection gives the appearance of the dove's bill. Two yellow concave pollinia are attached to a hollow triangular stipe, which slips over the projection below the anther cap.

CULTURE: Temperature, 60–70°F (15–21°C); light, 2400–3600 footcandles; humidity, 40–70%; medium, a mixture of 1 leaf mold : 1 peat moss; fertilization, monthly, with an 18–18–18 ratio.

COLOR PLATE: *Peristeria elata*

SPECIES	FLOWERING SEASON	GENERAL LOCALE
aspersa	S	Venezuela, Brazil
cerina	SS	Brazil, Venezuela, Guyana, Suriname, French Guiana, Peru
elata	SS	Costa Rica, Panama, Colombia, Venezuela
pendula	W–S	Panama, Guyana, Suriname, French Guiana

Peristeria elata

A: Plant in flower, × ⅛.
B: Flower, face view, × 1.
C: Flower, side view, × 1.
D: Lip, three-quarter view, × 1.
E: Lip, side view, × 1.
F: Flower, vertical section, × 1.
G: Column, ventral view, × 3.
H: Column, side view, × 3.
I: Column, vertical section, × 3.
J: Column, ventral view,
   anther cap lifted to show
   pollinia, × 3.
K, L: Pollinia, × 6.

Pescatorea _____

GENUS: *Pescatorea* Reichenbach f. (pes-kah-TOR-ee-uh)

TRIBE: Maxillarieae   SUBTRIBE: Zygopetalinae

IDENTIFICATION CHARACTERISTICS: The large, long-lived, showy flowers of *Pescatorea* are not only colorful, they also have strangely beautiful and complex lips. There are slightly more than a dozen species in this fine genus, which was first described by H. G. Reichenbach in 1852 and named in honor of M. Pescatore, a well-known French orchid grower of that era. Vegetatively, *Pescatorea* is very similar to *Huntleya* and other members of the subtribe; however, the genera are separated by some of their distinctive lip characteristics.

The sympodial epiphytes of this genus are pseudobulbless with the leaves loosely arranged in fans. The fans of leaves are closely arranged on the stem, so the plant forms a dense clump. Each fan has approximately six soft, lancelike leaves, each of which may be up to 2 feet (60 cm) long and 2 inches (5 cm) wide. The leaves are usually jointed a few inches above the base. The inflorescence, which bears a solitary flower up to 3.5 inches (8 cm) wide, arises from the axil of one of the lower leaves. Naked except for one or two leaflike bracts, the inflorescence may be as much as 6 inches (15 cm) tall; however, the average height is much lower.

Flower colors include white, yellow, lavender, and purple. The flowers have thick sepals and petals generally alike in size and color, with the petals sometimes more colorful than the sepals. The sepals and petals may form a hood around the rest of the floral segments. Although not the largest and showiest portion of the flower, the three-lobed lip has distinctive characteristics. It has a very large midlobe and two small side lobes. The midlobe is often covered with hairs on the upper two-thirds and has a very pronounced, keeled callus at the base. The callus may have up to 19 keels (e.g., *Pescatorea klabochorum*).

The erect column is almost straight sided but may narrow slightly near the anther cap. The very narrow, stigmatic surface, just behind the rostellum, often resembles a pair of human lips. The four yellow, almost-elliptical pollinia are borne on a single broad-footed stipe.

CULTURE: Temperature, 60°F (15°C); light, 2400–3600 footcandles; humidity, 40–60%; media, tree fern, peat and perlite, bark; fertilization, monthly, ratio depends on medium.

COLOR PLATE: *Pescatorea lehmannii*

SPECIES	FLOWERING SEASON	GENERAL LOCALE
cerina	F	Costa Rica, Panama
coronaria	S–SS	Colombia
dayana	W	Colombia
klabochorum	SS	Colombia, Ecuador
lehmannii	S–SS–F	Colombia, Ecuador
wallisii	W	Costa Rica

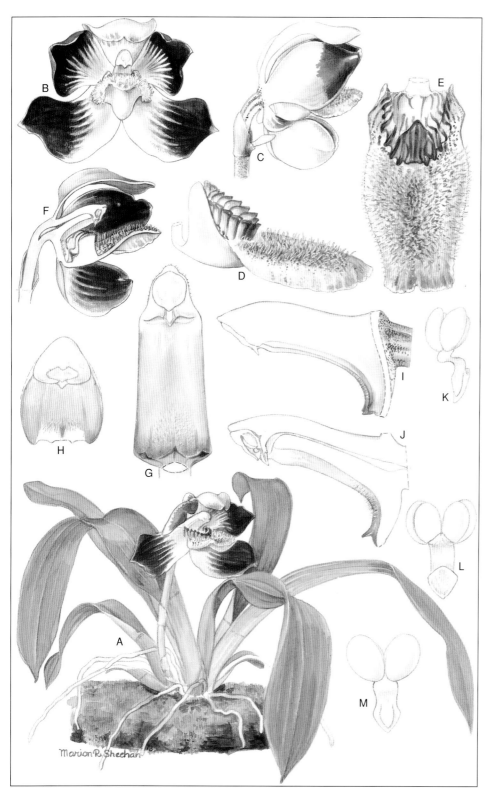

Pescatorea lehmannii
A: Plant in flower, × ½.
B: Flower, face view, × ¾.
C: Flower, side view, × ¾.
D: Lip, side view, × 1½.
E: Lip, face view, × 1½.
F: Flower, vertical section, × ¾.
G: Column, ventral view, × 2.
H: Column, end view, × 2.
I: Column, side view, × 2.
J: Column, vertical section, × 2.
K, L, M: Pollinia, × 5.

GENUS: *Phaius* Loureiro (FAY-us)

TRIBE: Arethuseae   SUBTRIBE: Bletiinae

IDENTIFICATION CHARACTERISTICS: *Phaius tankervilleae* was introduced into England in 1778 by John Fothergill, who brought the plant from China. The genus was identified by Juan Loureiro, who also named it using the Greek word *phaios* (swarthy), probably because of the yellow-brown flower color that dominates the genus. *Phaius tankervilleae* is commonly called the nun's orchid, possibly due to the lateral view of the column, which resembles a Madonna.

The genus contains about 20 pseudobulbous, sympodial, robust species with very short rhizomes. There are both terrestrial and epiphytic species with the terrestrials most widely known. *Phaius* is closely related to *Calanthe* and *Bletilla*.

The thickened, stocky pseudobulbs are hidden by the ensheathing leaf bases. Each pseudobulb is enclosed by two to eight large, thin, deeply grooved leaves, up to 4 feet (120 cm) long and 10 inches (25 cm) wide. Flower stalks arise from near the rhizome base between the point of attachment of two leaves. Many flowers are borne on the 3- to 4-foot (90- to 120-cm) tall inflorescences.

The 4-inch (10-cm) wide flowers are very showy and distinctive. The sepals and petals are alike in color and shape and are not united. The three-lobed lip has two lateral lobes folded over the column. The third or terminal lobe is broad-spreading, with a wavy margin and a slight indentation at the apex. The lip is spurred at the base. The inside of the spur of *Phaius tankervilleae* is slightly pubescent.

The column is broadest near the stigmatic region and often slightly hairy near the apex, which has four sharp lobes—two small ones near the upper surface and two larger flaring points near the rostellum. The column is wingless. The stigmatic surface on the underside of the column is almost circular in shape, being very rounded near the basal end. The anther cap of *Phaius tankervilleae* is pubescent. Each flower contains eight yellow pollinia borne in two groups of four each, attached to what appears to be a branched caudicle. Each group has two large and two smaller pollinia with the smaller near the apex of the caudicle. The pollinia are almost elliptical when viewed from the side.

Phaius is propagated in an unusual way. Once the flowers are spent, the flower stem can be used to increase the number of plants in a collection. The stem is cut above the base and just below where the first flower was attached. The remaining section is from one to several feet (30+ cm) long. Below each bract on the stem is a bud capable of producing a new plant. The stems are laid horizontally in a flat of moist sphagnum moss. Both ends are covered with moss to prevent drying out. The flat containing many stems is then placed under the bench and kept moist. As soon as the young plants have two or three roots, they can be snapped off the parent stem and placed in individual pots. Plantlets will require two to three years to attain flowering size.

CULTURE: Temperature, 55°F (12°C); light, 2400–3600 footcandles; humidity, 40–70%; media, (a) a mixture of 1 peat : 1 perlite : 1 soil or (b) a mixture of 1 loam : 1 rotted cow manure : 1 peat; fertilization, (medium a) monthly, with a 1–1–1 ratio as recommended on the container, (medium b) when the inflorescences appear, with a 1–1–1 ratio.

COLOR PLATE: *Phaius tankervilleae*

SPECIES	FLOWERING SEASON	GENERAL LOCALE
amboinensis	F	Indonesia to New Guinea
australis	S	Australia
flavus	S	India to Philippines
longipes	SS	South China to Malaya
pauciflorus	SS	Malaya to Java
pictus	F	Australia
pulchellus	SS–F	Madagascar
tankervilleae	S	India to Thailand, south to Australia & southwest Pacific Islands

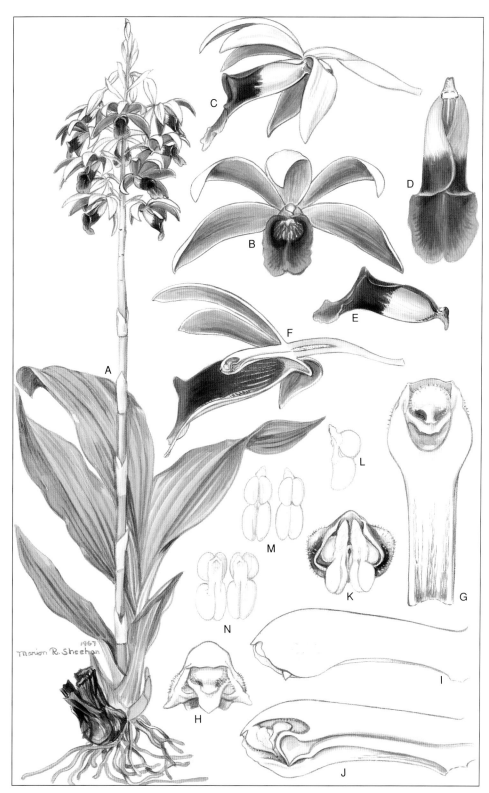

Phaius tankervilleae

A: Plant in flower, × ⅙.
B: Flower, face view, × ¾.
C: Flower, side view, × ¾.
D: Lip, face view, × 1.
E: Lip, side view, × ¾.
F: Flower, vertical section, × 1.
G: Column, ventral view, × 3.
H: Column, end view, × 3.
I: Column, side view, × 3.
J: Column, vertical section, × 3.
K: Anther cap with pollinia, × 6.
L, M, N: Pollinia, × 6.

Phalaenopsis

GENUS: *Phalaenopsis* Blume (fal-en-OPP-siss)
TRIBE: Vandeae SUBTRIBE: Aeridinae
IDENTIFICATION CHARACTERISTICS: Carl Blume is credited with founding the genus in 1825. He based his findings on *Phalaenopsis amabilis* which he found on the island of Nusa Kambangan. As early as 1750, however, G. E. Rumphius found the species on the island of Amboina, which he misidentified as *Angraecum*; thus he may have been the first to discover the genus. The generic name for these monopodial epiphytes was derived from the Greek words *phalaina* (moth) and *opsis* (appearance). This outstanding genus contains around 36 species, depending on the number of varieties given specific or natural hybrid status.

Phalaenopsis has a very short stem and appears to be stemless as the clasping leaves hide the stem (Fig. 23). Leaves are few in number, leathery, and up to 2 feet (60 cm) long and 6 to 8 inches (15–20 cm) wide (e.g., *P. gigantea*), shiny green or sometimes mottled silvery above, and green or purplish beneath. The inflorescence arises from the axil of the leaf and varies from a few inches to several feet in length depending on the species.

The flowers are predominantly white, pink, yellow, and mottled. Although they vary in size from 0.5 to 3 inches (1–7.5 cm) in diameter, the flowers are sufficiently alike to tie the genus together. The three sepals are alike in size and color. The two lateral petals are either much broader than the sepals (e.g., *Phalaenopsis amabilis*), equal to the sepals (e.g.,

P. equestris), or narrower than the sepals in size (e.g., *P. pulchra*) and are usually of the same color. The lip varies considerably in this genus. The midlobe of the three-lobed lip may have two antennae, or teeth, at the apex. The lip also exhibits various appendages or calluslike tissue depending on the species. Some species have an entire midlobe on the lip.

The column is short, narrow, and often the same color as the petals. The rostellum often has a pronounced beak in the center with an almost-similar beak on the anther cap. Two round yellow pollinia are borne on an almost-transparent stipe with a shield-shaped base (viscidium) that is very sticky.

CULTURE: Temperature, 70°F (21°C); light, 1500–1800 footcandles; humidity, 40–70%; media, tree fern, charcoal, bark; fertilization, monthly, ratio depends on medium.

COLOR PLATE: *Phalaenopsis schilleriana*

SPECIES	FLOWERING SEASON	GENERAL LOCALE
amabilis	F–W–S	Moluccas, Celebes, Australia, New Guinea, Java, Philippines
amboinensis	S	Moluccas
aphrodite	F–W–S	Philippines, Taiwan
cochlearis	W–S	Sarawak
corningiana	S	Borneo, Sarawak
cornu-cervi	S–SS–F	Malaysia, Java
equestris	F–W–S	Philippines
fasciata	W–S	Philippines
fimbriata	S–SS	Java
fuscata	S	Philippines
gigantea	S	Borneo
hieroglyphica	S–SS	Philippines
× *intermedia*	F–W–S–SS	Philippines
kunstleri	W–S	Malaysia
lindenii	W–S	Philippines
lowii	SS–F	Myanmar
lueddemanniana	S	Philippines
maculata	W–S	Sarawak, Malaysia
mannii	W–S	India
mariae	W–S	Philippines
micholitzii	W–S	Philippines
pallens	W–S	Philippines
parishii	W–S	Myanmar
pulchra	W–S	Philippines
sanderiana	W–S	Philippines
schilleriana	W–S	Philippines
speciosa	S	Andaman Islands
stuartiana	W–S	Philippines
sumatrana	W–S	Malay Peninsula, Sumatra, Java, Borneo
violacea	W–S–SS	Malay Peninsula, Sumatra, Borneo

Phalaenopsis schilleriana
A: Plant in flower, × ¼.
B: Flower, face view, × 1.
C: Flower, side view, × 1.
D: Lip, × 1½.
E: Flower, vertical section, × 1½.
F: Column, ventral view, × 5.
G: Column, end view, × 5.
H: Column, side view, × 5.
I: Column, vertical section, × 5.
J, K, L: Pollinia, × 8.

289

Phalaenopsis species, Plate 1

A: *P. pallens.*
B: *P. micholitzii.*
C: *P. gigantea.*
D: *P. amabilis.*
E: *P. pulchra.*
F: *P. fasciata.*
G: *P. sanderiana.*

290

Phalaenopsis species, Plate 2
A: *P. parishii.*
B: *Doritis pulcherrima.*
C: *P. equestris.*
D: *P. mannii.*
E: *P. lindenii.*
F: *P. mannii.*
G: *P. schilleriana.*
H: *P. lueddemanniana.*
I: *P.* Hymen.
J: *P. fimbriata.*
K: *P. stuartiana.*

Marion R. Sheehan

291

Phalaenopsis species, Plate 3

A: *P. cornu-cervi.*
B: *P. violacea* (Borneo).
C: *P. mariae.*
D: *P. fuscata.*
E: *P. cochlearis.*
F: *P. corningiana.*
G: *P. sumatrana.*
H: *P. maculata.*
I: *P. violacea* (Malaya).
J: *Paraphalaenopsis serpentilingua.*
K: *Paraphalaenopsis denevei.*
L: *Phalaenopsis amboinensis.*

Phalaenopsis

Pholidota

GENUS: *Pholidota* Lindley (pho-lih-DOH-tuh)
TRIBE: Coelogyneae SUBTRIBE: Coelogyninae
IDENTIFICATION CHARACTERISTICS: The rattle-snake orchids, as some pholidotas are called, are not widely cultivated although they are one of Thailand's most plentiful native orchids. As the inflorescences emerge from these interesting, multiflowered orchids, the buds are covered by brown papery bracts; the arrangement of these bracts is very similar to the rattles on the tail of the rattlesnake, hence, the common name.

The genus of approximately 40 species was founded by John Lindley in the early 1800s. The generic name is derived from the Greek word *pholidotos* (scaly). Lindley could have been referring either to the bracts that subtend the flowers or to the bracts that enclose the young pseudobulb. The genus is closely related to *Coelogyne* from which it differs in floral characteristics.

The pseudobulbs of these sympodial epiphytes may be widely spaced or arranged in tight clusters, up to 4 inches (10 cm) long, often conical, and ribbed. When the pseudobulbs are widely separated, the rhizome is covered by large bracts. As the new pseudobulb develops, it is protected by several green leafy bracts, which dry and become papery as it matures. In some species (e.g., *Pholidota articulata*) new pseudobulbs arise from the apex of old bulbs to form a chainlike growth. One or two stalked, leathery, pleated leaves emerge from the apex of the pseudobulb. Individual leaf blades may be up to 12 inches (30 cm) long and 3 inches (7.5 cm) wide. The pendulous or erect inflorescence, which arises from the apex of the developing pseudobulb, may be up to 18 inches (45 cm) long, twisted, and two-ranked usually, although sometimes with flowers irregularly arranged. It may bear over 75 dainty flowers, each subtended by a bract.

The small flowers are often scented with a musky odor and are seldom more than 0.5 inch (1 cm) wide. Basically, they are cream- or flesh-colored. The three sepals are alike in size and color and are usually a little larger than the two petals. The apices of the sepals are usually pointed and the petals are more blunt. In some species the sepals and petals never fully unfold and the flowers are almost cup-shaped. The lip is three-lobed with the midlobe often split; thus, at first glance the lip appears to be four-lobed. The two side lobes are small and partially enclose the column.

The short column, which may have a very distinct orange-brown anther cap at its apex, is broadest near the base. Two whitish, almost-teardrop-shaped pollinia are attached to a short, irregular, somewhat shield-shaped caudicle.

CULTURE: Temperature, 60–70°F (15–21°C); light, 2400–3600 footcandles; humidity, 40–60%; media, bark, tree fern, peat and perlite; fertilization, monthly, ratio depends on medium, a 1–1–1 ratio for tree fern, a 3–1–1 for bark.

COLOR PLATE: *Pholidota pallida*

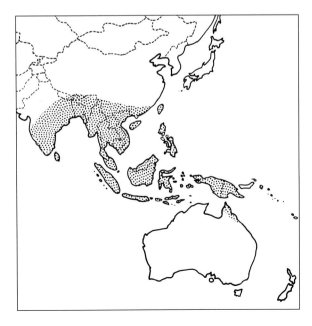

SPECIES	FLOWERING SEASON	GENERAL LOCALE
articulata	S–SS	Himalayas to Philippines, south to Australia
carnea	SS	Malay Peninsula, Sumatra, Borneo, Philippines
chinensis	SS	India, China
convallariae	S	Assam to Thailand
gibbosa	SS	Malay Peninsula, Sumatra, Borneo, Java
longibulba	SS	Malaya (Cameroon Highlands)
pallida	S–SS–F	Southern China, Himalayas, all tropical Asia, Australia
uraiensis	W	Taiwan
ventricosa	F–W–S–SS	Malay Peninsula, Sumatra, Java, Borneo

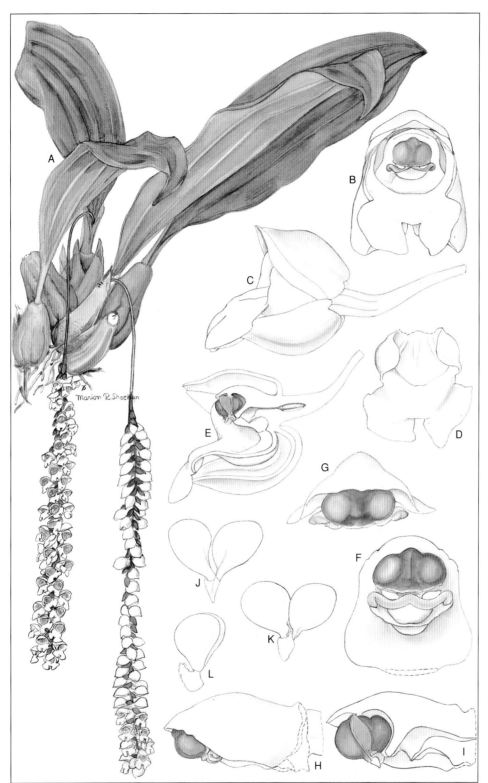

Pholidota pallida
A: Plant in flower, × ½.
B: Flower, face view, × 5.
C: Flower, side view, × 5.
D: Lip, × 5.
E: Flower, vertical section, × 5.
F: Column, ventral view, × 10.
G: Column, end view, × 10.
H: Column, side view, × 10.
I: Column, vertical section, × 10.
J, K, L: Pollinia, × 20.

295

Phragmipedium

GENUS: *Phragmipedium* Rolfe (frag-mih-PEE-dee-um)

TRIBE: Cypripedieae

IDENTIFICATION CHARACTERISTICS: Approximately a dozen delightful species of *Phragmipedium* are known today. They are part of the complex affectionately referred to as "Cyps" by many orchidists. Robert Rolfe separated the species known as *Phragmipedium* from the other genera on the basis of floral characteristics such as the appearance of the dorsal sepal and the configuration of the lip. The generic name was derived from the Greek words *phragma* (fence), a reference to the division of the ovary, and *pedilon* (slipper).

Phragmipedium species are either epiphytic or terrestrial. All are sympodial growers and have tight fans of leathery, dark green leaves. Each fan consists of six to eight flat leaves up to 3 feet (90 cm) long and 2 inches (5 cm) wide (e.g., *P. longifolium*). Inflorescences, which arise from within the fan of leaves, may be 3 feet (90 cm) tall, have leafy bracts, and bear as many as 15 flowers. In *P. longifolium*, usually one, at most two, flowers are open on a spike at one time.

The flowers may measure as much as 30 inches (75 cm) from the tip of the dorsal sepal to the tip of a lateral petal (e.g., *Phragmipedium caudatum*). Flower colors are greens and browns with yellow and purplish patterns. *Phragmipedium besseae* is a bright orange-red. The flowers of this genus are distinct and easy to separate from other genera in the "Cyp" complex. The dorsal sepal is more like the lateral petals and is not broad as its counterparts in *Cypripedium* and *Paphiopedilum*. The lateral petals are narrow, twisted, and sometimes extremely long (e.g., *P. caudatum*). The sac-shaped boot or lip is usually folded in.

The short column is unique and difficult to describe. Parts of it are covered by hairs, some of which are jointed. Two sets of pollinia are found on each column. Each laterally located set contains two cream-colored, almost-bean-shaped pollinia.

CULTURE: Temperature, 60–65°F (15–18°C); light, 2400–3600 footcandles; humidity, 40–60%; media, peat and perlite, osmunda, sphagnum moss for epiphytes, equal parts of garden soil, tree fern, and sphagnum moss for terrestrials; fertilization, monthly, ratio depends on medium.

COLOR PLATE: *Phragmipedium longifolium*

SPECIES	FLOWERING SEASON	GENERAL LOCALE
besseae	S–SS	Ecuador, Peru
boissierianum	F	Peru, Ecuador
caricinum	S	Peru, Bolivia, Brazil
caudatum	S–SS–F	Mexico to Venezuela, Peru
lindleyanum	F–W	Venezuela, Guyana
longifolium	F	Costa Rica to Colombia
sargentianum	S	Brazil
schlimii	S	Colombia
vittatum	S	Brazil

Phragmipedium longifolium
A: Plant in flower, × ³⁄₈.
B: Flower, face view, × ²⁄₃.
C: Flower, side view, × ²⁄₃.
D: Lip, × 1.
E: Flower, vertical section, × 1.
F: Column, ventral view, × 4.
G: Column, end view, × 4.
H: Column, side view, × 4.
I: Column, vertical section, × 4.
J, K: Two views of the pollinia in
     place, × 10.
L: One pollen mass removed,
     × 16.

Platanthera

GENUS: *Platanthera* L. C. Richard (pla-TAN-ther-uh)

TRIBE: Orchideae   SUBTRIBE: Orchidinae

IDENTIFICATION CHARACTERISTICS: From June to September, damp, grassy meadows and roadsides come alive with the brightly colored spikes of *Platanthera*. Unfortunately, these showy perennials have not enjoyed the popularity they deserve as temperate home garden subjects. Although recognized and first identified around 1700, the genus of over 200 species as known today was not fully described until 1918 when Louis C. Richard separated it from *Habenaria* on a small technical difference and native habitat distribution patterns. Richard coined the generic name from two Greek words meaning broad and anther, because of the very broad anthers found in this genus.

These sympodial terrestrials have underground tuberoids and/or thickened fleshy roots. Leaves vary considerably in number, shape, and size. One or more basal leaves up to 12 inches (30 cm) long are often reduced to bractlike appendages on the flower spike. The inflorescences, which arise from the crown of the plant, are up to 30 inches (75 cm) high and have dense clusters of flowers near the apex.

Although many of the flowers in this genus are small, 0.75 inch (2 cm) or less in diameter, they are very attractive and unusual. The flower color range includes orange, purple, greenish, and white. The dorsal sepal and two petals usually form a hood over the column. The two lateral sepals, usually larger than the petals, may be slightly curved to form part of the hood, or may even be reflexed like wings in the background. The lip is highly variable, ranging from entire (e.g., *Platanthera nivea*) to deeply and finely fringed (e.g., *P. cristata*). The spur on the lip is often very pronounced, being longer than the ovary in some species (e.g., *P. ciliaris*).

The short and broad column has a strikingly different anther cap. Two almost-granular pollinia on a long caudicle with a small viscidium are found under each cap.

CULTURE: Temperature, some species survive below freezing temperatures; light, 2400–3600 footcandles in greenhouses, will grow in full sun outdoors; humidity, 40–60%; media, rich, moist organic potting soils; fertilization, monthly during growing season, with a 1–1–1 ratio.

COLOR PLATE: *Platanthera ciliaris*

SPECIES	FLOWERING SEASON	GENERAL LOCALE
blephariglottis	F	Coastal Plain, New Jersey to Texas
ciliaris	S–SS–F	Texas to Illinois & eastward
clavellata	S–SS	Eastern United States, southern Canada
cristata	S–SS–F	Southeastern United States
flava	S–SS–F	Coastal Plain, Virginia to eastern Texas
integra	SS–F	Coastal Plain, New Jersey to Texas
nivea	S–SS–F	Coastal Plain, New Jersey to Texas
obtusata	S–SS–F	Canada, Alaska, eastern Rocky Mountains

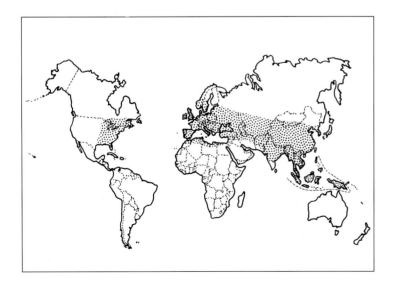

Platanthera ciliaris

A: Plant in flower, × ½.
B: Tuberoids and fleshy roots, × ½.
C: Flower, face view, × 4.
D: Flower, side view, × 2.
E: Lip, × 3.
F: Flower, vertical section, × 3.
G: Column, ventral view, × 8.
H: Column, end view, × 8.
I: Column, side view, × 8.
J: Column, vertical section, × 8.
K, L: Pollinia, × 10.

Marion R. Sheehan

Polycycnis

GENUS: *Polycycnis* Reichenbach f. (pol-ee-SIK-niss)

TRIBE: Maxillarieae SUBTRIBE: Stanhopeinae

IDENTIFICATION CHARACTERISTICS: The generic name tells it all. Derived from the Greek words *polys* (many) and *kyknos* (swan), *Polycycnis* is a very descriptive name to describe the many delicate, swanlike flowers that grace the mostly pendulous inflorescences. Florally, these attractive species resemble *Cycnoches* species but differ in having hermaphroditic flowers. Vegetatively, these species more closely resemble *Gongora* species, but again there are differences in the flowers.

The genus was first described by H. G. Reichenbach in 1885, who based his decision and established a new genus on the distinctive floral characteristics of this group. Reichenbach also picked a very descriptive generic name that readily recognized these distinctive birdlike flowers. Taxonomists have assigned up to seven valid species to this genus.

Vegetatively, the sympodial epiphytes of this genus are similar. The closely grouped pseudobulbs range from ovoid to almost-cylindric in shape and can be up to 6 inches (15 cm) in height. Each pseudobulb is topped by a single leaf, or occasionally two leaves, and is subtended by leafy bracts. The leaves, often petiolate, have blades up to 16 inches (40 cm) long and 5 inches (12.5 cm) wide, and have longitudinal folds. The few- to many-flowered inflorescences arise from the base of the pseudobulb. Most floral stems are pendulous and may be up to 24 inches (60 cm) long.

The base flower color ranges from pale yellow to buff, and flowers are heavily spotted with reddish to brownish dots. The diminutive swanlike flowers, up to 2 inches (5 cm) long, have narrow sepals and petals. The three sepals may be spreading or reflexed. In some cases they may be spreading when the flower first opens and then become reflexed as the open flower ages. The petals are usually a little narrower than the sepals and they, too, may be either spreading or reflexed. They may be slightly stalked at the base. The three-lobed lip is complex, causing it at first glance to appear to be double. It has a scattering of delicate hairs on the upper surface and is also adnate to the base of the column.

The elongate, gently curving, slender column is exerted for almost all its length. It widens in the area of the stigmatic surface and then tapers again towards the anther cap. There are two yellow, almost-cylindrical pollinia attached to a single stipe.

CULTURE: Temperature, 60°F (15°C) at night; light, 2400–3600 footcandles; humidity, 40–60%; medium, any good mix for epiphytes; fertilization, monthly, ratio depends on medium.

COLOR PLATE: *Polycycnis gratiosa*

SPECIES	FLOWERING SEASON	GENERAL LOCALE
aurita	S–SS	Colombia
barbata	S–SS	Costa Rica to Brazil
gratiosa	S–SS	Costa Rica
lehmannii	S–SS	Colombia
muscifera	S–SS	Colombia to Peru
ornata	S–SS	Colombia

Polycycnis gratiosa
A: Plant in flower, × ⅓.
B: Flower, face view, × 1½.
C: Flower, face view, at a
    younger stage, × 1.
D: Flower, side view, × 1½.
E: Lip, three-quarter view, × 3.
F: Flower, vertical section, × 1½.
G: Column, ventral view, × 4.
H: Column, ventral view, upper
    portion, × 6.
I: Column, end view, × 6.
J: Column, side view, × 4.
K: Column, side view, upper
    portion, × 6.
L: Column, vertical section of
    upper portion, × 6.
M, N, O: Pollinia, × 10.

301

Polyrrhiza

GENUS: *Polyrrhiza* Pfitzer (pol-ee-RYE-zuh)
TRIBE: Vandeae   SUBTRIBE: Angraecinae
IDENTIFICATION CHARACTERISTICS: *Polyrrhiza*, a very small genus, contains four to six unusual and interesting species of leafless orchids first described by Ernst H. H. Pfitzer in 1889. Pfitzer formulated the generic name by combining two Greek words meaning many and roots, thus very aptly describing the growth habit of this genus. The genus also has been called *Polyradicion* Garay and may be listed under either name.

These monopodial epiphytes consist of a modified stem and roots. The massive roots radiate out from the very shortened stem and either entwine themselves around and adhere to the stem on which they are growing or grow free from the branch. Since these orchids have no leaves to manufacture carbohydrates to sustain the plant, this function has been taken over by the roots, which are said to be chlorophyllous. Individual roots may be up to 30 inches (75 cm) long. The inflorescences arise from the shortened stem and may bear up to 10 flowers. Each flower opens independently; hence, usually only one flower is open at a time.

The greenish white flowers, up to 5 inches (12.5 cm) in diameter, are borne on greenish brown stems with leafy bracts at each node. The spurred flowers are most fascinating, especially in the configuration of the lip. In general, the three sepals and the two petals are alike in size, shape, and color and are usually reflexed. The three-lobed, spurred lip is the most outstanding feature of this flower. The two lateral lobes of the lip are small and turned upwards. The midlobe splits into two long, often twisted appendages, said by some to resemble the hind legs of an airborne frog. There is a long, narrow, tubular spur at the base of the lip. Some spurs are 6 to 7 inches (15–17.5 cm) long.

The column, which is exposed by the reflexed sepals and petals, is short and stubby. Two lateral appendages are folded down, making the column look very thick when viewed from either side. Two yellowish pollinia are borne on short simple stipes with small hairlike protrusions near the base.

CULTURE: Temperature, 55–60°F (12–15°C); light, 2400–3600 footcandles; humidity, 40–60%; media, palm logs, tree fern, cypress slabs; fertilization, monthly, with a 1–1–1 ratio. These plants should not be exposed to long periods without moisture but should be watered year round.

COLOR PLATE: *Polyrrhiza lindenii*

SPECIES	FLOWERING SEASON	GENERAL LOCALE
lindenii	W–S–SS	Southern Florida, West Indies

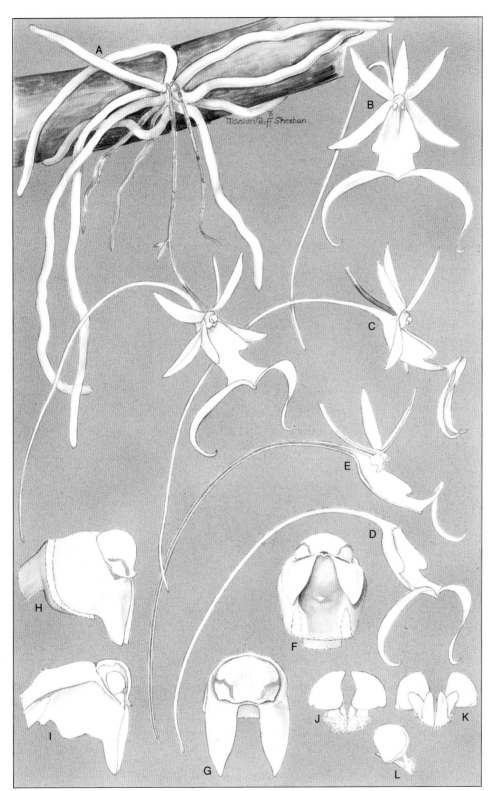

Polyrrhiza lindenii
A: Plant in flower, × ¾.
B: Flower, face view, × ¾.
C: Flower, side view, × ¾.
D: Lip, × ¾.
E: Flower, vertical section, × ¾.
F: Column, ventral view, × 6.
G: Column, end view, × 6.
H: Column, side view, × 6.
I: Column, vertical section, × 6.
J, K, L: Pollinia, × 10.

303

Polystachya _____

GENUS: *Polystachya* Hooker (poly-STAKE-ee-uh)
TRIBE: Epidendreae   SUBTRIBE: Polystachyinae
IDENTIFICATION CHARACTERISTICS: More than 100 species are known in this easy-to-cultivate pantropical genus. The greatest number and variety are found in tropical Africa. Since many of these species are small, they have not enjoyed the popularity they justly deserve for their charming, colorful flowers. The genus was first described by William J. Hooker in 1824, at which time Hooker derived the generic name from the Greek words *poly* (many) and *stachys* (ear of grain). He was probably referring to the many branches of some inflorescences that often are covered with minute, grainlike seed pods (e.g., *Polystachya flavescens*).

The pseudobulbs of these sympodial, epiphytic species are generally small, up to 2 inches (5 cm) tall, and grow either in clusters or chainlike rows. The clasping leaf bases often completely encompass the pseudobulb, which usually has two to four leathery, lancelike leaves measuring up to 8 inches (20 cm) long. The erect inflorescence arises from the apex of the pseudobulb and in some species often has a number of small branches near the apex. Flower colors include yellow-orange, white, pink, and green.

The flowers can be up to 2 inches (5 cm) in diameter but are generally much smaller. They are borne upside down (nonresupinate) and appear to be hooded due to positioning of the lip and the two lateral sepals. Some flowers are covered with fine hairs. The sepals, although similar in shape and color, are usually much larger than the petals. The three-lobed lip has two broad, lateral lobes and often a tongue-shaped, reflexed midlobe. A glandular, sometimes-hairy disc is formed near the base of the lip.

The short, erect column has a distinct foot at the base and is widest just behind the stigmatic surface. The column often is the same color as the flower. The four, almost-elliptical pollinia have very short stipes and are attached to a single, shieldlike foot.

CULTURE: Temperature, 60–65°F (15–18°C); light, 2400–3600 footcandles; humidity, 40–60%; media, tree fern, peat and perlite, bark; fertilization, monthly, ratio depends on medium.

COLOR PLATE: *Polystachya bella*

SPECIES	FLOWERING SEASON	GENERAL LOCALE
affinis	S–SS	West Africa
bella	S–SS	Kenya
concreta	F–W–S–SS	Florida, New & Old World tropics
cultriformis	S–SS–F	Tropical Africa, Madagascar, Mascarene Islands
fallax	W–S	Uganda, Zaire
flavescens	F–W–S–SS	Pantropical
odorata	W	Tropical Africa
pubescens	F–W–S	South Africa

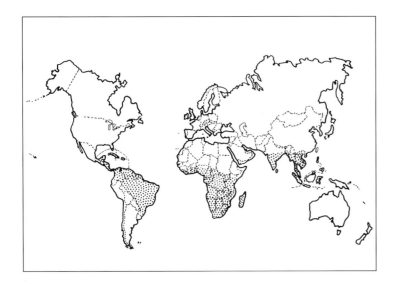

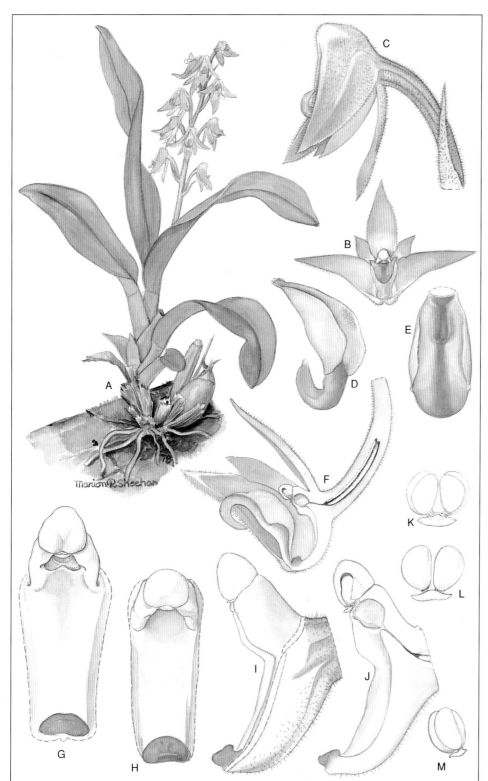

Polystachya bella
A: Plant in flower, × ½.
B: Flower, face view, × 2.
C: Flower, side view, × 3.
D: Lip, three-quarter view, × 5.
E: Lip, face view, × 5.
F: Flower, vertical section, × 3.
G: Column, ventral view, × 8.
H: Column, end view, × 8.
I: Column, side view, × 8.
J: Column, vertical section, × 8.
K, L, M: Pollinia, × 15.

Promenaea

GENUS: *Promenaea* Lindley (prom-en-EE-uh)

TRIBE: Maxillarieae   SUBTRIBE: Zygopetalinae

IDENTIFICATION CHARACTERISTICS: Whoever coined the phrase "good things come in small packages" must have had *Promenaea* in mind. The attractive miniature species of this genus have been popular over the years, probably not so much for their compact growth but for their bright, showy flowers. They are ideal miniatures.

Members of this small Brazilian genus consisting of approximately 15 species are primarily epiphytic but occasionally are found growing on rocks. The genus was described in 1843 by John Lindley, who was so impressed by its beauty that he named it for Promeneia, a priestess at Dodona. *Promenaea* is closely related to *Zygopetalum*, but differs in floral characteristics.

Vegetatively, these popular, cultivated species of sympodial plants form dense clumps of pseudobulbs and are very floriferous. The small, single-node pseudobulbs are approximately 1 inch (2.5 cm) long, 0.5 inch (1 cm) wide, and gray-green to green in color. The mostly slightly arching inflorescences arise from the base of the pseudobulb and have up to three flowers.

Captivating flowers, up to 2 inches (5 cm) in diameter in some species, are the striking feature of *Promenaea*. The base color of the flowers is yellow. The sepals and petals are similar in shape and color, with the sepals slightly larger in some species. The three-lobed lip is the largest floral segment and is the same base color as the other floral segments. The large midlobe and small lateral lobes contain various degrees of reddish spots and stripes. In our plant of *P. xanthina*, spots were restricted to the side lobes.

The stout, almost-straight-sided column has a pronounced foot and a very small stigmatic area. The underside of the column often has reddish marks. The four yellow pollinia are attached to a single small stipe with a large viscidium. The two smaller pollinia are superimposed on the two larger.

CULTURE: Temperature, 60°F (15°C) at night; light, 2400–3600 footcandles; humidity, 40–60%; medium, any well-drained organic medium such as tree fern and sphagnum moss; fertilization, monthly, ratio depends on medium.

COLOR PLATE: *Promenaea xanthina*

SPECIES	FLOWERING SEASON	GENERAL LOCALE
microptera	SS	Brazil
rolinsoni	SS	Brazil
stapelioides	SS–F	Brazil
xanthina	SS–F	Brazil

Promenaea xanthina

A: Plant in flower, × 1.
B: Flower, face view, × 1½.
C: Flower, side view, × 1½.
D: Lip, side view, × 3.
E: Lip, face view, × 3.
F: Flower, vertical section, × 2.
G: Column, ventral view, × 4.
H: Column, end view, × 4.
I: Column, side view, × 4.
J: Column, vertical section, × 4.
K, L, M: Pollinia, × 10.

Psychilis

GENUS: *Psychilis* Rafinesque (si-CHI-liss)
TRIBE: Epidendreae   SUBTRIBE: Laeliinae
IDENTIFICATION CHARACTERISTICS: Showy and very colorful flowers borne in clusters atop long, arching sprays make *Psychilis* species attractive to the hobbyist. This small genus comprising around 15 species is endemic to the West Indies. It was first recognized by Constantine S. Rafinesque in 1836, who coined the generic name from two Greek words, *psyche* (butterfly) and *cheilos* (lip), probably likening the lip with its two lateral wings to a butterfly. Unfortunately, for many years these species were lumped into *Epidendrum* and later *Encyclia*. In 1961 Robert Dressler recognized them as a distinct group and placed them into the "*Encyclia bifidum* group." Later studies by Ruben Sauleda (1988) moved the group back into the genus *Psychilis*, pointing out that the genus differs from *Encyclia* in a number of characteristics. Pseudobulbs of *Encyclia* are mostly pear-shaped (pyriform), while those of *Psychilis* are elongate (fusiform). There are also differences in method of leaf attachment, inflorescences, and attachment of the lip to the column. These differences are sufficient to separate certain species into this genus.

Vegetatively, *Psychilis* species are very much alike and difficult to separate when not in flower. The elongate pseudobulbs are tightly clustered; when mature, they have a number of equally spaced leaf scars indicating where the encircling leafy bracts were attached. Each pseudobulb is usu-ally topped by two narrow, leathery leaves. The leaves may be up to 10 inches (25 cm) long and 0.75 inch (2 cm) wide. The long, arching inflorescence, up to 30 inches (75 cm) tall, arises from the apex of the pseudobulb and bears up to 12 showy flowers, often producing new sprays of flowers for up to three years. Flower color varies among species and includes lavender, magenta, greenish yellow, and yellow.

The attractive flowers are easy to identify. The sepals and petals are very similar in shape and color. In general, the sepals are a little broader or may appear so because the petal bases in some species (e.g., *Psychilis atropurpurea*) tend to be more reflexed. The large lip is three-lobed, with very distinct side lobes that are adnate to the column at their bases. The large midlobe has a distinct, raised callus under the column.

The elongate column tapers slightly toward the base and is broadest in the stigmatic area. Depending on the species, the column may be white, lightly colored, or the same strong color as the flower. There are four yellow, elongate, elliptical pollinia, each with its own simple caudicle with erose margins.

CULTURE: Temperature, 60–65°F (15–18°C); light, 2400–3600 footcandles; humidity, 40–60%; media, plaques, tree fern, bark; fertilization, monthly, ratio depends on medium.

COLOR PLATE: *Psychilis atropurpurea*

SPECIES	FLOWERING SEASON	GENERAL LOCALE
atropurpurea	S–SS–F–W	West Indies
bifida	S–SS–F–W	Hispaniola
kraenzlinii	S–SS–F–W	West Indies
ragani	S–SS–F–W	West Indies

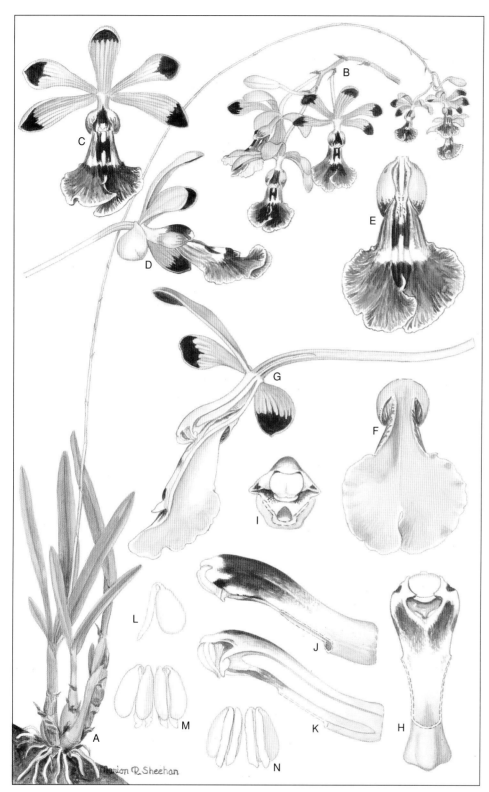

Psychilis atropurpurea
A: Plant in flower, × ¼.
B: Inflorescence, × ½.
C: Flower, face view, × 1.
D: Flower, side view, × 1.
E: Lip, face view, × 1½.
F: Lip, back view, × 1½.
G: Flower, vertical section, × 1½.
H: Column, ventral view, × 3.
I: Column, end view, × 3.
J: Column, side view, × 3.
K: Column, vertical section, × 3.
L, M, N: Pollinia, × 10.

Psygmorchis

GENUS: *Psygmorchis* Dodson & Dressler (sig-MORE-kiss)

TRIBE: Maxillarieae SUBTRIBE: Oncidiinae

IDENTIFICATION CHARACTERISTICS: *Psygmorchis* is a small genus of four miniature species with large attractive yellow flowers almost masking the plants. These plants, with delicate fans of thin leaves, are difficult to maintain in cultivation and often are very short lived in collections. Some authors (e.g., Alec Pridgeon 1992) report that *Psygmorchis* may be short-lived in nature, too. Despite their shortcomings, these species are worthy candidates for a collection as they challenge all who try to cultivate them.

For many years these species were included in *Oncidium*. In 1972, Calaway Dodson and Robert Dressler moved them to the new genus *Psygmorchis* due to differing vegetative characteristics that readily separated them from the other variegata types of *Oncidium* species (Fig. 21). The generic name was derived from two Greek words meaning fan orchid, a fit title for the vegetative characteristics of this genus. In tropical regions, *P. pusilla* is considered a weedy pest of citrus groves.

Vegetatively, these sympodial epiphytes consist of a small fan of up to 10 flat leaves. Each delicate, thin-leaved fan may be no more than 1.25 to 2.25 inches (3–6 cm) wide and may be almost hidden by the large flowers, which are up to 1 inch (2.5 cm) wide in some species (e.g., *Psygmorchis pusilla*). The inflorescences arise from the leaf axils and usually have one flower at a time, but the short flowering stem may have two or three buds that open in succession. The base color of the flowers is yellow.

The flowers are relatively large compared to the diminutive size of the plants. The small sepals and petals are greatly overshadowed by the very large, showy lip. The sepals and petals are usually yellow or greenish yellow, with reddish brown spots. The dorsal sepal often is hoodlike and is deflexed over the column. The yellow lip is three-lobed, with a very large midlobe and with reddish brown marks near the base and on the crest.

The short, pale yellow-green column is distinctly winged. Two yellow pollinia are borne on a long, thin stipe with a reddish brown viscidium at the base.

CULTURE: Temperature, 60°F (15°C); light, 2400 footcandles; humidity, 40–60%; media, tree fern plaques or citrus twigs; fertilization, monthly, with a 1–1–1 ratio. Some growers report that distilled water or rainwater prolongs the life of plants.

COLOR PLATE: *Psygmorchis pusilla*

SPECIES	FLOWERING SEASON	GENERAL LOCALE
glossomystax	W–S–SS	Mexico to Brazil
gnoma	S–SS	Costa Rica, Guatemala
pumilio	S–SS	Brazil, Paraguay
pusilla	W–S–SS–F	Mexico to Brazil & Bolivia, Trinidad

Psygmorchis pusilla
A: Plant in flower, × 1.
B: Flower, face view, × 2.
C: Flower, side view, × 2.
D: Lip, three-quarter view, × 2.
E: Flower, vertical section, × 5.
F: Column, ventral view, × 10.
G: Column, end view, × 10.
H: Column, side view, × 10.
I: Column, vertical section, × 10.
J, K, L: Pollinia, × 20.

Marion R. Sheehan

311

Renanthera

GENUS: *Renanthera* Loureiro (reh-NANN-ther-uh)

TRIBE: Vandeae   SUBTRIBE: Aeridinae

IDENTIFICATION CHARACTERISTICS: *Renanthera* was one of the earliest epiphytic orchids to be grown in England, although the first flowering was not reported until 1827 when, according to Bechtel et al. (1992), it was discovered that the genus had been first described in 1790 by Portuguese botanist Juan Loureiro in *Flora Cochinchinensis*. The generic name was derived from two Greek words, *renes* (kidney) and *antera* (anther), and refers to the somewhat kidney-shaped pollinia that help separate *Renanthera* from *Vanda*.

Some of the most rank-growing monopodial orchids, attaining heights of 15 feet (450 cm), are found among the 10 to 12 species belonging to this genus. The round, leafy stems become almost woody with age. The stiff, leathery leaves have uneven lobes at the apex and range from a few to 12 inches (30 cm) long and 1.5 inches (4 cm) wide. Aerial roots are produced abundantly from the stems of the plants. The inflorescences appear from the axils of the upper leaves and may bear as many as 150 flowers (e.g., *Renanthera storiei*) or as few as 10 (e.g., *R. monachica*). An individual flower spike may be 4 feet (120 cm) long (e.g., *R. storiei*).

The flowers, basically red or yellow, are up to 2.5 to 3.5 inches (6–8 cm) in diameter and may last a month or longer. They have unequal sepals; the two lateral sepals are the largest segments of the flowers and often have wavy margins. The two petals are similar in shape to the dorsal sepal but are usually longer and narrower. The lip is very small with a saclike spur at the base. The midlobe is often reflexed with a small callus area directly below the stigmatic surface.

The small column, almost as broad as it is long, usually extends slightly beyond the reflexed midlobe of the lip and may be partially hidden by the side lobes. Two yellow pollinia, kidney-shaped when viewed from one side or more like pocketbook rolls when seen from another angle, are borne on a small stipe with a broad shield-shaped base.

CULTURE: Temperature, 65–70°F (18–21°C); light, full sun for best flowering; humidity, 40–60%; media, tree fern, fir bark; fertilization, monthly, ratio depends on medium.

COLOR PLATE: *Renanthera philippinensis*

SPECIES	FLOWERING SEASON	GENERAL LOCALE
coccinea	S–SS–F	Southern China to Thailand
elongata	W	Java, Borneo, Sumatra, Malay Peninsula
imschootiana	SS	Assam, Laos, Vietnam
matutina	F	Malay Peninsula, Thailand, Sumatra, Java
monachica	W–S	Philippines
philippinensis	S	Philippines
pulchella	F	Assam, Myanmar, Thailand
sarcanthoides	SS	Sumatra, Celebes, Malaysia
storiei	SS	Philippines

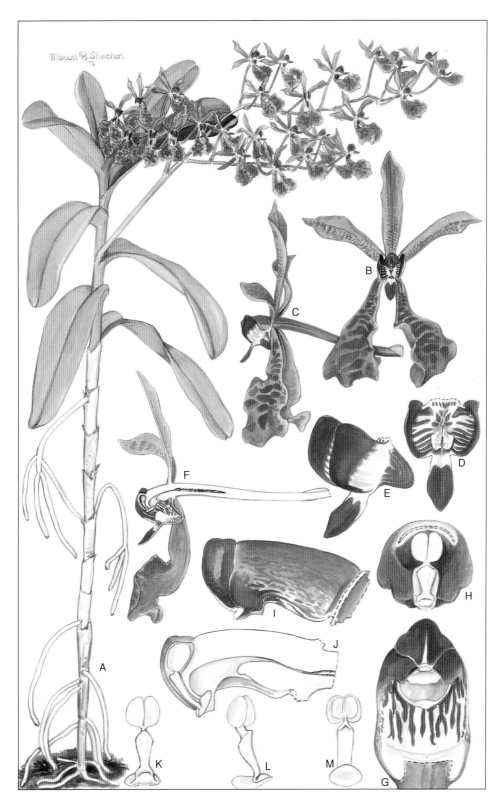

Renanthera philippinensis

A: Plant in flower, × ⅓.
B: Flower, face view, × 1½.
C: Flower, side view, × 1½.
D: Lip, face view, × 3.
E: Lip, side view, × 3.
F: Flower, vertical section, × 1½.
G: Column, ventral view, × 8.
H: Column, end view, anther
   cap removed to show pol-
   linia, × 8.
I: Column, side view, × 8.
J: Column, vertical section, × 8.
K, L, M: Pollinia, × 8.

Rhyncholaelia

GENUS: *Rhyncholaelia* Schlechter (rink-oh-LAY-lee-uh)

TRIBE: Epidendreae SUBTRIBE: Laeliinae

IDENTIFICATION CHARACTERISTICS: "To be or not to be *Rhyncholaelia*, that is the question." For more than 70 years, the question has been: What is the correct generic name for the plant depicted in the accompanying illustration and for other species like it? Is it *Rhyncholaelia*, *Laelia*, or *Brassavola*? In 1918, Rudolf Schlechter recognized that two species of spectacular flowering plants were sufficiently different taxonomically from *Cattleya*, *Laelia*, and *Brassavola* to be placed in a separate genus. He coined the generic name *Rhyncholaelia* from the Greek word *rhynchos* (snout) and the genus name *Laelia*, undoubtedly a reference to the seed capsule, which Schlechter considered a main point in his generic separation. Although still debated by taxonomists, *Rhyncholaelia* is considered by most as the proper generic name. From a horticulturist's standpoint, however, *Brassavola* probably will continue to be used as the generic name to be consistent with the hundreds of hybrids already recorded.

Vegetatively, these sympodial epiphytes are very easy to distinguish from their close relatives. They have club-shaped to spindle-shaped pseudobulbs that often are hidden by very glaucous, almost-white sheaths. Each pseudobulb is topped by a single stiff, leathery, gray-green, glaucous leaf that is usually elliptic and up to 8 inches (20 cm) long. Each growth bears a single flower subtended by a very large, leafy sheath.

The basic flower colors are light green to creamy white, with an occasional flower displaying a pale lavender-pink tint. The throats of the flowers range from emerald green in color to having a large rose-colored spot. The flowers, which can be up to 7 inches (17.5 cm) in diameter, are very similar as far as their sepals and petals are concerned, usually being alike in size, shape, and color, with the segments of *Rhyncholaelia glauca* a little more reflexed. The lips, however, are so distinctly different that these two species can be separated easily without question. *Rhyncholaelia digbyana* has an extremely large, slightly three-lobed lip, which has a very deeply fringed margin, whereas *R. glauca* has a broad, blunt, fringeless lip.

The column is almost straight sided with a small anther cap at the apex. There are eight pollinia, four large and four small, with two large and two small attached to each caudicle. Some caudicles have what appear to be small globules of pollen attached near the margins between the normal pollinia.

CULTURE: Temperature, 60–65°F (15–18°C) at night; light, 2400–3600 footcandles; humidity, 40–60%; media, tree fern, fir bark, tree fern plaques; fertilization, monthly, ratio depends on medium.

COLOR PLATE: *Rhyncholaelia digbyana*

SPECIES	FLOWERING SEASON	GENERAL LOCALE
digbyana	S–SS	Mexico to Guatemala
glauca	S	Mexico, Guatemala, Honduras

314

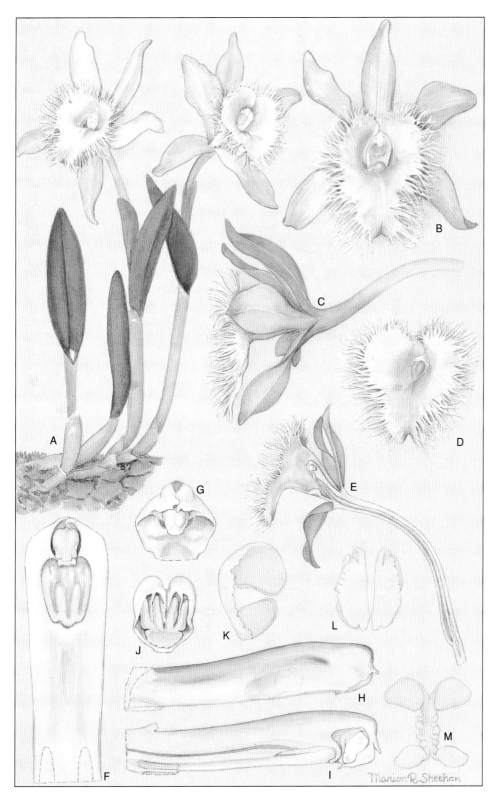

Rhyncholaelia digbyana
A: Plant in flower, × ⅓.
B: Flower, face view, × ½.
C: Flower, side view, × ½.
D: Lip, × ½.
E: Flower, vertical section, × ⅓.
F: Column, ventral view, × 2.
G: Column, end view, × 2.
H: Column, side view, × 2.
I: Column, vertical section, × 2.
J: Anther cap with pollinia, × 4.
K, L, M: Pollinia, × 5.

315

Rhynchostylis

GENUS: *Rhynchostylis* Blume (rink-oh-STY-liss)
TRIBE: Vandeae   SUBTRIBE: Aeridinae
IDENTIFICATION CHARACTERISTICS: This small genus of very floriferous plants was discovered by Carl Blume on a collecting trip in Java in the early 1880s. The species originally were assigned to *Saccolabium*, a closely related genus, and later transferred to *Rhynchostylis*. The foxtail orchids, as the four species of this genus are often called, are enjoyed and grown for their long, erect or pendent axillary inflorescences, which are densely covered with small colorful flowers. The generic name was derived from two Greek words, *rhynchos* (beak) and *stylos* (pillar), and refers to the beaked column. Unfortunately, the beaked column is not specifically limited to this genus.

The stout, monopodial epiphytes of this genus range in height from 8 inches (20 cm) to 4 feet (120 cm). The thick leathery leaves are very closely arranged on the stem. There are two unequal lobes at the apex of the leaves. The leaves of some species may be up to 12 inches (30 cm) long and 2.5 inches (6 cm) wide, while others are smaller, but all have a distinct keel beneath.

The large numbers and bright colors of the flowers more than compensate for their small size, 0.75 to 1 inch (2–2.5 cm) in diameter. The waxy sepals and petals vary slightly among species, but usually are much alike and often have wavy margins. The short lip is usually compressed and slightly curved with a saclike spur at the base. The flowers are basically white with red, magenta, or lavender-blue spots. Reddish lavender and white forms have been introduced into the trade.

The column is very short with a beaked anther at the apex. The almost-heart-shaped anther cap protects the two yellow pollinia. The round pollinia, with a slight cleavage on the front side, are borne on small stalks, attached to a broader stipe, which is attached to a broad, flat foot.

CULTURE: Temperature, 60–70°F (15–21°C); light, 2400–3600 footcandles; humidity, 40–70%; media, peat and perlite, tree fern, bark, or combinations of these; fertilization, monthly, ratio depends on medium.

COLOR PLATE: *Rhynchostylis gigantea*

SPECIES	FLOWERING SEASON	GENERAL LOCALE
coelestis	SS–F	Thailand
gigantea	F–W	Malaysia, Indochina, Myanmar, Thailand
retusa	S–SS	India & Sri Lanka to Southeast Asia, East Indies, Philippines

Rhynchostylis gigantea
A: Plant in flower, × ¼.
B: Flower, face view, × 1.
C: Flower, side view, × 1.
D: Lip, face view, × 1½.
E: Lip, side view, × 1½.
F: Flower, vertical section, × 1½.
G: Column, ventral view, × 4.
H: Column, end view, × 4.
I: Column, side view, × 4.
J: Column, vertical section, × 4.
K: Column, end view, anther
   cap and pollinia removed,
   × 4.
L: Anther cap with pollinia, × 6.
M, N: Pollinia, × 8.

317

Robiquetia

GENUS: *Robiquetia* Gaudichaud (roh-bih-KWET-ee-uh)

TRIBE: Vandeae   SUBTRIBE: Aeridinae

IDENTIFICATION CHARACTERISTICS: There are probably not more than 12 species of charming plants in the genus *Robiquetia*, few of which have found their way into orchid collections. The pendulous sprays of many very small, colorful flowers make these orchids most attractive. The genus was first described by Charles Gaudichaud-Beaupré in 1862 and named in honor of French chemist M. Pierre Robiquet. This signal honor was accorded Robiquet for his discovery of both morphine and caffeine. Although these Southeast Asian monopodial epiphytes do not have spectacular flowers, they are a delight and should be grown more widely.

Vegetatively, *Robiquetia* species resemble small *Aerides* species, except that they are pendent rather than upright. The thick, leathery leaves may be 7 to 8 inches (17.5–20 cm) long and 2 inches (5 cm) wide and are distinctly bilobed at the apex. The inflorescences arise from the leaf axis and are pendulous, up to 10 inches (25 cm) long and densely covered with small, 0.5-inch (1-cm) wide flowers. Basic flower colors are red-browns and yellows, with some purples and whites; many flowers are spotted.

The small but heavy-textured flowers are very attractive and are often overlooked because of their diminutive size. The sepals and two petals are almost alike in shape and color, but the petals are slightly smaller than the sepals. All flower segments are slightly curved, making the flower almost cup-shaped. The three-lobed, spurred lip appears almost sac-shaped. The two lateral lobes are erect and the pointed midlobe is slightly concave.

The column is very short and almost as broad with a very pronounced, pointed anther cap at the apex. The stigmatic surface lies behind the sharp-tipped rostellum. The two yellow, almost-round, cleft pollinia are borne atop a long, narrow stipe with a very small, shield-shaped foot.

CULTURE: Temperature, 60–70°F (15–21°C); light, 2400–3600 footcandles; humidity, 40–60%; media, tree fern, bark, also grows well on tree fern plaques; fertilization, monthly, ratio depends on medium.

COLOR PLATE: *Robiquetia spathulata*

SPECIES	FLOWERING SEASON	GENERAL LOCALE
hamata	W	New Guinea
mooreana	W	New Guinea
spathulata	SS	Myanmar to Philippines, Indonesia

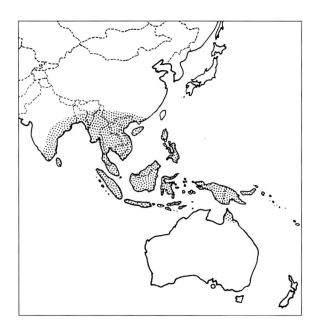

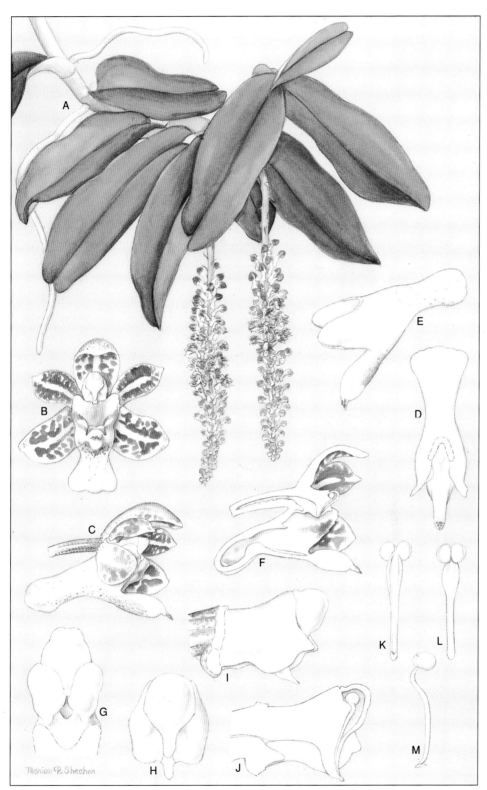

Robiquetia spathulata

A: Plant in flower, × ½.
B: Flower, face view, × 4.
C: Flower, side view, × 4.
D: Lip, face view, × 5.
E: Lip, side view, × 5.
F: Flower, vertical section, × 4.
G: Column, ventral view, × 12.
H: Column, end view, × 12.
I: Column, side view, × 12.
J: Column, vertical section, × 12.
K, L, M: Pollinia, × 15.

Rodriguezia

GENUS: *Rodriguezia* Ruiz and Pavón (rod-rih-GEEZ-ee-uh)

TRIBE: Maxillarieae   SUBTRIBE: Oncidiinae

IDENTIFICATION CHARACTERISTICS: *Rodriguezia*, a popular, well-known, and widely grown genus, contains about 20 species of dwarf plants, which have been in cultivation since the early 1880s. This genus was first studied and named by Hipólito Ruiz Lopez and José Antonio Pavón in 1794 and dedicated to an early Spanish botanist, Emanual Rodriguez.

Rodriguezias are small, sympodial, pseudobulbous epiphytes often with very elongate rhizomes. Some species (e.g., *Rodriguezia lanceolata*) produce large numbers of fine white roots that become a very conspicuous part of the plant. This genus is closely related to *Ionopsis* and *Comparettia*, differing primarily in floral characteristics. *Rodriguezia* and *Oncidium* have been hybridized.

The pseudobulbs are ovoid, to 1.5 inches (4 cm) long, and often compressed and furrowed when old. Some species have only one leaf per pseudobulb (e.g., *Rodriguezia batemannii*), while others have a half dozen per bulb (e.g., *R. lanceolata*). The leaves are leathery, narrow, to 9 inches (22 cm) long, and often folded at the base, similar to hands clasped in prayer. The flowers are borne on sprays that usually are as long as the leaves and bear from a few to 30 flowers. The flowers are often arranged on one side of the stem (e.g., *R. lanceolata*) and range from 0.75 to 1.5 inches (2–4 cm) wide.

The flowers of *Rodriguezia* have several distinct characteristics. The lateral sepals are united and form a boatlike structure concealed by the large, prominent lip, which has a much reduced spur at the base. The lip margin is wavy and a small indentation is often found at the apex of the lip. The dorsal sepal and two petals are similar in size, shape, and color. Rose and white are the predominant flower colors.

The small column is broadest near the stigmatic surface and tapers gradually toward both ends. The basal one-third of the column is covered by fine white hairlike projections in some species. The column may be winged or may have a hornlike projection on either side of the almost-oval stigmatic surface. Two whitish or yellowish pollinia are borne on a white stipe with a yellowish disc at the base of the stipe. The round pollinia are of uniform size and appear to be slightly split at the top.

CULTURE: Temperature, 60–65°F (15–18°C); light, 2400–3600 footcandles; humidity, 40–70%; media, peat and perlite, tree fern, bark; fertilization, monthly, ratio depends on medium.

COLOR PLATE: *Rodriguezia lanceolata*

SPECIES	FLOWERING SEASON	GENERAL LOCALE
batemannii	S	Peru
candida	F	Brazil, Guyana
compacta	S	Costa Rica, Panama
decora	S–SS	Brazil
lanceolata	W–S	Trinidad, Panama, tropical South America
pubescens	W–S	Brazil
strobelii	S–SS	Ecuador
venusta	S–SS	Brazil

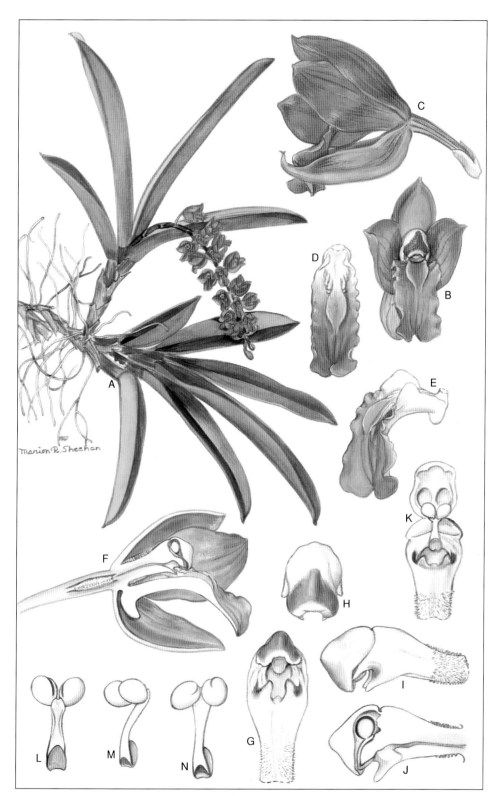

Rodriguezia lanceolata
A: Plant in flower, × ½.
B: Flower, face view, × 3.
C: Flower, side view, × 3.
D: Lip, face view, × 3.
E: Lip, side view, × 3.
F: Flower, vertical section, × 3.
G: Column, ventral view, × 6.
H: Column, end view, × 6.
I: Column, side view, × 6.
J: Column, vertical section, × 6.
K: Column, end view, anther
   cap lifted to show pollinia,
   × 6.
L, M, N: Pollinia, × 12.

321

Rodrigueziella

GENUS: *Rodrigueziella* Kuntze (rod-rih-geez-ee-EL-uh)

TRIBE: Maxillarieae   SUBTRIBE: Oncidiinae

IDENTIFICATION CHARACTERISTICS: In a crowded greenhouse, the diminutive flowers of *Rodrigueziella* might go unnoticed if it were not for their delightful fragrance revealing their presence among the leaves. This fine genus of miniature orchids is closely related to *Gomesa*, but naming it correctly poses a taxonomic dilemma. Do the plants belong to *Rodrigueziella* or *Theodorea*? The controversy has been going on since 1891 and even today these plants are listed under both generic names in literature on Brazilian orchids. The present volume follows Guido F. J. Pabst and Fritz Dungs, who accept *Rodrigueziella* as the proper generic name. Otto Kuntze named this genus of perhaps six species in 1891 to honor João Barbosa-Rodrigues, an avid plant collector in Brazil.

The sympodial epiphytic species of *Rodrigueziella* have small, slender, smooth pseudobulbs, each subtended by several leafy bracts and with a pair of soft, leaves, up to 5 inches (12.5 cm) long, at the apex. The arching, bracted inflorescences arise from the base of the pseudobulb, bear up to 10 flowers, and usually are shorter than the leaves and often slightly below them.

The base color of the small flower is pale yellow-green. Although diminutive, the 0.5-inch (1-cm) wide flowers are borne in considerable numbers, even on a small plant. This feature, combined with the fragrance of the flowers, makes the plants attractive subjects. The sepals and petals are very similar in size, shape, and color, with the dorsal sepal seemingly slightly broader. Floral segments usually curve forward. The three-lobed lip is almost fiddle-shaped, with the midlobe slightly recurved. The keels on the lip are yellow and covered with hairs.

The column is long, narrow, and slightly wider at the stigmatic surface. Two brownish pollinia are borne on a single stipe with a brownish viscidium.

CULTURE: Temperature, 60°F (15°C); light, 2400–3600 footcandles; humidity, 40–60%; media, tree fern plaque, branches, tree fern; fertilization, monthly, with a 1–1–1 ratio.

COLOR PLATE: *Rodrigueziella gomezoides*

SPECIES	FLOWERING SEASON	GENERAL LOCALE
gomezoides	S	Brazil
handroi	S–SS	Brazil

Rodrigueziella gomezoides
A: Plant in flower, × ¾.
B: Flower, face view, × 4.
C: Flower, side view, × 4.
D: Lip, face view, × 8.
E: Lip, side view, × 8.
F: Flower, vertical section, × 6.
G: Column, ventral view, × 10.
H: Column, end view, × 10.
I: Column, side view, × 10.
J: Column, vertical section, × 10.
K, L, M: Pollinia, × 20.

Rossioglossum

GENUS: *Rossioglossum* (Schlechter) Garay & Kennedy (ross-ee-oh-GLOSS-um)

TRIBE: Maxillarieae   SUBTRIBE: Oncidiinae

IDENTIFICATION CHARACTERISTICS: Originally part of the complex genus *Odontoglossum*, several large and colorful species were transferred to the new genus *Rossioglossum* by Leslie Garay and George Kennedy in 1976. The two men reasoned that there were enough differences in lip and column features to raise Rudolf Schlechter's section of the genus *Odontoglossum* to generic level. They retained part of the basic generic name, *glossum*, referring to the tonguelike lip, and added the prefix *rossio-* in honor of John Ross, who collected in Mexico in the early 1800s and discovered *R. insleayi* around 1839.

Vegetatively, the six sympodial, epiphytic species of this genus are very much alike. The mostly ovoid pseudobulbs are borne on a very short rhizome and form tight clusters. Each pseudobulb is topped by two elliptic-to-lanceolate leaves. Individual petiolate leaves may be up to 8 inches (20 cm) long and 2.5 inches (6 cm) wide. The lateral, erect inflorescences may be up to 6 inches (15 cm) long and bear up to eight flowers.

The 3.5-inch (8-cm) wide flowers are yellow with spots or blotches of varying shades of red-brown. The sepals and petals are alike in shape and color. The petals are slightly larger or appear so due to the rolled back margins on the sepals. The surfaces of the floral segments have a high glossy sheen and are most attractive. The three-lobed lip is free from the column. The two side lobes are very small with the midlobe comprising the major portion of the lip. There is a distinctly fleshy, mostly bilobed callus near the side lobes.

The column is short and erect, and sometimes has two incurving horns. Its underside may be slightly hairy. The two elongate yellow pollinia are borne on a small triangular stipe, which looks almost oval due to the inrolled margins. Each stipe has a very small viscidium.

CULTURE: Temperature, 50–55°F (10–12°C) at night; light, 2400–3600 footcandles; humidity, 40–60%; media, fir bark, tree fern, peat and perlite; fertilization, monthly, with a 1–1–1 ratio for tree fern, peat and perlite, and with a 3–1–1 ratio for fir bark.

COLOR PLATE: *Rossioglossum insleayi*

SPECIES	FLOWERING SEASON	GENERAL LOCALE
grande	F–W–S	Mexico, Guatemala
insleayi	F	Mexico
schlieperianum	F	Costa Rica to Panama
williamsianum	S	Guatemala, Honduras, Costa Rica

Rossioglossum insleayi
A: Plant in flower, × ½.
B: Flower, face view, × ¾.
C: Flower, side view, × ¾.
D: Lip, × 2.
E: Flower, vertical section, × ¾.
F: Column, ventral view, × 5.
G: Column, end view, × 5.
H: Column, side view, × 5.
I: Column, vertical section, × 5.
J, K, L: Pollinia, × 8.

Sarcochilus _____

GENUS: *Sarcochilus* R. Brown (sar-koh-KYE-luss)
TRIBE: Vandeae SUBTRIBE: Aeridinae
IDENTIFICATION CHARACTERISTICS: Although widespread through much of Southeast Asia and south to Australia, *Sarcochilus* has not had the attention it richly deserves. The attractive, flowering plants of this genus make handsome specimens. When Robert Brown first described the genus in 1810, he combined two Greek words, *sarcos* (flesh) and *cheilos* (lip), to describe the fleshy lips. The genus as now known contains over 50 species formerly scattered among several genera.

Sarcochilus species are mostly epiphytic, although some grow on rocks and others might be classed as semiterrestrial. The growth of some species (e.g., *S. stenoglottis*) is similar to that of *Phalaenopsis* species; the growth of other species (e.g., *S. hartmannii*) resembles that of miniature *Vanda* species although clumps are often formed. Each growth has five or more leathery leaves, with clasping leaf bases, up to 12 inches (30 cm) long and 1 inch (2.5 cm) wide. Some leaves have almost-straight sides. The inflorescences arise from the axils of the leaves and bear five or more flowers.

The flowers, which can be up to 2 inches (5 cm) in diameter, range in color from white to yellow, often with red speckling. The sepals and petals are alike in shape and color, although the sepals are usually broader than the petals. The three-lobed lip varies among the species and may be very showy (e.g., *Sarcochilus fitzgeraldii*) or very small. It is hinged to the footed column. In some species the flowers last only one day.

The short column has a very pronounced foot and an almost-circular, stigmatic surface. Two almost-elliptical pollinia are attached to a short-footed stipe.

CULTURE: Temperature, 60–65°F (15–18°C); light, 2400–3600 footcandles; humidity, 40–60%; media, fir bark, tree fern, peat and perlite; fertilization, monthly, ratio depends on medium.

COLOR PLATE: *Sarcochilus hartmannii*

SPECIES	FLOWERING SEASON	GENERAL LOCALE
australis	F–W	Australia
falcatus	F	Australia
fitzgeraldii	W	Australia
hartmannii	W	Australia
pallidus	F–W–S–SS	Malay Peninsula, Philippines, Indonesia
stenoglottis	F	Sumatra, Borneo, Malay Peninsula
virescens	F	Malay Peninsula

Sarcochilus hartmannii
A: Plant in flower, × ½.
B: Flower, face view, × 1½.
C: Flower, side view, × 1½.
D: Lip, side view, × 7.
E: Lip, face view, × 7.
F: Flower, vertical section, × 1½.
G: Column, ventral view, × 10.
H: Column, end view, × 10.
I: Column, side view, × 10.
J: Column, vertical section, × 10.
K, L, M: Pollinia, × 20.

327

Sarcoglottis _____

GENUS: *Sarcoglottis* Presl (sar-koh-GLOTT-iss)
TRIBE: Cranichideae SUBTRIBE: Spiranthinae
IDENTIFICATION CHARACTERISTICS: *Sarcoglottis* is considered by some taxonomists as merely a subsection of the large, complex genus *Spiranthes*; however, the two can be separated by differences in floral characteristics. Jan Presl first singled out the genus in 1827 and now there are more than 35 recognized species. The generic name was derived from two Greek words, *sarx* and *glotta*, meaning fleshy tongue, a reference to the fleshy lips on the flowers. Many of these terrestrial, sympodial species make very attractive foliage plants when not in flower. Unfortunately, the leaves die back each year so there is a short period when the plants are not attractive.

This group of pseudobulbless orchids has basal rosettes of large, soft leaves up to 14 inches (35.5 cm) long and 3 inches (7.5 cm) wide. Some leaves are attractively variegated green and white, while most are medium to dark green. They die back annually and are replaced by a new set soon after flowering. The tall, erect, leafless inflorescences arise from the center of the rosette of leaves. Each node and bud is subtended by a green, leafy bract. Most inflorescences bear 12 or more flowers, and flower color varies with the species.

The small, almost-tubular, elongate flowers, 2.25 × 0.5 inches (6 × 1 cm), are often hairy on the outside. The three sepals are unequal in size but the same in shape and color. The smaller sepal is the dorsal sepal; it is usually slightly concave but in some cases may be upright. The two petals are slightly larger than the dorsal sepal, converging with it. The three-lobed lip partially encloses the column between the two upright, lateral lobes. The midlobe is flared and reflexed. The flowers are spurred, but the spur is fused to the ovary and is often missed by the casual observer; in a vertical section of the flower, however, it is obvious.

The column is most unusual, being widest near the stigmatic area and tapering almost to a point at the apex. The stigmatic surface has two distinct divisions. The rostellum is thin and almost translucent. Two elongate pollinia, resembling rabbit's ears, are attached to a very short stipe with a shield-shaped foot.

CULTURE: Temperature, 60–68°F (15–20°C); light, 2400–3600 footcandles; humidity, 40–60%; media, a mixture of 1 leaf mold : 1 peat moss, or 1 peat moss : 1 soil : 1 perlite; fertilization, monthly, with a 1–1–1 ratio.

COLOR PLATE: *Sarcoglottis metallica* var. *variegata*

SPECIES	FLOWERING SEASON	GENERAL LOCALE
acaulis	S–SS–F	Mexico to Argentina
grandiflora	S–SS–F	Venezuela, Brazil, Ecuador
metallica	S–SS	Brazil
var. *variegata*	S–SS	Brazil
sceptrodes	S–SS–F	El Salvador to Panama

Sarcoglottis metallica var. *variegata*

A: Plant in flower, × ³⁄₈.
B: Flower, face view, × 1.
C: Flower, side view, × 1.
D: Column and lip, × 4.
E: Petals and upper sepal, × 1½.
F: Flower, vertical section, × 1½.
G: Column, top view, × 5.
H: Column, ventral view, × 5.
I: Column, side view, × 5.
J, K, L: Pollinia, × 5.

Schoenorchis

GENUS: *Schoenorchis* Blume (shoen-OR-kiss)
TRIBE: Vandeae   SUBTRIBE: Aeridinae
IDENTIFICATION CHARACTERISTICS: If plants were ever nominated as jewels of miniature orchids, some species of *Schoenorchis* would be top candidates on the list. Among the 24 known species in this genus, some delightful miniatures have flowers no larger than the blunt tip of a pencil. In some cases, flowers are borne in unusually large numbers and are often very colorful. Hence, what they lack in size is overcome by numbers and color. *Schoenorchis fragrans* serves as a prime example of these characteristics. Some species (e.g., *S. gemmata*) grow to about 1 foot (30 cm) tall and are almost out of the miniature class.

The genus was first described by Carl Blume in 1825, but over the years some species have been intermingled with *Saccolabium*. It was not until 1908, when J. J. Smith broke up the genus *Saccolabium*, that *Schoenorchis* was finally recognized by most authors as a distinct genus based on differing floral characteristics. The generic name was derived from the Greek words *schoenos* (reed, rush) and *orchis* (orchid), probably referring to the reedlike leaves on some species. Identifying species is difficult at best because they are often separated by minute characteristics. For example, *S. fragrans* and *S. seidenfadenii* are separated by the difference in the calluslike growth on the epichile of the lip and the angle between the spur and the epichile. These microscopic differences make it difficult for the average grower

to separate the species, therefore often leading to mislabeling. Eric Christenson (1985, p. 851) considers these two species to be conspecific, retaining *S. fragrans* as the species.

Vegetatively, this small genus consists of mostly pendent, epiphytic, herbaceous species. Whether the species are erect or pendent, the leaves may be linear and terete to short and flat, with the leaf bases clasping the stem. The smaller, broader leaves of some species (e.g., *Schoenorchis fragrans*) are often purplish beneath. Individual leaves may be up to 4 inches (10 cm) long but usually not over 0.25 inch (0.5 cm) wide. The many-flowered inflorescences arise from the axil of the leaf and are usually drooping or lax, simple or branched. In some species with multiple inflorescences on a plant, the leaves may be completely hidden by the flowers.

The main flower colors are purple and white, and flowers range from 0.15 to 0.5 inch (2–10 mm) across. The sepals and petals are similar in shape and color but may vary slightly in size. Since the sparkling flowers are so small, however, the minute differences in size often go undetected to the naked eye. The three-lobed lip is narrow and has a distinct spur. The side lobes are small and erect, while the spur is very large and pronounced.

The very short column is erect with a relatively large anther cap when compared to most other columns. The stigmatic surface is small. Four yellow pollinia are borne as two appressed pairs on a single stipe with a large viscidium.

CULTURE: Temperature, 60°F (15°C); light, 2400–3600 footcandles; humidity, 40–60%; media, tree fern plaques, cork bark; fertilization, monthly, with a 1–1–1 ratio.

COLOR PLATE: *Schoenorchis fragrans*

SPECIES	FLOWERING SEASON	GENERAL LOCALE
fragrans	S–SS	Thailand
gemmata	SS	India to Thailand
juncifolia	SS	Java, Sumatra
seidenfadenii	SS	Thailand
spatulata	S–SS	Thailand

Schoenorchis fragrans
A: Plant in flower, × 2.
B: Flower, face view, × 10.
C: Flower, side view, × 10.
D: Lip, face view, × 12.
E: Lip, side view, × 12.
F: Flower, vertical section, × 12.
G: Column, ventral view, × 30.
H: Column, end view, × 30.
I: Column, side view, × 30.
J: Column, vertical section, × 30.
K: Column, anther cap removed
   to show pollinia in place,
   × 30.
L, M, N: Pollinia, × 50.

331

Schomburgkia

GENUS: *Schomburgkia* Lindley (shom-BURG-kee-uh)

TRIBE: Epidendreae SUBTRIBE: Laeliinae

IDENTIFICATION CHARACTERISTICS: While Richard Schomburgk, a well-known German botanist, was a member of the boundary expedition to Guyana (then British Guiana) in 1840–1844, he found many new species of plants. John Lindley named one of the orchid plants *Schomburgkia crispa* (now *S. gloriosa*) in honor of the founding botanist. Although some taxonomists no longer consider this a valid genus and have transferred all species to the genus *Laelia*, many taxonomists and horticulturists disagree and list the plants under the original generic name. Some species (e.g., *S. tibicinis*) have been transferred to *Myrmecophila*, leaving about 12 species in *Schomburgkia*.

These sometimes-massive, sympodial epiphytes have very distinctive pseudobulbs resembling those of *Cattleya* but with a stalked base. Two or three leathery leaves surmount each pseudobulb. The terminal inflorescences, bearing upward to 15 flowers, attain lengths of 5 feet (150 cm) or more.

The flowers are 1.5 to 3.5 inches (4–8 cm) wide. Flower colors are cream, red-brown, reddish purple, and wine purple. Bigeneric hybrids have been produced with *Cattleya*, *Laelia*, *Caularthron* (*Diacrium*), and *Epidendrum*. The sepals and petals are almost equal in size and shape; some are narrow, some broad, but all have undulating margins. The lip is three-lobed, with the two lateral lobes partially enclosing the column.

The short, broad column has only one distinct lobe at the apex that protrudes over the anther cap. The stigmatic surface is almost heart-shaped. There is a large cavity between the stigmatic surface and the point of attachment of the floral segments, thus leaving most of the underside of the column almost hollow. The light yellow pollinia are borne in two groups of four pollinia each. Two pollinia are attached at each end of a short, broad caudicle with uneven margins.

CULTURE: Temperature, 60–70°F (15–21°C); light, 2400–3600 footcandles (survives under higher light intensities in some tropical areas); humidity, 40–70%; media, peat and perlite, tree fern, bark; fertilization, monthly, ratio depends on medium.

COLOR PLATE: *Schomburgkia undulata*

SPECIES	FLOWERING SEASON	GENERAL LOCALE
gloriosa	F–W	Venezuela, Guyana, Suriname, French Guiana, Brazil
humboldtii	W–S	Venezuela
lyonsii	SS–F	Cuba, Jamaica
rosea	W–S	Venezuela, Colombia
superbiens	W	Mexico, Guatemala, Honduras
thomsoniana	S	Cuba, Cayman Islands
undulata	W–S	Colombia, Trinidad, Venezuela
weberbauerana	W–S	Venezuela, Peru

Schomburgkia undulata
A: Plant in flower, × ¼.
B: Flower, face view, × ¾.
C: Flower, side view, × ¾.
D: Lip, face view, × 2.
E: Lip, side view, × 2.
F: Flower, vertical section, × ¾.
G: Column, ventral view, × 3.
H: Column, end view, × 3.
I: Column, side view, × 3.
J: Column, vertical section, × 3.
K: Anther cap and pollinia, × 5.
L, M: Pollinia, × 12.

marion R. Sheehan

Scuticaria

GENUS: *Scuticaria* Lindley (skoot-ih-CARE-ee-uh)

TRIBE: Maxillarieae   SUBTRIBE: Zygopetalinae

IDENTIFICATION CHARACTERISTICS: *Scuticaria* is a very small, captivating genus consisting of at least two and possibly as many as four unique species. At first glance the flowers are reminiscent of those of *Maxillaria*, to which they are closely allied. In 1843, John Lindley removed *S. steelii* from *Maxillaria* and founded the new genus. His reason for separating the species was that *Scuticaria* has more flowers per stalk and different pollinia. Lindley chose the generic name based on the Greek word *scutica* (lash), undoubtedly referring to the long, whiplike, terete leaves so typical of this genus. Unfortunately, *Scuticaria* is not as widely grown as a fine attractive genus should be.

This group of sympodial epiphytes has distinctive, grooved, terete, pendent leaves that may be up to 4 feet (120 cm) long, with most averaging 2 to 3 feet (60–90 cm), and not more than pencil thick. The leaves are borne in fairly tight clusters. Each leaf is borne atop a very short, sometimes knotty stem, usually as thick as the leaf and often swollen at the base. Each flowering scape may have two to three flowers.

Flower colors are basically combinations of browns and yellow-greens. The fleshy flowers are up to 3 inches (7.5 cm) in diameter (e.g., *Scuticaria steelii*). The sepals and two petals are alike in shape and color, but the two petals are slightly smaller than the sepals. The three-lobed lip has two lateral lobes turned up and almost enclosing the column. The flared midlobe is slightly cupped and is usually slightly cleft in the middle. There is a fleshy crest on the lip under the column.

The long, narrow column is slightly curved, footed, and spotted purplish brown. The base of the anther cap curves upward at the tip giving the appearance of a point in side view. Four yellow appressed pollinia are borne on an unusual stipe with two sharp-pointed projections, one on either side.

CULTURE: Temperature, 60–68°F (15–20°C); light, 3000–3600 footcandles; humidity, 40–60%; medium, tree fern plaques are best; fertilization, monthly, with a 1–1–1 ratio.

COLOR PLATE: *Scuticaria steelii*

SPECIES	FLOWERING SEASON	GENERAL LOCALE
hadwenii	S–SS–F	Brazil, Guyana
steelii	F	Venezuela to Brazil

334

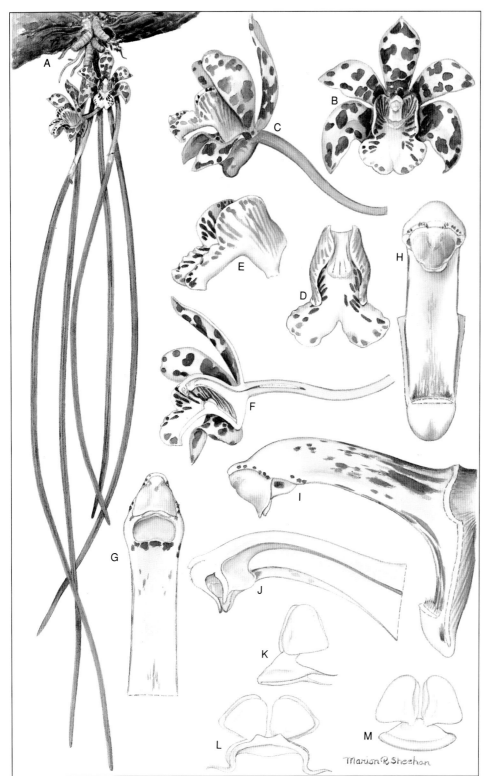

Scuticaria steelii
A: Plant in flower, × ¼.
B: Flower, face view, × ¾.
C: Flower, side view, × ¾.
D: Lip, face view, × 1.
E: Lip, side view, × 1.
F: Flower, vertical section, × ¾.
G: Column, ventral view, × 3.
H: Column, end view, × 3.
I: Column, side view, × 3.
J: Column, vertical section, × 3.
K, L, M: Pollinia, × 8.

GENUS: *Sedirea* (Linden & Reichenbach f.) Garay & Sweet (seh-DEER-ee-uh)

TRIBE: Vandeae   SUBTRIBE: Aeridinae

IDENTIFICATION CHARACTERISTICS: Miniature plants often are overlooked because the flowers as well as the plants are small. *Sedirea japonica,* however, is one miniature with a delightful display of very showy flowers.

Sedirea contains only one species, the plant of which, when young, resembles *Phalaenopsis.* The flowers, however, look similar to those of *Aerides.* Originally, *Sedirea japonica* was considered part of the genus *Aerides,* but Leslie Garay and Herman Sweet removed it in 1974, based mainly on differences in the reproductive structures. They established the new genus *Sedirea,* which is *Aerides* spelled backwards, undoubtedly because of the close resemblance of the two genera.

Vegetatively, this monopodial epiphyte has a very short, leafy stem, usually with three to five leaves. The short, leathery, strap-shaped leaves are medium green and up to 6 inches (15 cm) long and about 1 inch (2.5 cm) wide. They sometimes have a bilobed apex. Although monopodial in growth habit, lateral growths form from the base, and a mature plant may have two or more flowering growths. The short, slightly arched inflorescences arise from the leaf axils and bear from 10 to 12 flowers.

The attractive 1-inch (2.5-cm) wide flowers are creamy white or greenish white with rose spots. Interestingly, most of the rose patterns are confined to the lateral sepals and the lip, while the upper half of the flower (consisting of the dorsal sepal and petals) is devoid of marks. The petals are slightly smaller than the sepals and curve forward, making them appear even smaller. The spurred lip has two small lateral lobes and a larger, almost-spathulate midlobe.

The elongate column is almost as long as the petals, one of the characteristics that helps separate this genus from *Aerides.* The two oval, grooved yellow pollinia are borne on a single stipe with a triangular viscidium.

CULTURE: Temperature, 60–65°F (15–18°C); light, 2400–3600 footcandles; humidity, 40–60%; medium, tree fern plaques; fertilization, monthly, with a 1–1–1 ratio.

COLOR PLATE: *Sedirea japonica*

SPECIES	FLOWERING SEASON	GENERAL LOCALE
japonica	S–SS	Japan, Korea, Ryukyu Islands

Sedirea japonica

A: Plant in flower, × ½.
B: Flower, face view, × 1½.
C: Flower, side view, × 1½.
D: Lip, side view, × 2½.
E: Lip, face view, × 2½.
F: Flower, vertical section, × 2.
G: Column, ventral view, × 4.
H: Column, end view, × 4.
I: Column, side view, × 4.
J: Column, vertical section, × 4.
K, L, M: Pollinia, × 10.

Marion Ruff Sheehan

*Seidenfadenia*_____

GENUS: *Seidenfadenia* Garay (sye-den-fah-DEN-ee-uh)

TRIBE: Vandeae   SUBTRIBE: Aeridinae

IDENTIFICATION CHARACTERISTICS: At first glance *Seidenfadenia mitrata* looks like a terete *Oncidium* species, but it is soon noted that the roots are too large. In the spring when the multitude of small, fragrant flowers appear, the species is most attractive. It was originally called *Aerides mitrata* until 1972, when Leslie Garay transferred it to a new genus, based on the semiterete leaves and differences in floral characteristics, namely, the column structure. Actually Garay felt the species was taxonomically closer to *Rhynchostylis* than to *Aerides*. He named this monotypic genus in honor of Danish taxonomist Gunnar Seidenfaden, who has spent many years studying the orchid flora of Thailand.

This monopodial epiphyte has medium to dark green, pendent, semiterete leaves. The leaves, which are deeply grooved, may be up to 36 inches (90 cm) long but are more apt to be 12 to 16 inches (30–40 cm) long. *Seidenfadenia* produces a very extensive fleshy root system and grows best when mounted on a log or tree fern plaque. The axillary, densely flowered inflorescences, bearing 20 or more flowers, are shorter than the leaves and are usually erect but occasionally may be pendent.

The basic flower color is white to light magenta with the petals, sepals, and column tinted or having margins with varying amounts of red-purple. In some clones the entire flower may be red-purple.

The flowers are small, only 0.5 inch (1 cm) wide. The sepals and petals are alike in shape and color. The petal size varies and may be either slightly smaller or larger than the sepals. The three-lobed lip is attached to the base of the column. The flat midlobe is the most prominent part of the lip as the side lobes are very small and look very much like two small horns. The spur on the lip is short and slightly flattened on two sides.

The short column, 0.2 inch (4 mm) tall, is white or the same color as the flower. The anther cap is very distinct and usually darker in color than the surrounding tissue. The stigmatic surface is partially hidden by two small side lobes on the column. There are two orange, ovate pollinia borne on a single long, narrow stipe with an oval viscidium at the base.

CULTURE: Temperature, 60–65°F (15–18°C); light, up to 4000 footcandles; humidity, 40–60%; media, plaques, logs; fertilization, monthly, ratio depends on medium.

COLOR PLATE: *Seidenfadenia mitrata*

SPECIES	FLOWERING SEASON	GENERAL LOCALE
mitrata	S	Thailand, Myanmar, Laos

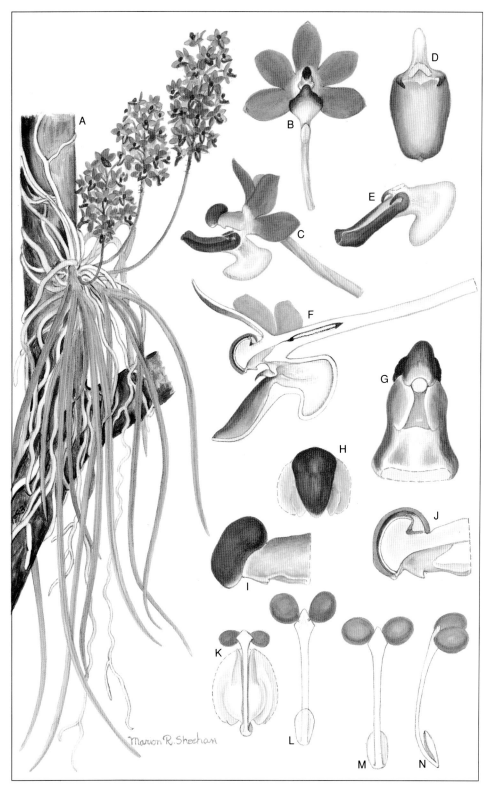

Seidenfadenia mitrata

A: Plant in flower, × ⅓.
B: Flower, face view, × 2.
C: Flower, side view, × 2.
D: Lip, top view, × 3.
E: Lip, side view, × 3.
F: Flower, vertical section, × 3.
G: Column, ventral view, × 8.
H: Column, end view, × 8.
I: Column, side view, × 8.
J: Column, vertical section, × 8.
K: Column detail, with pollinia
   in place and anther cap
   removed, × 8.
L, M, N: Pollinia, × 10.

339

Sobennikoffia

GENUS: *Sobennikoffia* Schlechter (soh-ben-ih-KOFF-ee-uh)

TRIBE: Vandeae   SUBTRIBE: Angraecinae

IDENTIFICATION CHARACTERISTICS: *Sobennikoffia* is an unusual and very attractive small genus endemic to Madagascar. It has relatively large, white to greenish white, typical angraecoid flowers borne on long, arching, many-flowered inflorescences. Comprising probably no more than three recognized species, this genus is found growing in a wide array of habitats, ranging from terrestrial to epiphytic and even sometimes lithophytic. The genus was first described by Rudolf Schlechter based on specimens of *S. robusta*. Schlechter named the genus in honor of his wife, whose maiden name was Sobennikoff.

Sobennikoffia has the typical monopodial habit common to the angraecoid group. It produces strong, robust stems, which may grow to a height of 2 feet (60 cm) and to a diameter of 0.75 inch (2 cm). Branching varies with species (e.g., *S. humbertiana* often branches freely, producing plantlets near the base of the stem). Once the keikis have produced several roots, they can be removed and potted up. As the plants mature and the older leaves abscise, the base of the stem remains encased in the dry, brown leaf bases. A well-grown plant has numerous leathery leaves up to 15 inches (38 cm) long and 1.5 inches (4 cm) wide. The leaves often have wavy margins, especially on the larger plants. The long, arching inflorescences, up to 24 inches (60 cm) tall, arise from the leaf axils, and each one has 15 or more delightful, white to greenish white, showy, long-spurred flowers. A mature plant may have as many as five inflorescences at a time, hence the plants can be most attractive when in flower.

The flowers of *Sobennikoffia* species are similar to each other and up to 2 inches (5 cm) in diameter. They are longer from petal and sepal tips to the tip of the spur than they are wide in face view. The sepals and petals are alike in size, shape, and color and usually are heavily reflexed near their tips. The long-spurred, three-lobed lip is a unique feature of the genus. Instead of turning downward, the spur turns upward and resembles a small horn of plenty. This is unusual for angraecoid orchids. The spur of *S. robusta* is light apple green both inside and out while the remainder of the flower is white, but as the flower ages, it often turns almost peach colored. The three lobes of the lip are often very distinct and sharp-pointed.

The white column is short and about as broad as it is long. It has a small, elliptical stigmatic surface. The anther cap may be white or a light apple green. Two yellow pollinia are attached to a single broad stipe.

CULTURE: Temperature, 60–65°F (15–18°C); humidity, 40–60%; light, 2800–3200 footcandles; media, coarse, open medium (e.g., large bark chunks), plaques; fertilization, monthly, ratio depends on medium.

COLOR PLATE: *Sobennikoffia robusta*

SPECIES	FLOWERING SEASON	GENERAL LOCALE
humbertiana	S–SS	Madagascar
robusta	SS	Madagascar

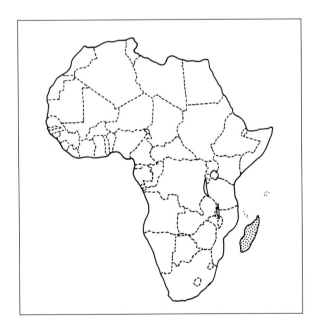

Sobennikoffia robusta
A: Plant in flower, × ⅜.
B: Flower, face view, × 1.
C: Flower, side view, × 1.
D: Lip, top view, × 1.
E: Flower, vertical section, × 1.
F: Column, ventral view, × 5.
G: Column, end view, × 5.
H: Column, side view, × 5.
I: Column, vertical section, × 5.
J, K: Pollinia, × 10.

Sobralia

GENUS: *Sobralia* Ruiz & Pavón (soh-BRAIL-ee-uh)

TRIBE: Coelogyneae   SUBTRIBE: Sobraliinae

IDENTIFICATION CHARACTERISTICS: It is a shame that the large, colorful flowers of *Sobralia* are so short-lived, some lasting only a day, as they are as showy as the flowers of *Cattleya* which they resemble. Fortunately, these large plants flower over a period of time. There are 35 species of terrestrial, sympodial plants in this genus, which was first described by Hipólito Ruiz Lopez and José Antonio Pavón in 1794 in a flora of Peru and Chile. They named the genus in honor of their friend Francisco Sobral, a Spanish physician and botanist.

Vegetatively, *Sobralia* forms large, dense clumps of leafy reedlike stems, which may be up to 6 feet (180 cm) tall in some species. *Sobralia dichotoma*, according to some accounts, attains heights of 18 feet (540 cm). The number of papery-to-leathery, oblong-to-almost-lanceolate leaves per stem varies among species, with individual leaves up to 15 inches (38 cm) long and 3 inches (7.5 cm) wide (e.g., *S. dichotoma*). The degree of venation in the leaves also varies; some species are very strongly nerved (e.g., *S. liliastrum*). The flowers are borne singly on a terminal inflorescence that frequently is subtended by a large, green leafy bract. Some complex inflorescences bear up to 10 flowers opening one at a time.

The flowers, which closely resemble those of *Cattleya*, may be up to 10 inches (25 cm) across. The base flower colors are pink, lavender, magenta, yellow, and white. The sepals and petals are usually alike in color, but vary in size and shape. The petals are usually larger and often have undulate margins while the sepal margins are not wavy. The large showy lip may be three-lobed or entire and encloses or partially encloses the column. The apical lobe is broad and spreading with deeply undulate or sometimes fimbriate margins. The discs vary from having a few to numerous keels in some species to being smooth in others.

The long, slender, tapered columns may be up to 1.5 inches (4 cm) long and may be winged at the apex. The eight soft, light yellow pollinia are borne in two cells and vary in shape and size.

CULTURE: Temperature, 50–60°F (10–15°C) at night; light, 3000–3600 footcandles; humidity, 40–60%; medium, any terrestrial potting mix; fertilization, monthly, with a 1–1–1 ratio.

COLOR PLATE: *Sobralia yauaperyensis*

SPECIES	FLOWERING SEASON	GENERAL LOCALE
candida	S–SS	Peru, Venezuela
cattleya	S–SS	Venezuela, Colombia
decora	S–SS	Mexico to Honduras
dichotoma	SS–F	Colombia, Ecuador, Panama
fimbriata	S–SS	Venezuela
infundibuligera	W–S	Venezuela
leucoxantha	S–SS	Costa Rica to Colombia
liliastrum	S–SS	Venezuela, Colombia, Brazil
macrantha	S–SS–F	Mexico to Panama
rosea	S–SS	Colombia to Bolivia
violacea	W–S–SS–F	Venezuela to Bolivia
yauaperyensis	SS–F	Venezuela

Sobralia yauaperyensis
A: Plant in flower, × ⅓.
B: Flower, face view, × ½.
C: Flower, side view, × ½.
D: Lip, top view, × ¾.
E: Flower, vertical section, × ½.
F: Column, ventral view, × 1½.
G: Column, end view, × 1½.
H: Column, side view, × 1½.
I: Column end, anther cap lifted, × 3.
J: Column, vertical section, × 1½.
K, L, M: Pollinia, × 6.

343

Sophronitis

GENUS: *Sophronitis* Lindley (sof-roh-NYE-tiss)
TRIBE: Epidendreae   SUBTRIBE: Laeliinae
IDENTIFICATION CHARACTERISTICS: A small genus of diminutive species, *Sophronitis* is probably best known for the red flower color it imparts to bigeneric hybrids with *Cattleya* and *Laelia*. The genus, which contains two species and possibly a third, according to some taxonomists, was named when Mrs. Harrison of Liverpool, England, flowered *S. cernua* in 1826. John Lindley derived the generic name from the Greek word *sophron* (modest), an appropriate descriptive word for *S. cernua*.

The pseudobulbs of these sympodial epiphytes are small, 0.5 to 1 inch (1–2.5 cm) tall, and ovoid, and each is topped by a small, solitary, leathery leaf up to 3 inches (7.5 cm) long. The leaves are either gray-green or dark shiny green. The pseudobulbs are thickly clustered on the rhizome. The flowers arise from the apex of the pseudobulb and are either solitary or two to five in number.

The flowers range from 1 (2.5 cm) to almost 3 inches (7.5 cm) in diameter and are very showy even though relatively small in size and few in number. The flower colors are orange-red, scarlet, and yellow. The sepals are alike in shape and color. The petals are usually broader than the sepals and sometimes more vivid in coloration. The lip is three-lobed, with the two lateral lobes partially encircling the column. The lip is smaller than the lateral petals and has a spur that is adnate to the ovary.

The short, broad column is almost-hook-shaped when viewed from the side. This is due to the two petallike wings that project from the sides of the column near the stigmatic surface. These are folded under and almost cover the stigmatic cavity. Eight pollinia of like size are divided into two groups of four each. The pollinia are steel blue in color and attached to a small caudicle.

CULTURE: Temperature, 60–70°F (15–21°C); light, 1500–2500 footcandles; humidity, 60–80%; media, tree fern, a mixture of 1 tree fern : 1 sphagnum moss; fertilization, monthly, with an 18–18–18 ratio.

COLOR PLATE: *Sophronitis cernua*

SPECIES	FLOWERING SEASON	GENERAL LOCALE
cernua	F–W	Brazil
coccinea	F–W	Brazil

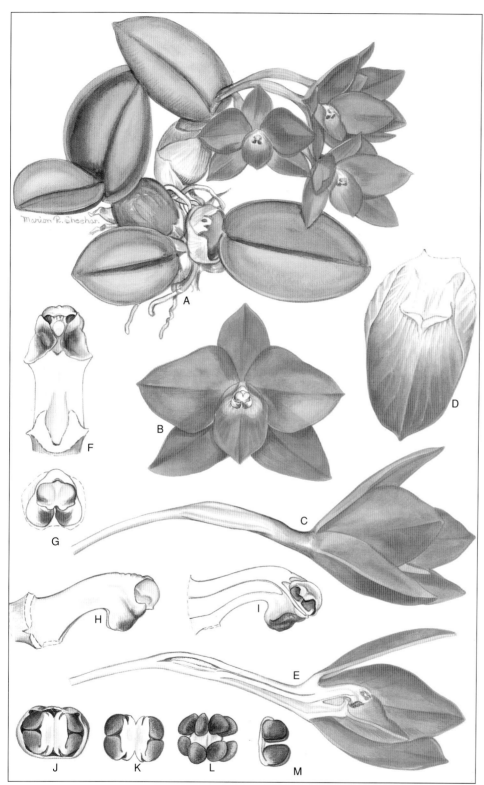

Sophronitis cernua

A: Plant in flower, × 1½.
B: Flower, face view, × 3.
C: Flower, side view, × 3.
D: Lip, × 5.
E: Flower, vertical section, × 3.
F: Column, ventral view, × 10.
G: Column, end view, × 10.
H: Column, side view, × 10.
I: Column, vertical section, × 10.
J: Anther cap with pollinia,
   × 20.
K, L, M: Pollinia, × 20.

Spathoglottis

GENUS: *Spathoglottis* Blume (spath-oh-GLOTT-iss)

TRIBE: Arethuseae   SUBTRIBE: Bletiinae

IDENTIFICATION CHARACTERISTICS: This interesting genus is often overlooked by some growers, possibly because of the deciduous nature of some species. Many of the 40 known species, however, are worth growing. *Spathoglottis* was first described by Carl Blume in 1825, who coined the generic name from two Greek words meaning spathe and lip, possibly to describe the sheath at the base of the leaves on some species and the distinctive lip of the genus.

The pseudobulbs look more like gladiolus corms than orchid pseudobulbs except that they are green and partially enclosed by dry leaf sheaths. Each pseudobulb is topped by up to four soft, somewhat lance-shaped, prominently veined, folded leaves up to 2 feet (60 cm) long. The leaves are often sheathed at the base for several inches above the pseudobulb, giving the appearance of a short stem. The tall, up to 2.5 feet (75 cm), inflorescences arise from the base of the pseudobulb.

The flowers (up to 25) are borne in a tight cluster near the top of the inflorescence and may be up to 3 inches (7.5 cm) in diameter. The sepals and inflorescence may be covered with soft hairs. The two petals, which are slightly larger than the sepals, vary in color from yellow (e.g., *Spathoglottis affinis*) to reddish purple (e.g., *S. plicata*). The lip is the unique segment of the flower. The narrow, upright lateral lobes of the lip partially enclose the column. The midlobe is the most interesting lobe. It is very narrow in the middle and flares at both ends. The basal third often has two small lobes and two ears with hairlike projections. Basically, the lip is the same color as the flower, often with red and yellow spots near the base.

The elongate column curves downward and is terminated by a tiny beaked anther cap. The column, which is widest just below the anther cap and has a very small stigmatic surface, is frequently the same color as the sepals and petals. Eight small, elongate, yellowish pollinia, arranged into two groups of four, are borne on thin caudicles.

CULTURE: Temperature, 60–65°F (15–18°C); light, 2400–3600 footcandles, also grows in full sun; media, a mixture of 3 peat : 1 sand, or 1 peat : 1 sand : 1 perlite; fertilization, monthly, with 1–1–1 ratio.

COLOR PLATE: *Spathoglottis affinis*

SPECIES	FLOWERING SEASON	GENERAL LOCALE
affinis	SS	Myanmar, Thailand, Java, Malaysia
aurea	S	Malaysia
bensoni	SS	Myanmar
chrysantha	S	Philippines
confusa	SS	Borneo
eburnea	SS	Thailand, Cambodia
elmeri	S	Philippines
fortunei	W	Hong Kong
gracilis	W	Borneo
grandifolia	W–S–SS–F	New Guinea
hardingiana	F–W	Myanmar
ixioides	SS	Himalayas
kimballiana	S	Borneo
lobbii	SS–F	Borneo, Indochina
microchilina	S	Sumatra, Malaysia
petri	S	Fiji Islands
plicata	S	Thailand, Pacific Islands, India, New Guinea, Malaysia, China
pubescens	SS	India, China, Indochina, Thailand
tomentosa	F	Philippines
vanoverberghii	W–S	Philippines
vieillandi	F	New Caledonia

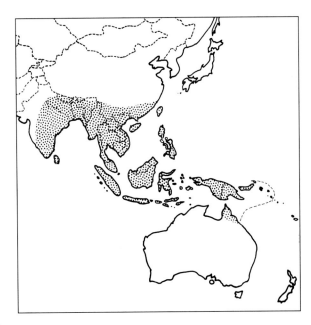

346

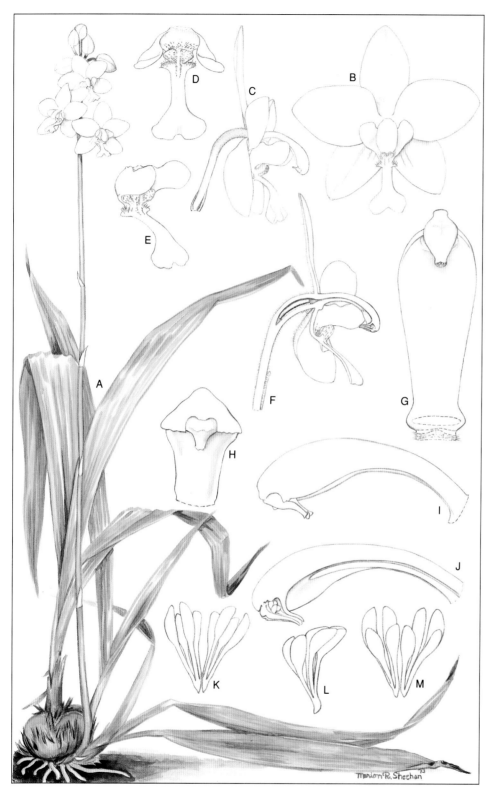

Spathoglottis affinis
A: Plant in flower, × ½.
B: Flower, face view, × 1½.
C: Flower, side view, × 1½.
D: Lip, face view, × 2.
E: Lip, three-quarter view, × 2.
F: Flower, vertical section, × 1½
G: Column, ventral view, × 5.
H: Column, end view, × 5.
I: Column, side view, × 5.
J: Column, vertical section, × 5.
K, L, M: Pollinia, × 12.

Stanhopea

GENUS: *Stanhopea* Frost ex Hooker (stan-HOPE-ee-uh)

TRIBE: Maxillarieae   SUBTRIBE: Stanhopeinae

IDENTIFICATION CHARACTERISTICS: When it comes to interesting flowers and unusual fragrances, few orchid genera can surpass *Stanhopea*. This unique tropical American genus, probably encompassing around 25 or more species, was first flowered in Kew Gardens, England, by John Frost in 1829. Frost gave the information to William Hooker who described the plant as *S. insignis*. The generic name honored the Earl of Stanhope, then president of the Medica-Botanical Society of London. In Mexico, where several species are native, *S. insignis* is affectionately called "el toro," the bull. This nickname is undoubtedly due to the two hornlike projections on the midsegment (mesochile) portion of the lip.

Vegetatively, *Stanhopea* species are very much alike. The short, ovoid pseudobulbs are borne in tight clusters on these sympodial epiphytes. Each 2- to 3-inch (5- to 7.5-cm) high, deeply ribbed pseudobulb has leafy scales at its base and is topped by a single leaf. Each lanceolate leaf with its petiole may be up to 15 inches (38 cm) long and 4 to 6 inches (10–15 cm) wide. The soft leaves are very prominently veined beneath. The inflorescence appears at the base of the pseudobulb and grows downward, often growing right through the medium and out of the bottom of the container. Each inflorescence bears three to seven short-lived flowers up to 7 inches (17.5 cm) in diameter.

Basically, flowers are white to creamy yellow with reddish, yellow, and brownish spots and blotches. The three sepals and two petals usually are alike in color, but vary in other aspects. The three sepals are the largest segments of the flower and are slightly reflexed. The two petals are deeply reflexed and often have wavy margins. The lip is the striking part of this flower. It can be divided into three very distinct segments. The basal third (hypochile) usually is hollowed out or boot-shaped where it is attached to the base of the column. The middle third (mesochile) has two very pronounced, horn-like projections, usually parallel to the upper third of the lip but sometimes bent around it. The upper third (epichile) is highly variable, ranging from cordate to oblong in shape. The lower two-thirds of the lip appears very waxy. The whole lip may be highly colored or almost colorless.

The long, winged column extends almost to the apex of the lip in a very graceful arch. Often bearing patterns similar to the petals, the column is widest near the apex where the wings are most pronounced. Each flower contains two yellowish elliptical pollinia attached to a single stipe with an almost-circular foot.

CULTURE: Temperature, 60°F (15°C); light, 2400–3600 footcandles; humidity, 40–60%; media, any well-drained epiphytic mixture, but best if grown on tree fern plaques or in hanging baskets; fertilization, monthly, with a 1–1–1 ratio.

COLOR PLATE: *Stanhopea oculata*

SPECIES	FLOWERING SEASON	GENERAL LOCALE
costaricensis	SS	Costa Rica
ecornuta	SS	Guatemala, Honduras
grandiflora	SS	Colombia, Venezuela, Guyana
graveolens	SS	Mexico, Guatemala, Honduras to Brazil
insignis	SS	Brazil, Peru
martiana	SS	Mexico
oculata	SS	Mexico to Panama
platyceras	SS	Colombia
shuttleworthii	SS	Colombia
tigrina	SS	Eastern Mexico
tricornis	SS	Ecuador
wardii	SS	Mexico to Venezuela

Stanhopea oculata
A: Plant in flower, × ⅓.
B: Flower, face view, × ½.
C: Flower, side view, × ½.
D: Lip, × 1
E: Flower, vertical section, × ½.
F: Column, ventral view, × 1½.
G: Column, end view, × 1½.
H: Column, side view, × 1½.
I: Column, vertical section,
      × 1½.
J, K, L: Pollinia, × 6.

Stenia

GENUS: *Stenia* Lindley (STEN-ee-uh)

TRIBE: Maxillarieae   SUBTRIBE: Zygopetalinae

IDENTIFICATION CHARACTERISTICS: The attractive, pale yellow, almost-translucent, waxy flowers of *Stenia* make this small South American genus highly desirable. Although it has only a few known species and is considered a rarity by some authors, the genus is appearing in orchid shows more often in recent years than it has in the past.

The genus was first described by John Lindley in 1837, who derived the generic name from the Greek word *stenos* (narrow), undoubtedly describing the narrow pollinia on which the genus is based. *Stenia* is closely related to *Maxillaria* but separated from it by differences in the lip and pollinia. The genus is also closely related to *Bollea*, *Huntleya*, and *Chondrorhyncha*, but differs in column and pollinia characteristics.

Vegetatively, the sympodial, epiphytic species of this genus are very similar. The small pseudobulbs are hidden by the leaves, which have clasping bases. Each growth comprises one to three medium to dark green leaves up to 5 inches (12.5 cm) long and 2 inches (5 cm) wide. Leaf shape varies from obovate to elliptic. The lateral inflorescences arise from the leaf axil and are recurved or prostrate. An inflorescence bears one relatively large, 2.5-inch (6-cm) wide, light yellow flower. If the plant is crowded by other plants in a greenhouse, flowering may often go unnoticed since flowers are borne close to the rim of the pot.

The sepals and petals are very similar in size, shape, and color. In some cases, the dorsal sepal and the two petals are the same size, while the two lateral sepals are slightly larger and more acute at the apex. The lip with reddish dots is the most colorful floral segment. Because it is deeply concave and its lobes are not very distinct, the lip appears to be almost-saccate at first glance. There are seven or more teeth on the disc.

The short, angular, slightly pubescent column tapers slightly toward the base and has a distinct stigmatic area. The four, very elongate, pale yellow pollinia, in two sizes, are attached to a stipe with a viscidium.

CULTURE: Temperature, 60°F (15°C); light, 2400–3600 footcandles; humidity, 40–60%; media, tree fern, bark, peat and perlite; fertilization, monthly, ratio depends on medium.

COLOR PLATE: *Stenia pallida*

SPECIES	FLOWERING SEASON	GENERAL LOCALE
guttata	SS–F	Peru
pallida	SS–F	Guyana, Suriname, French Guiana, Trinidad

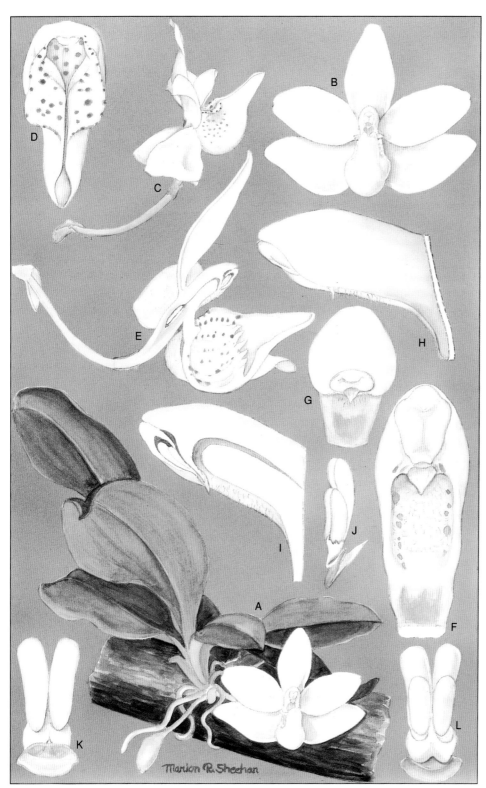

Stenia pallida

A: Plant in flower, × ¾.
B: Flower, face view, × 1.
C: Flower, side view, × 1.
D: Lip, × 2.
E: Flower, vertical section, × 1½.
F: Column, ventral view, × 4.
G: Column, end view, × 4.
H: Column, side view, × 4.
I: Column, vertical section, × 4.
J, K, L: Pollinia, × 8.

351

Stenoglottis

GENUS: *Stenoglottis* Lindley (sten-oh-GLOT-tiss)
TRIBE: Orchideae   SUBTRIBE: Habenariinae
IDENTIFICATION CHARACTERISTICS: There are possibly only three known species in this elusive African genus, an unfortunate circumstance as these plants are delightful fall-blooming terrestrials. Although deciduous in nature, *Stenoglottis* species, which are easily cared for, respond by producing tall inflorescences of dainty flowers during late autumn.

The genus was first described by John Lindley in 1836 based on specimens of *Stenoglottis fimbriata* collected by J. F. Drège in South Africa. Lindley coined the generic name from the Greek words *stenos* (narrow) and *glottis* (tongue), undoubtedly referring to the shape of the lip.

In spring or early summer, the plants produce a basal rosette of leaves. The leaves, which may be up to 8 inches (20 cm) long, may be soft and bright green (e.g., *Stenoglottis longifolia*) or darker green with dark brown blotches (e.g., *S. fimbriata*). In early fall, a slender inflorescence, up to 18 inches (45 cm) high, develops in the center of the rosette and produces up to 50 delicate flowers over several weeks. The small flowers, 0.3 inch (0.8 cm) wide, are basically varying shades of rose to pale purple with darker purplish spots on the lips, sepals, and petals. After flowering, these orchids die back, losing all their leaves, which often turn brown very rapidly. The tuberlike roots lie dormant in the soil over the winter and produce another set of leaves and flowers the next year. During the dormant period, water should be reduced but the potting mixture should not be allowed to dry out completely.

The three sepals and two petals are alike in shape and color, with the petals often a little smaller. The sepals are slightly fused at the base. The lip is the most attractive portion of the flower and is much larger than the sepals and petals. Long and narrow, it is broadest near the apex. The lips of some species are spurless whereas others may have a very short, spurlike projection at the base. Lacerations at the apex of the lip vary, but usually there are three to five distinct, taillike lobes.

The very short column is hidden by a hood formed by the petals and has an unusual apex. There are two yellow, club-shaped, granular-looking pollinia. Each is attached to a short caudicle with a small viscidium.

CULTURE: Temperature, 65–80°F (18–26°C) summer and 50°F (10°C) winter; light, 2400–3600 footcandles; humidity, 40–60%; medium, any good mix for terrestrials with up to 30% organic matter; fertilization, monthly during the growing season, with a 1–1–1 ratio.

COLOR PLATE: *Stenoglottis longifolia*

SPECIES	FLOWERING SEASON	GENERAL LOCALE
fimbriata	SS–F	Tanzania to South Africa
longifolia	SS–F	South Africa

Stenoglottis longifolia
A: Plant in flower, × ½.
B: Flower, face view, × 4.
C: Flower, side view, × 4.
D: Lip, × 4.
E: Petal, × 4.
F: Flower, vertical section, × 4.
G: Column, face view, × 15.
H: Column, side view, × 15.
I: Column, vertical section,
   × 15.
J, K, L: Pollinia, × 16.

Marion R Sheehan

Stenorrhynchus

GENUS: *Stenorrhynchus* L. C. Richard (sten-oh-RINK-uss)

TRIBE: Cranichideae SUBTRIBE: Spiranthinae

IDENTIFICATION CHARACTERISTICS: Among the many attractive terrestrial orchids are some *Stenorrhynchus* species. Their clusters of showy, often brick-red flowers are borne on bracteate inflorescences that appear to arise from nowhere. Since these orchids are often leafless at flowering, the emerging inflorescences give the plants an almost-mystical air. Soon after flowering, the deep rich green rosette of leaves appears, only to disappear before the next flowering. Pots of some *Stenorrhynchus* species in the greenhouse may look empty for a period of weeks in early spring between flowering and leaf emergence, so growers should take care not to eliminate the pot at this time.

This widely spread genus of both terrestrial and epiphytic orchids contains up to 60 species. It was first identified by Louis C. Richard in 1818 and given the generic name *Stenorrhynchus*, derived from the Greek words *stenos* (narrow) and *rhynchos* (snout) and undoubtedly a reference to the narrow rostellum. Over the years, different members of this genus have been transferred in and out of the genus *Spiranthes*, although distinct taxonomic differences separate the two genera, such as the lack of a spiraled inflorescence in *Stenorrhynchus*. Even today some *Stenorrhynchus* species are listed under *Spiranthes* in some books.

Vegetatively, most species consist of a basal rosette of mostly lanceolate leaves. The six to ten leaves, which may be up to 16 inches (40 cm) long and 2.5 inches (6 cm) wide, are much reduced on the inflorescence and are often bractlike. The flower color varies from greenish white to a variety of red tones.

Each elongate flower is subtended by a bract and measures 0.75 × 2.75 inches (2 × 7 cm). The flowers are very interesting. The sepals and petals are alike in size, shape, and color, with the sepals often a little darker in color and pubescent on the outside. The tips of the petals are often strongly reflexed. The slightly three-lobed lip is almost equal in size to the other floral segments, but it is pubescent on both sides, the hairs under the column near the spur are larger than those on the outside.

The short column is also unique in the area of the anther cap. The underside of the column is mostly stigmatic surface. The four elongate, almost-white (in our plants) pollinia are paired, with each pair attached to a single caudicle with a viscidium.

CULTURE: Temperature, 50°F (10°C) for best growth, some species tolerate much lower temperatures; light, grows in full sun to partial shade outdoors, 3000–3600 footcandles in the greenhouse; humidity, 40–60%; medium, any rich organic medium; fertilization, monthly, with a 1–1–1 ratio.

COLOR PLATE: *Stenorrhynchus lanceolatus*

SPECIES	FLOWERING SEASON	GENERAL LOCALE
lanceolatus	S–SS	Florida, West Indies to northern South America
navarrensis	S–SS	Panama
speciosus	S–SS	Mexico to northern South America, West Indies

Stenorrhynchus lanceolatus

A: Plant in flower, × ½.
B: Flower, face view, × 2.
C: Flower, side view, × 2.
D: Lip, face view, × 2.
E: Lip, side view, × 2.
F: Flower, vertical section, × 2.
G: Column, ventral view, × 3.
H: Column, end view showing stigmatic surface, × 5.
I: Column, side view, × 3.
J: Column, dorsal view showing anther cap, × 5.
K: Column, anther cap removed, × 5.
L, M: Pollinia, × 5.

Tetramicra _____

GENUS: *Tetramicra* Lindley (teh-truh-MIKE-kruh)
TRIBE: Epidendreae   SUBTRIBE: Laeliinae
IDENTIFICATION CHARACTERISTICS: The dainty butterfly-like flowers of this genus are borne in a row at the end of a long, wiry stem. This small genus of approximately 12 species is found only in the West Indies and in a very limited area on the east coast of southern Florida. John Lindley first described the genus in 1831. He derived the generic name from two Greek words, *tetra* (four) and *micros* (small), possibly a reference to the four small pollinia or to the four depressions in the anther.

The sympodial species of this genus grow on rocks (as lithophytes) or shrubs (as epiphytes) or in sandy soils (as terrestrials). In short, they grow just about anywhere. The small clusters of leaves resemble the leaves of small *Ascocentrum* species. Each fan of leaves is separated by a slender rhizome, often spacing the fans 3 to 6 inches (7.5–15 cm) apart. The small leaves are thick, stiff, leathery, and may be almost terete. They often are recurved gracefully and up to 7 inches (17.5 cm) long. The tall, wiry inflorescence, up to 2 feet (60 cm) in some species, is topped by a few to many flowers.

The flowers, up to 1 inch (2.5 cm) wide, often have greenish red sepals and petals and purple lips. The sepals and petals are generally alike in shape and color, with the petals somewhat smaller than the sepals. The large three-lobed lip almost obscures the sepals and petals when the flower is observed in face view. The two lateral lobes appear to be two large lateral petals to the untrained observer. The midlobe of the lip is the largest lobe and may have three to five longitudinal stripes, depending on the species.

The column is the same color as the lip and has two broad, earlike lobes near the anther cap. There are eight yellow pollinia and four caudicles. Each caudicle has one large and one small pollinium attached to it.

CULTURE: Temperature, 60°F (15°C); light, 2400–3600 footcandles; humidity, 40–60%; medium, tree fern (grows well in a variety of media); fertilization, monthly, ratio depends on medium.

COLOR PLATE: *Tetramicra canaliculata*

SPECIES	FLOWERING SEASON	GENERAL LOCALE
canaliculata	S–SS–F	Florida, Antilles
elegans	F–W	Haiti, Dominican Republic
parviflora	W–S	Bahamas, Jamaica, Dominican Republic

Tetramicra canaliculata

A: Plant in flower, × ⅓.
B: Flower, face view, × 2.
C: Flower, side view, × 2.
D: Lip, midlobe only, × 3.
E: Flower, vertical section, × 3.
F: Column, ventral view, × 6.
G: Column, end view, × 6.
H: Column, side view, × 6.
I: Column, vertical section, × 6.
J, K, L: Pollinia, × 30.

357

Thunia

GENUS: *Thunia* Reichenbach f. (THOON-ee-uh)
TRIBE: Arethuseae   SUBTRIBE: Thuniinae
IDENTIFICATION CHARACTERISTICS: *Thunia* species possess some unique characteristics that make them interesting to grow. The biennial nature of large leafy stems coupled with large colorful flowers are two good reasons why these species are worth growing in a greenhouse. The stark tan stems of these deciduous orchids, which are ensheathed by the dry leaf bracts, and the persistent leaf bases are not very attractive; to the uninformed grower, they might appear to be candidates for the orchid world beyond. Actually, the barren stems belie the potential of these plants. When the new growths appear, they elongate rapidly and soon produce their attractive pendent sprays of flowers.

The genus was first described by H. G. Reichenbach in 1852, based on specimens of *Thunia alba*. Reichenbach named the genus in honor of Count Thun Hohenstein of Tetschin, Bohemia. The genus is closely related to *Phaius*, from which it is easily distinguished because *Thunia* lacks pseudobulbs. There are approximately six species in this genus.

Vegetatively, *Thunia* contains both semiepiphytic and terrestrial species that form clumps of erect stems, some up to 50 inches (125 cm) high. The biennial stems are covered with foliage when young and are enshrouded with dry leaf bases when the leaves fall with age. The deciduous, lanceolate, alternate leaves, up to 8 inches (20 cm) long, clasp the stem and are light green to gray-green,

soft, and pliable. The midrib of the leaf blade is often very pale, being almost white on some plants. The terminal inflorescence is reflexed to pendent and bears up to nine short-lived flowers, 3 to 3.5 inches (7.5–8 cm) in size. Each flower is subtended by a showy bract. The base colors are purple and white, with some yellow-orange lips.

The flowers of *Thunia* species are very similar, but vary slightly in size and color. The sepals and petals are alike in shape and color, with the two petals often a little narrower. The lateral sepals curve slightly toward the dorsal sepal, causing the angle between the dorsal sepal and the lateral sepals to appear to be less than 90 degrees. The lip, which has a very fine dentate margin and is adorned with numerous hairs, is the most attractive segment of the flower. It is spurred, encircles the column, and flares out.

The long and narrow column is broadest near the stigmatic surface. The anther cap and stigmatic area are partially enclosed by the small wings on the column. There are four elongate, light yellow pollinia with very short stipes. Each pollinium appears to be two pollinia (bipartite) folded together.

CULTURE: Temperature, 55°F (12°C); humidity, 40–60%; light, 2400–3600 footcandles; medium, any good mixture containing at least 40% organic matter for terrestrials; fertilization, monthly, with a 1–1–1 ratio.

COLOR PLATE: *Thunia marshalliana*

SPECIES	FLOWERING SEASON	GENERAL LOCALE
alba	S–SS	India to Thailand
bensoniae	S–SS	Myanmar
marshalliana	S–SS	Myanmar, Thailand, South China

Thunia marshalliana

A: Plant in flower, × ⅓.
B: Flower, face view, × ½.
C: Flower, side view, × ½.
D: Lip, face view, × 1.
E: Flower, vertical section, × 1.
F: Column, ventral view, × 3.
G: Column, end view, × 3.
H: Column, side view, × 3.
I: Column, vertical section, × 3.
J, K, L: Pollinia, × 6.

Trichocentrum

GENUS: *Trichocentrum* Poeppig & Endlicher (trick-oh-SEN-trum)

TRIBE: Maxillarieae SUBTRIBE: Oncidiinae

IDENTIFICATION CHARACTERISTICS: This captivating group of miniature orchids is characterized by spurred flowers with extremely prominent lips. In some species (e.g., *Trichocentrum tigrinum*), the flower may be almost as large as the plant.

There are approximately 12 species in this desirable genus described in 1838 by Eduard F. Poeppig and Stephen L. Endlicher. The generic name was coined from the Greek words *tricho* (hair) and *kentron* (spur), referring to the long, very narrow spur of some species (e.g., *Trichocentrum panduratum*).

Vegetatively, these sympodial epiphytes have all the earmarks of small mule's ear *Oncidium* species, which causes confusion when the plants are not in flower. Each very small pseudobulb, which often goes unobserved, is topped by one thick, leathery leaf. The green, obtuse-to-elliptic leaves often are spotted with purplish color on the upper surface and may be almost completely purple beneath. They persist for many years, so the plants often form small clumps. The basal inflorescence bears one to several 1.75-inch (4-cm) wide flowers with mottled colors on the sepals and petals.

The flowers vary from fully open (e.g., *Trichocentrum tigrinum*) to almost cup-shaped with an exerted lip (e.g., *T. panduratum*). The sepals and petals are very similar in size, shape, and color, and range from sharp-pointed to blunt at the apex. The indistinctly three-lobed lip is by far the largest segment of the flower. It is spurred, with the size of the spur varying among the species and being very short in *T. tigrinum*.

The short column may have two very pronounced lacerate wings almost surrounding the entire column. The column has a very large stigmatic surface. The two yellow, elliptical, pocketbook-like pollinia of this genus are borne on a single stipe with a very distinct viscidium.

CULTURE: Temperature, 55–60°F (12–15°C); light, 2400–3600 footcandles; humidity, 40–60%; media, tree fern plaques, cork; fertilization, monthly, ratio depends on medium.

COLOR PLATE: *Trichocentrum tigrinum*

SPECIES	FLOWERING SEASON	GENERAL LOCALE
albococcineum	SS–F	Brazil, Peru
fuscum	F	Brazil
panduratum	F–W	Peru
pfavii	F–W	Costa Rica, Panama
tigrinum	S–SS	Ecuador

Trichocentrum tigrinum
A: Plant in flower, × 1.
B: Flower, face view, × 1½.
C: Flower, side view, × 1½.
D: Lip, face view, × 1½.
E: Lip, side view, × 1½.
F: Flower, vertical section, × ½.
G: Column, ventral view, × 5.
H: Column, end view, × 5.
I: Column, side view, × 5.
J: Column, vertical section, × 5.
K, L, M: Pollinia, × 8.

361

Trichoglottis

GENUS: *Trichoglottis* Blume (trick-oh-GLOT-tiss)
TRIBE: Vandeae SUBTRIBE: Aeridinae
IDENTIFICATION CHARACTERISTICS: *Trichoglottis* is an excellent genus that deserves to be grown more widely. Although there are over 30 species of fine plants, only two species are commonly grown. The genus was first described by Carl Blume in 1825. The generic name was derived from two Greek words meaning hairy tongue and refers to the very pronounced hairs found on the lips of the flowers (e.g., *T. luzonensis*). The genus is separated from other closely allied genera (e.g., *Vandopsis*) by floral structure.

Vegetatively, these monopodial epiphytes resemble *Vanda* species but have much shorter leaves and larger internodes so the leaves are spaced a little further apart. Growth may be erect (e.g., *Trichoglottis luzonensis*) or pendent (e.g., *T. rosea*). Plants may be as much as 5 feet (150 cm) tall with leaves 2 to 6 inches (5–15 cm) long. Aerial roots are produced in abundance from the stem. The flowers are borne in small axillary clusters, containing one to a few flowers.

The 0.25- to 2-inch (0.5- to 5-cm) wide flowers range in color from deep purple-maroon to pink to yellow with brown marks. The sepals and petals are almost identical. The petals may be slightly smaller than the sepals, but are the same color. The lip is usually smaller than the petals and may be five-lobed (e.g., *Trichoglottis brachiata*) with two small, basal lobes and three distinct apical lobes. The api-cal lobes may be very hairy (e.g., *T. brachiata*).

The small column is not enclosed by the lip and stands almost perpendicular to the lip. It is slightly hairy and broadest just below the stigmatic area. The anther cap is somewhat roughened. Two yellow pollinia, somewhat resembling pocketbook rolls from one angle, are borne on a narrow, elongate stipe with a shield-shaped base.

CULTURE: Temperature, 65–70°F (18–21°C); light, 3600–4000 footcandles; humidity, 40–60%; media, tree fern, fir bark; fertilization, monthly, ratio depends on medium.

COLOR PLATE: *Trichoglottis brachiata*

SPECIES	FLOWERING SEASON	GENERAL LOCALE
brachiata	S–SS–F	Philippines
ionosma	S	Philippines, Taiwan
lanceolaria	F–W–S–SS	Malay Peninsula, Sumatra, Java
luzonensis	S–SS	Philippines
philippinensis	S–SS	Philippines
retusa	SS	Malay Peninsula, Java, Sumatra, Borneo
rosea	F–W–S–SS	Philippines
sagarikii	SS	Thailand
wenzelii	SS	Philippines

Trichoglottis brachiata
A: Plant in flower, × ½.
B: Flower, face view, × 1.
C: Flower, side view, × 1.
D: Lip, × 1½.
E: Flower, vertical section, × 1.
F: Column, ventral view, × 5.
G: Column, end view, × 5.
H: Column, side view, × 5.
I: Column, vertical section, × 5.
J, K, L: Pollinia, × 10.

363

Trichopilia

GENUS: *Trichopilia* Lindley (trick-oh-PlLL-ee-uh)
TRIBE: Maxillarieae SUBTRIBE: Oncidiinae
IDENTIFICATION CHARACTERISTICS: John Lindley founded the genus *Trichopilia* in 1836 based on specimens collected in Mexico, and George Barker introduced the genus into England in 1835. The generic name is coined from two Greek words, *tricho* (hair) and *pilos* (cap), and refers to the ciliated hood around the anther cap. *Trichopilia* is composed of about 25 species of small plants characterized by large fragrant flowers.

These sympodial, epiphytic orchids have almost-flattened pseudobulbs from 2 to 10 inches (5–25 cm) long. The rhizome between the pseudobulbs is very short, hence the pseudobulbs are tightly clustered. Each pseudobulb bears one or more leathery leaves at its apex. The leaf blade may be oblong to lanceolate and from a few inches to 1 foot (30 cm) in length, sometimes with wavy margins. Pendulous inflorescences originate at the base of the pseudobulb and bear from a few to 10 flowers, with individual flowers up to 6 inches (15 cm) in diameter. The open flowers often rest on the rim of the pot.

Although the species vary vegetatively, they are very similar in floral characteristics. The sepals and petals are similar in size, shape, and color. They are generally long and narrow and may have wavy margins, or may even be corkscrew-like (e.g., *Trichopilia tortilis*). The large, often funnel-shaped lip, which is the showiest portion of the flower, usually is perpendicular to the other floral segments and often has a wavy margin.

The long, narrow column is usually hidden within the lip and is widest near the stigmatic area. One of the distinguishing features of this genus is the fringe that encircles the anther cap at the apex of the column. The two yellow pollinia are almost heart-shaped when viewed from the side and are borne on a short curved stipe with a very small foot.

CULTURE: Temperature, 60–65°F (15–18°C); light, 2400–3600 footcandles; humidity, 40–60%; media, tree fern, fir bark; fertilization, monthly, ratio depends on medium.

COLOR PLATE: *Trichopilia suavis*

SPECIES	FLOWERING SEASON	GENERAL LOCALE
brevis	F	Peru
fragrans	W	West Indies, Venezuela, Colombia, Ecuador, Peru, Bolivia
galeottiana	SS–F	Mexico
hennisiana	S–SS	Colombia
laxa	F–W	Colombia, Venezuela, Ecuador, Brazil
leucoxantha	SS	Panama
maculata	W	Guatemala, Panama
marginata	S	Guatemala, Costa Rica, Panama, Colombia
oicophylax	SS	Venezuela, Colombia
suavis	S	Costa Rica, Panama, Colombia
tortilis	W	Mexico, Guatemala, El Salvador, Honduras
turialbae	SS	Costa Rica, Panama

Trichopilia suavis

A: Plant in flower, × ½.
B: Flower, face view, × ¾.
C: Flower, side view, × ¾.
D: Lip, × ¾.
E: Flower, vertical section, × ¾.
F: Column, ventral view, × 2.
G: Column, end view, × 2.
H: Column, side view, × 2.
I: Column, vertical section, × 2.
J: Column, end view, anther
   cap removed showing pol-
   linia in place, × 2.
K, L, M: Pollinia, × 4.

Trigonidium _____

GENUS: *Trigonidium* Lindley (trig-oh-NID-ee-um)

TRIBE: Maxillarieae   SUBTRIBE: Maxillariinae

IDENTIFICATION CHARACTERISTICS: *Trigonidium* is a small genus of not more than 12 easy-to-grow, sympodial, epiphytic species. The genus is closely related to *Maxillaria*, which it resembles vegetatively, but once in flower the two genera are unique: the broad-sepaled flowers of *Trigonidium* are triangular in shape when they are fully open. When John Lindley first described the genus, he undoubtedly had this characteristic in mind, as he based the generic name on the Greek word *trigonos* (three-cornered). Several other floral segments are also triangular; hence the name is apropos.

Vegetatively, *Trigonidium* forms dense clumps of pseudobulbs. The short, ovoid pseudobulbs are ridged and topped by one to three lanceolate leaves up to 2 feet (60 cm) long and about 1 inch (2.5 cm) wide. Usually the leathery leaves are reflexed near their midpoint and acute at their apex. The inflorescences, often more than one per pseudobulb, arise from the base of the pseudobulb and are up to 18 inches (45 cm) tall. Each consists of a solitary, long-lived flower.

The flowers, up to 1.5 inches (4 cm) wide, are greenish yellow to light brown in color, often with darker colored marks. They have to be observed closely to appreciate their unique qualities. In face view, the flower resembles a comic mask with two purple eyes and a green nose. The three sepals are the largest segments of the flower. Their bases form a tube, almost obscuring the remaining floral segments, while their tips are reflexed, giving the flower a triangular look. The small, linear petals often have a distinct, dark eye at their apex. The three-lobed lip is the smallest segment of the flower. The two lateral lobes are erect and usually darker in color. The midlobe is often warty and lighter in color.

The small, very narrow column has a minute foot at the base. The anther cap has a distinct, reflexed horn at its apex. The four yellow almost-elliptical pollinia are borne on a very short stipe with a small, inverted, V-shaped foot.

CULTURE: Temperature, 60–70°F (15–21°C); light, 2400–3600 footcandles; humidity, 40–60%; media, peat and perlite, tree fern, bark; fertilization, monthly, ratio depends on medium.

COLOR PLATE: *Trigonidium egertonianum*

SPECIES	FLOWERING SEASON	GENERAL LOCALE
egertonianum	S	Mexico to Panama
lankesterii	S–SS	Costa Rica, Panama
obtusum	S–SS	Venezuela, Brazil, Bolivia

Trigonidium egertonianum
A: Plant in flower, × ½.
B: Flower, face view, × 1.
C: Flower, side view, × 1.
D: Lip, face view, × 4.
E: Lip, side view, × 4.
F: Petal, × 2.
G: Flower, vertical section, × 1.
H: Column, ventral view, × 6.
I: Column, end view, × 6.
J: Column, side view, × 6.
K: Column, vertical section, × 6.
L, M, N: Pollinia, × 15.

Marion R. Sheehan

367

Vanda

GENUS: *Vanda* R. Brown (VAN-duh)

TRIBE: Vandeae SUBTRIBE: Aeridinae

IDENTIFICATION CHARACTERISTICS: *Vanda* is a very popular genus and is widely grown in the tropics as a garden subject, especially for the wide range of flower colors. There are approximately 60 species, many of which are commonly cultivated. The genus was founded by Robert Brown when *V. roxburghii* flowered in England in the autumn of 1819. *Vanda* is a Sanskrit word describing orchid plants of vandaceous growth habit in their native area. The specific epithet was given in honor of William Roxburgh, director of the Calcutta Botanic Garden from 1797 to 1814.

These monopodial, mostly epiphytic species have strap-shaped leaves (Fig. 24) 2 to 12 inches (5–30 cm) long and dark green above and lighter beneath. The leaves are conduplicate, and the leaf base clasps the stem. The apex of the leaf is very irregular and appears as if a small segment was torn from the tip. The simple, few- to many-flowered inflorescence arises from the axil of the leaves.

There is a wide range of flower color in the genus, including lavender blue. The 1- to 4-inch (2.5- to 10-cm) wide flowers are popular not only because of their color range, size, and longevity, but also because of their adaptability for use in corsages and arrangements. The sepals are similar in shape and color with the dorsal sepal usually broader. The petals are shaped like the sepals, but are smaller in size; they may be reflexed and often turned at right angles to the plane of the sepals. The spurred or sac-shaped base of the lip is a distinct characteristic of the genus. The two lateral lobes of the lip near the spur vary in size. Some almost encircle the column and others are sometimes greatly reduced to small earlike appendages. The apical lobe also varies in size, but is often broad and lobed; it bears a fleshy disc.

The short column is broadest at the base and tapers rapidly toward the apex. The three-lobed anther cap gives the column a beaklike apex. The stigmatic surface has only a narrow slit as an opening. Two yellow pollinia, each shaped like half a sphere, are attached to a broad, flat stipe with a round, translucent foot.

CULTURE: Temperature, 60–70°F (15–21°C); light, 2400–3600 footcandles (also will grow in full sun); humidity, 40–70%; media, tree fern, bark, charcoal; fertilization, monthly, ratio depends on medium.

COLOR PLATE: *Vanda tricolor*

SPECIES	FLOWERING SEASON	GENERAL LOCALE
bensonii	SS–F	Myanmar
brunnea	F–W	Thailand, India
coerulea	F–W	Himalayas, Myanmar, Thailand
coerulescens	S–SS	Myanmar
concolor	W–S	China
dearei	SS	Borneo
denisoniana	S	Myanmar, Arakan Mountains
foetida	SS	Sumatra
insignis	F	Moluccas, Timor, Alor Islands
lamellata	F–W	Philippines, Marianas Islands
lilacina	SS	Laos, Thailand
limbata	SS	Java
luzonica	S	Philippines, Luzon Island
merrillii	S	Philippines, Luzon and Negros Islands
parviflora	SS	Himalayas, India to Sri Lanka, Myanmar
roeblingiana	F	Philippines, Luzon Island
spathulata	F–W–S–SS	South India, Sri Lanka
sumatrana	SS	Sumatra
tessellata	F–W	Sri Lanka, India, Myanmar
tricolor	F–W	Java, Bali
watsoni	W–S	Vietnam, Annam

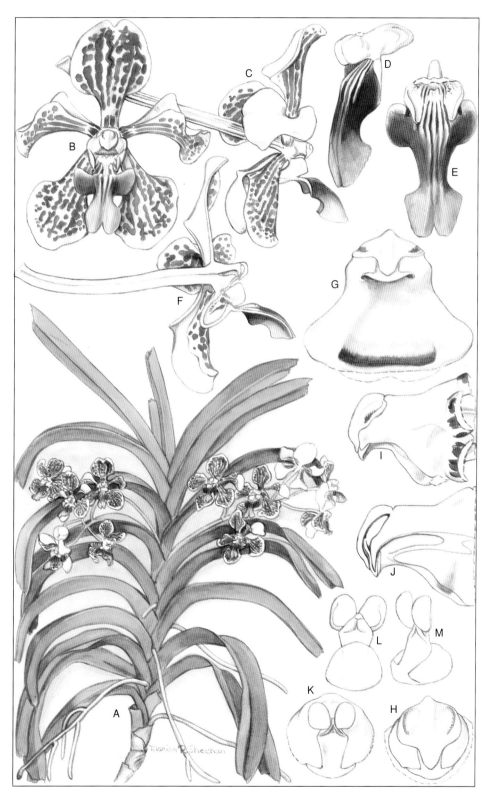

Vanda tricolor

A: Plant in flower, × ⅛.
B: Flower, face view, × ½.
C: Flower, side view, × ½.
D: Lip, side view, × ¾.
E: Lip, face view, × ¾.
F: Flower, vertical section, × ½.
G: Column, ventral view, × 2.
H: Column, end view, × 2.
I: Column, side view, × 2.
J: Column, vertical section, × 2.
K: Column, end view, anther cap removed showing pollinia, × 2.
L, M: Pollinia, × 3.

369

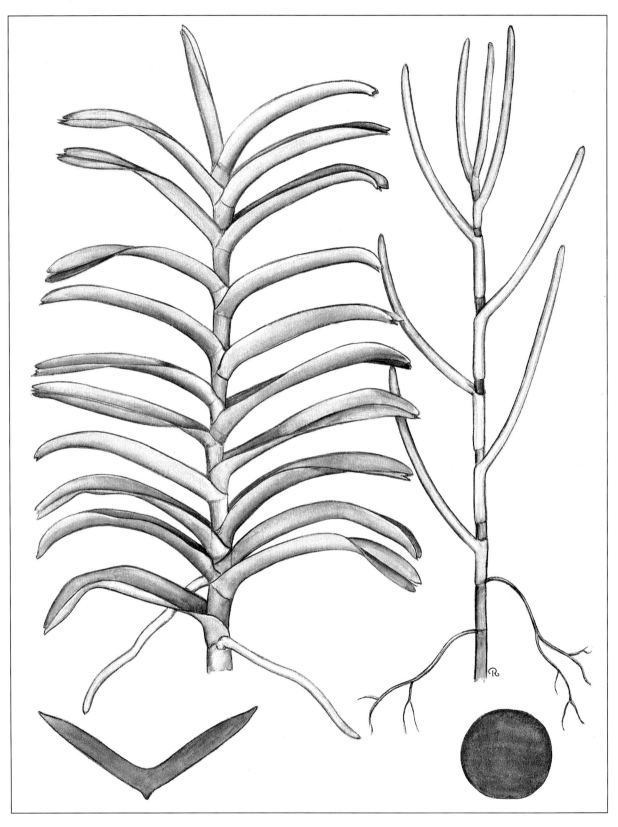

Figure 24. Vegetative forms of *Vanda* and *Papilionanthe* showing plant habit and leaf cross section. *Vanda tricolor* (left) and *Papilionanthe teres* (right).

370

Vanda species

Vandopsis

GENUS: *Vandopsis* Pfitzer (van-DOPP-siss)
TRIBE: Vandeae SUBTRIBE: Aeridinae
IDENTIFICATION CHARACTERISTICS: *Vandopsis* is a genus of approximately eight robust, monopodial, epiphytic species. The genus was probably first recognized by the French botanist Charles Gaudichaud-Beaupré around 1817, when he discovered *V. lissochiloides*, which he named *Fieldia lissochiloides*. It was not until 1850 that Ernst H. H. Pfitzer established the genus *Vandopsis*. During the intervening years, Carl Blume, John Lindley, and George Bentham shifted the species from one genus to another. Pfitzer named the genus using the Sanskrit word *nanda* (orchid) and the Greek word *opsis* (looks like), because the plants resembled vandas.

Vandopsis is a very stout grower, attaining heights of several feet. The thick, leathery strap leaves are up to 24 inches (60 cm) long and 2 to 3 inches (5–7.5 cm) wide. The bases of the leaves clasp the stem, and the tips of the leaves are often slightly recurved and have bilobed apices. The inflorescences, up to 6 feet (180 cm) long and bearing as many as 20 flowers, arise from the leaf axils.

The thick, fleshy or sometimes almost-leathery flowers of this genus open over a period of time, thus extending the blooming season. The 2-inch (5-cm) wide flowers of *Vandopsis lissochiloides* may last for three to four months. Those of *V. gigantea* have a substance very similar to that of a banana peel and are almost as thick. The sepals are alike in size and color. The two petals are similar to the sepals but slightly smaller. The small lip has three lobes, with the two small lateral lobes joined by a tissue bridge. The third lobe of the lip is elongate and fleshy. The flowers are yellow with brown or purple blotches.

The column is very short and almost as broad as it is long. A small anther cap covers the apex of the column. The stigmatic surface is separated from the pollinia by a very thin rostellum. There are two yellow, almost-elliptical pollinia attached to a single stipe with a broad base. Each pollinium has a very distinct cleavage line.

CULTURE: Temperature, 60–70°F (15–21°C); light, 2400–3600 footcandles, can stand full sun under certain conditions; humidity, 40–70%; media, charcoal, bark, tree fern; fertilization, monthly, ratio depends on medium.

COLOR PLATE: *Vandopsis gigantea*

SPECIES	FLOWERING SEASON	GENERAL LOCALE
gigantea	S–SS	Myanmar, Thailand
lissochiloides	SS	Philippines to Thailand
undulata	SS	Himalayas
warocuqueana	SS–F	New Guinea

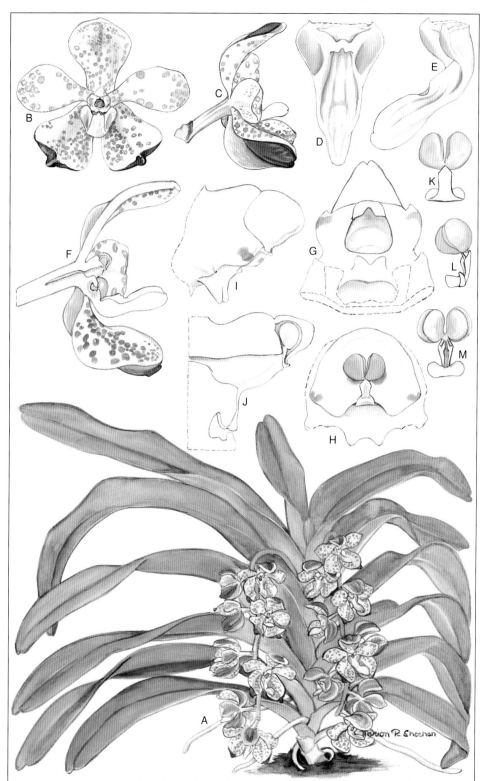

Vandopsis gigantea

A: Plant in flower, × ¼.
B: Flower, face view, × ¾.
C: Flower, side view, × ¾.
D: Lip, face view, × 2.
E: Lip, side view, × 2.
F: Flower, vertical section, × 1.
G: Column, ventral view, × 4.
H: Column, end view, anther
   cap removed, × 4.
I: Column, side view, × 4.
J: Column, vertical section, × 4.
K, L, M: Pollinia, × 6.

Vanilla

GENUS: *Vanilla* Miller (vah-NILL-uh)
TRIBE: Vanilleae   SUBTRIBE: Vanillinae

IDENTIFICATION CHARACTERISTICS: *Vanilla* is the only genus in the vast orchid family of economic importance (other than for its flowers). This genus is the source of vanillin, a chemical obtained from the seed pod and the basis of vanilla flavoring used so widely in baked goods and other desserts and candies. It is a genus of approximately 60 species of vinelike plants found throughout the tropical world. According to Bechtel et al. (1992), Philip Miller first described the genus in 1754, although the name is often attributed to O. Swartz who described the genus in 1799. The word *vanilla* was derived from Spanish and means pod or small sheath. The plants are grown as a commercial agricultural crop in several areas of the world.

Vanilla species climb as their aerial roots, arising at the nodes, attach to or encircle twigs to hold fast. The shiny leaves vary and are up to 9 inches (22 cm) long and 3 inches (7.5 cm) wide depending on the species. Some species have large, alternate, leathery leaves (e.g., *V. planifolia*) whereas in others the leaves are reduced to scalelike appendages giving the vine a leafless appearance (e.g., *V. barbellata*).

The flowers, which are borne in axillary inflorescences of a few to many flowers, open separately and last for one day. They are large, up to 3 inches (7.5 cm) wide, showy, and fleshy. Flower colors are pale yellow, greenish, or white, with lips having orange or lavender patterns. The large sepals are equal in size, shape, and color, and are similar to the petals. A complex lip is attached to the column and encircles it. The flaring apical lobe of the lip has a wavy margin and bears various appendages.

The long, narrow column has a very complex apex. The anther cap is under the tip of the column rather than at the apex. The underside of the column is pubescent. A very pronounced rostellum separates the pollinia from the stigmatic surface. A tissue flap protects the stigmatic surface and must be lifted to insure pollination. The pollinia, which are not always distinct, are sometimes difficult to remove. In some instances, four indistinct pollinia can be removed from a flower; however, in many instances, the pollen masses crumble as they are removed.

CULTURE: Temperature, 40–70°F (4–21°C); light, 2400–3600 footcandles; humidity, 40–70%; media, rich organic compost or an epiphytic medium; fertilization, monthly, ratio depends on medium.

COLOR PLATE: *Vanilla planifolia*

SPECIES	FLOWERING SEASON	GENERAL LOCALE
africana	SS–F	Tropical western Africa
aphylla	SS	Southeast Asia, Java
barbellata	S–SS	Southern Florida, Caribbean Islands
chamissonis	S–SS	Brazil
dilloniana	S–SS	Southern Florida, Caribbean Islands
griffithii	S–SS	Borneo, Sumatra, Malay Peninsula
humblotii	SS	Comoro Islands
moonii	S	Sri Lanka
phaeantha	S–SS	Southern Florida, West Indies
phalaenopsis	SS	Seychelles Islands
planifolia	F	Florida, West Indies, Mexico to South America
pompona	SS	Mexico to Peru
walkeriae	S–SS	Sri Lanka

Vanilla planifolia

A: Plant in flower, × ¼.
B: Flower, face view, × ½.
C: Flower, side view, × ½.
D: Lip, face view, × 1.
E: Lip, side view, × ½.
F: Flower, vertical section, × ¾.
G: Column, side view, × 1.
H: Column end, ventral view,
   × 3.
I: Column end, ventral view,
   anther cap lifted, × 3.
J: Anther cap, later stage, × 3.
K: Column end, side view, × 3.
L: Column end, vertical section,
   × 3.
M: Pollinia in place, young stage,
   × 3.
N: Pollen mass, × 6.

Zygopetalum

GENUS: *Zygopetalum* Hooker (zye-goh-PET-uh-lum)

TRIBE: Maxillarieae SUBTRIBE: Zygopetalinae

IDENTIFICATION CHARACTERISTICS: *Zygopetalum* at one time was a polymorphic genus of 50 species. It has been reclassified into a distinct genus containing less than 20 species. William Hooker established the genus when he received a plant from Mr. Mackay of Trinity College Botanic Garden, Dublin. The plant had been introduced from Brazil in the early 1800s by Mackay. Hooker named the genus in 1827 using two Greek words, *zygon* (yoke) and *petalon* (petal, sepal), to identify the lip callus tissue that appears to be a yoke uniting the sepals and petals.

The genus has ovoid pseudobulbs with distinct sheaths. As the pseudobulbs age and become wrinkled, the sheaths turn brown and degenerate into strong fibers. Individual bulbs of these sympodial epiphytes are 2 to 3 inches (5–7.5 cm) tall and have up to six lanceolate leaves, 18 inches (45 cm) long and 2 inches (5 cm) wide. The leaves have pronounced veins and the blades taper toward the folded bases. The inflorescences arise from the pseudobulb base at the sheath's axil and bear three to ten flowers, each 2 to 3 inches (5–7.5 cm) wide.

The fragrant flowers have sepals and petals that are green or greenish with brown or purple blotches. The lips are white with lavender or brownish purple marks on the veins. The flowers of *Zygopetalum* species are very similar. The sepals and two petals are alike generally in size and color and have undulating margins. Some species, however, have sepals that are larger than the two petals. The lip is three-lobed with two very small lateral lobes, usually erect and adjacent to or encircling the column. The third or apex lobe is very broad with a wavy margin. The base of the small spurred lip is attached to the base of the column.

The short column is terminated by a distinct anther cap with a beaked rostellum. The concave underside of the column is often pubescent. Four pollinia are attached by a broad stipe to a disc that rests on the rostellum.

CULTURE: Temperature, 60–70°F (15–21°C); light, 2400–3600 footcandles; humidity, 40–70%; media, tree fern, bark, peat and perlite, some treated as terrestrials; fertilization, monthly, ratio depends on medium.

COLOR PLATE: *Zygopetalum mackayi*

SPECIES	FLOWERING SEASON	GENERAL LOCALE
brachypetalum	F–W	Brazil
bolivianum	W	Bolivia, Peru
burkei	F–W	Venezuela, Guyana, Suriname, Brazil
crinitum	SS–F	Brazil
intermedium	F–W	Brazil
mackayi	F–W	Brazil
maxillare	W–S	Brazil, Paraguay
mosenianum	W–S	Brazil

Zygopetalum mackayi
A: Plant in flower, × ¼.
B: Flower, face view, × ¾.
C: Flower, side view, × ¾.
D: Lip, × 1.
E: Flower, vertical section, × ¾.
F: Column, ventral view, × 3.
G: Column, end view, × 3.
H: Column, side view, × 3.
I: Column, vertical section, × 3.
J, K, L: Pollinia, × 5.

Zygosepalum _____

GENUS: *Zygosepalum* Reichenbach f. (zye-goh-SEEP-uh-lum)

TRIBE: Maxillarieae SUBTRIBE: Zygopetalinae

IDENTIFICATION CHARACTERISTICS: It is difficult to understand why species such as those of the genus *Zygosepalum* with their large, attractive, long-lived flowers are more or less a rarity in collections today. Although they are rare in nature also, with modern technology these plants could be made available. This small genus of possibly five species originally was described in 1863 by H. G. Reichenbach, who coined the generic name from two Greek words, *zygon* (yoke) and *sepalum* (sepal), probably referring to the connate nature of the sepals. There is still some confusion in the literature because some taxonomists have included *Zygosepalum* in the genus *Menadenium*. Thus, it may be necessary to search under both names in a given book to find members of the genus.

The creeping rhizomes of these sympodial epiphytes have widely spaced pseudobulbs often 2 inches (5 cm) apart. The small, single-noded pseudobulbs are subtended by several often-large, leafy bracts and usually have two leaves at their apex. The leafy bracts may be as large as the leaves atop the pseudobulb. The lanceolate leaves, which are usually up to five-nerved, are 12 inches (30 cm) long and 1.5 inches (4 cm) wide. The single-flowered (occasionally two-flowered) inflorescence arises from the base of the pseudobulb.

The elongate flowers may be up to 2 inches (5 cm) wide and 3.5 inches (8 cm) long. They are fragrant, have excellent substance, and are large compared to the size of the plant. Individual flowers last up to two weeks on the plant. Flower color is white with peachy brown and green highlights. The sepals and petals are very similar in shape and color, with the petals slightly narrower. The large, flaring lip has a very distinctive crescent-shaped callus beneath the column.

The long, slightly curved column, which tapers in the middle, has a distinct hood with a lacerated margin at its apex. The four pollinia are borne on a single stipe with a very pronounced viscidium.

CULTURE: Temperature, 65–70°F (18–21°C); light, 2400–3600 footcandles; humidity, 60%; medium, any good mix for epiphytes; fertilization, monthly ratio depends on medium.

COLOR PLATE. *Zygosepalum labiosum*

SPECIES	FLOWERING SEASON	GENERAL LOCALE
labiosum	S–SS	Colombia, Venezuela, Brazil
lindeniae	W	Venezuela to Brazil, Peru
tatei	S	Venezuela to Brazil

Zygosepalum labiosum

A: Plant in flower, × ½.
B: Flower, face view, × 1.
C: Flower, side view, × ¾.
D: Lip, three-quarter view, × 1.
E: Flower, vertical section, × 1.
F: Column, ventral view, × 2.
G: Column, end view, × 2.
H: Column, side view, × 2.
I: Column, vertical section, × 2.
J: Anther cap in place, face
   view, × 4.
K: Anther cap removed, back
   view, × 4.
L, M, N: Pollinia, × 5.

Marion R. Sheehan

Glossary

Abaxial (ab-AX-ee-ul) (Fig. 26): The side of an organ, such as a leaf, facing away from the main stem or axis; the underside.

Acaulescent (ah-kaw-LESS-ent) (Fig. 28B, E): Refers to plants that are, or appear to be, stemless.

Acuminate (Figs. 25, 35A): Having a very sharp apex with long, straight or slightly concave sides.

Acute (Figs. 25, 35B, 47A, I): Having a very sharp, but not long and tapered, point.

Adaxial (Fig. 26): The side of an organ, such as a leaf, facing the main stem or axis; the upper side.

Adnate (Figs. 48, 63M): Refers to the attachment of two plant parts, whether partially or completely fused.

Adventitious (ad-ven-TISH-us) (Fig. 28C): Refers to buds and roots that appear from abnormal locations on the stem of a plant.

Aerial root (Fig. 30F): A root produced along the stem above ground, mainly by monopodial plants. This kind of root usually does not enter the medium.

Agglutinate: To glue together.

Aggregate (Fig. 38A): Forming a dense mass or grouping.

Albino: Refers to a plant lacking chlorophyll or a flower lacking pigment (e.g., a white flower).

Alternate (Fig. 28C, F): Refers to plant parts placed individually at different heights on a stem or inflorescence.

Amorphous: Having no regular form; formless.

Amphigean (am-fih-JEE-an): Any plant distributed in both hemispheres of the Old and New Worlds.

Anastomosing (an-NAS-toh-mohz-ing) (Figs. 28E, 37G, I): Interlacing or running together (e.g., the network of veins on a leaf).

Ancipitous (an-SIP-ih-tus) (Fig. 20): Having two edges and being flattened (e.g., pseudobulbs of *Laelia rubescens*).

Androecium (an-DREE-see-um) (Fig. 60): The male portion of the flower (e.g., the stamens).

Angiosperm (AN-jee-oh-sperm): A plant with the seed enclosed in a case or fruit.

Annual: A plant with a life cycle of one year (i.e., a plant that grows from seed to flower to seed in one growing season).

Antennae (Figs. 25, 58B, 63G): Slender, elongate appendages (e.g., as on lips of *Phalaenopsis*).

Anther (Figs. 59, 60, 61): The pollen-bearing portion of the stamen.

Anther cap (Figs. 59, 60Aa, 61Bc): The covering over orchid pollinia.

Anthesis (an-THEE-sus): The period of time when the flower is opening.

Antipodal (an-TIP-oh-dal): Refers to a plant that grows on opposite sides of the world.

Antrorse (AN-trorse) (Fig. 27C): Growing upward or even forward.

Aphyllus (Fig. 28B): Leafless (e.g., *Polyrrhiza lindenii*).

Apical: At the apex. Refers to a leaf or bud at the tip of a stem.

Apiculate (Figs. 35I, 47C, F): Ending in a sharp point.

Asexual: A form of propagation using vegetative segments of the plant rather than seed to increase the population.

Attenuate (Fig. 47H, J): Gradually narrowing to a point.

Auriculate (Fig. 25): Having appendages that are earlike in appearance.

Awl-shaped (Fig. 35A): Tapering gently from the base to a stiff point.

Axil (Fig. 26): The angle formed between a leaf and the stem to which it is attached.

Axile (Fig. 64A): Of the axis; a form of placentation in which the ovules are borne on a central axil or on protrusions from it.

Axillary (Fig. 43Aa): Refers to flowers that arise from the axil of a leaf (e.g., some species of *Dendrobium*).

Axis (Figs. 30F, 31): The main stem of a plant.

Backbulb (Fig. 26): The older pseudobulbs, usually three, four, or more behind the lead, having lateral buds and sometimes leaves. When severed from the parent, these bulbs produce new plants.

Banded (Figs. 37C, 55E): Said of flowers and leaves that have strong lines of color, ribs, or similar marks.

Basal (Fig. 43Ab): Said of an inflorescence that arises from the base of the pseudobulb (e.g., *Lycaste*).

Beak (Fig. 63N): A long, pronounced point, such as the stigma projection that forms the rostellum; a beaklike projection.

Beard (Fig. 57Ca, Cb, Ea, Eb): A limited area with hairs, often found on flowers.

Biennial: A plant with a life cycle spanning two growing seasons, usually growing vegetatively the first season and flowering and seeding in the second.

Bifarious (bye-FAHR-ee-us) (Fig. 28D): Refers to plant parts arranged in two rows.

Bifoliate (Fig. 28A): Having two leaves.

Bifurcate (BYE-fur-kayt) (Fig. 52H): Divided into two branches, forked (e.g., the midlobe of the lip of many orchids but also said of stigma, styles, lip, or some hairs).

Bigeneric: Refers to a hybrid made between two genera, such as *Laeliocattleya* (*Laelia* × *Cattleya*).

Bisexual: Having both sexes. Refers to flowers having both male and female parts (i.e., stamen and pistil).

Blade (Figs. 31, 32): The flattened, expanded portion of a leaf.

Bloom: A whitish gray waxy coating found on some leaves (e.g., *Brassavola glauca*).

Blotch (Figs. 25, 37C, D, 55C): An irregular color spot on sepals or petals.

Boot (Fig. 50): Pouchlike lips (e.g., flowers of Cypripedioideae).

Botanical: An affectionate term used by orchidologists to denote species with small flowers or species not commonly cultivated. Also, having to do with botany.

Bract (Figs. 26, 31, 41): A leaflike structure that subtends a flower, leaf, or stem.

Bracteole: A very small bract; a bractlet.

Breaking (Fig. 26): The point at which a new or lateral bud begins to grow; the lead.

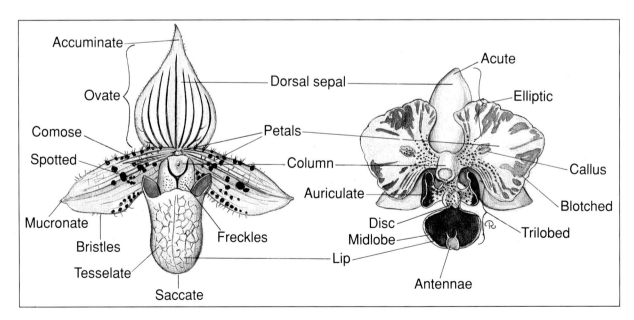

Figure 25. *Paphiopedilum lowii* (left) and *Phalaenopsis* × *intermedia* var. *diezii* (right) showing that a variety of terms can be applied to the same plant part.

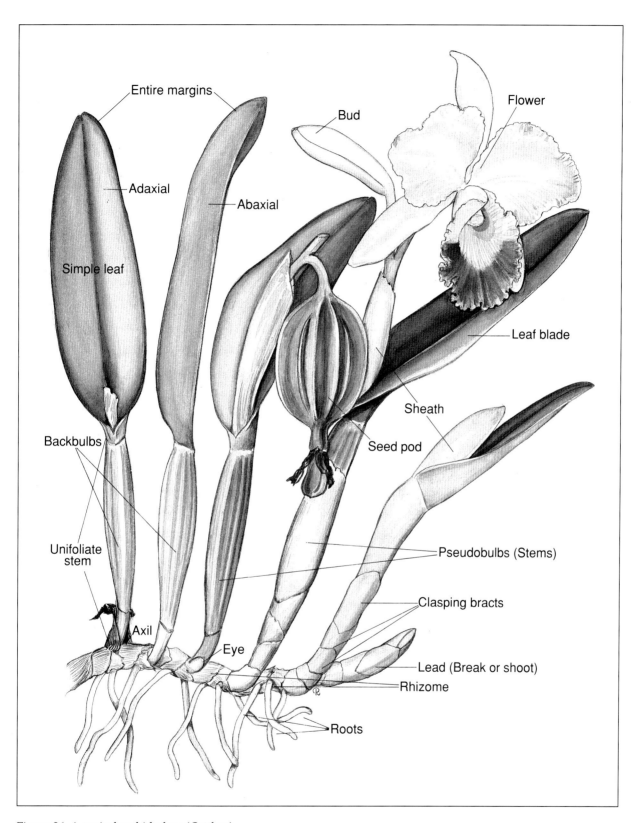

Figure 26. A typical orchid plant (*Cattleya*).

383

Figure 27. Growth habits. A: Epiphytic (*Encyclia tampensis*). B: Terrestrial (*Cypripedium acaule*). C: Monopodial (*Arachnis*). D: Monopodial (*Ascocentrum*). E: Monopodial (*Phalaenopsis*). F: Sympodial (*Encyclia*). G: Sympodial (*Dendrobium*). H: Sympodial (*Paphiopedilum*).

384

Figure 28. Growth habits. A: Pseudobulbous orchid. B: Leafless (*Polyrrhiza*). C: Reed-type with offset (*Dendrobium*).
D: Distichous (*Dendrobium*). E: Whorled leaves (*Goodyera*). F: Vine (*Vanilla*).

Bristly (Figs. 25, 57Ba, Bb): Having stiff hairs.

Bud (Figs. 26, 41): An unopened flower or an initiated new shoot before it elongates.

Bulb (Fig. 26): An enlarged or swollen stem. See **Pseudobulb**.

Caducous (ka-DOO-kus): Falling or dropping off early, as sepals or petals.

Callus (Figs. 25, 58): A hard, often waxy projection found on an orchid lip (e.g., *Phalaenopsis*).

Calyx (Figs. 41, 46): The outermost segments of the flower; the sepals.

Cap (Figs. 59, 60, 61): The removable cover over the pollinia (e.g., anther cap).

Capsule (Fig. 65): The fruit of orchids; a fruit from a compound ovary, usually dry and opening at one or more sutures at maturity.

Carpel (Fig. 64): A cell in a compound ovary.

Cauda (Fig. 60D, E): A slender appendage.

Caudate (Fig. 57Fa): Having long, taillike appendages (e.g., floral parts of *Brassia*).

Caudicle (KAW-dik-ul) (Fig. 60E): The stalk of a pollinium.

Cauline (KAW-line): Belonging to a stem.

Cell (Fig. 64): An opening in the ovary also known as a locule. Also, the smallest unit of plant structure.

Chlorophyllous: Having chlorophyll.

Chlorotic (klor-ROT-ik): Refers to a yellowish plant as opposed to a normal green one.

Ciliate (Figs. 54B, 58C): Having stiff hairs on the margin.

Circumboreal: Refers to any plant found in the Northern Hemisphere.

Cirrus (SEER-rus) (Fig. 58B): The antennae found on the lips of some orchids (e.g., *Phalaenopsis amabilis*).

Clasping (Figs. 26, 28C): Refers to a leaf base or a bract that enfolds the stem or pseudobulb.

Clavate (Fig. 39O): Club-shaped with increased thickening towards the apex.

Clavellate (Fig. 57Ca, Cb): Club-shaped but small.

Claw (Fig. 47D, E): The stemlike base of a petal or sepal.

Clinandrium (kly-NAN-dree-um) (Fig. 4): The anther bed; the tissue at the apex of the column under the anther.

Column (Figs. 25, 59, 61, 63): The waxy structure in the center of the flower. An organ formed by the union of the male and female portions of the flower, also called the **gynandrium**.

Clone: A group of plants asexually propagated from one plant.

Column foot (Figs. 59, 63E): An extension at the base of the column, often attached to the lip.

Comose (Figs. 25, 56 right): With hair in tufts.

Compact (Fig. 28E): Short or compressed.

Compressed (Figs. 39C, 40D, E): Flattened, usually laterally.

Concave (Fig. 59): Basin-shaped (e.g., many stigmatic surfaces).

Conduplicate (Fig. 33B): Folded together lengthwise (e.g., leaves or other plant parts).

Conical: Cone-shaped.

Connate (Fig. 48C): Joined, said of two similar segments joined at their bases (e.g., the synsepal of the Cypripedioideae).

Connective tissue: Refers to tissue that unites the two cells of the anther.

Constricted (Fig. 39N): Compressed or drawn together at some point.

Convex: Curving upward, the opposite of concave.

Convolute (Fig. 33A): Rolled up.

Cordate (Fig. 34J): Heart-shaped (e.g., leaves).

Coriaceous: Having a thick, leathery texture (e.g., leaves).

Corm (Fig. 30C): A swollen stem base, usually underground. A storage organ.

Crest (Fig. 58D): Having a raised, irregular toothed area, often found on the lips of orchids.

Crested (Fig. 58D): Bearing a crest.

Crispate (Figs. 53C, 54D): Having very strong, wavy margins; the ultimate form of undulate.

Cultivar: A horticultural variety often cultivated for its unique characteristics.

Cupped (Fig. 49F, G): Dish-shaped, or resembling a small cup.

Cylindrical (Fig. 39J, K): Round and equal from top to bottom.

Cyme (SYME): A determinate inflorescence where the central flower opens first; usually a wide, almost-flat-topped inflorescence.

Cymose (SY-mohs): Having inflorescences that are cymes or cymelike.

Deciduous (de-SID-yew-us): Refers to a plant that sheds its leaves annually and is leafless for a period of time (e.g., *Cypripedium*, *Platanthera*, and *Bletia*).

Decumbent (Fig. 29B): Reclining. Refers to a stem with the tip turned up.

Dentate (Fig. 52T): Having toothlike margins that are usually sharp and coarse (e.g., leaves and petals).

Denticulate (Figs. 37J, 54A): Minutely dentate.

Determinate (Fig. 43Ba): Said of an inflorescence when the terminal flower opens first, thus

Figure 29. Growth habits. A: Procumbent (*Dendrobium*). B: Decumbent (*Ludisia*). C: Erect (*Caularthron*).

preventing any further elongation of the inflorescence.

Diandrous (dye-AN-drus) (Figs. 14, 60Ba, Bb, 61Aa, Ab, 62A, 63Q): Having two anthers (e.g., in Cypripedioideae).

Dichotomous (dye-KOT-oh-mus): Continually dividing into twos. Said of branches when they fork into pairs (e.g., *Pholidota*).

Dimorphous (dye-MOR-fus): Having two forms. Said of plants (e.g., *Grammatophyllum*) with two forms of vegetative or floral parts.

Dioecious (dye-EE-shus): Having male and female flowers on separate plants.

Diphyllous (dye-FILL-us) (Fig. 28A): Having two leaves; bifoliate.

Diploid: Having two sets of chromosomes; the usual complement of chromosomes.

Disc (Figs. 25, 58A): A fleshy structure found on the basal portion of some orchid lips.

Distichous (DIS-tik-us) (Fig. 28D): Having flowers or leaves in two ranks, usually on opposite sides of a stem.

Diurnal: Refers to flowers that open or are fragrant only during the day.

Dorsal (Fig. 25): Pertaining to the back (e.g., the dorsal sepal or uppermost sepal).

Downy (Figs. 37A, 57Aa, Ab): Having a dense cover of very soft hairs.

Elliptic (Figs. 25, 34A, 39G, H, 47I): Somewhat oval in shape and equally rounded at the base and apex.

Elongate (Figs. 39H, 47J): Very long or drawn-out (e.g., leaf or pseudobulb).

Emarginate (Fig. 35E): Refers to a leaf with a shallow notch at its tip.

Embryo: The tiny plant found within a seed.

Endemic: Refers to a plant from a given area that is found nowhere else (e.g., endemic to Florida means found only in Florida).

Endosperm (EN-doh-sperm): The carbohydrates, usually stored in seed but lacking in orchid seed.

Ensiform (Figs. 34G, 47J): Sword-shaped.

Entire (Fig. 26): Said of margins that are not broken, toothed, or serrated.

Ephemeral (ee-FEM-er-al): Of very short duration (e.g., flowers of *Dendrobium crumenatum* that are open only for one day).

387

Epichile (EP-ih-kile): The terminal part of a complex, often segmented lip (e.g., the lip of *Stanhopea*).

Epidermis: The layer of cells that forms the covering of all plant parts.

Epiphyte (EP-ih-fite) (Fig. 27A): A plant that lives on another but does not draw nourishment from the host plant (e.g., *Cattleya*).

Equitant (EK-kwi-tant) (Fig. 28D): Refers to leaves overlapping and forming two ranks (e.g., *Psygmorchis pusilla*).

Erect (Fig. 29C): Growing upright.

Erose (Fig. 35G): Said of a leaf tip that appears to have a torn margin or that looks like an insect chewed on it (e.g., *Vanda tricolor*).

Evergreen: A plant that retains its leaves for more than one year and that does not lose them all at one time.

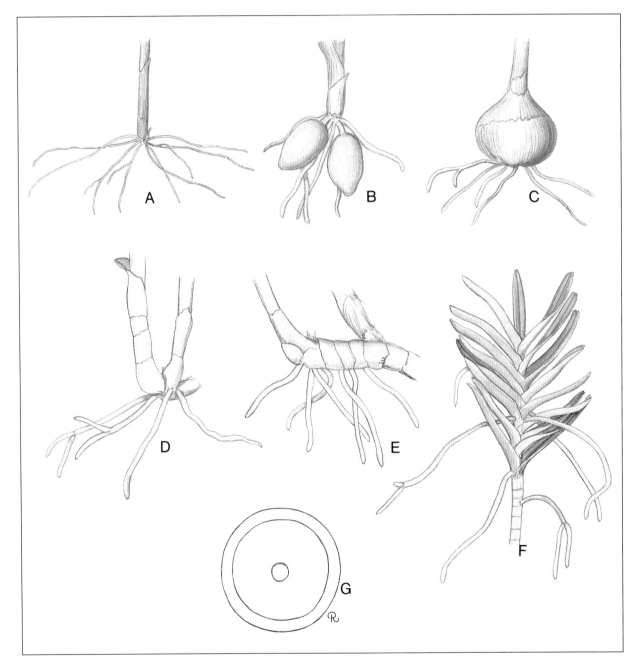

Figure 30. Variations in orchid roots. A: Fibrous (*Pogonia*). B: Tuberoids (*Ophrys*). C: Corm (*Bletilla*). D: Fleshy roots; no rhizome (*Dendrobium*). E: Rhizome and fleshy roots (*Cattleya*). F: Aerial roots (*Aerides*). G: Fleshy root in cross section showing velamen layer.

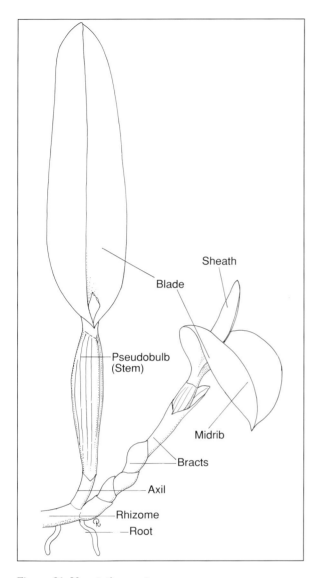

Figure 31. Vegetative parts.

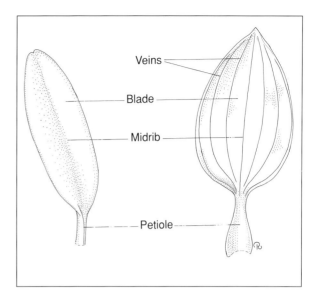

Figure 32. Leaves.

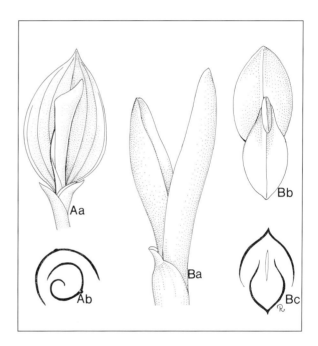

Figure 33. Leaf emergence. A: Convolute (*Ludisia*).
Aa: New leaf emerging. Ab: Cross section showing
inrolled new leaf. B: Conduplicate (*Cattleya*). Ba: Side
view. Bb: Top view. Bc: Cross section showing
overlapping.

Eye (Fig. 26): The vegetative bud at the base of the
pseudobulb of sympodial orchids.

Falcate (Figs. 34M, N, 47F): Sickle-shaped.

Family: A natural unit in taxonomy wherein one
or more genera are combined because of a
number of similar characteristics (e.g., Orchidaceae).

Fertilization: The fusion of the male (pollen) and
female (ovule) that gives rise to the seed. Also,
the act of applying nutrients (fertilizer) to
plants.

Fetid: Having a disagreeable, usually offensive
odor.

Fibrous (Fig. 30A): Resembling fibers in structure
(e.g., roots).

Filament: The stemlike structure that supports
the anther; a part of the stamen, fused into the
column in orchids.

Fimbriate (Fig. 54E): Having a fringe.

Fleshy root (Fig. 30D): A large, thick, succulent
root.

389

Flora: All the plants native to a given area or country. A book containing descriptions of plants from such an area is also called a **flora**.

Floriferous (flo-RIFF-er-us): Having flowers. Often said of a plant that flowers freely or has many flowers.

Flower (Figs. 26, 41): A stem bearing a pistil or stamens or both generally surrounded by petals or sepals or both.

Foliage: Leaves.

Foot (Figs. 59, 63E): See **Column foot**.

Forked (Fig. 52E, G, H): Having two or more prongs. Used of plants to mean divided into two equal segments.

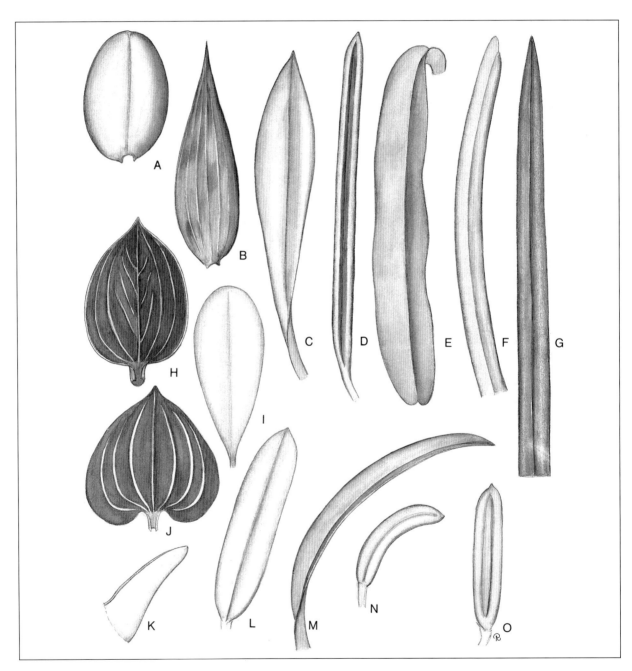

Figure 34. Leaf shapes. A: Elliptic (*Sophronitis*). B: Lanceolate (*Sobralia*). C: Oblanceolate (*Gongora*). D: Linear (*Brassavola*). E: Lorate (*Aerides*). F: Ligulate (*Cymbidium*). G: Ensiform (*Epidendrum*). H: Ovate (*Calypso*). I: Obovate (*Stellis*). J: Cordate (*Pogonia*). K: Triangular (*Lockhartia*). L: Oblong (*Rodriguezia*). M: Falcate and keeled (*Neofinetia*). N: Falcate, fleshy, or thick (*Dendrobium*). O: Lingulate (*Dendrobium*).

390

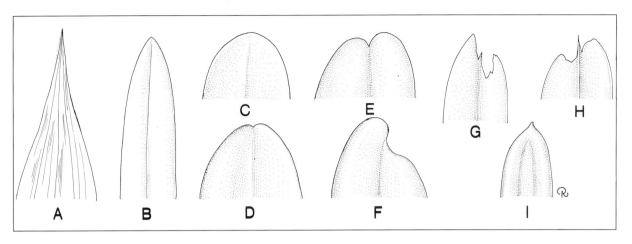

Figure 35. Leaf tips. A: Acuminate. B: Acute. C: Obtuse. D: Retuse. E: Emarginate. F: Unequally two-lobed. G: Erose (torn). H: Mucronate. I: Apiculate.

Freckled (Figs. 25, 55A): Said of petals or sepals covered with small, usually darker colored spots.

Fringed (Figs. 54C, 63H, Q): Having a border or margin with an edging of fine hairs.

Fruit (Fig. 65): The capsule in orchids; any structure that bears or contains seeds.

Furrowed (Fig. 39F, G, I): Having long grooves.

Fusiform (Fig. 39L, P): Spindle-shaped.

Gamopetalous (gam-oh-PET-uh-lus) (Fig. 48B): Having fused petals.

Gamosepalous (gam-oh-SEEP-uh-lus) (Fig. 48): Having fused sepals.

Genera: Plural of genus.

Genus: A taxonomic subdivision of a family composed of one or more species with similar characteristics.

Glabrous (Fig. 26): Without hairs; often misdescribed as smooth.

Gland: A secreting organ (e.g., nectary).

Glaucous: Having a whitish or grayish waxy bloom on the foliage (e.g., *Rhyncholaelia glauca*).

Globose (Fig. 39A): Almost round.

Glutinous: Very sticky.

Gregarious (greh-GAYR-ee-us): All plants of a given population flowering at the same time, a phenomenon often triggered by an environmental factor such as temperature change (e.g., *Dendrobium crumenatum*).

Grex: Collectively the progeny of a given cross; the group of offspring.

Grooved (Figs. 36C, 39F, G, H, I, L, M): Having furrows or ridges.

Gynandrium (jye-NAN-dree-um) (Figs. 61, 62): An organ containing the male and female portions of the orchid flower; also called the **column**.

Gynandrous (jye-NAN-drus): Having the stamens attached to the stigma and style in one unit.

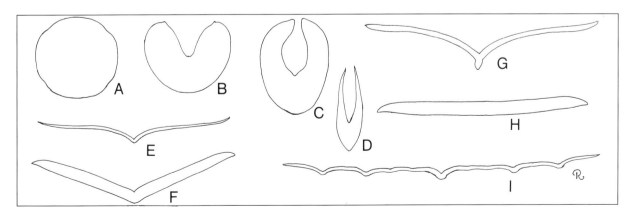

Figure 36. Leaf cross sections. A: Terete. B: Semiterete. C: Semiterete, deeply grooved. D: Semiterete, compressed. E: Thin. F: Thick. G: Keeled. H: Flat, no midvein depression. I: Pleated (or plaited).

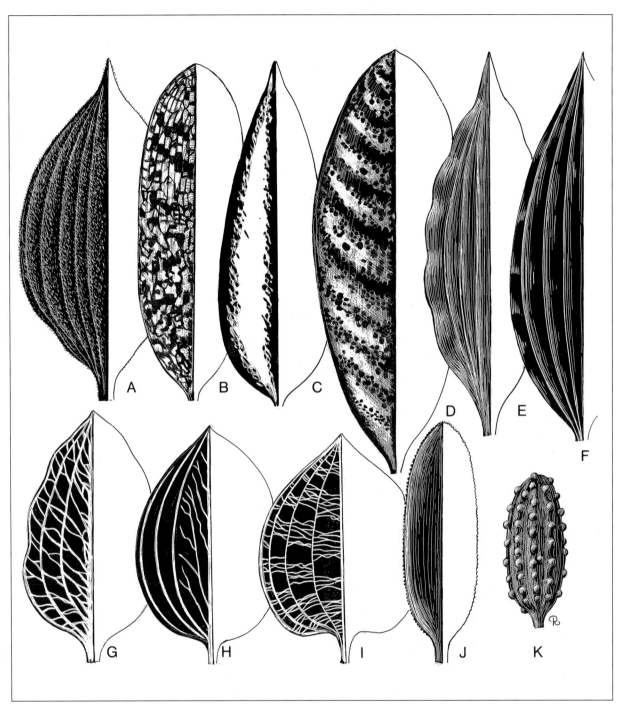

Figure 37. Leaf patterns and surfaces. A: Pleated and downy (*Cypripedium*). B: Tessellate (*Paphiopedilum*).
C: Irregularly banded or blotched (*Spiranthes*). D: Blotched, spotted, marbled, or mottled (*Phalaenopsis*). E: Undulate
(*Calanthe*). F: Pleated (*Eulophia*). G: Netted with oblique webbing (*Goodyera*). H: Veined and striped (*Ludisia*). I: Netted
or webbed (*Macodes*). J: Denticulate margin (*Dendrobium*). K: Tuberculate surface (*Dendrobium*).

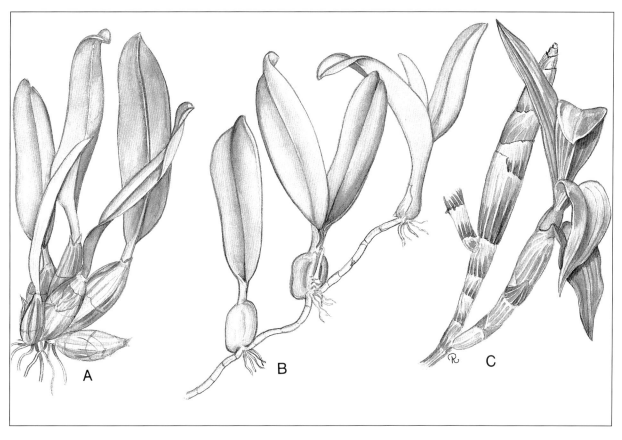

Figure 38. Pseudobulb growth habits. A: Aggregate (*Dendrobium*). B: Widely spaced or chainlike (*Bulbophyllum*). C: New pseudobulbs emerging from old (*Pholidota*).

Gynoecium (jye-NEE-see-um) (Figs. 61, 62): The female portion of a flower.

Habit (Figs. 25, 26, 27): The form or shape of a plant.

Habitat: The area where a plant grows native.

Hair: Threadlike growths on plant parts (e.g., pubescence, beards). See also **Hirsute**.

Head (Fig. 42D): Having flowers in a tight cluster at the top of the flower spike; a type of inflorescence; a short compact inflorescence (e.g., *Epidendrum ibaguense*).

Hermaphrodite (her-MAF-roh-dyte): A perfect flower (i.e., having both male and female organs).

Hirsute (Fig. 57Ba, Bb): Having coarse, usually long hairs.

Hooded (Figs. 49C, D, E, 63F): Said of floral parts that form a hood (e.g., *Catasetum*).

Horned (Figs. 49B, 63I): Having a hornlike projection (e.g., the lip of *Stanhopea*).

Hybrid: A plant that results from the crossing of two species. Many orchid hybrids also result from crosses between and among genera.

Hybridization: The act of producing hybrids.

Hypochile (HY-poh-kile): The basal part of a complex, often segmented lip (e.g., *Stanhopea*).

Imbricate (Fig. 28D): Overlapping in a shinglelike arrangement (e.g., leaves of *Lockhartia*).

Imperfect: An incomplete flower, lacking part or all the reproductive structures (e.g., without stamens).

Incised (Fig. 54E, Fa, Fb): Having a deep, usually irregular cut.

Indeterminate (Fig. 43Bb): Said of an inflorescence when the lower flowers open first and the apex of the inflorescence remains vegetative (e.g., *Phalaenopsis*).

Indigenous (in-DIJ-en-us): Refers to a plant native to a specific area or country.

Inferior (Fig. 4): Beneath; refers to ovaries where the floral segments are attached at the apex of the ovary.

Inflorescence (Fig. 41): A stem bearing a flower or flowers; the flowering portion of a plant.

Inrolled (Fig. 50A, B): Having margins rolled in (e.g., the lip in *Cypripedium*).

393

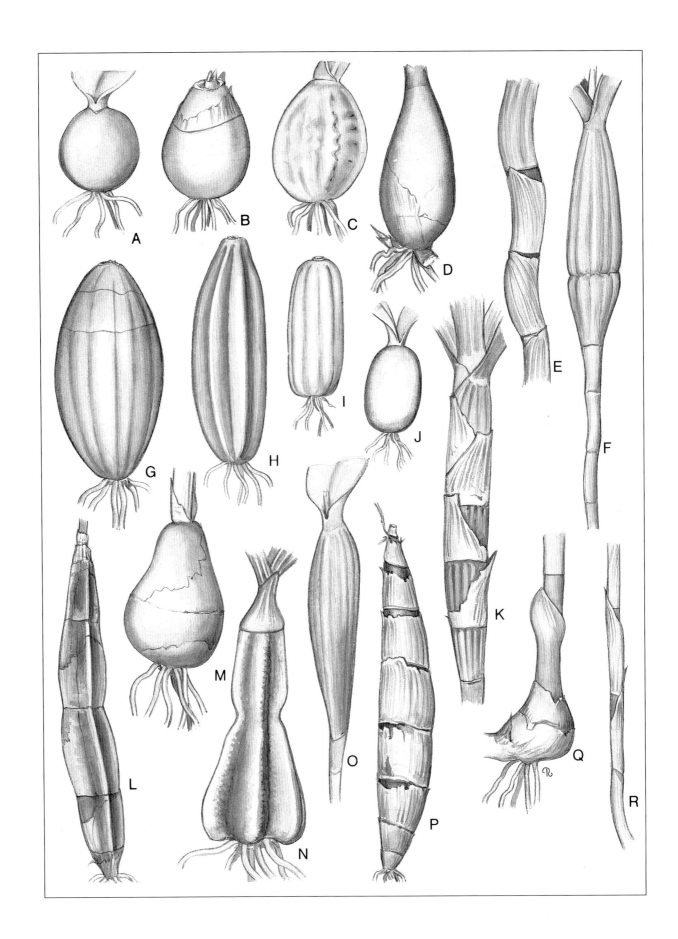

Internode (Fig. 27C, G): The segment of a stem between two nodes (leaves).

Irregular: Refers to a flower where a series of parts (e.g., petals) are not alike.

Jointed (Figs. 28C, 39E): Having very distinct nodes.

Keel (Figs. 34M, 36G): The main dorsal vein (midrib) found on many leaves.

Keiki (KEE-kee): See **Offset**.

Labellum (lah-BEL-lum) (Figs. 25, 41, 46, 52, 58): The highly modified petal of an orchid flower; the lip.

Lacerate (Fig. 54Fa, Fb): Appearing torn, or cut irregularly.

Laciniate (Fig. 57Ga, Gb): Cut into narrow, ribbonlike segments.

Lanceolate (Figs. 34B, 47C): Lance-shaped; longer than broad and tapering towards the apex.

Lateral (Figs. 25, 44): Coming from the side.

Lax (Fig. 49A): Having loose, flexible, drooping segments.

Lead (Fig. 26): The new growth on sympodial orchids.

Leaf (Fig. 26): The green, usually flat segment that grows from a stem.

Leafless (Fig. 28B): Without leaves.

Ligulate (Fig. 34F): Strap-shaped.

Limb (Fig. 52N): The flat, expanded portion of any segment, such as the lip.

Linear (Fig. 34D): Said of long, narrow leaves with parallel sides; grasslike.

Lingulate (LING-yew-late) (Fig. 34O): Tongue-shaped.

Lip (Figs. 25, 41, 46, 52, 58): The labellum.

Lithophyte (LITH-oh-fyte): A plant that grows on rocks.

Lobed (Figs. 40B, D, 51F): Having lobes.

Locule (LOK-yewl) (Fig. 64): One of the compartments of the ovary of an orchid.

Lorate (Figs. 34E, 47E): Strap-shaped.

Figure 39. Pseudobulb shapes. A: Globose, round, or orbicular (*Sophronitis*). B: Ovoid (*Neomoorea*). C: Ovoid-compressed (*Laelia*). D: Oblong- or ovate-elongate (*Encyclia*). E: Jointed (*Dendrobium*). F: Unguiculate (*Myrmecophila*). G: Elliptic (*Grammatophyllum*). H: Elliptic-elongate, sulcate or furrowed (*Gongora*). I: Oblong-sulcate or furrowed (*Pholidota*). J: Oblong-cylindrical (*Bulbophyllum*). K: Cylindrical (*Ansellia*). L: Fusiform-tetragonal or four-sided (*Dendrobium*). M: Pyriform (*Encyclia*). N: Constricted or hourglass-shaped (*Calanthe*). O: Obovoid, clavate, or club-shaped (*Cattleya*). P: Fusiform or spindle-shaped (*Catasetum*). Q: Swollen base (*Cattleya*). R: Stemlike or reedlike (*Isochilus*).

Massula (MAS-sul-uh): A small group or clump of pollen grains occurring in some orchid genera (e.g., *Vanilla*).

Media: Plural of medium.

Medium: The material in which an orchid is grown. Also, the nutrient solutions, both solid and liquid, used in seed germination and tissue culture.

Mentum (MEN-tum) (Fig. 63E): A protrusion, often chinlike, at the base of the flower, composed of the lateral sepal bases and column foot.

Meristem: The actively growing cell tissue of young stems, leaves, and roots. Also, a vernacular name for a plant derived from tissue culture.

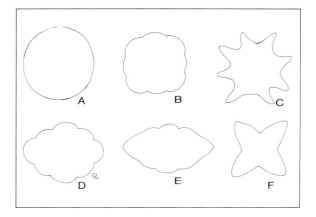

Figure 40. Pseudobulb cross sections. A: Round or orbicular (*Bulbophyllum*). B: Round, lobed (*Pholidota*). C: Round, ridged or furrowed (*Gongora*). D: Slightly compressed, lobed (*Myrmecophila*). E: Compressed (*Laelia*). F: Tetragonal, four-sided, or lobed (*Dendrobium*).

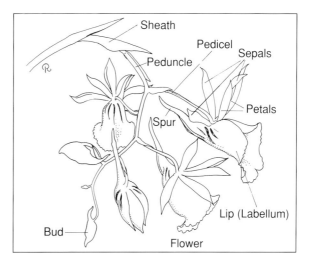

Figure 41. The inflorescence and its parts.

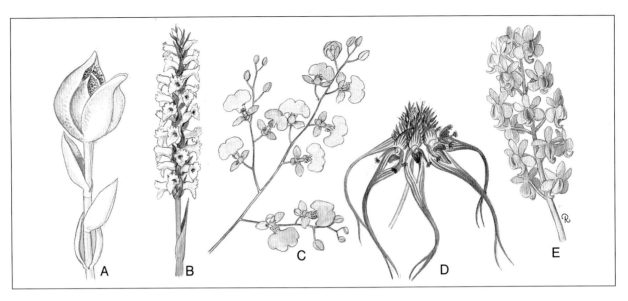

Figure 42. Inflorescence types. A: Single or solitary flower or uniflorate (*Anguloa*). B: Spike (*Spiranthes*). C: Panicle or spray (*Oncidium*). D: Umbel or head (*Bulbophyllum*). E: Raceme (*Aerides*).

Figure 43. A: Inflorescence origins. Aa: Axillary (*Dendrobium*). Ab: Basal (*Lycaste*). Ac: Terminal (*Encyclia*). B: Methods of flowering. Ba: Determinate (*Angraecum*). Bb: Indeterminate (*Ascocentrum*).

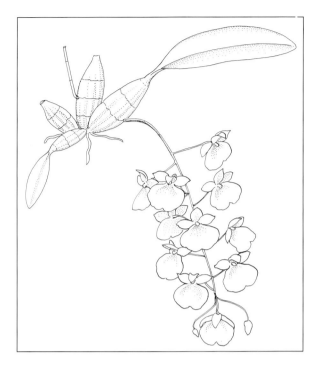

Figure 44. Inflorescence from the side of the pseudobulb (*Dendrobium*).

Figure 45. Inflorescence (*Dendrobium*) showing resupination.

Mesochile (MEZ-oh-kile): The middle part of a complex, often segmented lip (e.g., *Stanhopea*).

Midlobe: The center lobe of a three-lobed lip.

Midrib (Figs. 31, 32): The main vein of a leaf.

Mimicry: The resemblance of an organism to a totally unrelated organism, usually to bring about pollination by deception (e.g., *Ophrys apifera* resembles a bee to attract the bee as a pollinator).

Monandrous (mo-NAN-drus) (Figs. 60A, 61B, 62B): Having one anther.

Monoecious (moh-NEE-shus): Having male and female organs in separate flowers, but both appearing on the same plant.

Monopodial (mon-oh-POH-dee-al) (Fig. 27C, D, E): Having one foot. Refers to a plant growing perpendicular to the horizon with strong apical dominance; flowers are borne on axillary inflorescences, and terminal buds remain vegetative (e.g., *Phalaenopsis*, *Vanda*).

Mucronate (Figs. 25, 35H): Having a small, short, sharp tip at the apex of a leaf.

Multigeneric: Refers to hybrids made from three or more genera.

Nectar: The sugary exudate of various glands on a plant that attracts insects and sometimes birds, and helps bring about pollination.

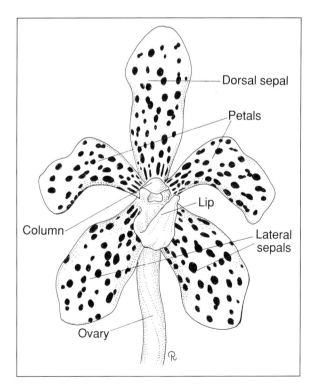

Figure 46. The flower and its parts.

397

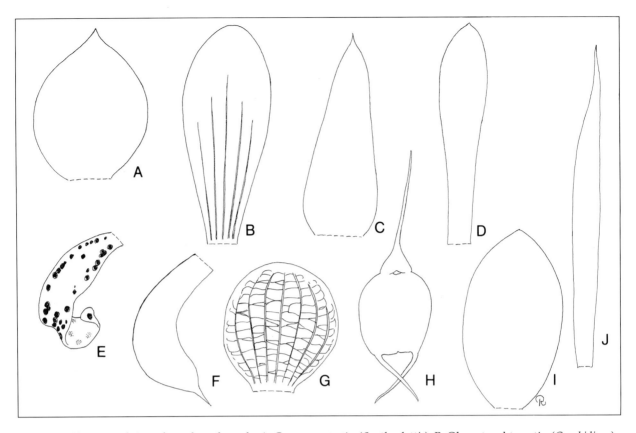

Figure 47. Shapes and tips of sepals and petals. A: Ovate, acute tip (*Spathoglottis*). B: Obovate, obtuse tip (*Cymbidium*). C: Lanceolate, acute apiculate tip (*Sophronitis*). D: Oblanceolate, obtuse tip (*Vanilla*). E: Lorate, recurved (*Grammatophyllum*). F: Falcate, apiculate (*Trichoglottis*). G: Orbicular or round, obtuse tip (*Vanda*). H: Attenuate cauda (*Masdevallia*). I: Elliptic, acute tip (*Cymbidium*). J: Ensiform, elongate, attenuate tip (*Brassia*).

Nectary (Fig. 51): The gland that produces nectar, often found at the base of a lip.

Nerve (Fig. 32): The small vein of a leaf.

Netted (Fig. 37G, I): Said of veins forming a connected network.

Nocturnal: Refers to flowers that open or are fragrant only at night.

Node (Fig. 27C, G): The point on the stem or pseudobulb where the leaves or bracts are attached.

Obcordate: Having heart-shaped lobes at the apex of the leaf (e.g., *Ascocentrum*).

Oblanceolate (Figs. 34C, 47D): Lance-shaped but widest at the apex.

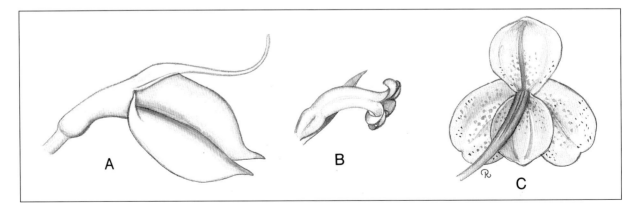

Figure 48. Connate flower parts. A: Gamosepalous (*Masdevallia*). B: Gamopetalous and gamosepalous (*Spiranthes*). C: Gamosepalous (*Paphiopedilum*).

398

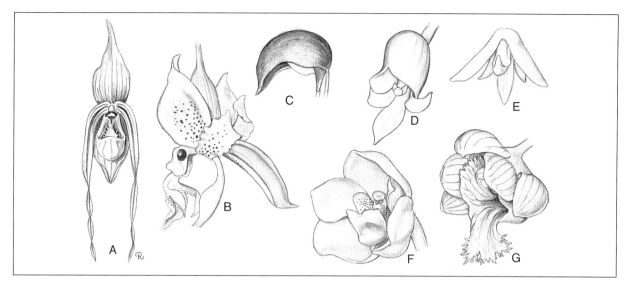

Figure 49. Some unusual floral characteristics of orchids. A: Drooping (lax) twisted petals (*Paphiopedilum*). B: Horned lip (*Stanhopea*). C: Hooded, total flower (*Corybas*). D: Hooded, lip (*Schlimia*). E: Hooded, lateral sepals (*Polystachya*). F: Open cupped segments (*Peristeria*). G: Cupped segments (*Catasetum*).

Oblong (Figs. 34L, 39D): Longer than wide.

Obovate (Figs. 34I, 39O, 47B): Ovate but narrowest at the base.

Obtuse (Figs. 35C, 47B, D, G): Rounded at the tip.

Offset (Fig. 28C): A lateral shoot, above ground, that produces roots while still attached to the parent stem, common in some *Dendrobium*, *Epidendrum*, and *Phalaenopsis* species.

Orbicular (Figs. 39A, 40A, 47G): Round.

Orchidaceae (or-kih-DAY-see-ee): The Latin name for the orchid family.

Orchidist: A person who is very interested in orchids and their culture.

Orchidology: The study of orchids.

Outrolled (Fig. 50C, D, E): Having margins rolled out (e.g., the lip in some paphiopedilums).

Oval (Figs. 39G, 47A, I): Shaped like a thickened ellipse.

Ovary (Fig. 46): The basal portion of the pistil containing the ovules; if pollinated and fertilized, the ovary develops into the fruit.

Ovate (Figs. 25, 34H, 47A): Egg-shaped in outline.

Ovoid (Fig. 39B, C): Egg-shaped as a solid form.

Ovule (Fig. 64): A small protuberance in the ovary, capable of forming a seed when fertilized; an embryonic seed.

Panicle (Fig. 42C): Having a branched inflorescence (e.g., some *Oncidium* species).

Papillae (pa-PILL-ee) (Figs. 56 left, 58, 63E): Small pimplelike projections on a surface.

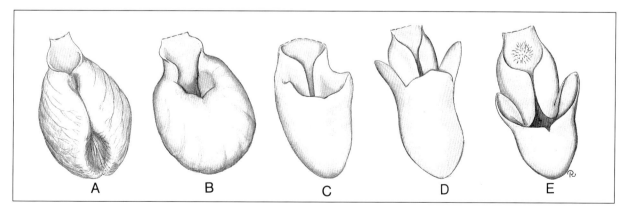

Figure 50. Some slipper- or boot-shaped lips. Inrolled top: A: *Cypripedium acaule*. B: *C. calceolus*. Outrolled top: C: *Paphiopedilum concolor*. D: *P. glaucophyllum*. E: *P. insigne*.

399

Parasite: A plant that derives its sustenance from another living plant.

Parietal (pa-RYE-eh-tal) (Fig. 64B, C): A form of placentation in orchids where ovules are borne on the walls or on protrusions of the walls of the ovary.

Pedicel (Fig. 41): The stem of a single flower on an inflorescence.

Peduncle (PEE-dung-kul) (Fig. 41): The stem of a cluster of flowers or a solitary flower, where the inflorescence is reduced to a single flower (e.g., *Maxillaria*).

Peloric (pel-LOHR-ik): Having an abnormal flower form in which the petals resemble the lip or the lip assumes a petallike form, thus creating a regular appearing flower; not the usual two petals and a lip.

Perennial: A plant with a life cycle that continues for more than two years.

Perfect: Refers to a flower having both male and female organs.

Perianth (Fig. 46): Figuratively, around the anther; a collective term for the two outer whorls of floral segments (i.e., sepals and petals).

Petal (Figs. 41, 46): The inner whorl of the perianth; the segments, of which there are usually three with one highly modified; the lip.

Petaloid: Having the appearance of a petal (e.g., bracts of *Cyrtopodium*).

Petiole (Fig. 32): The stalk of a leaf.

Pilose (Fig. 57Ea, Eb): Having a covering of soft hairs.

Figure 51. Variations in orchid spurs and nectaries. A: *Phaius*. B: *Rangaeris*. C: *Angraecum*. D: *Ludisia*. E: *Platanthera*. F: *Aerides*. G: *Ascocentrum*. H: *Galeandra*.

Figure 52. Variations in orchid lips. A: *Aerangis*. B: *Miltonia*. C: *Sophronitis*. D: *Cycnoches*. E: *Tridactyle*. F: *Calanthe*. G: *Orchis purpurea*. H: *Orchis simia*. I: *Oncidium*. J: *Spathoglottis*. K: *Cyrtopodium*. L: *Bifrenaria*. M: *Vandopsis*. N: *Trichopilia*. O: *Vanilla*. P: *Phaius*. Q: *Catasetum*. R: *Calypso*. S: *Stanhopea*. T: *Gastrochilus*. U: *Mormodes*.

Pistil (Fig. 4Aa): The female organ of the flower which produces the seed; a collective term for the stigma, style, and ovary.

Placenta: The ovule-bearing portion of the ovary.

Placentation (pla-sen-TAY-shun) (Fig. 64): The arrangement of the ovules in an ovary.

Pleated (Figs. 27B, 36I, 37A, F): Folded as a fan (e.g., leaves of *Calanthe*).

Plicate (Figs. 36F, 39I): Folded (e.g., leaves).

Pod (Fig. 65): A rather general term for a dry, dehiscent fruit.

Pollinarium (poll-in-AR-ee-um) (Fig. 5): The entire set of pollinia from a flower including the caudicle, stipe, and viscidium, when present.

Pollination: In orchids, the act of placing pollinia onto the stigmatic surface of the flower.

Pollinator: The agent bringing about the pollination of a plant (e.g., a bee, moth, bird).

Pollinia (Figs. 5, 6, 59, 60, 61): The compact packets of pollen found in orchid flowers.

Pollinium: Singular form of pollinia.

Polyploid: Having more than the normal two sets of chromosomes.

Porrect: Directed outward and forward.

Proboscis (proh-BAH-siss): The long, flexible mouth parts of an insect.

Procumbent (Fig. 29A): Lying flat; said of a stem growing horizontally on a surface.

Proliferation: The act of bearing offsets.

Prostrate: See **Procumbent**.

Pseudobulb (SOO-doh-bulb) (Figs. 26, 31): A false bulb; the aboveground, thickened portion of a lateral branch of sympodial orchids.

Pseudobulbous (soo-doh-BUL-bous) (Fig. 28A): Having pseudobulbs.

Pubescence (Figs. 57, 63O): A covering of short, soft hairs.

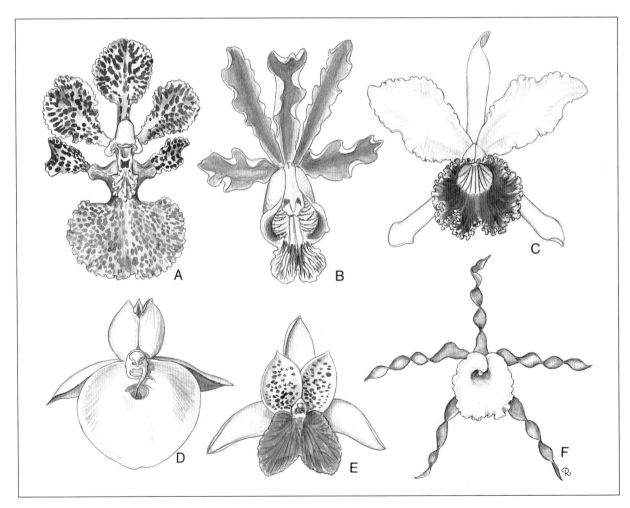

Figure 53. Sepal, petal, and lip margins. A: Ruffled (*Oncidium*). B: Wavy (*Myrmecophila*). C: Crispate (*Cattleya*). D: Smooth or plain (*Catasetum*). E: Lip bilobed and slightly ruffled (*Cymbidiella*). F: Twisted or spiraled (*Trichopilia*).

Pubescent (Fig. 63O): A general term referring to hairs on plants.

Pyriform (Fig. 39M): Pear-shaped (e.g., pseudobulbs).

Raceme (Fig. 42E): An inflorescence with flowers on short stalks.

Racemose: Having inflorescences that are racemes or racemelike.

Rachis (Fig. 41): The main stem of an inflorescence.

Radicle: The primary root of a germinating seed.

Ramicaul: The term applied to the leaf- and flower-bearing stem portion of pleurothallid plants.

Rank (Figs. 27D, 30F): Refers to the arrangement of flowers or leaves in vertical rows. A plant with two ranks has two vertical rows of leaves.

Receptacle: The enlarged apex of a stem upon which some of the floral segments are attached.

Recurved (Fig. 58C): Bending backwards.

Reed-type (Fig. 28C): A type of sympodial orchid with long lateral branches of uniform thickness bearing many leaves (e.g., *Dendrobium*).

Resupinate (ree-SOO-pin-ayt) (Fig. 45): Said of some orchid flower buds that emerge upside down and turn 180 degrees to right themselves before opening (e.g., *Vanda*).

Retrorse: Pointing backward and downward.

Retuse (Fig. 35D): Rounded at the end with a shallow notch in the center.

Revolute: Said of a leaf having its margins rolled back.

Rhizome (Figs. 26, 30E, 31): A horizontal stem, either on or just below the ground, with roots and erect lateral branches.

Ridged (Figs. 39L, N, 40C, F): Said of plant parts having strips of raised tissue (e.g., pseudobulbs of *Gongora*).

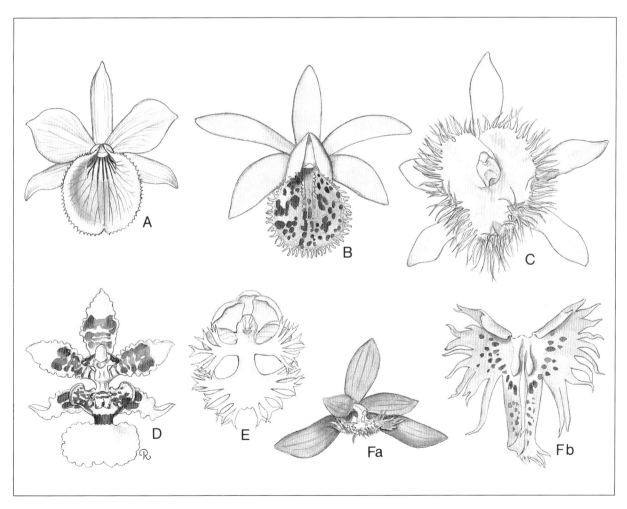

Figure 54. Lip margins. A: Finely toothed or denticulate (*Broughtonia*). B: Ciliate (*Pleione*). C: Fringed (*Brassavola*). D: Crispate (*Oncidium*). E: Fimbriate (*Platanthera*). Fa: Lacerate (*Encyclia*). Fb: Lacerate, detail of same.

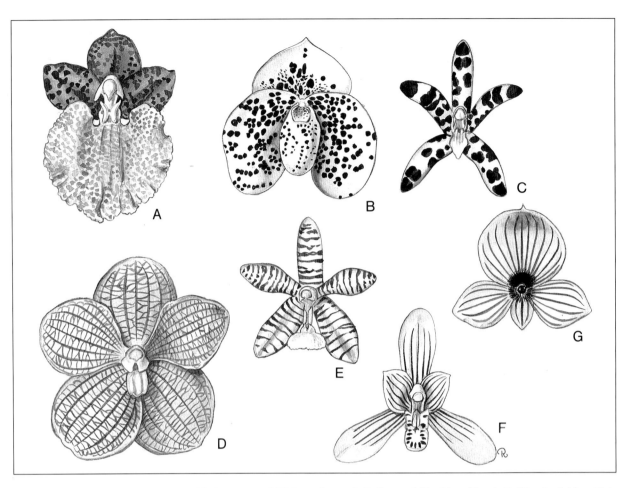

Figure 55. Flower markings. A: Freckled or spotted (*Odontoglossum*). B: Spotted (*Paphiopedilum*). C: Blotched (*Ansellia*). D: Tessellated (*Vanda*). E: Cross-banded or barred (*Phalaenopsis*). F: Parallel-striped (*Cymbidium*). G: Curved-striped (*Telipogon*).

Figure 56. Vestiture. Papillae on the lip of *Dendrobium phalaenopsis* with detail (left) and comose hairs on the petal margins of *Paphiopedilum callosum* with detail (right).

404

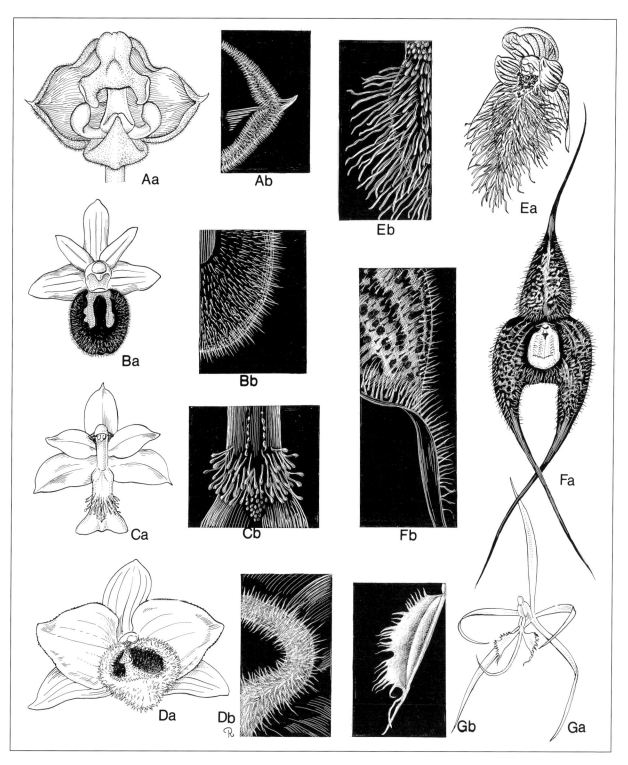

Figure 57. Vestiture and margins showing detail of same. Aa, Ab: Downy pubescent (*Polystachya*). Ba, Bb: Hirsute, bristly, or setose (*Ophrys sphegodes*). Ca, Cb: Beard of clavellate hairs (*Calopogon*). Da, Db: Velutinous or densely pubescent with velvety hairs (*Dendrobium*). Ea, Eb: Bearded with pilose hairs (*Calochilus*). Fa, Fb: Villous or long, shaggy-haired (*Dracula*). Ga, Gb: A finely laciniate margin erroneously described as ciliate by the species name (*Epidendrum ciliare*).

Root (Figs. 26, 30, 31): A leafless plant segment, usually underground, but often aerial in epiphytic orchids. An underground storage organ in some terrestrials (e.g., *Ophrys*).

Rosette (Fig. 28E): Said of stemless plants, the leaves of which radiate out from a central axis and form a circle.

Rostellum (ros-TELL-um) (Figs. 59, 62B, C): Figuratively, a little beak; the sharp apex of the stigma that separates the pollinia from the stigmatic surface; a gland.

Ruffled (Fig. 53A, E): Having a wavy margin.

Rupicolous (ruh-PICK-oh-lus): Growing on or among rocks, ledges, or cliffs.

Saccate (Figs. 25, 50): Sack-shaped (e.g., the pouchlike lip of *Paphiopedilum*).

Saprophyte (SAP-roh-fite): A plant that derives its sustenance from the decomposition of old plant parts and that usually lacks chlorophyll.

Scape: A leafless flower stalk, often arising from the ground, with or without scales or bracts in place of leaves, and bearing one or more flowers.

Scapose: Having flowers on a scape.

Scarious: Dry and papery (e.g., bracts).

Sectile: See **Massula**.

Secund: Having flowers arranged on one side of an inflorescence (e.g., *Dendrobium secundum*).

Seed (Fig. 7): A matured ovule capable of producing a plant.

Seed pod (Figs. 26, 65): The mature ovary containing the mature ovules (seeds).

Seedling: Any plant formed from a seed that has not yet attained flowering size. An orchid seedling may be five to seven years old before it flowers.

Segment: One of the parts of a plant (e.g., leaf, root, sepal, petal, etc.).

Semipeloric (sem-ee-pel-OR-ik): Having an abnormal flower in which the petals have some liplike characteristics.

Semiterete (Fig. 36B, C, D): Said of the leaves of hybrids (e.g., *Vanda*) formed by crossing strap-leaved plants with terete-leaved.

Sepal (Figs. 41, 46): A segment of the outer whorl of the perianth that protects the unopened flower bud; in orchids the sepal usually is trimerous, with two of the sepals fused in the *Paphiopedilum* group.

Sessile (Fig. 31): Stalkless; having the leaf blade attached directly to the stem (e.g., *Cattleya*).

Sheath (Figs. 26, 31, 41): Any leaflike structure on an orchid that envelops a developing bud and emerging pseudobulb.

Shoot (Fig. 26): The new growth of a plant, usually a portion of the stem with its attached leaves.

Simple (Fig. 26): Not compound (e.g., a leaf without leaflets or a nonbranched inflorescence).

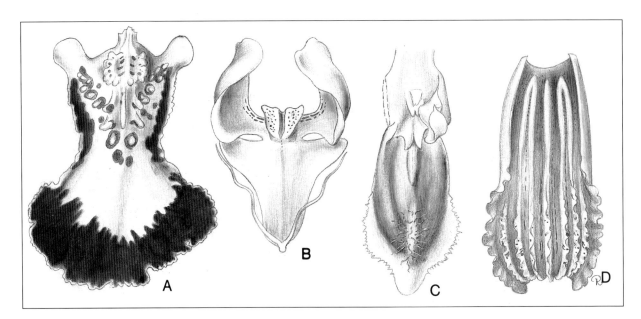

Figure 58. Lip decorations and protuberances. A: Lip with ears, papillae, and a disc of irregularly lobed tissue (*Oncidium*). B: Trilobed lip with a smooth, waxy callus and antennae (*Phalaenopsis*). C: Recurved side lobes, a raised curved callus, beard of villous hairs, and a finely ciliate margin (*Phalaenopsis*). D: Ruffled margins and wavy crests with thickened ridges (*Bletia*).

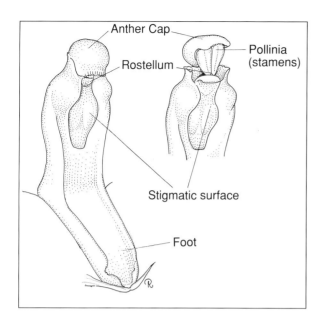

Figure 59. The column.

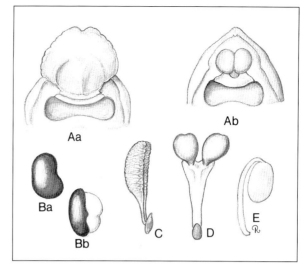

Figure 60. Androecium parts. A: Column end (*Grammatophyllum*). Aa: Anther cap in place. Ab: Anther cap removed to show pollinia. Ba, Bb: Diandrous pollinia, two views (*Paphiopedilum*). C: Pollinia (*Ludisia*). D: Pollinia with foot on stipe (*Trichopilia*). E: Pollinia and plain caudicle (*Broughtonia*).

Sinus (Figs. 52E, F, G, H, I, 53A): The area or space between two lobes of a lip, leaf, or other plant part.

Smooth (Fig. 53D): Refers to a surface free of blemishes; not hairy, not rough, and not scabrous.

Solitary (Fig. 42A): Having only one flower per inflorescence.

Spathe (Fig. 26): A bract or leaf that subtends or encompasses an inflorescence; the sheath.

Spathulate: Spoon-shaped.

Species: A plant or group of plants separated from other plants or groups by one or more distinct characteristics.

Speculum (SPECK-yew-lum): The central shiny area of the labellum as in *Ophrys*.

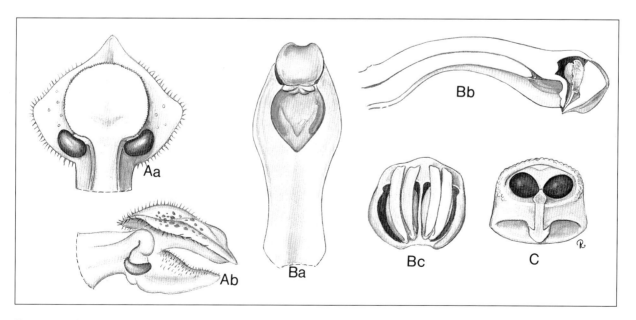

Figure 61. The gynandrium or column. A: Diandrous (*Paphiopedilum*). Aa: Column, ventral or bottom view. Ab: Column, side view. B: Monandrous (*Cattleya*). Ba: Column, ventral or bottom view. Bb: Column, vertical section. Bc: Anther cap with pollinia in place. C: End of column with anther cap removed to show pollinia in place (*Ascocentrum*).

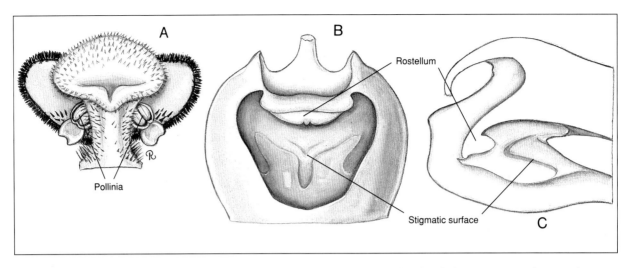

Figure 62. Gynandrium. A: Diandrous (*Phragmipedium*). B: Monandrous (*Schomburgkia*), stigmatic surface much enlarged, ventral view. C: Side view.

Spike (Fig. 42B): An inflorescence with sessile flowers.

Spiral (Figs. 28E, 53F): Having leaves arranged on the stem like a corkscrew.

Spotted (Figs. 25, 52N, 54B, 55B): Having irregular areas of color on sepals, petals, or leaves.

Spray (Fig. 42C): A general term used to describe all types of inflorescences.

Spur (Figs. 42, 51): The tubular extension found on the lips of many orchids (e.g., *Angraecum*), which usually contains a nectary.

Stalk: See **Stem**.

Stamen (Figs. 59, 60B, C, D, E): The male portion of the flower composed of a filament and an anther containing pollen.

Staminode (STAM-in-ohd): A pollenless or sterile stamen.

Stem (Fig. 41): The aboveground segment of a plant. A main axis that bears leaves and that eventually flowers and fruits.

Stemlike (Fig. 39R): Appearing like a stem.

Stigma (Fig. 63R): The apex of the pistil, often sticky; the receptive portion of the pistil.

Stigmatic surface: The sticky area on the underside of the column where the pollinia are placed and the pollen germinates.

Stilidium (pl. Stilidia) (Fig. 63K,L): A winglike appendage on the column.

Stipe (Figs. 5, 60D): A thin stalk that connects the pollinia to the viscidium.

Strap leaf (Fig. 35E): A long and narrow leaf (e.g., *Vanda*).

Striped (Figs. 37H, 55F, G): Having lines of color on sepals, petals, or leaves.

Style: The portion of the pistil connecting the stigma to the ovary.

Sub: Almost (e.g., subcordate or almost heart-shaped).

Subgenus: A natural division or group within a genus.

Substance: Refers to the thickness and longevity of floral segments.

Succulent: Refers to leaves, stems, or other plant organs that are very soft, fleshy, and moist.

Sulcate (Fig. 39F, G, I, K): See **Furrowed**.

Swollen (Fig. 39Q): Larger than other similar parts; distended or enlarged.

Sympodial (sim-POH-dee-al) (Fig. 27F, G, H): Refers to a plant, the main stem of which grows horizontally and has determinate lateral branches; inflorescences are terminal or axillary (e.g., *Laelia*).

Figure 63. Variations in orchid columns. A: Slender, long, curved (*Cycnoches*). B: Short and wide (*Gastrochilus*). C: Flaring "skirt" below cap (*Angraecum*). D: Shouldered (*Vandopsis*). E: Footed, papillate (*Dendrobium*). F: "Hood" over anther cap (*Pholidota*). G: Anther cap pointed, antennae (*Catasetum*). H: Fringed "collar" (*Trichopilia*). I: Two-horned (*Trichoglottis*). J: Two side appendages, large back lobe, tiny anther cap (*Dendrochilum*). K: Winged (*Oncidium*). L: Wide wings (*Lockhartia*). M: Long, perianth parts partly adnate (*Vanilla*). N: Beaked cap (*Rhynchostylis*). O: Pubescent (*Lycaste*). P: Twisted (*Ludisia*). Q: Diandrous, fringed (*Phragmipedium*). R: Large erect stigma, twin anther sacs (*Satyrium*). S: Short with pair of club-shaped pollen masses (*Plantanthera*). T: Broad with pair of erect pollinia (*Orchis*).

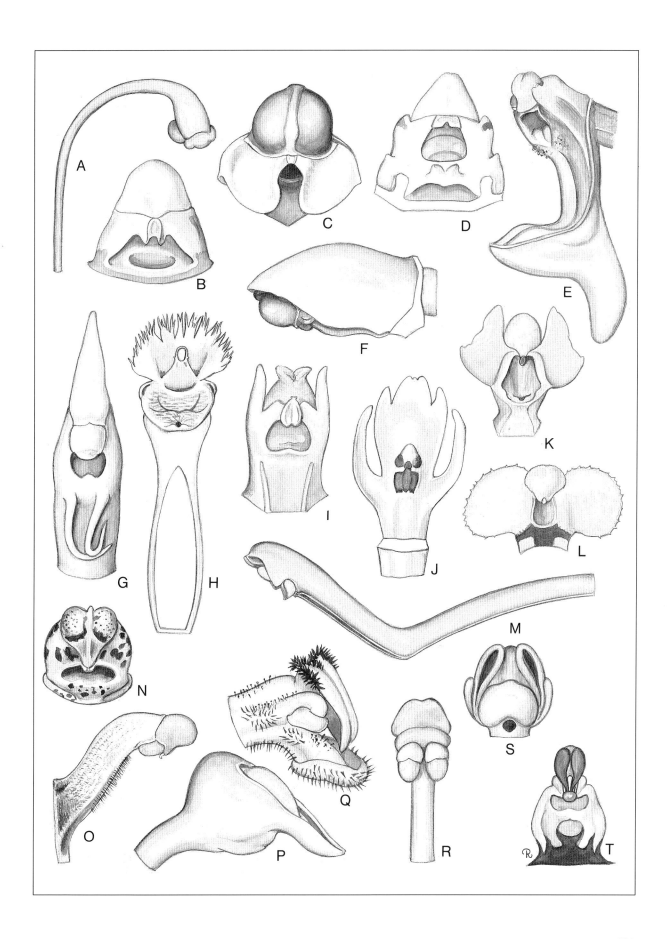

Synsepal (SIN-see-pul) (Fig. 48C): The fused lateral sepals found in the subfamily Cypripedioideae.

Taxon: A taxonomic term applying to a related group of plants (e.g., a genus or species).

Taxonomy: The science of plant classification.

Terete (Figs. 36A): Said of leaves that are round in cross section (e.g., *Brassavola nodosa*).

Terminal (Figs. 26, 43Ac): Refers to a flower arising from the tip of the growth (e.g., *Cattleya*); the uppermost flower or the apex of the stem.

Terrestrial (Fig. 27B): A plant that grows in soil or similar medium (e.g., *Phaius*).

Tessellate (Figs. 25, 37B, 55D): Checkered or evenly netted (e.g., flowers of *Euanthe sanderiana*, *Vanda coerulea*).

Tetragonal (Figs. 39L, 40F): Four sided.

Tetraploid: Having four sets of chromosomes or double the usual two sets.

Texture: The surface quality of flowers or leaves (i.e., crystalline, waxy, scaly).

Throat (Fig. 52N, O): The basal, usually almost-tubular portion of the lip of an orchid flower.

Tissue culture: An asexual method of propagating plants using meristematic tissue to produce like plants. A form of cloning.

Tomentose (Fig. 57D): Having a very dense covering of hairs; almost woolly.

Triangular (Fig. 34K): Three sided.

Tribe: A group of closely related genera.

Trilobed (Figs. 25, 52F): Having three lobes.

Triploid: Having three sets of chromosomes; the usual two plus one additional set.

Truncate: Said of a leaf that appears to have been cut off at the apex; having a flat apex.

Tuber (Fig. 30B): A shortened, thickened stem containing eyes and usually found underground; often misused with orchids. See Tuberoid.

Tubercle (Fig. 37K): A small tuber not necessarily underground (e.g., a small tuber on a leaf or petal).

Tuberoid: A thickened underground storage organ having both stem and root tissue.

Tubular: Having a round cylindrical shape (e.g., fused sepals in some *Masdevallia* species).

Tunicate (Fig. 33Ab): Having concentric or sheathing layers of tissue.

Twisted (Figs. 49A, 63P): Having parts that are spiraling or corkscrewlike.

Umbel (Fig. 42D): An inflorescence in which the flowers appear to arise at one point.

Undulate (Figs. 37E, 53B): Having an up-and-down wavy margin on a leaf or petal; not waving in and out.

Unequally two-lobed (Fig. 35F): Said of leaf tips with unequal apical lobes.

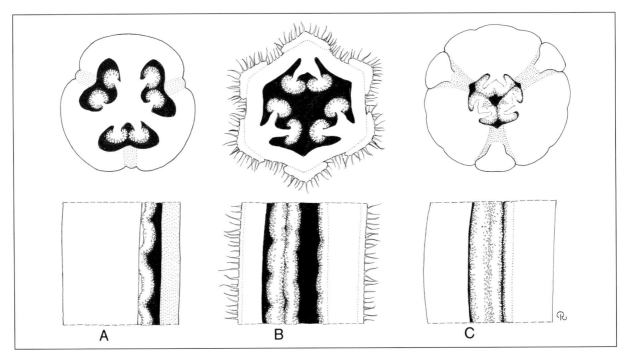

Figure 64. Placentation. A: Axile, cross section and vertical section (*Phragmipedium*). B: Parietal, diandrous orchid, cross section and vertical section. C: Parietal, monandrous orchid, cross section and vertical section.

410

Unguiculate (un-GWIK-yew-late) (Fig. 39F): Drawn out at the base, often drawn into a thin stalk or even clawlike.

Unifoliate: Having only one leaf.

Valves (Fig. 65A, Ea): The segments of a seed pod.

Variety: A plant within a species that has a minor, distinct characteristic (e.g., *Cattleya dowiana* var. *aurea*).

Vegetative: Refers to asexual methods of reproduction (e.g., division in *Cattleya*). Also refers to the leafy portion of the plant.

Vein (Fig. 32): Vascular tissue that transports water, nutrients, and carbohydrates throughout a leaf and/or a plant.

Velamen (vel-A-men) (Fig. 30G): The thick, spongy layer of cells that surrounds the roots of epiphytic orchids.

Velutinous (vel-LOO-tin-us) (Fig. 57Da, Db): Having a cover of erect, somewhat-firm hairs.

Venation (ven-A-shun) (Figs. 32, 34, 37): The arrangement of the veins.

Ventral (Fig. 61Aa, Ba): On the lower side, opposite of dorsal.

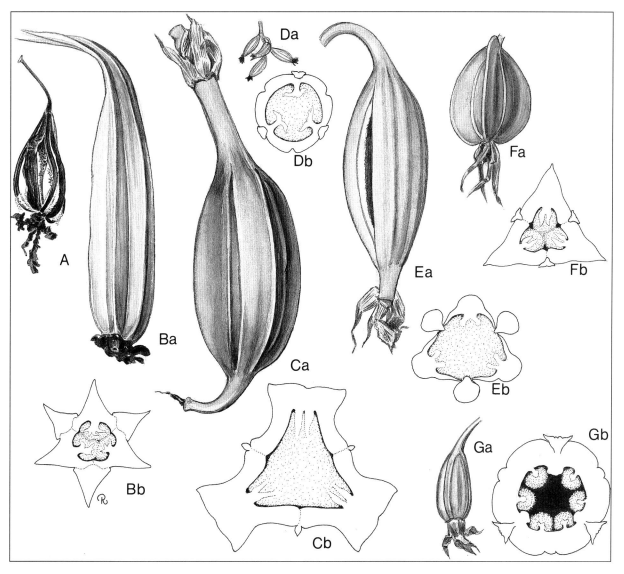

Figure 65. Mature seed pods showing habit and cross sections. A: *Dendrobium* pod split open and seeds disseminated. Ba, Bb: *Vanda* pod and cross section. Ca, Cb: *Cattleya* pod and cross section. Da, Db: *Polystachya* pods and cross section. Ea, Eb: *Phaius* pod split along one suture and cross section. Fa, Fb: *Encyclia* pod and cross section. Ga, Gb: *Dendrobium* pod and cross section.

Vestiture: A covering of hairs, papillae, or other protuberances on a surface.

Villous (Figs. 57Fa, Fb, 58C): Having long, soft hairs covering the surface.

Vine (Fig. 28F): A plant that climbs.

Viscid: Very sticky.

Viscidium (vis-SID-ee-um): The sticky disc attached to the pollinia (e.g., *Catasetum*) which adheres to the pollinator to insure removal of the pollinia from the flower and to another flower for cross-pollination.

Whorl (Fig. 28E): Three or more plant parts attached at the same point.

Winged (Fig. 63K, L): Having an organ with a usually flat projection on one or more sides.

Woolly: Having long, soft, sometimes matted hairs.

Xerophyte: A plant native to an arid area.

Zygomorphic (zye-go-MOR-fik) (Fig. 3): Capable of being divided into equal halves in one plane only; said of flowers having bilateral symmetry.

Bibliography

Allen, P. H. 1953. *The Orchids of Panama*. Rpt. *The Orchid Journal*. Vol. 2. N.p.

American Orchid Society Bulletin. 1945–1993. Vols. 19–62.

Ames, B., and O. Ames. 1939. *Drawings of Florida Orchids*. 2nd ed. Cambridge, Massachusetts: n.p.

Ames, O., and D. S. Correll. 1952. *Orchids of Guatemala*. Fieldiana: Botany, vol. 26, no. 1. Chicago, Illinois: Chicago Natural History Museum.

Ball, J. S. 1978. *Southern African Epiphytic Orchids*. Johannesburg, South Africa: Conservation Press (PTY).

Bateman, J. 1843. *The Orchidaceae of Mexico and Guatemala*. London, England: John Ridgeway and Sons.

Bechtel, H., P. Cribb, and E. Launert. 1992. *Manual of Cultivated Orchid Species*. 3rd ed. Cambridge, Massachusetts: Massachusetts Institute of Technology Press.

Braem, G. T. 1984. *Cattleya, Die bifoliaten Cattleyen Braziliens*. Hildesheim, Germany: Brücke-Verlag Kurt Schmersow.

_____. 1986. *Cattleya, Band 2, Die unifoliaten (einblättrigen) Cattleyen*. Hildesheim, Germany: Brücke-Verlag Kurt Schmersow.

Braga, N., and S. Simao. 1983. *Native Orchids of Brazil*. São Paulo, Brazil: Editora Grafica Topan-Press LTDA.

Caballero, R. L. R., D. E. Mora, M. E. Barahona, and N. H. Williams. 1986. *Generos de Orquideas de Costa Rica*. San José, Costa Rica: Editorial Universidad de Costa Rica.

Cady, L., and E. R. Rotherham. 1970. *Australian Native Orchids in Color*. Sydney, Australia: A. H. and A. W. Reed.

Cheng, C. 1970. *Taiwan Native Orchids*. Taichung, Taiwan: Chow Cheng Orchids.

_____. 1979. *Formosan Orchids*. Taichung, Taiwan: Chow Cheng Orchids.

Christenson, E. 1985. Sarcanthine Genera—2. The Genus *Schoenorchis*. *American Orchid Society Bulletin* 54(7): 850–854.

Constantin, J. 1927. *Atlas en Couleurs des Orchidees Cultivees*. Paris, France: Libairie Générale de L'Enseignement.

Correll, D. S. 1950. *Native Orchids of North America*. Waltham, Massachusetts: Chronica Botanica Company.

Correvon, H. 1923. *Album des Orchidees d'Europe*. Geneva, Switzerland: H. Correvon, «Floraire,» Chêne-Bourg.

Cribb, P. 1987. *The Genus Paphiopedilum*. Portland, Oregon: Timber Press.

Curtis, C. H. 1950. *Orchids: Their Description and Cultivation*. London, England: Putnam and Company.

Darwin, C. 1904. *The Various Contrivances by Which Orchids are Fertilized by Insects*. 2nd ed. London, England: John Murray.

Davis, R. S., and M. L. Steiner. 1952. *Philippine Orchids*. New York: The William Fredrick Press.

Dockrill, A. W. 1969. *Australian Indigenous Orchids*. Sydney, Australia: The Society for Growing Australian Plants.

Dodson, C. H., and D. E. Bennett, Jr. 1989. *Orchids of Peru. Icones Plantarum Tropicarum*, series 2. Fascicles 1–2. St. Louis, Missouri: Missouri Botanical Garden.

Dodson, C. H., and P. M. Dodson. 1980. *Orchids of Ecuador. Icones Plantarum Tropicarum*. Fascicles 1–4. St. Louis, Missouri: Missouri Botanical Gardens.

Dodson, C. H., and R. Vásquez Ch. 1989. *Orchids of Bolivia. Icones Plantarum Tropicarum*, series 2. Fascicles 3–4. St. Louis, Missouri: Missouri Botanical Garden.

Dressler, R. L. 1981. *The Orchids: Natural History and Classification*. Cambridge, Massachusetts: Harvard University Press.

_____. 1993. *Phylogeny and Classification of the Orchid Family*. Portland, Oregon: Dioscorides Press.

Dressler, R. L., and G. E. Pollard. 1976. *The Genus Encyclia in Mexico*. Mexico City: Asociación Mexicana de Orquideologia, A.C.

Dunsterville, G. C. K., and L. A. Garay. 1959. *Venezuelan Orchids Illustrated*. London, England: Andre Deutsch Limited.

_____. 1979. *Orchids of Venezuela: An Illustrated Field*

Guide. Cambridge, Massachusetts: Botanical Museum, Harvard University.

Escobar, R. 1990. *Native Colombian Orchids*. Vols. 1–4. Medellin, Colombia: Compañia Litografica National.

Fawcett, W., and A. B. Rendle. 1910. *Flora of Jamaica*. Vol. 1, *Orchidaceae*. London, England: Longmans and Company.

Florida Orchidist. 1961–1993. Vols. 4–36.

Foldats, E. 1969. *Flora of Venezuela*. Vol. 15, *Orchidaceae*. Parts 1–5. Caracas, Venezuela: Edicion Especial del Instituto Botanico.

Fowlie, J. A. 1970. *The Genus Lycaste*. Pomona, California: Day Printing Corporation.

_____. 1977. *The Brazilian Bifoliate Cattleyas and Their Color Varieties*. Pomona, California: Day Printing Corporation.

Garay, L. A. 1978. *Orchidaceae. Flora of Ecuador*, 225 (1). Stockholm, Sweden: University of Göteborg.

Garay, L. A., and H. R. Sweet. 1974a. *Flora of the Lesser Antilles: Orchidaceae*. Jamaica Plain, Massachusetts: Arnold Arboretum, Harvard University.

_____. 1974b. *Orchids of the Southern Ryukyu Islands*. Cambridge, Massachusetts: Botanical Museum, Harvard University.

Ghose, B. N. 1959. *Beautiful Indian Orchids*. Calcutta, India: Vaskar Press.

Grant, B. 1966. *The Orchids of Burma*. Rangoon, Burma: Central Press.

Hall, A. V. 1965. *Studies of the South African Species of Eulophia*. Newland, South Africa: Journal of South African Botany. Supplementary vol. 5.

Hamilton, R. M. 1977. *When Does It Flower?*. British Colombia, Canada: Robert Hamilton Publisher.

_____. 1979a. *Orchid Flower Index (1736–1966)*. British Colombia, Canada: Robert Hamilton Publisher.

_____. 1979b. *Orchid Flower Index (1966–1979)*. British Colombia, Canada: Robert Hamilton Publisher.

Harrison, E. R. 1972. *Epiphytic Orchids of Southern Africa*. Natal, South Africa: Wildlife Protection and Conservation Society of South Africa.

Hawkes, A. D. 1965. *Encyclopedia of Cultivated Orchids*. London, England: Faber and Faber.

Hennessy, E. F., and T. A. Hedge. 1989. *The Slipper Orchids*. Randburg, South Africa: Acorn Books CC.

Hillerman, F. E., and A. W. Holst. 1986. *Introduction to the Cultivated Angraecoid Orchids*. Portland, Oregon: Timber Press.

Hoehne, F. C. 1930. *Album de Orchidaceae Brasileiras*. São Paulo, Brazil: Impressao da "Graphiears," Romiti, Lanzara and Zanin.

_____. 1940. *Flora Brasilica*. Vol. 12, nos. 1–12, *Orchidaceas*. São Paulo, Brazil: Impressores "Graphicars," Romiti and Lanzara.

_____. 1949. *Iconografia de Orchidaceas do Brasil*. São Paulo, Brazil: S. A. Industrias "Graphicars," F. Lanzara.

Hoffman, N., and A. Brown. 1984. *Orchids of South-West Australia*. Nedlands, Australia: University of Western Australia Press.

Holttum, R. E. 1953. *Flora of Malaya*. Vol. 1, *Orchids of Malaya*. Singapore: Government Printing Office.

Jones, D. L. 1990. *Exotic Orchids of Australia*. Balgowlah, Australia: Reed Books (PTY).

Kamemoto, H., and R. Sagarik. 1975. *Beautiful Thai Orchid Species*. Bangkok, Thailand: The Orchid Society of Thailand.

Kupper, W., and W. Linsenmaier. 1953. *Orchidées*. Zurich, Switzerland: Service d'Images Silva.

Lindley, J. 1840. *Sertum Orchidaceum*. London, England: John Ridgeway and Sons.

Lindleyana. 1988–1993. Vols. 1–6.

Little, R. J., and C. E. Jones. 1980. *A Dictionary of Botany*. New York: Van Nostrand Reinhold Company.

Luer, C. A. 1972. *The Native Orchids of Florida*. New York: New York Botanical Garden.

_____. 1975. *The Native Orchids of the United States and Canada*. New York: New York Botanical Garden.

McQueen, J., and B. McQueen. 1992. *Miniature Orchids*. Portland, Oregon: Timber Press.

Millar, A. 1978. *Orchids of Papua New Guinea*. Seattle, Washington: University of Washington Press.

Morris, B. 1970. *The Epiphytic Orchids of Malawi*. Malawi: The Society of Malawi.

Nagano, Y. n.d. *Oriental Miniature Orchids*. Tokyo, Japan: Kashima Shoten.

Nicholls, W. H. 1951. *Orchids of Australia*. Adelaide, Australia: An Australiana Society Publication.

Nilsson, S. 1979. *Orchids of Northern Europe*. Middlesex, England: Penguin Books.

Northen, R. T. 1970. *Home Orchid Growing*. 3rd ed. New York: Van Nostrand Reinhold Company.

_____. 1980. *Miniature Orchids*. New York: Van Nostrand Reinhold Company.

The Orchid Digest. 1946–1993. Vols. 10–57.

Ospina, M. 1958. *Orquideas Colombianas*. Bogota, Colombia: Publicaciones Tecnicas LTDA.

Ospina, M., and R. L. Dressler. 1974. *Orquideas de las Américas*. Bogota, Colombia: Litografia Arco.

Pabst, G. F. J., and F. Dungs. 1975. *Orchidaceae Brasiliensis*. Vols. 1–2. Hildesheim, Germany: Brücke-Verlag Kurt Schmersow.

Peterson, J. B. 1952. *Some New or Little Known Orchids from the Cameroon*. Rpt. from Saertryk AF Botanisk Tiolsskrift. 158–171. N.p.

Piers, F. 1968. *Orchids of East Africa*. Lehre, Germany: Verlag Von J. Cramer.

Pridgeon, A., ed. 1992. *The Illustrated Encyclopedia of Orchids*. Portland, Oregon: Timber Press.

Quisumbing, E. N.d. *Philippine Orchids and Their Culture*. N.p.

Rupp, H. M. R. 1943. *Flora of New South Wales, The Orchids of New South Wales*. Sydney, Australia: Australian Medical Publishing Company.

Sanchez, C. G. 1930. *Las Mejores Orquideas de Mexico*. Mexico, D.F.: Talleres Tipograficos "La Pluma Fuente."

Santapua, H., and Z. Kapadia. 1966. *The Orchids of Bombay*. Calcutta, India: Government of India Press.

Sauleda, R. P. 1988. A revision of the genus *Psychilis* Rafinesque. *Phytologia* 65(1) (June).

Schelpe, E. A. C. L. E. 1966. *An Introduction to the South African Orchids*. London, England: Macdonald and Company.

Schlechter, R. 1927. *Die Orchideen*. Berlin, Germany: Verlagsbuchandlung Paul Parey.

Schuler, S., ed. 1988. *Simon and Schuster's Guide to Orchids*. New York: Simon and Schuster.

Schultes, R. E. 1960. *Native Orchids of Trinidad and*

Tobago. New York: Pergamon Press.

Schultes, R. E., and A. S. Pease. 1963. *Generic Names of Orchids: Their Origin and Meaning*. New York: Academic Press.

Schweinfurth, C. 1958. *Orchids of Peru*. Fieldiana: Botany, vol. 30, nos. 1–4. Chicago, Illinois: Chicago Natural History Museum.

Segerbäck, L. B. 1992. *Orchids of Malaya*. Rotterdam, Netherlands: A. A. Balkema.

Seidenfaden, G., and T. Smitinand. 1959. *The Orchids of Thailand*. Bangkok, Thailand: The Siam Society.

Shuttleworth, F. S., H. S. Zim, and G. W. Dillon. 1970. *Orchids: A Golden Guide*. New York: Golden Press.

Soon, T. E. 1980. *Asian Orchids*. Singapore: Times Books International.

Spatzek, J. F. 1984. *Orchid Species Source Book 2*. N.p.

Sprunger, S., ed. 1986. *Orchids from Curtis's Botanical Magazine*. London, England: Cambridge University Press.

Stewart, J., and R. Campbell. 1970. *Orchids of Tropical Africa*. New York: A. S. Barnes.

Stewart, J., and E. F. Hennessy. 1981. *Orchids of Africa*. Johannesburg, South Africa: Macmillan South Africa.

Su, H-J. 1975. *Native Orchids of Taiwan*. Taipei, Taiwan: Harvest Farm Magazine.

Summerhayes, V. S. 1951. *Wild Orchids of Britain*. London, England: Collins.

_____. 1968a. *Flora of Tropical East Africa. Orchidaceae*. Part 1. London, England: Crown Agents for Oversea Governments and Administrations.

_____. 1968b. *Flora of West Tropical Africa. Orchidaceae*. Vol. 3, part 1. London, England: Crown Agents for Oversea Governments and Administrations.

Sweet, H. 1980. *The Genus Phalaenopsis*. Pomona, California: Day Printing Corporation.

Valdivisieso, P. O. 1976. *Orquideas de Colombia*. Bogota, Colombia: Universidad Javeriana.

Valmayor, H. L. 1984. *Orchidiana Philippiniana*. 2 vols. Manila, Philippines: Eugenio Lopez Foundation.

Van Royen, P. 1980. *The Orchids of the High Mountains of New Guinea*. Vaduz, Germany: J. Cramer.

Veitch, J. 1894. *A Manual of Orchidaceous Plants*. Chelsea, England: James Veitch and Sons.

Werkhoven, M. C. M. 1986. *Orchids of Suriname*. Paramaribo, Suriname: Vaco N. V. Uitgeversmaatschappij.

Wiard, L. A. 1987. *An Introduction to the Orchids of Mexico*. Ithaca, New York: Comstock Publishing Associates.

Williams, J. G., and A. E. Williams. 1983. *A Field Guide to the Orchids of North America*. New York: Universe Books.

Williams, L. O. 1939. *Las Orquidaceas del Noroeste Argentino. De Lilloa*. Tomo. 4. Buenos Aires, Argentina: Imprenta Y Casa Editora «Coni.» 337–375.

_____. 1951. *The Orchidaceae of Mexico*. Ceiba. Vol. 2, nos. 1–4.

_____. 1956. *An Enumeration of the Orchidaceae of Central America, British Honduras, and Panama*. Ceiba. Vol. 5, nos. 1–4.

Williamson, G. 1977. *The Orchids of South Central Africa*. London, England: J. M. Dent and Sons.

Winterringer, G. S. 1967. *Wild Orchids of Illinois*. Chicago, Illinois: Illinois State Museum.

Withner, C. L. 1988. *The Cattleyas and Their Relatives*. Vol. 1, *The Cattleyas*. Portland, Oregon: Timber Press.

_____. 1990. *The Cattleyas and Their Relatives*. Vol. 2, *The Laelias*. Portland, Oregon: Timber Press.

Index

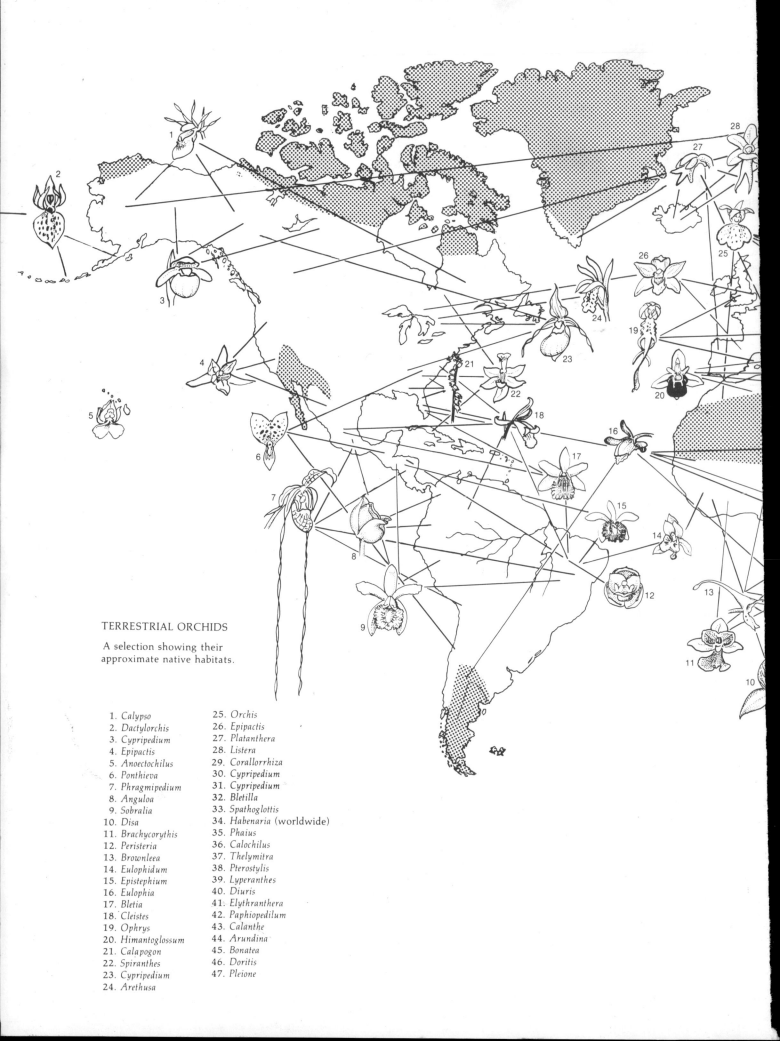

TERRESTRIAL ORCHIDS

A selection showing their
approximate native habitats.

1. *Calypso*
2. *Dactylorchis*
3. *Cypripedium*
4. *Epipactis*
5. *Anoectochilus*
6. *Ponthieva*
7. *Phragmipedium*
8. *Anguloa*
9. *Sobralia*
10. *Disa*
11. *Brachycorythis*
12. *Peristeria*
13. *Brownleea*
14. *Eulophidum*
15. *Epistephium*
16. *Eulophia*
17. *Bletia*
18. *Cleistes*
19. *Ophrys*
20. *Himantoglossum*
21. *Calapogon*
22. *Spiranthes*
23. *Cypripedium*
24. *Arethusa*

25. *Orchis*
26. *Epipactis*
27. *Platanthera*
28. *Listera*
29. *Corallorrhiza*
30. *Cypripedium*
31. *Cypripedium*
32. *Bletilla*
33. *Spathoglottis*
34. *Habenaria* (worldwide)
35. *Phaius*
36. *Calochilus*
37. *Thelymitra*
38. *Pterostylis*
39. *Lyperanthes*
40. *Diuris*
41. *Elythranthera*
42. *Paphiopedilum*
43. *Calanthe*
44. *Arundina*
45. *Bonatea*
46. *Doritis*
47. *Pleione*